The Artful Universe

SUNY Series in Hindu Studies
Wendy Doniger, Editor

The Artful Universe

An Introduction to the Vedic Religious Imagination

William K. Mahony

State University of New York Press

Cover photo by Frank W. Bliss.

Published by
State University of New York Press, Albany

Printed in the United States of America

For information, address State University of New York Press, State University Plaza, Albany, N.Y., 12246

Production by E. Moore
Marketing by Dana Yanulavich

Library of Congress Cataloging-in-Publication Data

Mahony, William K.
The artful universe : an introduction to the Vedic religious imagination / William K. Mahony.
p. cm. — (SUNY series in Hindu studies)
Portions of several chapters have been delivered at various colleges.
Includes bibliographical references and index.
ISBN 0-7914-3579-2 (hardcover : alk. paper). — ISBN 0-7914-3580-6 (pbk. : alk. paper)
1. Vedas—Criticism, interpretation, etc. 2. Hinduism.
I. Title. II. Series.
BL1112.7.M35 1997
294.5′921046—dc21 97-9205
CIP

10 9 8 7 6 5 4 3 2 1

Contents

Preface

This book serves as an introduction to the Vedic religious tradition of ancient and classical India, a tradition that in many ways has stood as the foundation for much of Indian spirituality for 3,500 years and more. The discussions in the following pages emphasize Vedic ideas regarding the nature of divinity and its relationship to the natural and human worlds; Vedic cosmology and metaphysics; the nature and process of revelation and its relationship to poetry and other forms of expression; the structure and purpose of ritual performance and other forms of hallowed activity; and the function and practice of meditation. Consideration of such topics leads to a presentation of other related Vedic ideas and aspirations as well: the connection between liturgy and contemplation; the relationship between the soul and ultimate reality; the yearning for and experience of transcendence, freedom, and immortality.

These are key components of the Vedic religious world. Accordingly, they have been the focus of many studies by astute scholars in both India and the West. However, most of these books tend to be rather opaque to those who are relatively unfamiliar with the material at hand, and few of them have directed their readers' attention to all the components of the Vedic religious world just mentioned. I hope that this book makes these important aspects of Vedic thought more accessible to interested nonspecialists, thereby contributing to the wider understanding and continuing study of Vedic religion.[1]

As a way to frame these important but in some ways diverse aspects of Vedic thought, *The Artful Universe* denominates and highlights a particular theme that links all these components together, namely, the important role of the divine and human imagination in the formation, transformation, and reformation of a meaningful world. Religious functions of the imagination are woven throughout the Vedic world. The imagination here refers not only to the power and process by which an image is formed in and by the mind and heart, but also to a number of ways in which that inwardly formed image is drawn outward or expressed, as well as to that process by which images of seemingly external forces and truths are internalized or experienced within one's own being. This book shows that, according to Vedic thought, imaginative human beings create, cognize, and recognize a world of significance and value or a structure of truth precisely because they have the ability to imagine such a world or truth and that, in fact, this effective power is similar to the gods' very ability to fashion a meaningful universe by imagining it into being. The imaginative human being—poet, liturgist, contemplative sage—thus shares with the deities, or at least yearns to share with them, the ability to fashion, understand, and order an otherwise confusing and broken world. It is the creative, revelatory, and restorative imagination that makes human beings most like the gods.

Professional scholars of the Veda will recognize themes that have attracted the interest of eminent twentieth-century academics for some time: the notion that language has the power to create and maintain a world of meaning, for example; the metaphysics of creativity; the parallelism between divine creativity and human poetic expression; the similar aims of poetry and ritual; the role of the imagination in the contemplative experience of the sublime. But it is precisely these and related ideas which I sense might be of interest to people who do not specialize in Vedic scholarship but who nevertheless have become interested in Vedic thought and practice and who might find an introductory discussion of these ideas relevant to their own pursuits. I would in fact be most pleased if inquisitive poets, artists, dramatists, meditators, or *sādhaka*s of one form or another find in the following pages information and perhaps even inspiration as they seek to know more about one of the oldest and most venerated of the world's spiritual traditions.

Initial research for this book was supported by a Fellowship from the National Endowment for the Humanities and by funding supplied by Davidson College. I am most appreciative of the kindness and welcome given to me by the officers of the Bhandarkar Oriental Research Institute in Pune; a special note of appreciation in this regard goes to R. N. Dandekar and S. D. Laddu. Thanks, too, go to M. D. Bhandare of the American Institute of Indian Studies, for the logistical support he gave to my family while we lived in Pune.

Many people have offered me their constructive criticism and have given me encouragement while I have undertaken the writing of this book. My thanks go first to Wendy Doniger, whose continuing interest in my work over the years means a great deal to me. Paul B. Courtright, Laurie L. Patton, Joanne Punzo Waghorne, Edward Levy, and several anonymous referees read the entire manuscript and offered suggestions for improvement. Of course, any mistakes in the following pages are my own.

For their collegial support at Davidson College I thank Mark Csikszentmihalyi, Trent Foley, Burkhard Henke, Herb Jackson, Samuel Maloney, Mark McCulloh, Alexander McKelway, Karl Plank, Lynn Poland, Max Polley, Daniel Rhodes, Catherine Slawy-Sutton, Homer Sutton, Job Thomas, Robert Williams, and Price Zimmermann. Scott Denham of Davidson's German department gave me valuable help one full morning as I worked through some Vedic songs I found particularly difficult to translate. I have enjoyed many hours of conversation on a wide range of topics on the poetic imagination, from Aristotle to Abhinavagupta, with Professor A. Vishnu Bhat of the English department at Madras Christian College.

With gratitude I acknowledge the encouragement given to me over the years by Professors Constantina Rhodes Bailly, Douglas Renfrew Brooks, and Paul Muller-Ortega.

I reserve my final, deepest thanks for my family—Pamela, Abigael, and Olivia—whose love and patience stand behind every word in the following pages. And it is with profound appreciation beyond the range of words that I offer my reverence to the artful source of all that is real and precious and valuable in this mysterious and awe-inspiring universe. I offer the fruits of my work to that incomprehensible wisdom that brings all things into being, sustains them, nourishes them, and transforms them into the splendor of the Absolute; I honor the divine imagination itself and its perfect embodiment in the play of the universal consciousness that pulses and dances through all beings.

Pronunciation of Sanskrit Words

The pronunciation of Sanskrit words is made easier than it might at first seem by the fact that the language is extraordinarily consistent. Unlike English, each distinct sound is represented in only one way. Therefore, any given letter of the alphabet, even in transliteration, is to be pronounced in one—and only one—manner.

The alphabet begins with the vowels and diphthongs. The *a* is always pronounced like the *u* in the English word b*u*t, the *ā* as in the English f*a*ther, *i* as in st*i*ll, *ī* as in machi*ne*, *u* as in sm*oo*th, and *ū* as in l*u*te. Sanskrit also includes a vocalic *r* and *l*, represented by *ṛ* and *ḷ* and pronounced as in the English bitt*er* and litt*le*, respectively. Pronounce the Sanskrit diphthongs *e, ai, o*, and *au*, as you do the English g*a*te, *ai*sle, sl*ow*, and c*ow*, respectively.

The alphabet then moves through the various consonants, regarding which there are several points to keep in mind:

The sound represented by the Roman *c* is always pronounced as the *ch* in the English word *ch*erish and never like the soft *c* in receive.

The *h* following a consonant is always pronounced with a slight aspiration. Thus, *kh* is pronounced as in the English bac*k-h*oe, *gh* as in do*gh*ouse, *ch* as in chur*ch-h*ouse, *jh* as in sle*dgeh*ammer, *th* as in goa*t-h*erder, *dh* as in ma*d-h*ouse, *ph* as in u*ph*ill, and *bh* as in cra*b-h*ouse.

When you see a consonant with a dot under it (*ṭ, ṭh, ḍ, ḍh, ṇ, ṣ*), curl your tongue against the roof of your mouth while pronouncing it. This does not always come easily to English-speakers. The sound is similar to the *t* in the English *ant*, the *d* in *end*, and so on.

The sibilant *ś* is pronounced as in the English *sh*oe while *s* (without the diacritical mark) is the same as that in the English *s*un.

The symbol *ñ* is pronounced as in the word ca*ny*on. The *ṁ* nasalizes the preceeding vowel and *ṅ* is pronounced as in the English si*ng*.

Finally, *ḥ* represents an aspiration of the preceding vowel and, if at the end of a word, an ever-so-slight repetition of that same vowel.

Introduction

The phrase *Vedic religion* refers to a complicated yet systematic set of religious values, ideas, and practices from ancient India, many of the salient themes of which came to serve as central if unstated components of classical Hinduism. Although there is not universal agreement, historians tend to feel that the origins of Vedic religion lie among the religious sensibilities of slowly migrating Indo-European pastoralists who, beginning around 1500 BCE, entered the Punjab from the northwest. By the sixth century BCE, the Vedic presence had extended eastward onto the Ganges River Plain, assimilating and responding to various other religious worldviews as it did so but nevertheless maintaining a distinct quality of its own; within two or three centuries it had moved across the Deccan Plateau and into the southern regions of the subcontinent. By the third century BCE, the Vedic perspectives reached across most of what today we call India. Because of the important place Vedic ideologies held in Indian civilization at the time, historians often call this period of Indian history the Vedic Period. But this nomenclature is somewhat misleading. Throughout the past 3,500 years, Vedic sensibilities have continued to contribute to and in some ways to define Hindu Indian religious, philosophical, social, and cultural thought as a whole.[1]

Vedic religion in general revolved around the ideas that the wondrous marvels and powers of nature, the diverse personalities and behavior of the many gods and goddesses who gave form to and enlivened the world, the composition and dynamics of the human community, and the structure and destiny of the individual person are all somehow linked to one another through a transcendent universal order and harmony of being; that the power of this hidden principle could be harnessed and expressed in effective language; that, because of the interconnectedness of all being, actions performed in any one of such realms therefore affect the status of all others; and that by inwardly knowing the nature and structure of that timeless unifying principle one might thereby free one's spirit from the vicissitudes of life and the constraints of death. Such a vision of the world found expression in Vedic religion in an intricate system of mythic narratives sung in metrical verse, in the performance of complicated yet similarly systematic ritual performances, and in the practice of contemplative meditation.

As I hope to show, Vedic literature and practice also gave expression to the related ideas that the meaningful universe based on this transcendent principle of harmony comes into being through the power of the imagination; that it is by means of the imagination that this universal harmony is revealed; that it is the imagination that sustains that harmony when it is threatened and reconstructs it when it is destroyed.

Just where this creative, revelatory, and restorative imagination is said to reside varies. Most texts imply that it lies in the minds of the gods and goddesses, who are understood to have fashioned the world in their own image by thinking it into existence, to have entered into and enlivened it, and to have re-formed it when necessary. But Vedic texts suggest, too, that the power of imagination by which the gods as divine artists create the physical world is the same effective force by which a human poet forms verbal images in the mind and sings them forth in the form of metrical verse; a priest establishes a ceremonial domain and constructs thereon a dramatic universe; and a contemplative sage recognizes within his own heart the identity of the soul with the eternal, divine ground of being. Thus, it is the imagination that joins the human spirit with ultimate reality itself.

Those texts further imply the idea that each of these divine and human forms of expression reflects in its own way that transcendent, hidden, unified principle of harmony and order that supports and directs the movements of all things. According to this view, even the many gods and goddesses are diverse images of this universal artfulness of being. From this perspective, the universe in all its marvelous mystery yet fragile complexity, and including both inward as well outward realms, is a divine work of imaginative art.

THE UNIVERSE AS ART

To Vedic visionary poets, the world is—or could be—an integrated whole, a unified structure and process of being in which there are no unbridgeable distances separating the divine, natural, and human worlds: for them, the sacred world is an encompassing whole in which everything exists in an interconnected totality; it is a seamless universe rather than a disjointed multiverse.[2]

Songs sung by those poetic bards present a number of metaphors to represent that integral principle and ground of being on which that universe rests and from which all things arise: it is, for example, the cosmic wheel on which all things of the universe turn; it is the universal pillar that supports all beings; it is the universal Word of which all words are different expressions; it is the single divine body whose various limbs and organs form the different realms and diverse aspects of the divine, physical, social, and moral cosmos. In any case, it is through this ordered yet dynamic unifying principle that everything in the universe fits together properly. Sometimes Vedic hymns refer to it as the "One" or the "One Reality," or simply as "It."

Earlier Vedic texts tend to describe that unified integrative principle with the term *Ṛta*, a rich and multivalent Sanskrit word often translated into English by such phrases as "universal law" or "cosmic order."[3] (Because it refers to a Vedic term for the Absolute, this word will be capitalized and appear in roman rather than italic script throughout the following pages.) Ṛta is that hidden structure on which the divine, physical, and moral worlds are founded, through which they are inextricably connected, and by which they are sustained. The cosmic order which holds all things together, Ṛta has also been translated as "truth."[4]

As the foundational principle of order as well as the source and reference of normative behavior, the Vedic concept of Ṛta can rightly be understood to stand as the precursor to the classical South Asian notion of *dharma*, the ontological principle of integrity and set of ethical prescriptions that sustain the universe as a whole.

But perhaps such translations of Ṛta as "cosmic order" or "universal truth" are in a way too static. The word could also be rendered into English by phrases suggesting an integrated and even artistic principle of being, for it connotes a universal quality in which different elements fit together in a balanced and structured yet dynamic way. The word *ṛta* literally means "that which has moved" in a fitting manner.[5] It thus suggests both a correctness or smooth compatibility of things as well as the principle of balance and integrity that gives foundation to that compatibility. It may be of interest to note in this regard that the word *ṛta* is a distant relative not only of the English *rite* and thus of *ritual* (both of which signify actions that lend or establish dramatic order to the disorder of life as it is often experienced), but also of the English *harmony* as well as of *art* and thus of *artful*.[6]

The title of this book—*The Artful Universe*—therefore presents a play on words. By using the word *universe* I refer to the Vedic idea that all things in the various realms of a sacred, meaningful existence are in some way connected to each other in a mysterious and complicated yet systematic whole. By *artful* I want to suggest not only the general notion that Ṛta is universal truth and ritual order, but also that this structure of being is one in which all things fit together properly, smoothly, and harmoniously—"artistically," if you will. As the universal (artistic) principle that gives rise to and joins all things together into a smoothly fitting whole, Ṛta stands as the foundation of the world as universe rather than as chaotic multiverse. As we will see, the key elements of the early Vedic idea of Ṛta—arguably one of the most important of all Vedic concepts[7]—find expression in later Vedic literatures as Brahman, the expansive and pervasive ground of being that supports all things, and as Ātman, the universal Self standing as the single subject of which the many objects of the world are different embodiments.

Drawing on this play on words, one of the points I will make in the following pages, then, is this: because Ṛta establishes a harmonious whole, the perfect and perfected world is, in a sense, an "artful universe." Similarly, that person—deity, poet, priest, contemplative sage—who sees, expresses, adheres to, and supports Ṛta thereby participates in this universal artistry and may be said therefore to be an "artist" whose actions support and strengthen that world as universe against the fracturing forces that pull it into a multiverse.

VEDA AS VISIONARY SACRED KNOWLEDGE

The adjective *Vedic* is based on the Sanskrit word *veda*, the latter of which reflects the same ancient linguistic root meaning to "see" that also eventually gave rise to the English words *wise* and *wisdom* as well as to *idea, vision,* and *view*. It is also distantly related to the English word *wit*.[8] When we speak of one's wit, we refer to the way that person perceives and thus understands the world in general: to lose one's wits is to lose one's comprehension of a situation as it really is and to become confused or muddled by what it merely appears to be; to be at wit's end is to be unable to formulate coherent views or modes of understanding. A person's wit also allows him or her to see connections between experiences and ideas that normally may not be associated, and to represent those associations with a felicitous and enlightening choice of words or images; a witty person thereby not only is able to understand a situation more clearly than others because he or she is able to see beyond the surface of things, but is also able to communicate that understanding in such a way that less insightful people may similarly come to see things from a different perspective. Accordingly, the word *wit* also suggests poetic skill or ability to solve mysterious puzzles.

Most of the connotations of these English words apply generally to the Sanskrit word *veda* as well, for it, too, referred in ancient India to a special mode of seeing beyond the surface, a vision that not only allowed the seer to comprehend things as they truly are or should be, but also to contemplate or reflect on their deeper meaning and thereby truly to know them.[9] But *veda* implied more than a person's ability to see things in a way that others do not. It allowed a visionary to see through a process of direct perception, ecstatic experience, or inner vision what were regarded as fully sacred modes and structures of being, even ultimate reality itself. *Ya evaṁ veda*, sages asserted:[10] "one who thus knows" sees hidden, timeless, and powerful divine forces and principles within the ephemeral or otherwise incomprehensible contours of the world of existence.

As a noun, *veda* refers to that perfected, sacred knowledge; it is that which the visionary knows. Tradition holds that the content of that sacred knowledge is the timeless truth itself, *satya*, gained and expressed in ancient India by poets, ritualists, and philosophers whom orthodox tradition regards as wise seers. "One who thus knows" sees divinity itself. "One who thus knows" understands holy truths.

We may think of *veda* not only as "knowledge of the sacred" but also as "sacralizing knowledge," for truth, in ancient India, was a powerful, active, and transformative force. It could be enacted and constructed through liturgical drama, formulated through the effective sounds of the chant, given voice through language, revealed by listening. Various practices supported truth; other actions injured it. Visionary knowledge was power, embodied in act and word.

When we speak specifically of *the* Veda we refer to particular collections of sacred and sacralizing poetic songs, ritual instructions, and philosophical or speculative mystical teachings that are believed to reflect or reveal that hidden, transcendent, or inner truth and which were memorized and transmitted through the generations by visionary sages in ancient India. (A short summary of those literatures appears in a later section of this Introduction.)

THE POWER OF THE IMAGINATION

In this work I will bring attention to passages from Vedic texts that refer in various ways to mental abilities or processes associated with what I will call the imagination. The term is a rather general one, to be sure. It derives, of course, from the word *image*, which refers to a reproduction, likeness, reflection, counterpart, or duplicate of something that is not otherwise immediately present to the senses at the time. The word also refers to a mental revival or inward duplication of outward, sensual experience. Accordingly, the verb *imagine* generally refers to the process of conceiving an image in the mind. But the imaginative process often includes more than the inward reflection of an outward form. To imagine is also to express that which has been conceived in the mind; and to express an image is to press it outward, to *ex–press* it, to draw it out from within. An external image is thus an expression or drawing forth of an inward model. The imagination thus both internalizes the outer world and externalizes the inner world.

Similar ideas find reflection in Vedic literatures. We will read, for example, of the Vedic idea of *māyā*, a term which in the Vedic period was already rich and full with meaning and which, accordingly, has brought from translators a number of renditions in European languages. The word has entered the English lexicon as a "mental fabrication," primarily in the sense of the "appearance through fantasy" and thus of "illusion." This is indeed the connotation of the word as it tends to be used in some Hindu philosophical schools of thought, particularly those traditions associated with the influential nondualist philosophy that has come to be known as the Advaita Vedānta, which focuses on the effort required to see through what this philosophical perspective regards as the unreality of the objective world. But this was not the word's meaning in earlier, Vedic India. Here, *māyā* referred in general to the gods' mysterious ability to construct objective forms where previously there were none. The gods' *māyā* was associated particularly with the events and seeming marvels of nature, such as the appearance of the sun's bright form at dawn from what previously had been a deep and encompassing darkness[11] or the formation of thunderclouds in an otherwise empty sky.[12] According to Vedic thought this is no ordinary process; it reflected an unfathomable and even miraculous power of creativity and transformation. The deities are said to form those objects, first, by conceiving them in their minds, second, by expressing or projecting those inward conceptions outward into time and space and, third, by dwelling in those forms they had thus created. One scholar has justly concluded that, in the Vedic period, *māyā* referred to the gods' mysterious "special ability to create forms, or rather to the inexplicable power of a High Being to assume forms, to project itself into externality, to assume an outward appearance, to appear in, or as, the phenomenal world"; that the deities could perform such wondrous feats was due to their "mental equipment" that made such "awe-inspiring abilities" possible.[13] The fourteenth-century CE Vedic commentator, Sāyaṇa, associated *māyā* not only with the divine "power to accomplish" something (*śakti*), but also with "wisdom" (*prajñā*) and "superior wisdom" (*abhijñā*).[14]

The deities' *māyā* was an extraordinary imaginative art[15] through which they drew forth and thereby gave reality to the objective world itself. Vedic poets described the gods and goddesses as "possessing *māyā*," and thus as powerful magicians or artists of sorts.[16]

From the Vedic perspective, the world we live in is therefore a projection of the gods' imaginative minds. The Vedic concept of *māyā* thus stands as a precedent for the later Hindu ideas of *īśvara-saṁkalpa* and *icchā-śakti*, the former referring to God's ability to effect change in the world through the force of divine thought and the latter to God's power to do or bring about whatever God wishes.

Vedic thought holds that not only the deities possess this constructive power of the imagination. Human poets, priests, and meditating sages are also said to make use of the same formative and transformative power. As we will see, such imaginative people were understood to be able to form images in their minds of the otherwise invisible forces and structures that direct the movements of the universe and that hold that universe together, and then to express those images either in the form of words or as physical bodily movements. In the former case, those verbal images took the form of poetic songs. In the latter instance, they were expressed in the staged drama of the sacred ritual. "The singing priest goes forth to perform the rite," an ancient verse reads, "sending forth the brilliant song through *māyā.*"[17]

We will also mention the Vedic concept of *dhī*, which refers to the visionary's ability to see the gods' and goddesses' presence in the world and to respond to that divine company through imaginative songs of praise sung during sacred ceremonial rites. The Vedic contemplative practiced meditation, *dhyāna*—a word related to *dhī*—as a way both to recognize and to envision those divine powers residing deep within his or her own heart.

In the Vedic worldview, deities and human beings thus share a common quality: both possess the power of imagination. Both live in and give meaning to a world formed and re-formed by means of the imaginative process. We might therefore say this: because it arises from the gods' creative and constructive power of the imagination, and because it is recognized and understood by imaginative human beings, the universe is therefore an imaginary universe. By this I do *not* mean that Vedic thinkers would hold that such an imaginary universe is false. In fact, I mean just the opposite: I will show in this book that, in the Vedic worldview, it is the imagination, especially the divine imagination, that gives image to the transcendent artfulness of the universe; and it is the human imagination—especially the poetic, sacerdotal, and contemplative imagination—that sees through the apparently deadened and perplexing chaos of the objective world, recognizes within it the hidden, unified, and unifying principle of being, and draws that principle and power into effect. Whether divine or human, it is precisely the imagination that fashions and recognizes the universe as meaningful, abiding, and valuable, that is to say, as real.

LITERARY SOURCES

Nearly eleven thousand verses Vedic tradition holds were first sung by visionary poets in ancient India are collected in the slightly more than one thousand poetic hymns and songs[18] that form what is known as the *Ṛgveda-Mantra-Saṁhitā*, the "collection of verses expressing sacred visionary knowledge," usually known more simply as the *Ṛgveda*. They are composed in Sanskrit (*saṁskṛta*: "well-formed"), the ancient and sacred language of Vedic India. The collection is traditionally grouped into either ten or eight separate books of varying length;[19] references in the following pages to Vedic songs and verses will be according to the division of the text into ten books. (Those references will consist of three parts. The first number refers to the book, the second to the hymn in that book, and the third to the verse in that hymn. For example, *Ṛgveda* 1.61.2—"[the seers] have dressed their visionary songs with heart, and mind, and intellect"—refers to Book One, Hymn 61, verse 2.)

First sung on the Indian subcontinent around 1500–1200 BCE, but perhaps reflecting much earlier ideas, images, wording, and themes, the songs of the *Ṛgveda* were memorized through the generations, finally to be codified in Vedic Sanskrit sometime before 1000 BCE.[20] From a historical perspective they thus comprise the oldest extant literature from the larger Indo-European world in general. Throughout those songs appear a number of riddles, enigmatic phrases, and rhetorical questions put to verse that probably were sung in the context of the performance of sacred rites. An "answer" to such a riddle, enigma, or speculative question was known as a *brahman*, and verses that expressed a *brahman* therefore gave voice to the mysterious and hidden power that held together the universe as a whole. Those who could discern and understand the meaning of a *brahman* understood the mystery of being itself and were thus understood thereby to be worthy of performing those sanctifying rituals that linked the human community to the structures and forces of the universe in general. The Vedic visionary could "see" and thus "know" a *brahman* and then express that vision in verse form. It was the seer, then, to whom the *brahman* was revealed.

Most of those poets said to have seen the revealed truths are believed to have lived in distinct families, the patriarchs of each being the seers Gṛtsamāda, Viśvāmitra, Vāmadeva, Atri, Bharadvāja, and Vasiṣṭha. Each of Books Two through Eight of the *Ṛgveda* consists entirely of poems by these sages or their patrilinear descendants, respectively. Book Nine is composed only of hymns sung by various seers to Soma Pavamāna, the deity embodied in an ambrosial drink of immortality gained by pressing and clarifying the essence of the *soma* plant.[21] Soma Pavamāna is also known as the Lord of Visions, for he is said to open the seer's inner eye. Books One and Ten each consist of 191 hymns attributed to a variety of seers. Such balance of composition and the larger number of seers associated with the hymns, along with the fact that they include philosophical elements not shared by the other books, has suggested to many scholars that the hymns gathered into Books One and Ten were first sung somewhat later than were those of the other eight.

It is to be noted at the outset, however, that Vedic tradition holds that the truths presented by this literature are eternal in nature and that the content of the Veda therefore constitutes divine revelation.[22] Accordingly, these songs and verses cannot from the Vedic perspective be said to have been composed at any particular historical moment.[23] They certainly cannot be said to have been written any time in the centuries just mentioned: members of Vedic families memorized word for word the songs, lessons, and insights giving voice to those truths and transmitted them orally throughout the generations across the many centuries. They were not actually written down until just a few hundred years ago.

According to Vedic tradition, therefore, the truth is to be sung, not merely stated. In fact, an entire body of sacred verse equivalent in many ways to the *Ṛgveda* has been transmitted orally by traditional Vedic families throughout the generations over the past three thousand years and more. This is the *Sāmaveda*, the tradition of which revolves around the proper singing of the Vedic metrical hymns. Words accompanying those melodies come from the *Ṛgveda*, as do those from a third collection, the *Yajurveda*, the "knowledge of the prayers and instructions" recited during the rituals.

These three collections—the *Ṛgveda, Sāmaveda,* and *Yajurveda*—constitute what is known as the sacred and immutable "Triple Veda." A fourth collection, the *Atharvaveda*, consists of magical charms, spells, and incantations of specific use to monarchial and ruling classes but also of hymns reflecting high philosophical speculation sung by the Atharvans, who were priests officiating at performances of ancient Indian fire rituals.

Since its verses and songs serve as the basis for the *Sāmaveda* and the *Yajurveda*, most of our attention in the first three chapters will be given to selections from the *Ṛgveda*, with some reference given also to the *Atharvaveda*.

In the years following roughly 1000 BCE, various priestly families within the Vedic clans systematized complicated sets of instructions regarding the performance of solemn public rituals and explained what was understood to be the cosmically important function of those ceremonies. Such ritual performances were founded on two related ideas. One such notion was that the world of the gods and the world of human activity stood in analogical or homologous relationship to each other, the human world being a smaller and more constrained or perhaps somewhat degraded version of the divine world. The other idea was that the two realms were connected to each other in an effective way. It was because of this connection that the acts of the gods in the divine world affected the nature and quality of life in the human world. The reverse was also true: human activity affected the status and quality of the divine world. The two realms were linked by means of the universal thread on which the tapestry of being was said to be woven. This unifying power was none other than the *brahman* itself, the hidden structure that holds the complicated and diverse world together as a whole. Knowing the *brahman*, Vedic priests enacted ritual dramas as a way to align their action in the world of human beings with those of the gods and goddesses in the invisible worlds and thus with the universal order of being itself. Their sacerdotal instructions and expositions form a collection of ritual texts that have come to be known collectively as the Brāhmaṇas ("pertaining to the *brahman*"). Instructions regarding the performance of the rituals interpreted by the Brāhmaṇas were codified in the period roughly between the fifth and third centuries BCE in a number of technical works known as the Dharma Sūtras.

As early as the ninth century BCE, small groups of people began to leave the life of the villages to meditate in the forest, where, unwilling or financially unable to perform the grand and expensive public rituals, they contemplated the nature of the various homologies and equivalences between divine and human as well as outer and inner worlds. Their teachings formed the basis of texts known as the Āraṇyakas ("forest-books"). The generally mystical perspective driving the composition of the Āraṇyakas came to fuller expression beginning as early as the eighth century BCE, when the earliest collections of another genre of contemplative texts, the Upaniṣads ("secret teachings, mystic doctrines"), were first passed through the generations. The most influential of those Upaniṣads date from that time through roughly the 1st century BCE. Ascetic contemplatives meditating in the forests held the notion that one who truly knew the *brahman* thereby knew not only the powerful bond that joined the human to the divine world but also—in an important development in Vedic thought—the hidden yet powerful, sublime, unified essence of all things, the eternal ground of being itself. To Upaniṣadic thinkers, Brahman was the ontological Absolute. (When referring to the Absolute, the word will henceforth be capitalized and appear in roman script.) It was therefore through their inward knowledge of Brahman rather than through their outward performance of ritual activity that such sages were said to gain access to the immortal powers previously regarding as enlivening the heavenly world. Possessed of such understanding, the contemplative was, in the words of one of the Upaniṣads, "liberated from the jaws of death."[24]

In my discussion in Chapter Five I have drawn on a number of Upaniṣads beyond what have been called the "principal" or "major" Upaniṣads of the Vedic canon. Some of those lesser-known and often more sectarian works date from well into the first millennium of the Common Era and thus entered the canon after what often is regarded as the Vedic Period of Indian history. Many of those later Upaniṣads reflect the influence of a number of extra-Vedic ideas and practices such as the cosmological perspective associated with the Sāṁkhya tradition of philosophy, which recognizes an ontological hierarchy of being in which "awareness" or "intelligence" (*buddhi*) plays an important role in the evolution and devolution of being; or the practice of the "eight-limbed spiritual discipline" systematized by Patañjali and his followers; or the practice of inward visualization and other contemplative disciplines associated with Hindu Tantra. I have included many of those later Upaniṣads in this study for two reasons. First, although they present teachings and insights that are consistent with Vedic thought in general, they have not received the attention that the earlier Upaniṣads have long attracted. Second, they expand and make explicit some ideas that remain implicit or somewhat inchoate in the major Upaniṣads. This is particularly the case regarding the use of the imagination in the *yogī*'s practice of envisioning the divine within the structures and dynamics of his or her inner being.

These literatures, then—the *Ṛgveda* and *Atharvaveda* and various of the many Brāhmaṇas, Āraṇyakas, Upaniṣads, and (to a lesser extent) Dharma Sūtras—serve as the sources[25] on which the discussion in the following pages will be based.[26] The reader will note that virtually all references in the body of this book are to primary texts; those to secondary literatures may be found in the Notes. Unless otherwise noted, all translations are mine.

TO FIND THE UNIVERSAL "BOND OF BEING WITHIN NONBEING"

When I speak of their participation in an "artful universe," I do not wish to imply that Vedic poets, philosopher-priests, and meditating sages were unaware of the often difficult struggles and uncertainties of existence. Far from it: their songs, ritual instructions, and contemplative teachings refer not infrequently to a fractured discord of being. They saw about them, and at times participated in, manifold expressions of competition among people: rivalries of different kinds; jealousy and fear and distrust; different groups of people struggling for power over one another, leading at times to battles of conquest and defeat. They experienced fierce famine and debilitating disease. Although they held them in awe, Vedic visionaries were sometimes frightened by some of the gods and goddesses enlivening the world, just as they were of the demonic forces they envisioned as constraining the forces of life in that world. Confused at times about the meaning of their lives, some felt trapped in cycles of suffering and pain. Faced by the undeniable fact of death, they wished to understand the nature and purpose and significance of life. Their texts indicate that Vedic poets, priests, and meditators yearned to know just what it was that held this whole uncertain and often fragile universe together and somehow to align themselves with that deeply mysterious power and truth.

I would want to say, however, that from the Vedic point of view the two apparently opposite vectors pulling at life and existence—the forces of dissonance and disintegration on the one hand and those of consonance and integration on the other hand—are not mutually exclusive. In fact, as we will see, Vedic thought holds that a true vision of a divine universe must necessarily include the brokenness of the world, and that in fact it is precisely the imagination that is able to see the way the whole fits together despite the often disjointed nature of the parts. Furthermore, there is considerable evidence in the texts at hand to suggest that, from the Vedic perspective, imaginative creativity and transformation do not take place without considerable danger at times. Vedic creation myths tell of the disintegration of a unified truth into innumerable broken parts: in one such sacred story, for example, the world comes into being as a result of the ritual dismemberment of god's universal body;[27] in another, the single divine Word is broken into the many diverse words spoken by the human tongue;[28] in others, the deities who bring the world into being are said to struggle mightily but at times unsuccessfully against the deadening forces of powerful demons.[29] Vedic literatures are filled with expressions of conflicting powers and thus of power relationships. For the Vedic mind, the primary forces were those which gave rise to and supported being (*sat*) and those which led to and dissolved into nonbeing (*asat*). Sometimes the powers of life prevailed; sometimes not. The overcoming and defeat of being by nonbeing was a constant possibility. As one scholar has noted, the Vedic world was one that was "forever hovering on the brink of collapse."[30]

Visionary poets heard the primordial, divine Word sounding in the background of all existence, even an existence that was "forever hovering on the brink of collapse." They then gave voice to that Word in poetic songs that carried such force that they buttressed even the often-waning power of the gods of light and expansive life in their struggles against the demons of darkness, inertia, and death. The successful poet thereby linked the human community to the divine world. Accordingly, it was centrally important for the Vedic community to be able to recognize such inspired visionaries. Hence the competition among seers in poetic contests held in conjunction with the performance of large public rituals. The development of the Vedic ritual was closely and inextricably connected to the hope that the bitter uncertainties of life and death could be regularized and controlled in such a way that the underlying harmony and balance of the universe could be maintained. In some ways the performance of the Vedic ritual ceremonies were attempts to routinize the struggle between being and nonbeing and thereby to take control over the forces of death by subsuming them within the forces of life.[31]

To the Vedic mind, the power of transformation was drawn from the forces of chaos: for, just as the brilliance of light shines most noticeably from the depths of darkness, so, too, the establishment of a world of meaning and significance must at times arise precisely out the experience of powerless insignificance and disjointed meaninglessness. The *Atharvaveda* notes that existence itself is grounded in nonexistence,[32] and that the universal pillar on which rest all things in the world consists of both that which is and that which is not.[33] The emergence and development of Vedic visionary poetry, sacral drama, and meditation not only included, but in some ways depended on, such experience of the interrelatedness of existence and nonexistence. By means of his intuition and power of imagination the visionary saw the mysterious and powerful unity that linked the fullness of existence with the depths of nonexistence. "Searching within their hearts with the power of their minds," a sacred Vedic song asserts, "poets found the bond of being within nonbeing."[34] The priest's actions on the ceremonial stage duplicated the sacrificial incorporation of the power of death within the self (*ātman*) of the universal Lord of Creatures, Prajāpati. The meditator realized that the universal, divine *ātman* resided deep within his own heart and saw that the powers of nonexistence lose their force when one returns to and merges with that eternal and all-encompassing Self.

That which supported the profound interconnectedness of all things, even of existence and nonexistence themselves—this is to say, the *brahman*—was for Vedic visionaries a mysterious, hidden structure and force. This is why the *brahman* could not be comprehended by normal or ordinary modes of thinking or described in straightforward language. Discussions and disputations regarding the nature of the *brahman* often took the form of questions, enigmas, riddles, and esoteric imagery. Perhaps the most condensed set of such imagery appears in *Ṛgveda* 1.164, the "Song of this, the Beloved" or "The Riddle of the Universe," attributed to the philosopher-poet Dīrghatamas. We will look at parts of this long hymn in several places in the following chapters. The song presents a number of circumlocutions, unexplained visual images, puzzles, and questions asked by Dīrghatamas in the context of what appears to be a competition of sorts between poets. It was through the use of these enigmatic verses that Vedic poets like Dīrghatamas expressed their vision into the otherwise ineffable structures and forces that drive the world.[35] Such verses expressed a visionary poet's recognition of significance or meaning in a setting that remained insignificant and meaningless to others. Vedic poet-priests seem to have challenged each other with various linguistic tropes in order to discern which priests were capable of insight into the true meaning of things, for only such visionary, imaginative liturgists could perform the ritual in a way that would be effective in the invisible world of the gods. Furthermore, the successful initiate was one who did not turn away from this challenge but remained in contemplation until he reached the necessary intuitive insight. Like the Zen Buddhist who ponders and comes to understand a *kōan*, the Vedic contemplative poet-priest who came to understand the significance and meaning of the *brahman* came thereby to understand the nature and meaning of reality itself.

The priests whose lessons form the Brāhmaṇa literatures did not mention Ṛta as much as the Vedic poets did. But they did speak repeatedly of the various connections and correspondences between different aspects and functions of the universe, when others could only see what I am calling a disconnected multiverse. In this connection they spoke of the *brahman* as the invisible link that bound, or could bind, all things together, the power of which could be known and manipulated as a way to reintegrate the sacred world. Vedic priests felt that, if they knew the *brahman*, their actions within the ritual domain would affect the world of the gods as well. The texts hold that the priestly overseer who watched over the entire performance of the complicated rites performed the entire ceremony in his mind and that, indeed, it was in this mental offering where the transformative power of the rite actually resided. Not insignificantly, this priest who silently performed the rite in his mind was known as the *brahman*-priest.

By the time of the Upaniṣads, some Vedic thinkers had come to teach that one's knowledge of the *brahman* was more important than the outward performance of the ritual itself, for it was in knowing the power that connected all things that one came to experience the unity of being itself. They spoke of Brahman—the ontological Absolute—in distinctly reverential terms; for them, it was ultimate reality, the single source and unifying foundation of all things. The Upaniṣadic idea of Brahman was thus in a way a restatement of the earlier notion of Ṛta. The difference is that, while Vedic poets saw Ṛta as the dynamic principle of harmony on which the universe runs, Upaniṣadic philosophers regarded Brahman as the unchanging ground of being that pervades and supports all things. Upaniṣadic sages came to experience the unity of being through the process of disciplined meditation, for it was through inward contemplation that they recognized the presence of the Absolute within their own being. To them, Brahman was the single "Self" (*ātman*) of the universe. Knowing Brahman, the sage tasted the nectar of that divine, universal Self—Ātman—dwelling within his or her own heart. For the teachers whose lessons form the theistic Upaniṣads, that divine Self was the supreme deity himself or herself, regarded by different traditions as Śiva, Viṣṇu, or the universal Goddess.

Neither Ṛta, nor Brahman, nor Ātman, nor the supreme deity possessed a form distinctly its own. The Absolute was not regarded as an object among other objects. It was that deeply mysterious reality, power, and truth that made it possible for anything to exist to begin with. Although having no form, its presence was revealed by the fact that there is even such a thing as being itself. Since the truth of being is reflected in this existence of beings, all beings are in some way *images* of the Absolute. The process by which those beings come into existence and are sustained is therefore a process of *imagination.*

In Vedic thought, then, it is the imagination that gives form to the formless. The imagination reveals the sublime. Doing so, the imagination thereby gives a living body, as it were, to the invisible universal structure of harmony (Ṛta) and unifying ground of being (Brahman/Ātman) which precedes and transcends form itself.

But the imagination did more than this. In giving form to the formless, the imagination brought light to darkness, as it were. It brought order to chaos. Where there was disintegration, the imagination brought wholeness. Where there was death, imagination brought life. It was the power of imagination that enabled Vedic poets to sing forth songs that gave voice to Ṛta. The imagination allowed Vedic ritualists to perform sacred rites, which were understood to contribute to and even establish or reestablish the integrity of the divine universe itself.[36] And, through the contemplative imagination, the meditator recognized the shining image of the divine—the immutable integrity of being itself—deep within his or her own heart.

From the Vedic perspective, the power of visionary knowledge and experience thus allows the seer, liturgist, and contemplative *yogī* to envision, retrieve, and express a powerful wholeness of being despite and within the apparent contradictions and disjunctions of life. Such knowledge and experience both draw on and foster the ability to *imagine* the divine. I want to say, again, that this does *not* mean that the divine is "imaginary" in the sense that it is not real. In its own and various ways, Vedic religion teaches that, when everything is said and done—when layer after layer of being has been discovered, uncovered, and revealed—ultimate reality is beyond manifest form. According to Vedic thought, the single ground of being is the very beingness of being itself, a splendid and transcendent truth that stands as the universal subject of which all objects are images. It is through the universal process of imagination, therefore, that the formless Absolute takes form. As the reflection or image of the divine, the world is therefore not false; it is *satya*: "true."

As we will see, from the Vedic perspective, the world is constantly threatened by forces of disintegration and dissolution. But, again, it is precisely the imagination—this time the human imagination—which allows the visionary whose mind is clear and whose heart is open to recognize the image of the divine even when the world is filled with the diabolical. It may be said, therefore, that the Vedic imagination reunifies, or attempts to reunify, a broken world. It is the visionary who, through intuition and imagination, can envision and then experience abiding truths when there may appear to be none. The imagination allows a person to remember the otherwise dismembered holiness of being.

It is in this, its reintegrative function, that the imagination plays a fundamentally religious role. By "religious" I mean, literally, "pertaining to that which re-links."[37] Like that unifying process known in Sanskrit as *yoga*, religion is that multifaceted, effective process that binds together the totality of an otherwise disintegrated, dissipated, or deadened existence to form an integrated and vital whole. In Vedic India, the sacred imagination serves a similar function. In refreshing the debilitated power of life, in healing the fractured harmony of being, in recognizing the presence of the divine in the world and within one's own being, the imagination thereby relinks this, the artful universe.

Chapter 1

The Gods as Artists: The Formative Power of the Divine Imagination

Well-established in the world, he was a skillful artist:
he who formed these twins, heaven and earth.
Skilled in visionary imagination, with his power
he joined together both realms, spacious and deep,
well-formed, and unsupported.

— Ṛgveda *4.56.3*

A WORLD OF SHIMMERING LIGHT

To the Vedic Indian bards who in the second millennium BCE first gave voice to the hymns that form the *Ṛgveda*, the universe seems not to have been merely a complicated collection of inert objects moving randomly through time and space. During moments of poetic inspiration, the world, for them, came to be seen as a place of wonder, of amazement, of puzzlement; it was a shimmering, almost translucent world which, at once, veiled and revealed hidden sublime forces that, though their effects could be known initially through the senses, finally transcended the empirical realms.

The universe in which the life-giving sun moved through the sky, the silvery moon swelled and diminished through the month's nights, the stars delighted the heavens, bright and fearful darts of lightning punctured the dark thunderclouds, fecundative rain brought new life to the earth below, and streams and rivers chattered boisterously down their valleys and across the plains to the immense and restless oceans: this world was, to these poetic singers, a universe of sparkling light and energy, glimmering with creative power and splendor, and shining with transformative, powerful brilliance.[1]

Light, especially, captured their attention. Since it was through the illuminative power of light that objects were known to exist, all things therefore were seen to consist of light: the light of the sun revealed the objects on earth as much as it revealed the sun itself; physical objects were, to these seers, crystallized light. In a sense, therefore, sublime light was the universal essence of every and all particular things. Furthermore, in a way, light gave rise to all things: forms previously laying inchoate and vague in the darkness emerged in the presence of light into their unique shape and texture. As the universal essence and creator of everything, light was seen to be equivalent to being itself, and thereby to truth. To perceive light was thus to gain knowledge of reality.[2]

Reality itself: this was revealed by the play of light. The universe as a whole glowed with the inner creative power of light, which suffused and gave being to all things. Since creative light played on the many surfaces and forms it created, the world as a whole was a world of play;[3] it was a cosmic game, a universal riddle, the meaning of which few could understand. The visionary, poetic sage saw that play, understood those riddles, and sang forth his song in response to the brilliant creation.

Not surprisingly, those seers tended to describe the foundational, formative, and transformative forces that give form and movement to the universe with language that connotes not only effective power but also a kind of shimmering luminance or glow that seems to reflect a deeper and more powerful splendor and brightness. Since the primary luminous objects shining their light onto the world resided in the skies as the sun, moon, lightning, and stars, verbal images of celestial brilliance are particularly prevalent in Vedic songs. Thus, for example, the Vedic noun *div*, which means "sky" and thus "heaven," likely derives from an Indo-European verbal root meaning to "shine."[4] From the root *div* comes the important Sanskrit word *deva*, which as an adjective means "divine" and thus "heavenly." As a noun, *deva* means "divine power" and thus "deity."[5]

To the Vedic seers, then, the light-filled objects that gave shape to the universe as a whole were images of hidden forces, the formative power of which gave substance and life to that universe. Those images were regarded as the many *deva*s and *devī*s—that is, the various gods, goddesses, and demigods—who were said to live and act in the various earthly, aerial, and celestial domains.[6] Different poets saw different numbers of divinities in the world. One sang, for example, of the "thirty and three gods,"[7] while another praised 339 deities who had served the shining god of fire alone.[8] Later Hinduism was to declare that the number totaled 330 million. A sense of the ubiquity of the divine is succinctly stated in one sage's admission that wise people had

sought you,
O fire that knows all beings,
O god of wondrous splendor,
in many places.[9]

Since it was suffused with light, the world was filled, for these poets, with the presence of the gods. The stars that illumined the nocturnal heavens were not merely dots in an impersonal sky, but the shimmering eyes of the goddess of the night, Rātrī. Of her we hear a seer's proclamation:

Here comes the Night!
Adorned once more in all her beauty,
she has looked about with her eyes.
The goddess has seen many places.[10]

The rivers were not merely water moving toward the ocean; rather, they were sparkling revelations of Sarasvatī, the chattering, flowing goddess who brought life and prosperity to the world. A Vedic verse delightfully described the rivers as

young unmarried girls who,
knowing the true harmony of the universe,
flow forth, streaming and bubbling
like fountains.[11]

The lightning that jumped across the sky was not simply an impersonal, jagged flash of energy; it was the thunderbolt of Indra, the king of the gods, who battled the cloud-dragon living on the mountaintops. Pierced by those bolts, the demonic serpent gave forth the life-giving waters it had trapped within its body. Indra

. . . killed the serpent who lay on the peaks.
The mighty waters rushed downward, falling into the sea,
As if they were lowing cows.[12]

The wind was Vāyu or Vāta, a powerful and free deity who traveled wherever he wished and who gave colorful rise to the storm's flashing bolts and the red clouds of swirling dust. A verse from a song to Vāyu reads:

The Wind's chariot: its power!
It runs, crackling.
Its voice: thunder.

It ruddies the many regions
    and touches the heavens. As [the Wind] moves,
    the dust of the earth is scattered.[13]

The dawn on the eastern horizon was not merely the beginning of the day: she was Uṣas, the daughter of Father Sky and the divine Earth and the older sister of the goddess Night. To Vedic poets she was beautiful and playful. Look, for example, at *Ṛgveda* 1.124.8–9:

Leaving,
    but to return,
Night gives up her place
    to her older sister who
    beaming with the sun's rays,
    dresses splendidly,
like a girl
    on her way to a festival.

Or *Ṛgveda* 7.77.1–2:

Dawn arrives, shining—like a lady of light—
stirring all creatures to life. . . .
Dawn's light breaks the shadows.
Her face turned to all things across this wide world,
she rises in splendor, enwrapped in bright clothes.
Shining in golden colors, dressed with rays of light,
she guides forth the day like a cow leads her calves.

The Vedic poets thus seem at first glance to have held the objects of nature in reverence:[14] they sang songs to the wind, to the lightning, to the rivers, to the stars and the dawn. But closer attention to their songs shows that those verses reflect the idea that the objects and events of the natural world gave form to more profound, hidden truths. The actual objects of their praise were not the things of the world, but the forces that brought those things into existence, for to them the real brilliance of being lay not in the shimmering surface of things, but in the effective power of life itself, which somehow linked the many objects to one another in a universal tapestry. Physical forms did not reflect external light; they revealed inner light, the glow of which brought them into view. Similarly, the brilliant gods did not shine onto the world's various objects as much as they lived within them. "Entering into this world through their hidden natures,"[15] the gods adorned the universe as a whole.

So, for example, while the Vedic community venerated the fire (*agni*) that burned in the heavens as the sun and flashed in the sky as lightning as well as that which crackled in the household hearth and cooked the food, the *real* fire the Vedic poets held in reverence was Agni, the divine power of heat itself, the hidden god who lived in and gave brilliant form to all such distant and nearby fiery things at one and the same time. The same Agni who warmed the hearth also bedecked the skies. As one poet said, "He, the friend of the household, has dressed the heaven's vault with stars."[16] According to another,

> he who is made to grow within our own homes,
> whose beauty is praised at sunset and sunrise,
> whose truth is unconquerable:
> the glowing one, whose flames do not die,
> shines forth his brilliance
> as the sun does its splendor.[17]

The single Agni "of many forms" served as the universal energy of life itself:

> O Agni, much acclaimed!
> It is you, O god of many forms,
> who, as in ancient times, gives the power of life
> to all people.
> Because of your power of life you live in all food.
> When you shine forth, your light glows
> without defeat.[18]

Hearing their songs, one senses that the poets not so much worshiped the processes of nature as much as they pondered the larger and seemingly more miraculous emergence of truth and being ("light") from evil and nonbeing ("darkness"). This is how one such seer described the arrival of the hidden goddess of the dawn given form by the softly glowing morning light:

> As if aware
>   that her arms shine
>   from her morning bath,
> she rises
>   so that we may see her.
> Dawn, the daughter of Heaven,
> has come to us
>   with light,
> driving away
>   evil and darkness.[19]

THE GODS AS UNIVERSAL CREATORS

Their songs thus suggest that the visionary seers who first sang the verses that came to be collected and memorized as the *Ṛgveda* saw the world to be populated and enlivened by the many hidden deities revealed, in part, by the play of light. Without those deities, in fact, the world in a sense would not exist, for without light there would be nothing to see. The use of the English word *exist* here is intentional. It literally means to "stand out" (from the Latin *ex-sistere*)—that is, to emerge or come forth from an indistinguishable and vague background—and is distantly related therefore to a number of Sanskrit words that imply the coming into being and preservation of something firm and durable, or that suggest an enduring and abiding firmness.[20] From the Vedic perspective, the objective world was brought into existence by the bright and shining gods, who established and stabilized that world by forming and then entering into its many shapes, which they took as their homes.[21]

The world thus established by the shining deities revealed the creative power of the gods, just as the light of the sun revealed the sun itself. However, while the world's many bright and luminous forms revealed the gods' formative power, the deities themselves remained hidden, just as light is invisible until it finds reflection in an object.

But, in the Vedic vision, the gods did more than shape and enter into objects, thus bringing them into existence. They also created the dimensions of space itself. Why might this be so? Again, the experience of light is elucidating. Stretching in some mysterious way, invisibly, across empty space, the light that defines the shape of the sun rising in the east simultaneously comes into view again in, say, the shape of a tree on the western horizon. The hidden light thus measures off that distance, as with a ruler, and separates objects from one another, thereby creating the world in a way similar to that in which builder builds a house by marking off its length and width and separating the walls from each other. So it was with the Vedic gods, who not only entered into the many and various forms, but also measured off the distances and thereby created space. We see a suggestion of this idea in the following lines from a hymn sung in praise particularly of the god Indra, but which offers homage to the gods and goddesses in general:

> With firm minds, and virtuous, they fashioned the heavens;
> they have come to be the foundations of the earth. . . .
> Entering into this world through their hidden natures,
> they adorned the regions for [Indra's] control;
> measuring with rulers, they fixed the wide expanses and
> separated and secured the immense worlds.[22]

We see it, too, in another paean, also to Indra:

> You, who by eternal law has spread out
> flowering and seed-bearing plants, and streams of water;
> you, who has given form
> to the incomparable bolts of lightning in the sky;
> vast, and encompassing the vast universe:
> you are a fit subject for our song.[23]

Vedic sages were especially intrigued by this, the gods' mysterious and wondrous power to form something where previously there apparently was nothing, an inexplicable power the seers held in wonder and understood to reflect a certain mysterious divine wisdom. One such seer sang this to Indra:

> With your wisdom and power, and
> through works of wonder,
> you have placed nourishing milk in the raw cow's udders. . . .
> You, Indra, have spread out the wide earth—a mighty marvel—
> and, high yourself, propped up the high heaven.
> You have supported both worlds—
> young mothers from the timeless, universal harmony whose
> sons are gods.[24]

Another asked the god Tvaṣṭṛ (the "Fashioner") to form children within women's wombs: "At the time when our wives draw near us, may Tvaṣṭṛ give us heroic sons."[25]

Sometimes the deities were said to use that skill to form objects and to effect extraordinary transformation in order to perform rather mundane magical feats, as when, for example, the celestial Aśvins were said to free two poets who had been tied up, thrown into a wall, and covered with water;[26] to release a poet who had somehow become encompassed by the growth of a tree; to have given milk to a cow's dried udder in order to quench a weary man's thirst; to return an old man to youth; and to bring a dead boy back to life so his father could look at him.[27]

Most of the time, however, the poets praised the gods' wondrous abilities when thinking of the marvels of the natural universe. According to one seer, the gods Mitra and Varuṇa used their miraculous ability to form objects in the dimensions of space, as when they brought the rising sun ("the powerful one") into the skies:

> Firmly established in cosmic order,
> the powerful one swiftly follows each of the dawns

and enters into the worlds:
great is Mitra's and Varuṇa's
magical power!
Dawn spreads her splendor in all directions![28]

The god Varuṇa is the sole object of similar reverence for the singer of the following verses from *Ṛgveda* 5.85, which give a good sense of the manner in which Vedic poets praised the gods in general. We might note also the delightful poetry here: that the poet saw Varuṇa to have "woven the air between the tree branches," for example, reflects a fresh and evocative vision.

1. Sing forth
        a deeply resonant, sublime hymn,
        grateful to the celebrated Lord of lords,
    Varuṇa,
    who has opened the earth
        for the sun to spread out,
    as one would stretch
    the skin of an animal.

2. It is Varuṇa who
        put milk into cows and
        mighty speed into horses, and has
    woven the air between the tree branches.[29]
    It is Varuṇa who
        has placed fire in the waters,[30]
        the sun in the heavens,
        ambrosia in the mountains, and
    effective imagination within hearts.

5. I will proclaim
        this wondrous act
        of the mighty Varuṇa,
        the Lord immortal.
    It is he, who,
        standing in the skies,
        has measured the earth with the sun
        as if with a ruler.

6. Truly, no one has ever
        hindered or prevented
        this most wise god's
    mysterious, transformative power,

through which,
        despite all their waters,
        the rivers fill not even one sea,
into which they flow.[31]

We again see in this song the Vedic idea that the gods, Varuṇa in this case, formed the world by measuring off its dimensions and by placing the various objects in their proper place: the deity has stretched out the earth like an animal skin and marked off its contours as if with a ruler; he also has placed the sun in the skies and *soma* in the mountains. Such is his mysterious creative ability. Furthermore, according to the vision represented by this song, Varuṇa himself is the source of inspiration in the human community, for it is Varuṇa who puts imagination within the human heart.

To the Vedic seers, the many objects of the world thus were not merely separate and insignificant things: they were exactly what they were because they had been brought to light by the gods; they had been measured, placed in position, and impelled to do just what they did by hidden divine forces and powers, which preceded, sustained, and enlivened them. It was the gods who brought out the stars at night, who clothed the mountains with clouds, and who pulled the rivers to the sea, the latter of which miraculously never overflowed. The objects of the world found their individual particularity, their inner integrity or support, in the various gods' creative will; for the world, and all things in it, had been given shape and enlivened by the many deities' clever dexterity and shimmering, transformative splendor.

THE GODS' INNER TRANSFORMATIVE POWER

For the Vedic seers, the world populated and directed by divine powers was therefore a world of mystery, puzzlement, and wonder. Such a perspective found expression in *Ṛgveda* 4.13, a truly beautiful song in praise of the mysterious and brilliant beauty of the dawn. The poet saw the sun as an image of Agni, whom he called here by the more specific names Sūrya (the Shining One) and Savitṛ ("he who sets in motion"). He noted the presence of other deities as well. We have already heard of the Aśvins the poet mentions in the first verse. They were celestial gods, twin offspring of the sun, who were said in many of the *Ṛgveda*'s hymns to ride through the sky in an aerial chariot pulled by flying horses or birds and to bring fortune and health to the world below:

1. Agni has gazed benevolently
   on the radiant, wealth-giving dawn.

Come, Aśvins, to the homes of the pious.
The sun, the divine power, rises with splendor!

2–3. The divine Savitṛ
spreads wide his brilliance,
waving his banner on high,
like a victor searching for spoils.
Following the established law,
Varuṇa and Mitra, the rulers of secure realms,
raise the sun into the heavens.
With unceasing consistency
they impel Savitṛ to drive away the darkness.
Seven strong and shining steeds
bear upward the sun,
whose eye sees all things.

4. His mighty horses spread outward
like a spider's web,
tearing the night's dark robe.
The shimmering rays of the sun
submerge the darkness beneath the waters,
like a heavy tide.

5. How is it that—neither tethered nor supported—
the sun stays in space?
Why does he not fall?
Who has seen what inner power moves him?
A celestial pillar, he guards the vault of heaven.

Putting aside a discussion of the delightful imagery and use of poetic tropes in this hymn (this *is* vivid language, even in translation: "waving his banner on high, like a victor searching for spoils . . . His mighty horses spread outward like a spider's web, tearing the night's dark robe"), we can see in these verses that the seer's interest was caught by the brilliance of the rising sun, which he praised as an embodiment of the god of fire, Agni. But he sang of more than the Aśvins and of Agni. We note in the second verse that the poet referred to the gods Varuṇa and Mitra, heavenly deities who throughout the hymns of the *Ṛgveda* receive praise due in part to their ability to guide the movements of the universe as a whole. Here, they are said to raise the sun into the heavens, "following the established rule."

By the fifth verse of the song we sense that perhaps the visionary sage was even more deeply impressed by this established rule than he was of either the sunrise or the gods, for here he reflected his amazement at the perplexing fact that the sun does not fall from the sky. Agni may well have "spread wide his brilliance" as he "gazed kindly on the radiant dawn"; Varuṇa and Mitra may have watched over the proper movements of the sun into and through the heavens; but what, the seer asked, was that hidden, sustaining force—that invisible "inner power"[32]—that supports even the god Agni himself and by which the sun travels across the skies? How is it that the sun does not fall, although there seems to be nothing supporting it? The singer could see in the sun the heavenly image of the god; but, he asked: Who has seen that hidden inner power that supports even the god himself?

The Fervent Transformative Power of Tapas

Vedic texts often depict the deities' inward transformative power as an energetic, forcefully fervent heat they describe as *tapas*. In the natural world, the primordial heat of such *tapas* lies principally in the element of fire. The powerful energy of life-giving and life-sustaining fire may exist inherently, as it does, for example, in the god of the sun, Sūrya, who burns with vital and transformative force. Such *tapas* may need to be cultivated and generated through diligent inward fervor, as is the case for the warrior god, Indra, who must fuel his inner fury in order to do heated battle with the various demonic enemies of the sacred universe. *Tapas* is also revealed in the fire, *agni*, which burns in the sacred altars in Vedic ritual arenas.

In any case, *tapas* is understood in the Vedic world to be an effective, energetic power closely associated with creative or transformative activity. As such, it is most closely identified with intense ascetic fervor. Vedic thought holds that the god Prajāpati's power of *tapas* is so strong that, through it, the Lord of Creatures creates the world itself. A sacred story holds that, in the beginning, Prajāpati existed by himself. He wished no longer to be alone, so he created the universe and all creatures in it. He did so by cultivating his inward heat and, bursting with that blazing energy, exploded outward, just as a well-stoked fire produces innumerable sparks that rise into the darkness. The luminous parts of Prajāpati's disseminated body formed the various regions and beings in the world. His same *tapas* subsequently served as the vital energy that brought those newly formed creatures to life. According to the Brāhmaṇa literatures of the Vedic canon, the Vedas themselves were born in a like manner. Accounts of such a process appear rather frequently. Here is an example:

> Prajāpati wished, "May I be propagated, may I be multiplied." He practiced *tapas*. Having practiced *tapas* he emitted these worlds: the earth, the atmosphere, and heaven. He warmed up these worlds, and when he did so, the bright ones [that is, the luminous deities] were born. Agni

> was born of the earth, Vāyu from the atmosphere, Āditya from heaven. He warmed up these bright ones, and when he had done so the Vedas were born.[33]

Vedic thought was to associate *tapas* not only with cosmogonic heat, but also with other forms of transformative energy: it is an intense purifying force as well as initiatory heat, revelatory light, contemplative fervor, and blazing ecstatic power.[34] Because it was the energetic heat by which the world was fashioned (we might say "cooked"), *tapas* was a universal force that preceded even the gods and through which the world came into being. Referring to an unnamed, unified deity or primordial state of being he called simply "the One" which came into being from the depths of nonbeing through the force of *tapas*, one Vedic seer sang these verses as part of a cosmogonic hymn:

> In the beginning, darkness was obscured by darkness;
> all was water, indiscriminate.
> Then, stirring, that which was hidden in the void—the One—
> emerged through *tapas*.[35]

In fashioning and sustaining the world through *tapas*, the gods therefore necessarily drew on an inward power through which they themselves had come into being. They "cultivated" or "practiced" *tapas*. Such ascetic practices were usually described in physical terms: the gods were said, for example, to toil and struggle in their creative work. But at times the cultivation of that power was said to occur in the mind and to take fruit in the form of mental activity itself. The same visionary whose verses we just read also noted that the *tapas* through which the world emerges from the chaotic darkness is closely connected with the generative power of the mind:

> . . . that which was hidden in the void—the One—
> emerged through *tapas*.
> Desire entered into the One, in the beginning:
> That was the first seed of thought.[36]

COSMIC CREATIVITY AS DIVINE IMAGINATION

For Vedic seers, then, the world was real not simply because it existed; for them, the world was real because it had been *brought into* existence.[37] It had been conceived and constructed, formed and performed by the gods themselves. This idea is suggested by the following verses from *Ṛgveda* 10.72:

1. Let us now with poetic skill proclaim
these the generations of the gods,
so that others too may see them
when these songs are sung in future ages.

2. Brahmaṇaspati formed [this world],
firing and smelting [it together], like a smith.
In an earlier era of the gods,
from nonexistence existence came. . . .

3. In the earliest era of the gods
existence came of nonexistence.
Then, the cardinal directions arose
from within the swelling creative power. . . .

7. O gods! When, like austere artists,
you made all things grow:
just then you brought forward the sun
who had been lying, hidden, in the sea.

Another song, *Ṛgveda* 10.81, traces all of creation to the work of a divine architect, whom it addresses as Viśvakarman, the Maker of All Things. How the cosmic artist did so remained a mystery. With what materials did Viśvakarman make it? How did he do it? If he made all things, including the dimension of space itself, then where did he stand while he made them? Here are some selections from that song:

1. Taking the role of a priest, the Seer, our Father,
once offered all these worlds in a sacred ceremony
and endeavored to attain munificence.
Through his own power of will, he himself
entered into subsequent creations,
thus cloaking the first creative moment in mystery.

2. Where did he stand when he took his position?
What supported him?
How was it made?
From what did the Maker of All Things,
beholding all things, fashion the earth and
shape the splendor of the skies?

3. With eyes looking in every direction,
with faces everywhere,
with arms and feet extending to all places,

The god,
—alone—
creates the heavens and the earth,
He welds them together with [air blown by]
his arms and wings.

4. From what lumber, and from what tree
were the heavens and the earth carved?
Ponder this, wise people!
Inquire within your minds:
On what did he stand when he made all things?

In the first verse, the poet expressed the view that the mysterious universal progenitor created the world from the depths of eternity (before all "subsequent creations") and then entered into the forms he had shaped, thereby hiding himself within the structures of the world as a whole. We might note also in verse 1 that the poet regarded the god to be not only a cosmic architect but a visionary poet as well; he was also a cosmic priest, a liturgical actor whose drama both formed and performed the world. According to that same verse, the universal artist is said to build the world in and through the power of his will. In other words, the force driving such creation resides in the god's mind. As the same poet said of that universal creator: "exceptional of mind and of exceptional creative power is Viśvakarman, the establisher, the disposer, and most lofty presence."[38] We have already seen a suggestion of this same idea in a seer's proclamation of the gods: "with firm minds . . . they uphold the sky."[39] Another poet similarly sang of the artistic ability of a deity he did not name but who, too, formed heaven and earth through the force of the imagination:

Well established in the world, he was a skillful artist;
He who formed these twins, the heaven and the earth.
Skillful in visionary imagination, with his power,
he joined together both realms, spacious and deep,
well-formed, and unsupported.[40]

Vedic poets used several words to describe the gods' creative power of the mind. For example, in this last passage Vāmadeva described the unnamed deity who forms the heaven and the earth as *dhīra*, a word built on the verbal root *dhī-* (to "envision mentally," that is, to "see" in the mind) and thus referring to one skilled in the power of imagination. Another poet similarly proclaimed this of the god Soma:

This sage who is skilled in visionary imagination [that is, this *dhīra*]
has measured out the six wide realms

in which no beings are excluded.
This—yes this—is he
who has made the width of the earth and
the high heights of the heavens.
He formed the nectar in the three sparkling rivers.
Soma supports the wide atmosphere.[41]

A third said this of Indra, the king of the gods:

Indra! You are splendid:
mighty in mental power and
skilled in visionary imagination [*dhīra*]!
Strengthen us, too, with such might, O Lord of Power.[42]

The poet here associated Indra's nature as *dhīra* with his possession of resolute mental power. The word is *kratu*, which refers to one's effective skill based on one's deeper force of intention, purpose, or determination. By means of this ability Indra and the other gods inwardly planned the dimensions of an object, drew those mental plans outward, and projected them into the world of space and time, thus forming the world of objective shapes. We see an example of this in *Ṛgveda* 1.39.1, in which, thinking perhaps of bolts of lightning or rays of sun crossing the sky, the poet pondered the mental power of the gods that such brilliance expresses. The Maruts here are Vedic gods of the storm.

Maruts! Movers of the earth! When you spread forth your measure
from far away, like flame, O Maruts,
to whom do you go, to whom, [and]
by whose *kratu*, through whose image?

We might paraphrase these questions in this way: "What is that divine imaginative power, O Maruts, by which you bring things into existence?"

The *Ṛgveda* associates such a transformative power of the will with a certain dexterity, not only in the sense of physical strength and artistic skill but also of adroit intelligence, clarity of mind, and mental power. Such dexterity is itself associated not only with imaginative skill but also with a certain shimmering brilliance.[43] The gods' power of imagination constituted a creative force the texts sometimes characterize as "all-pervading, far-extending, powerful, creative."[44] It took extraordinary strength to effect such change.[45] Nevertheless, Indra himself claims that "my power alone is all-pervading; I am able to accomplish whatever I wish through my mental expression."[46] The gods therefore were understood to be bright, dexterous, and strong artists who drew the universe into being through the power of their imagination.

So, in the *Ṛgveda* there are many ways to indicate the deities' powerfully transformative, effective, and creative mental power.[47] The most important of such means, however, would be that represented by the word *māyā*. Later Indian philosophers were often to use this word in the sense of the mind's pernicious and misleading tendency to fabricate unreal worlds; for them, *māyā* was equivalent to what we might call illusion or even delusion. But early Vedic seers used this rich and important word to describe the marvelous and mysterious power by which the gods and goddesses were able through the power of the mind to create dimensional reality seemingly out of nothing. The power of the gods' *māyā* allowed them to convert their divine ideas into manifest forms. Through the power of their imagination they constructed or fashioned the many and various physical objects that constitute the world as a whole. And it was through their *māyā* that they projected themselves into those forms as a way to enliven them and to direct their activities.[48] We have already seen instances of the word: "great is Mitra and Varuṇa's magical power [*māyā*]," for example[49] and (we could also translate this as "incomprehensible mental power"), "truly, no one has ever hindered or prevented this god's wondrous transformative power [*māyā*], through which, despite all their waters, the rivers fill not even one sea into which they flow."[50] Their *māyā* was thus the gods' effective power at converting an idea into physical reality, a marvelous power the poets regarded as derived from and expressing the gods' inner wisdom and insight.[51] For those poets, divine *māyā* was a profound art beyond ordinary comprehension.

The derivation of the word *māyā* remains somewhat uncertain. It may come from the root *mā-*, meaning to "measure" or "give dimension to" something. If so, then the term is related to the verbal root *mā-*, to "mark off, mete out, apportion, arrange, show, display" and thus to a number of verbs[52] referring to the making, building, fashioning, shaping, or constructing of something by conceiving its dimensions within the mind and then—in the process of "measuring" what has thus been imagined—projecting or converting those plans into three-dimensional space. Converting their mental plans into the plan of the universe, they stretched out the physical world, so to speak. This is the meaning of the verb in *Ṛgveda* 8.41.10, in which the poet sang of the god Varuṇa as he who, "following his sacred vow, spread over the dark ones with a robe of light; he who measured out the ancient place, who propped the worlds apart." This is also the sense in which the verb is used in 8.42.1, in which Varuṇa is declared to have "measured out the breadth of the earth." In both instances, Varuṇa mentally conceives the dimensions of the earth and then projects those plans outward, giving them three-dimensional form.

Alternatively, the word *māyā* may derive from the verbal root man-, to "think."[53] If so, the implications regarding the role of the deities' imagination in the formation of the world are obvious. In either case, however, in early Vedic thought the word *māyā* signified the wondrous and mysterious power to turn an idea into a physical reality; the power of *māyā* is the power to realize one's conceptions, specifically through the formative power of the imagination. The gods were described as *māyin*, that is, as "possessed of the power of *māyā*."[54] Imaginative human beings possessed the same power. We will return to this latter point at length in subsequent chapters, but we might at this time look again for a moment at *Ṛgveda* 3.38, wherein the poet played with terms signifying such a creative process. While Sanskritists will recognize in this translation the repeated use of words built on *mā-* and *man-*, those not familiar with the language will still see the close relationship between imagination and cosmogony. We have already read from verses 2 and 3 of this hymn; we repeat them here, and add others, to emphasize the point that it is the divine imagination that measures off the dimensions of the different realms of the universe, thereby bringing all forms into being.

1. Like a strong horse good at pulling, like a skilled workman,
I have formed a prayerful thought.
Pondering what is the most cherishable and noble,
filled with inspiration, I yearn to see the [divine] poets.

2. With firm minds, and virtuous, they fashioned the heavens;
they have come to be the foundations of the earth.
These are those expansive realms for which the heart longs;
they have come to support the skies.

3. Entering into this world through their hidden natures,
they adorned the regions for [Indra's] control;
measuring with rulers, they fixed the wide expanses
and separated and secured the immense worlds.

4. They adorned him even as he climbed upward.
Self-luminous he moves, dressed in brilliance.
That is the bull's—the divine being's—mighty form:
consisting of all forms, he bears immortal names.

5. First, the primordial bull produced progeny.
These are the many drinks that gave him strength.
Since time immemorial you two kings, two sons of heaven,
have gained dominion by means of insightful songs.

6. O Lords, three seats do you hold in the sacred assembly.
Many, even all, do you honor with your presence.
Having gone there in my mind, I saw
celestial beings with windblown hair.

7. They fashioned the milk-cow [that is, the dawn] and
her friend the strong bull's [the sun's] many various forms.
Providing yet other new celestial figures,
those with wondrous creative ability shaped a form around him.

Their *māyā* allowed the gods to produce what were, from the Vedic perspective, the genuinely wondrous marvels of nature. According to *Ṛgveda* 5.63, to pick just one example, it is through their *māyā* that the gods Varuṇa and Mitra not only somehow placed the sun in the heavens, but also by which they mysteriously brought heavy thunderclouds into a previously empty sky, hiding that same sun but bringing life-giving rain to the earth. The singer of the song seems to have been amazed at the ease with which the Maruts, too, undertook a similarly miraculous art. Indeed, it is through their *māyā* that the gods governed the events of the universe in general. In verses 4, 6, and 7 from that hymn of praise we read:

Mitra and Varuṇa! Your *māyā*
stretches itself up to heaven.
The sun—that sparkling weapon—moves forth as light.
You hide him with clouds and with rains in the sky.
O Lord of the Rainfall, your sweet drops burst forth.
Mitra and Varuṇa! With care, the Lord of the Rainfall lets resound
his refreshing, loud, and mighty voice.
With their *māyā* the Maruts delicately clothe themselves in clouds:
you cause the ruddy, spotless sky to rain.
Wise Mitra and Varuṇa! Through your *māyā*
and with your laws
you watch over the ordained way.
You govern all the world by means of eternal order:
you placed the sun in the heavens
as a chariot recognized by all.

Vedic seers understood the gods' *māyā* to be of truly universal import, for without it the world would not exist, nor would it be capable of sustaining itself. We see this idea clearly in a verse to Indra:

He made firm the sloping hills and
determined that the waters flow downhill.
Through his *māyā*
he supported the earth that gives food to all living beings and
kept the heavens from falling.[55]

That the physical world as a whole in all of its wondrous complexity was seen to have been formed and enlivened by the inexplicable, creative artistry of the gods and goddesses suggests that, in Vedic India, the universe as a whole was an artifact, an image of the divine deities' incomprehensible wisdom and creative mental skill to convert nothingness into three-dimensional form. Viewed from this perspective, the world is an artifact of the divine imagination.

DIVINE IMAGINATION AS COSMIC BEAUTY

If the world of the Vedic poets was one of shimmering light that revealed or reflected hidden divine forces, it also was, in some ways, a world of sublime beauty.[56] Not surprisingly, these poets often described such beauty with terms that suggest a shimmering luminescence[57] or the pleasing play of light.[58] Those terms also suggest the process of sight and the appearing of something into the realm of vision.

To note the appearance of something was to perceive its emergence into being, that is, to recognize the fact that it has been created. Viewed from this perspective, all of creation has been formed by the brilliant gods and goddesses and is, in a literal sense, beautiful. Referring to Agni in the form of lightning, *Ṛgveda* 3.1.5, for example, proclaims that, "clothing himself in light, the life of the waters, he measures off his expansive and perfect beauty." Not infrequently, a poet's experience of visual beauty therefore was conjoined with his recognition of the hidden, dynamic harmony of the universe as well as of the gods' creative power. So, for instance, noting Varuṇa's sublime presence in the sky's magical change from darkness to light at the sunrise, one poet sang:

> He has encompassed the night and
> by means of his *māyā*
> has formed the mornings:
> he is transcendently beautiful!
>
> Following his sublime law, his beloved ones
> have brought the three dawns to fullness for him.
> Strikingly beautiful over all the earth,
> He has formed the regions of the sky.[59]

Another visionary praised Agni, here in his celestial forms as the night's moon and the morning's sunrise:

> At night, Agni is the world's head, then
> as the sun, takes birth and rises into the morning.

The prompt Priest goes about his work,
intuitively knowing the *māyā* of the gods, who are to be honored.
Beautiful is he who,
glowing in his magnificence,
has shined forth, resplendent,
well stationed in the heavens.[60]

For his part, another seer described the god Indra as the

creator of the earth and he who has formed the heavens:
he whose laws are sure
has brought forth
the swelling, shimmeringly beautiful waters.[61]

Praising the presence of Agni in the sun and moon (the "eyes of heaven") as well as in the rays of light that stream from them, one seer proclaimed:

O, Agni!
When the immortal gods
made both eyes of heaven
to him they gave the gift of resplendent, delightful beauty.
Now they flow forth
like rivers set in motion.[62]

Of the sunrise and sunset, another sang:

In golden, gorgeous brilliance, well-adorned,
they shine forth
with wondrous beauty!
May dusk and dawn remain with us![63]

Since divine power and light were seen to be equivalent in many ways to beauty, the gods were often understood to be the source of beauty itself as well as the source of inspiration through which beauty is appreciated. "You, the divine Maker, have made beauty perfect!" exclaims a verse to the god Tvaṣṭṛ,[64] while another notes that "under the god Savitṛ's influence, we contemplate all that is beautiful."[65] Sometimes that divinely created beauty was described in delightfully personal imagery, as in a song to the goddess of the dawn:

You make your attractive form visible to everyone,
as alluring as a bride dressed by her mother.

How brilliantly sacred you are, O Uṣas!
Shine more expansively!
No other dawns have achieved what you have achieved.[66]

For Vedic poets, to see light was therefore to see the gods, and to see the gods was to see mysterious beauty. To see the gods was also to see the appearance of being, and to see the appearance of being was to see the process of creation itself. The gods, the creative process, mystery, beauty: all this was revealed to the Vedic poets through images of light. The world was a brilliant image brought into being by the splendid universal imagination.

THE CREATIVE VOICE AND THE EXPANSIVE WORD OF THE GODS

Vedic sages not only saw the divine; they also heard it, and they sang what they heard in the form of verses, songs, and chants. Just as light was seen to be the creative essence of all things, so sublime sound was heard to be the foundation and essential nature of all that is. As such, sublime sound was honored and revered as a goddess, who not only formed all things but stood within them as their essential nature as well. Vedic poets heard the divine as *vāc*, "word"—or, more accurately, as "voice"[67]—and identified it as the goddess Vāc, the universal "Voice" herself, who through the power of her creative Word forms the universe in its entirety. Vāc was the universal Poetess who, like the ancient Greek *poiētēs*, was known to be a "maker," a "creator" of worlds, through the power of her language and speech.[68] Understood in this way, the cosmos was a poetic work of art, for it was, itself, a universal poem.[69]

Just as the bright and shining gods were revealed, in part, by the shimmering luminance of atmospheric and celestial bodies, so too the voice of the goddess Vāc was heard, for example, in the thunderous roar of the stormclouds and songs of the wind blowing through the many regions: "My home is in the [heavenly] waters," she sang to one seer. "From there I spread out on all sides all over the universe. . . . I breathe as the breeze and support all the worlds."[70] Raining from the skies and blowing through the air, her voice became all creatures. The sage Dīrghatamas likened Vāc to a lowing buffalo cow from whose

thousand-syllabled [voice] in the sublimest heaven . . .
    descend in streams the oceans of water;
It is from her whence
    the four cardinal directions derive their being;

It is from her whence
flow the immortal waters:
It is from her whence
the universe assumes life.[71]

Her association with the flowing waters that brought fertility to the earth and to lowing cows whose milk gave life and nourishment linked Vāc with other Vedic goddesses. One poet described Aditi, the mother of the gods, as a milk cow, for example;[72] so did another, who praised that same goddess as the "heavenly mother" who "pours forth sweet milk" and "healing waters."[73] Vedic seers frequently described Uṣas, the goddess of the dawn who escorts the day's light over the eastern horizon, as a cow returning to the pen. One poet noted that all things in the universe were given life by the divine cow he called Viśvarūpā: "she whose form is all things."[74] Singers of a hymn in the Paippalāda or Kashmir rescension of the *Atharvaveda* offered praise to the wondrous and generative universal cow and identified her not only with expansive cosmic space and the earth itself, but also with the invigorating goddess Iḍā ("she who streams forth," "she who refreshes") and with Virāj, the cosmic principle and power of a multiplying and multiform creation and thus an embodiment of the creative process itself.[75]

Her role as divine creator linked the goddess Vāc with a number of other deities of the Vedic pantheon who are said to fashion the world by one way or another. We might mention here the similarity between Vāc and the god Dhātṛ, who found praise from Vedic poets as "he who establishes" and thus as "he who creates" the world; with Tvaṣṭṛ, "he who fashions"; and with Savitṛ, whose name means "he who sets in motion" or "he who vivifies." The creative power of Vāc's divine Word is reminiscent also of that power held by the god Bṛhaspati, whose name means "Lord of the Expansive Power."[76]

But it is particularly the goddess Sarasvatī with whom Vāc was most closely associated in Vedic literature. In the song offered in praise of Vāc, Dīrghatamas referred to the goddess as Sarasvatī when he sang:

O Sarasvatī, present to us your inexhaustible breast
so that we may suck from it:
that source of pleasure with which
you allow all choice things to flourish,
which gives wealth, bestows treasure, and grants good gifts.[77]

In later Hindu traditions, Sarasvatī was to become the muse of the imaginative arts and of creativity in general. Her name literally means "she who possesses the quality of flowingness."[78] It is not difficult to see the connection here: from both cows and rivers flows nourishing liquid, and both cows and rivers produce mellifluous sounds. Although she was at times identified as a lowing cow,[79] Sarasvatī is particularly praised in the *Ṛgveda* as a goddess of the divine waters in which she dwells: the flowing streams that brought nourishment to the countryside, the celestial oceans in which the heavenly bodies rest, and the ethereal streams that bring life to various realms as they move throughout the many regions of the universe. "Descending from heaven" and "pervading all regions," she flows in both "heaven and earth"; she "distribute[s] welfare to the entire vast world."[80] Dependent on no other god for her life-giving power, she is described as "virginal" and "autonomous," in other words, as independent and whole.[81] One seer addressed her as "O Sarasvatī! Supreme mother, supreme river, supreme goddess!"[82]

As the goddess residing within the vitalizing, revitalizing, and cleansing waters, Sarasvatī received adoration as "she who purifies."[83] Vedic poets understood the sacred waters' purifying power to have inner as well as outer effect. One of them proclaimed, for example, that "our mother, the waters, will render us bright and shining," for "they carry way all impurities. O goddesses! I rise from them purified and brightened!"[84]

It is because of her inwardly creative and clarifying function, in part, that the flowing goddess Sarasvatī found praise as "she who inspires excellent ideas,"[85] a role that placed her in a position of much reverence for Vedic priests singing the poems and songs as part of the ceremonial performance of Vedic rituals, for she was the divine source of and the inspiration for those generative and therefore sacred words, verses, prayers, and hymns. According to the poets, it was Sarasvatī therefore who "perfects our inspired thoughts."[86]

As a muse who inspired Vedic seers, Sarasvatī was frequently associated in Vedic songs[87] with two other goddesses who played important roles in the sacred drama. Iḍā, who was representative of the sacral food offered to the gods, and Bhāratī, who directed the priests' prescribed movements and sanctifying actions during the ritual.[88] Because (as we will see in Chapter Three) the ritual was the way the Vedic priests aligned human action with divine harmony and order, it is not surprising therefore that Sarasvatī would be known as "she who is possessed of sacred order"[89] and "she who inspires speech that is in perfect harmony with sacred order."[90]

In slightly later Vedic literatures, Sarasvatī was not only associated with, but actually identified as, Vāc. The *Vājasaneyī-Saṁhitā*, for example, literally conflates the two and refers to her simply as Sarasvatī-Vāc.[91] Quoting this passage, the *Śatapatha Brāhmaṇa* adds the assertion, "for Sarasvatī is Vāc,"[92] a line that is repeated elsewhere as well.[93] As such, it is not surprising that Vāc—the universal Word who enlivens, refreshes, and inspires all things—is regarded as residing in the flowing rivers and in the rains falling from the atmosphere, which then give life to all beings. Moving through the world as the 1ife-giving waters, the divine Word dwells in and supports all things.

Although residing within the creation, Vāc was more often proclaimed to abide in a transcendent realm above both the skies and the heavens. Even the deities living in those worlds were said to emerge from her creative voice. Her supremacy is indicated in a verse in which the poet described the goddess as "the sacred syllable in which all of the heavenly deities have found their home."[94] Another heard her exclaim that "through my power I have come beyond this great earth, beyond the sky itself."[95] At times she is said specifically *not* to reside within the objective world, as in the declaration that "above the distant sky, they say, is Vāc, who knows all things but does not enter into all things."[96] The goddess's immortal abode rested above even that of the sun, which some poets saw as residing on a lower level of heaven.[97]

Fully present in the world and yet at the same time fully transcendent, Vāc subsumed all things. She was thereby equivalent to the "one true reality" whom the poet called simply "the One."[98]

In a sense, then, it was Vāc's voice that the Vedic sages heard when they opened their hearts and minds to listen to the eternal truth, and it was Vāc's sublime voice to which they gave human expression when they sang the hymns of the *Ṛgveda*. Their songs revealed the universal Word herself.

As we will see, Vedic visionaries associated what they regarded as that hallowed Word with a principle of harmony and order that preceded even the many gods and goddesses themselves. What was this transcendent, integrated principle of universal balance and order? What was its relationship to the gods, and to the world, and to the human spirit?

These and similar questions lie behind the discussion in the following chapter.

Chapter 2

Reality Veiled and Revealed: On the Artistic Order of the Universe

What was the model?
What was the image?
What was the connection between the two?
— Ṛgveda *10.130.3*

THE UNIVERSE AS IMAGE

Their poems suggest that the Vedic seers did not regard the universe simply as a collection of inert objects randomly occupying space and time with no particular connection to each other. For those visionaries, the world was real precisely because the gods and goddesses—divine artists—had actively and purposely formed it. Through their mysterious power to create and enter into the three dimensions, the deities assumed the various forms that together constitute the world of being. We have already seen that this formative power resided within the gods' minds and gave form to their mental activity. Singing of Indra, for example, a Vedic poet proclaimed that the powerful god was "skilled at assuming many forms,"[1] a declaration shared by another such visionary: "performing mysterious transformations of his body through the power of his *māyā*, the munificent one becomes any and all forms at will."[2] According to a third, Indra "made firm the sloping hills and ordained the waters to flow downhill. Through his *māyā*, he supported the earth that gives food to all living beings and kept the heavens from falling."[3] Still another heard Indra himself declare that "mine alone is miraculous power. I am able to accomplish whatever the power of my mind wishes."[4]

The gods formed and inhabited the world through the mysterious power of their imagination. Each particular component of that intricate, divinely fashioned world possessed its own shape, *rūpa*, a word that might be translated more exactly as "phenomenal form."[5] Each component also had its own distinguishing quality or unique characteristic that in some way made it different from others. This characteristic or quality was expressed in its *nāman*, its "name."

An object in the world necessarily consisted of both "name" and "form," for without a name it had no identity and without a shape it had no place in the world. An object's "name-and-form," was therefore its particular existence: that the sun, for example, or a cow, or a river was what it was and not something else was because of its unique outward shape and distinct inward character. An object's underlying essence and its own manifest form allowed it to stand out from the vague homogeneous background of nonbeing.

To the Vedic seer, the objective world in its entirety was a complicated system of name-and-form, produced by the gods' imagination. Vedic seers therefore regarded such a world as an image or duplicate of some sort of mental model. Relevant words here (*pramā*: "model," and *pratimā*: "duplicate") are built from the same verbal root meaning to "measure" or "mark off," which may lie at the base of the word *māyā*.[6] The prefix *pra-* means "onward, outward, forth," while *prati-* means "returning back toward." Thus, a *pramā* serves as a measured model, and a *pratimā* functions as a reflection of the measurements of that model. In other words, a *pratimā* is an "image" of a *pramā*.

But since an image must imitate something, what was it that the world of discernible forms thus duplicated or represented? What was the model the gods used when they first imagined what the objects of the world were to look like?

We could say that the world as phenomenological image reflected the noumenal or sublime form of the gods. But it did not do so directly; for (as we noted earlier) the gods remained hidden within the manifest forms of the world. Although their effects could be seen in the universe, the gods themselves could not be seen.[7]

From the Vedic perspective, therefore, the physical universe at once both revealed and veiled its sublime source. We remember that it was precisely the visionary sage who was able to see divine paradigms hidden in and revealed by physical forms. That these underlying models were not to be perceived directly is suggested by the fact that, as we will see, Vedic poets were understood to see a divine model's true form and to hear its true name only in their minds and hearts. Such sages—those who knew that the "doors of the mind may be opened"[8]—were described as having gained insight into the hidden truth that resided behind the world of physical form. As one verse asserts, "those who know the highest truths have perceived what is hidden."[9]

A METAPHYSICAL PROBLEM: THE RELATIONSHIP BETWEEN IMAGE AND MODEL

But a problem arises: as we have noted, in the Vedic worldview a manifest shape was seen to be a reflection of a hidden, paradigmatic form of some sort. However, if we take the ideas represented by the relevant terminology seriously, the transcendent model itself was necessarily a reflection of something else. For, just as a phenomenal image reflected the contours of a noumenal model, the world as *rūpa* ("displayed form") must necessarily have reflected some sort of *pratirūpa* ("counterform"). The problem resides in the object of the prefix *prati-*, which we remember means "returning toward" or "reflecting": understood from one perspective, the phenomenal world as *pratimā* is the reflection, while from another view, the noumenal world as *pratirūpa* is the reflection.

What, then, reflects what? What is the relationship between manifest form and paradigmatic model? Do the gods make the world in their image, or does the world make the gods in its image?

Vedic thought suggests that, in a way, it is both. In a most interesting verse, the seer Garga described the god Indra as being both the inherent form and the reflected image of all things:

> . . . the counterform of every form;
> his form is to be seen in all things.
> By means of his *māyā* Indra moves in various forms.[10]

We might ask: To what was it—form or counterform—that Indra's *māyā* gave image? Using other terms in a similar way, another philosopher-poet expressed a similar query:

> What was the model?
> What was the image?
> What was the connection [between the two]?[11]

Either Indra and the other gods were "reflections of the reflections"—creator and creature therefore being the same thing—or both the world and the gods somehow reflected something completely beyond form itself. In either case, the true source must somehow have been a form with no contours, an essence without a name. Although both the world and the gods reflected that transcendent model, the model itself reflected neither the gods nor the world. That primordial paradigm of being must therefore have preceded not only the creation of the world but also the appearance even of the gods.

What, then, was that ultimate reality of which even the gods were reflections? What was its relationship to the gods? What was its relationship to the world? To repeat a query addressed specifically to the Maruts, but which could rightly be put to the gods in general, "By whose pattern do you extend forth your measure?"[12]

In his own delightful way, one Vedic seer pondered a similar question in *Ṛgveda* 10.81, a song to the divine architect, Viśvakarman, whose cosmic artistry the poet understood to have formed the universe as a whole. Because we have already quoted from it at some length in another context we need not repeat this song here. We might simply remember that, realizing that the Maker of All Things established the dimensions of space themselves, the poet then asked: "From what lumber, and from what tree were the heavens and the earth carved? On what did he stand"[13] when he formed the cosmos as a whole?

We see in these passages a suggestion of a very important idea: the gods depended for their creative abilities on something within yet paradoxically beyond themselves. In *Ṛgveda* 4.13.5, quoted in Chapter One, the sun is said to be moved by an inner power: the language suggests the sun's autonomy, but also its ability to align itself inwardly with a force that has an effect on him. Something sustains even the gods themselves. Sustaining them, it must in some way be different or larger than them. Although they give expression to it, something else gives the gods their power and authority, and directs their movements. That hidden or transcendent source of the creative power must not, itself, have been an objective thing, for (as we have seen) objective things must necessarily have been made by the gods. It must have been a principle, namely, the principle of creativity itself.

The figure of Viśvakarman is just one of a number of images Vedic seers used to depict the transcendent yet interior ground of being. Other poets referred to the preexistent and unified source of being as a single "embryo" which, though itself unborn, gives rise not only to the physical universe as a whole but also to all divine powers in the form of the many gods and goddesses. As one seer sang, "it is from this golden embryo that the gods' single spirit came into being."[14] Because it was the sublime and invisible source of all that is, Vedic poets found it difficult to see that unborn embryo itself. Thus:

> That which precedes the earth and the heavens,
> that which always is—
> even before the divine spirits and divine powers had their being:
> just what was that original embryo
> which was received by the waters and
> in which all of the gods were seen together?[15]

It seems that Vedic seers struggled to find words to express their intuition regarding the nature of this hidden principle and power of being. As the poet to whom the previous verse is attributed was to note,

> You will not find that which produced these creatures;
> something else has come into being among you.
> Shrouded by dense fog, and with mouths stuttering,
> singers of songs wander about, frustrated.[16]

Since it gave rise even to the structures of time and space, that creative principle was necessarily eternal and infinite in presence and scope. It was of this—the unmanifest, unified, timeless, ubiquitous, and omnipotent principle of creativity—that the poet of *Ṛgveda* 10.82 sang in the following verses:

> 2. Mighty in mind and exceedingly powerful is the Maker of All
> Things:
> the builder and disposer, the epiphany supreme.
> People rejoice that their sacred offerings are welcomed:
> there, beyond the seven seers, where they say is the One.
>
> 3. The father who gave us our being, who,
> as disposer, knows all things that exist, each and every creature:
> it was he alone who gave to the gods their names.
> To him come all other beings with their questions.
>
> 5. Earlier than this earth, earlier than the heavens,
> before the gods and divine spirits had their being:
> what was this primordial embryo which the waters received and
> on which all the gods, together, gazed?
>
> 6. He was the primordial embryo borne by the waters
> when the gods gathered together.
> The One rested on the navel of the uncreated,
> he in which all created beings abide.

The seer here did not regard Viśvakarman to be a god among the many gods, but rather to be that preexistent power and principle which "knows all things that exist, each and every creature" and which therefore stands as the source of all beings; it is that single primordial Reality which became all the various and myriad things. Furthermore, the poet asserted here that this principle of being preceded even the gods and goddesses themselves: the deities emerged from it, and they directed their vision to it after their birth. He characterized that original, unified, and unifying source as existing "beyond the seven seers," that is, as unbound by time and space. It was "he alone" who gave the gods their names and to whom all return with their questions.

THE VEDIC NOTION OF ṚTA AS THE BEGINNINGLESS PRINCIPLE OF COSMIC HARMONY

We are not to understand by the song just quoted that Vedic poets regarded such a universal principle of harmony and being as a personal god. The image of Viśvakarman here gives personal expression to that impersonal law or foundation which precedes all things, including the gods. The idea behind this hymn finds expression in songs to the many gods and goddesses. Their songs show, therefore, that Vedic seers saw expressions of a deeper (or higher), impersonal, universal principle of balance, concord, and harmony, not only in the personalities of the gods and goddesses but also in the ordered rhythms of life: the daylight's regular emergence from and immersion back into the night, the periodic swelling and disappearance of the moon, the cyclical transitions among hot, wet, and dry seasons. It is on this mysteriously hidden, transcendent, world-forming, and world-sustaining principle that the universe as a whole was grounded, around which it turned, and through which all things in the world had their own inner principle of being. Even the gods themselves must necessarily have lived according to this timeless and eternal principle of universal harmony.

Vedic visionaries referred to this cosmic order, this divine law, by the word *ṛta*, one of the most important in all of the *Ṛgveda*. Throughout the following pages we will capitalize this term as a way to mark its importance and will keep it in roman rather than italic script. As we noted in the Introduction, the word itself literally means "that which is gone" in the sense of "the way things have always been," and thus "the way things truly are." It also implies a certain smooth and harmonious relationship among things that "fit together" properly and well (as we mentioned earlier, it is related to the English word *art*). We might therefore translate the word as "universal harmony." The etymology here suggests the idea that the many and various manifest changes undergone by the world are reflections of an underlying yet transcendent, timeless yet dynamic, cosmic integrity that girds, directs, coordinates, and ordains the movements of the universe as a whole. The day alternates with the night because that is the way the universe "fits together," as it were; that is what the day and night have always "done" or where they have always "gone." As one scholar has written, Ṛta signifies "what has gone on forever, what has always existed without beginning."[17]

The idea that Ṛta precedes even the gods themselves is suggested by the fact that, throughout their songs, the poets whose verses form the *Ṛgveda* described the gods and goddesses not only as aligned with or conjoined to Ṛta,[18] but also to be derived from or born of that very cosmic order.[19] Describing the dawns as the daughters of Heaven, a seer sang: "O Goddesses! With horses harnessed to Ṛta, you travel swiftly around the worlds"; another described Indra, who "lit up the many mornings by means of Ṛta" and who "travels with horses yoked to Ṛta." Vedic poets described Agni as "of the womb of Ṛta" and noted of him that, "emerging from Ṛta, he grew like some young creature, powerful, shining far."[20]

Emerging from and then reflecting the principle of universal order, the gods fashioned the world and watched over it to make certain that it, too, moved smoothly and in consonance with that order. While this latter protective function fell to all the gods and divine spirits in general, it was the central concern for a group of celestial brothers known as the Ādityas, and, among that group, particularly for the god Varuṇa (the "Encompasser"),[21] whom the songs of the *Ṛgveda* honor as one of the most august of divine personalities in the Vedic pantheon.[22] Second in prestige to Varuṇa among the Ādityas was the god Mitra (the "Friendly One"), an aerial deity so closely associated with Varuṇa that, as we noted earlier, in Vedic hymns they sometimes form a dual deity of sorts to whom Vedic seers referred as Mitra-Varuṇa. Poets repeatedly described Varuṇa, Mitra, and the other Ādityas, not as the "creators" of Ṛta, but as its "guardians" or "protectors." In *Ṛgveda* 7.66—a song primarily to Varuṇa and Mitra, but referring also to another Āditya, Aryaman—a poet-priest noted the regular cycles through which the days and seasons of the universe move; recognizing this rhythm, he participated in that universal order by performing sacred rites. Selections from that hymn read:

11. The cycles of the year and the month, the day and the night,
    the proper time to sing the sacred verses and to perform the
        sacred rituals:
    All of this have they made stable. . . .

12. So, at the risen sun today,
    we bring you to mind with sacred hymns[23]. . . .
    You are the charioteers of Ṛta.

The seer then offered praise for the deities who guaranteed and watched over such universal harmony:

13. True to Ṛta, born of Ṛta, strengtheners of Ṛta,
    fearful haters of unholy chaos:
    May we and our patrons live under their guidance. . . .

This seer's vision of the transcendent principle of Ṛta and of the gods' place in the universe in the context of that principle—as well as his own place and, he hopes, that of his patrons—was shared by Vedic poets in general. These visionaries saw the world in all of its intricate complexity as a majestic cosmic artifact in which all objects and events of the universe somehow mysteriously fit together in time and space in a finely tuned and pervasive harmony of being.

ṚTA AS THE FOUNDATIONAL ARTFULNESS OF THE UNIVERSE

Vedic philosopher-poets felt that each element in the cosmos, even each of the deities, was in it own way a work of art, the model for which was not a form but a principle. This principle was the principle of harmony itself: Ṛta.

Similar in some respects to the ancient Chinese philosophers who understood the rhythms and patterns of the world as a whole to reveal an underlying cosmic "Way" (*Dao*), Vedic poets in ancient India felt that Ṛta defined the relationship in which various objects or events, as well as all the aspects of one particular object or event, fit together harmoniously.[24] In a few instances in the *Ṛgveda*, references to Ṛta appear in association with words explicitly meaning "the way" or "the path,"[25] suggesting the idea that (like the Chinese *Dao*) Ṛta is an established and effective truth that girds all that is.

Vedic sages thus understood Ṛta to be the inherent universal principle of balance and concord, a dynamic rule or order in which all things contribute in their own unique way to the smooth running of the cosmos as a whole. If they were aligned with Ṛta, therefore, all things would be true to their own given nature and, in so doing, would properly express their particular function in that intricate and delicately aligned system of order. As the source of the inner integrity of all things and as the foundation of cosmic order, Ṛta was seen by Vedic poets to be inherent in or expressed by all things in the structured universe.

Indeed, to these sages, any particular thing (divine or otherwise) was real or true only to the extent that it displayed its own given or inner principle and thereby aligned itself in consonance with universal harmony. Vedic poets associated Ṛta with *satya*, a word which, as an adjective, may be translated as "real" or "true" and, as a noun, as "reality" or "truth." They sometimes used the words *ṛta* and *satya* virtually synonymously. They praised the god Soma, for example, as "speaking Ṛta, shining in Ṛta, speaking *satya* [and whose] actions are *satya,*"[26] and Agni as "wise, knowledgeable of Ṛta, aware of *satya.*"[27]

That the world was real and true at all was reflected in events that from one perspective are rather mundane and commonplace but, from another view, present a deep mystery. Why does the sun rise in the east every morning? How is it that rivers run downhill? The ancient seers give us a Vedic answer to such questions: "that the waters flow is Ṛta; that the sun extends its light is *satya*";[28] if they were to do otherwise, they would be untrue to their inner nature. False to their given function, they would thereby destroy cosmic order and universal harmony: they would be *anṛta* ("without Ṛta," thus unholy "chaos")—a word Vedic poets often associated with *asatya* ("false, untrue, unreal"). For Vedic thinkers, then, Ṛta not only characterized reality and truth; Ṛta was the principle on which reality and truth were based.

For Vedic poets, then, Ṛta was that eternal truth, that universal artfulness of being, which preceded even the gods themselves, to which the gods aligned and harnessed themselves, and through which they and the universe as a whole have always "gone." One visionary heard Varuṇa himself report that it was

> I [who] made the fluid nourishment of the waters flow forth
> and set the heavens firmly in the seat of Ṛta.
> True to Ṛta and by means of Ṛta,
> the son of Aditi, I have spread out the threefold universe.[29]

Because they saw it to be the normative foundation of reality and truth, Vedic poets sometimes used the word *dharman* ("support, proper conduct") as a near-synonym for Ṛta. One such visionary heard Indra say,

> Following *dharman*, I have spread forth the rivers [across the land]
> and, in the field, the plants that blossom and bear seed;[30]

and responded to that vision by declaring that

> you [O Indra], who has formed the incomparable bolts of lightning
> in the vast, encompassing and immense sky:
> you are a fit subject for our song.[31]

Here, *dharman* is to be understood to be that foundational principle—that obligation or responsibility to the world—to which Indra aligned himself, thus allowing him to bring into existence the different constitutive components of the universe as a whole.

Later Hinduism was to draw on the Vedic notions of Ṛta and *dharman* in formulating and enacting the classical idea of *dharma*, which generally represents a state of a stabilizing "correctness," in both a descriptive and a prescriptive sense. The word *dharma* is in some ways an appropriate classical Sanskrit equivalent for the English word *religion*. We will return to this point in Chapter Six. We might note briefly here, however, that to be "religious" is to be *dharmika*, or "of the nature of *dharma*"; and to be *dharmika* is consistent with what the Vedic poets described as *ṛtayuj-*, "joined to Ṛta."

ṚTA AND THE IMAGINATIVE ARTISTRY OF THE CREATION

To review for a moment: guided and sustained by Ṛta, the universe as a whole thereby followed a universal order of being, a cosmic truth in which all things existed in a balanced harmony with each other. In a sense, the universe was therefore a work of art. As the preexisting formless and thus sublime principle of generative being itself, Ṛta found manifest expression when anything whatsoever in the world was formed, sustained, or transformed. As we have seen, Vedic poets understood such activity to take place by means of the gods' and goddesses' power of imagination. In other words, the deities' *māyā* revealed the structure of Ṛta; the divine imagination revealed the artful universe.

In a verse offered in praise of Mitra and Varuṇa as the guardians of Ṛta and in which he described the sun as a bull who follows the dawn into the sky, a visionary noted the close relationship between Ṛta and *māyā*:

> Based on the firm foundation of Ṛta,
> the bull who pushes the mornings forward
> has entered between the mighty earth and heaven.
> Wondrous is Mitra's and Varuṇa's *māyā*,
> which, shining brightly, has spread its brilliance
> in all directions.[32]

In the following lines from *Ṛgveda* 5.63, a hymn in praise of Mitra and Varuṇa, we see themes not only of the shining quality and celestial home of Ṛta, but also of the equivalence of Ṛta with truth and with moral order (verse 1); we see, too, the association between Ṛta and *māyā* as the effective power of the gods' formative imagination. The poet—who in verse 7 described the deities themselves as poets—sang of the rising sun, which the gods bring into being through the eternal truth of Ṛta and by means of *māyā,* and asked for the gift of life-giving rain formed by similar divine creativity.

1. O Guardians of Ṛta!
   You whose laws are ever true:
   you raise your chariot into the highest heavens
   O Mitra and Varuṇa!
   The rain falls sweetly from the heavens
   onto whomever you wish.

2. O Mitra and Varuṇa! The kings of this world's kings.
   You govern together,
   gazing on the light.
   We ask for your gift of rain, the essence of immortality.
   The rains move
   through heaven and over earth.

7. Wise Mitra and Varuṇa! Through your *māyā*
   and with your law
   you watch over the ordained way.
   You govern all the world by means of Ṛta:
   you placed the sun in the heavens
   as a chariot recognized by all.

Since it was seen to be the foundation and essential harmony of all things in relationship with one another, Ṛta usually was not said to reside in any particular place or in any particular object, nor was it understood to have any particular physical shape. The closest Vedic poets came to assigning a physical quality to Ṛta was to describe it in ways that suggest a kind of glow or brilliance. For example, one poet sang out: "I invoke Mitra and Varuṇa, those who by means of Ṛta strengthen Ṛta, lords of the shining light of Ṛta."[33]

When Vedic visionaries did see Ṛta as residing in a "place," they tended to locate it in the heavens through which the shining celestial bodies moved in rhythmic harmony. So, for example, a seer described the sun as the "pure and lovely face of Ṛta," which, upon its rising, had "shined like gold of heaven;"[34] another saw a celestial home for universal truth when he sang of the periodic, rose-colored dawns, who refreshed their bodies in the "womb of Ṛta";[35] a third described the dawns as awakening and coming to the world from their heavenly home, namely, "from the seat of Ṛta."[36] That this transcendent source of universal harmony was understood to reside beyond the dimensions of the universe as a whole is suggested by such descriptions of Ṛta as located "in the highest heaven."[37]

Vedic poets at times suggested the idea that Ṛta not only was the principle of creativity, but also the power of creativity itself. Several poets characterized Ṛta in ways similar to that in which they described the force or energy of transformation (*sahas*). So, for example, just as the poets regarded Agni as "born of Ṛta,"[38] so they characterized that god as "born of *sahas*" as "made by *sahas*" and as "begotten of *sahas*."[39]

Vedic poets also came to associate Ṛta with *tapas*, which is the powerfully transformative universal "heat" or creative "fervor," the energy of which was understood to bring the world into being and which renewed life. In the following verses from what appears to be a funeral hymn,[40] Yamī encouraged a departed soul to return to the realm of those primordial poets, the gods and goddesses:

> Yes! Let him leave to join those,
> the original followers of Ṛta,
> the pure and holy strengtheners of Ṛta,
> those who were enlivened by *tapas*.
> To those who are skilled in a thousand ways ;
> to those poetic sages who protect the sun; to the lord of the dead;
> to those who are born of *tapas* and enlivened by *tapas*:
> to those, let him depart.[41]

Vedic poets made use of terms implying a powerful "artistic" quality to describe Ṛta. For example, a bard described the gods Mitra and Varuṇa, the traditional divine reflections of Ṛta, as "exceedingly dexterous" deities who had "dexterity as [their] father."[42]

According to this perspective, all things in the cosmos, including the deities themselves, came into being from their preexisting potential as determined by the cosmic principle of Ṛta and emerged into existence through the creative dynamics of that same principle. Allowing for the formation of all things, Ṛta also infused all things. Preexistent and transcendent, yet infusive and immanent in all things, Ṛta was regarded as "great" and as "expansive" or "pervasive" and thus as "mighty."[43]

Described in this way, the principle of Ṛta was similar to the *brahman*, the expansive, mysterious, powerful force that pervades and links all things in the universe. (We will return repeatedly to the central importance of the Vedic concept of the *brahman* in subsequent discussions.) And, as we have already noted, Ṛta was associated with truth, with creative fervor, lustrous energy, and transformative power.[44] Those qualities that characterize Ṛta thus were also identical in many ways with those that characterize the transcendent-yet-immanent creative "Word" of which we have already seen many references and which Vedic poets heard in personal form as the voice of the universal goddess Vāc.[45] We will soon read some specific passages that make this association between Ṛta and Vāc explicit.

ṚGVEDIC IMAGES OF THE EMANATION OF MULTIPLICITY

Their hymns suggest that Vedic poets saw the objective world to be formed in the image of the gods, and those deities themselves as giving image to the formless principle of Ṛta. The whole process by which the universe came into being and through which it came to be known was thus, in a way, one of formative or creative imagination.

If we restate that process in reverse and change the vocabulary somewhat, we may say this of the creative process: the sublime, formless, and unified artfulness of the universe first gives rise to the personalities of the various gods, and then the many gods' formative actions create the diverse components of the objective world.

According to this view, ultimate reality is a unified and sublime whole, the plethoral nature of which emanates or flows outward, forming the world as it does so.[46] Just as the water of a river forms various swirls, bubbles, and waves as it moves forth, or just as light breaks into different colors and shapes as it reflects off dust, so too the unified ultimate reality sends forth (produces or loosens from within) its infinite potential forms, and thus engenders or breaks down into the increasingly diverse and distinguishable objects of the spatial and temporal world. Such an emanation of the One creates the many.

Images of such a transformation of the One into the many appear throughout the *Ṛgveda*. In the previous chapter we read from *Ṛgveda* 3.38, which depicts the One as the "primordial bull," perhaps a suggestion that the actions of all things are directed by the One, the way a bull pushes a herd of cows along the path. This primary mover was the unmanifest sublime in which all things find their hidden model and from which all things emerge. The poet said it better: "consisting of all forms, he bears immortal names."[47]

A variant of this theme, from Brāhmaṇa literatures, asserts that it was the *brahman* that gave rise, first to the gods, and then to the manifest world. The *brahman* created the gods, whom it made ascend into the heavens. It then joined them in the celestial realm, but wished to descend again to the manifest worlds. The *brahman* did so by assuming different "names" and "forms." We read in the *Śatapatha Brāhmaṇa* that

> truly, in the beginning this [universe] was the *brahman*. It created the gods and, having created the gods, made them rise into the following realms: Agni, into this [earthly] world; Vāyu, into the atmospheric world; and Sūrya, into the heavenly world.
>
> [The *brahman*] made those deities who are above those three worlds ascend into the [even] higher realms. For, truly, just as these [three] worlds and these [three] deities are manifest, so too are those worlds and those deities manifest into which he made those gods rise.
>
> Then, the *brahman* itself ascended into the transcendent realm. Having gone to the transcendent realm, it thought, "How may I descend

again into these worlds?" It then descended again in two ways: as 'name' and 'form.' . . . As far as there is anything with a name and a form, to that extent is this [universe.][48]

Earlier, Dīrghatamas had used similar and additional imagery in his complicated hymn, *Ṛgveda* 1.164. That the poet wished to give praise to a single divine whole is suggested by the fact that the song was sung, not to any one god in particular, but rather to the Viśvadevas, the "gods-in-totality." Rich, difficult, and densely packed with various riddles and symbols, the hymn has fascinated Vedic commentators for well over a thousand years as well as contemporary Vedic scholars over the past several generations.[49] It is a long hymn, too long to present here in its entirety (we will include some of its verses in subsequent chapters). Of its several themes, three pertain to our present concern: (i) the ordered universe as a whole is said to descend from a single, highest mode of being the poet describes as Ṛta; (ii) Ṛta is identified as the eternal Word, personified as the goddess Vāc; and (iii) all the various objects and events of the divine and physical worlds are thus different embodiments—articulations, if you will—of the single divine Voice herself. The passages translated below seem to refer on the surface to the emergence of the sun at dawn and to the revolving wheel of the seasons. From *Ṛgveda* 1.164:

6. Ignorant and uncomprehending,
I ask for knowledge from poets who understand:
what was the One who in the form of the unborn
propped apart these six regions? . . .

8. In accordance with Ṛta, the mother yielded the father his share;
for, in the beginning, she joined with him
by means of her mind, reverent in heart.
Recoiling, she was pierced and became filled
with the essence of the embryo.
Reverent worshipers came to offer praise. . . .

10. Alone, he has risen,
firmly bearing three mothers and three fathers who never tire him out.
Above the distant sky, so they say, is Vāc,
who knows all but does not enter into all.

11. Around and around the twelve-spoked wheel of Ṛta turns
as it moves across the sky, never aging.
In pairs, seven hundred and twenty sons stand on it, O Agni. . . .

41. The buffalo cow lowed
producing the tumultuous chaotic floods.
She who is in the highest heaven has a thousand syllables,
having become one-footed, two-footed, eight-footed, and
nine-footed.

42. It is from her whence
the four cardinal directions
derive their being.
It is from her whence
flow the immortal waters.
It is from her whence
the universe assumes life. . . .

45. Vāc was divided into four parts: these
those insightful priests know.
Three parts, hidden in mystery,
mortals do not render into motion;
they speak only the fourth part of Vāc.

46. They name it Indra, Mitra, Varuṇa, Agni, and
it is the heavenly Garutmant.
Inspired poets speak of the One Reality
in many ways. They call it Agni, Yama, Mātariśvan. . . .

47. Yellow birds, clothed in the waters,
fly up to the sky along the dark path.
They have now returned from
the foundation of Ṛta.

In this song Dīrghatamas admits his inability to know the origin of the world and asks for help from those visionary poets who can indeed see into the form of ultimate reality. Like other seers, he calls this unified whole simply the One or the One Reality. He wonders how it was that this uncreated or "unborn" one could have separated the different realms and thus established the dimensions of space as a whole.[50] Verse 8 suggests that the sun is born of the mother (the earth, but perhaps the dawn), who "in accordance with Ṛta," through the power of her mind had joined the father (the sky) in conjugal embrace, then turned from him, pregnant with the solar seed.

The rising of the sun into the eastern sky—the emergence of being from the void—is thus an expression of Ṛta itself. The fact that Ṛta is to be found in the heavens is suggested in verse 47, where Dīrghatamas notes that "yellow birds, clothed in the waters, fly up to the sky along the dark path," that is, the sun's bright rays rise from the aerial ocean of the vague and indistinguishable night; perhaps the line refers to lightning jumping from thick clouds, or to sparks rising from a fire into the darkness.

We will remember from the previous chapter that another poet heard the universal voice of Vāc calling from highest heaven: "My home is in the (heavenly) waters," the goddess sang, "from there I spread out on all sides all over the universe. . . . I breathe as the breeze and support all the worlds."[51] It should not surprise us, then, that in our current hymn, *Ṛgveda* 1.164, Dīrghatamas associates Ṛta with that universal Poetess, whom he says resides "above the distant sky" (verse 10). In verse 41, Dīrghatamas depicts Vāc as a female water buffalo whose lowing voice of a thousand syllables takes form as the flowing waters that surge into the world: speaking in the rhythms of different poetic meters or "feet," the goddess forms all possible sounds. Her single voice, emanating in various creative words, speaks the ordered universe into being: "From her flow forth the [heavenly] oceans," thus establishing the four cardinal directions of dimensional space; from her "flows the universal syllable through which the entire universe assumes life."[52]

Reading these verses together allows us to see that Dīrghatamas seems to have understood all the various components and elements of existence, in all of its multifarious diversity, to give voice to a single principle of creativity, Ṛta, which the poet understands to be the unified nature of ultimate truth, the eternal Word itself. Dīrghatamas notes, however, that wise priests who know the truth realize that human language can give expression to only one-fourth of Vāc's powerfully creative universal voice. The rest must necessarily remain ineffable: "three parts, hidden in mystery, mortals do not render into motion."

For Dīrghatamas, the created world thus gives form to the harmony and order of Ṛta. Some Vedic sages, however, tended to regard the emergence of multiplicity as a fracturing of the primordial harmony of the One into the disjunction and disharmony of the many. For these latter visionaries, the birth of the many gods and thus the formation of the objective world potentially breaks the unified structure of Ṛta itself. This idea carries significance in regards to the performance of ritual, which, briefly stated, enacts the healing of those cosmic fractures and thus relinks that broken order. (We will return to this idea at length in Chapters Four and Six.)

Another Vedic philosopher-poet pondered such a process in quite abstract ontological terms. For him, the timeless and unmanifest One is an unnameable quality-less foundation to all that is, a creative principle that links nonbeing to being as well as transcends both being and nonbeing. First sung at least three thousand years ago, the hymn—*Ṛgveda* 10.129—records a truly profound philosophical musing:

1. There was neither nonbeing nor being then.
   There was no region of air nor sky beyond it.

What moved? Where? Under whose protection?
Was there water, deep and unfathomable?

2. There was neither death nor immortality then.
There was no distinction between night and day.
By its own inner power the One breathed, windless.
Beyond it, there was nothing whatsoever.

3. In the beginning, darkness was obscured by darkness;
All was water, indiscriminate.
Then: stirring, that which was hidden in the void—the One—
Emerged through the power of creative fervor.

4. Desire entered into the One, in the beginning:
That was the first seed of thought.
Searching within their hearts with wisdom
Poets found the bond of being within nonbeing.

5. Their ray extended light across the darkness:
But was there [anything] "above"; was there [anything] "below"?
Generative power was there, and creative force.
Underneath was energy. Above was impulse.

6. Who really knows? Who will proclaim it?
Where was this creation born? Where did it come from?
The gods were born after the creation of the universe:
Who, then, can know whence it comes?

7. No one knows whence this creation has come into being.
Perhaps it formed itself. Perhaps not.
Only he who looks down from the highest heaven truly knows.
Or maybe he does not know.

The philosopher-poet wondered just how it is that existence as a whole came into being to begin with: "Where was this creation born?" he asked. "Where did it come from?" He realized that the answer he sought was beyond comprehension; indeed, even the highest god himself may not fully understand the process. He was puzzled by the apparent fact that being can in any way arise from nonbeing, since "in the beginning, darkness was covered with darkness," and pondered the mysterious and transformative connection between the two. Noting that such a relationship between nonbeing and being necessarily lies outside the established structures of time and space ("there was neither death nor immortality then. There was no distinction between night and day"), he implied that the dualism of nonbeing and being itself arises from an underlying or transcendent unity that subsumes both.

This hymn calls that unnameable source of both being and nonbeing the "One" which precedes even the gods themselves, who are said to be "born after the creation of the universe." That he understood the One to be a dynamic principle is suggested by the visionary's reference to its transformative energy ("generative power was there, and creative force") and by the imagery of breath and of breathing, even though there was no air to breathe: "by its own power the One breathed, windless." Somehow ("perhaps it formed itself") creative fervor stirred in the absolute emptiness (verse 3), giving substance to the One. It is significant that in verse 4 the poet not only associated such formative force with the universal will he characterized as desire, but also saw such creative power to be equivalent to the functioning of the mind.

According to this thoughtful ancient hymn, then, it is the timeless and transcendent One which, in some mysterious way, willfully imagines the universe into being. Even the gods cannot fully understand their own source since they are themselves products of such a process. And yet, imaginative poets who looked "within their hearts with wisdom" and whose insight "extended light across the darkness" were said to have "found the bond of being within nonbeing."

Such is the artful nature of the universe as a whole: all forms and all names whatsoever , divine or manifest, derive ultimately from a unified principle of harmony and power of creativity and transformation. The manifold world of name-and-form reflects the transcendent reality, characterized as the dynamic Ṛta, the principle of which emanates into the divine world as the various sonorous and brilliant gods and goddesses of the Vedic pantheon. Those deities continue this universal production of being through their own secondary power of imagination, thus forming the objective world as a complicated, marvelous image of themselves. This understanding of the nature of creativity reflects an important cosmological concept that, to paraphrase a contemporary scholar, centers on the idea that before the creation of the world all of the many manifest forms were but one universal and unmanifest divine body, and that all names were but one unspoken name, namely, the divine Word itself.[53]

It was the visionary poet who heard that sublime Word and saw that sublime form, and thus aligned himself with the structure and movements of that universal, formative, and sustaining principle itself. It is to the poet, then, that we now turn our attention.

Chapter 3

The Poet as Visionary:
The Artistry of the Verbal Imagination

My ears unclose to hear, my eye to see him.
The light that is placed within my heart brightens.
Far roams my mind, its vision extending into the distance.
What shall I say? What shall I now imagine?

— Ṛgveda *6.9.6*

That they saw the dynamic harmony of Ṛta to give structure and movement to the universe as a whole does not mean that Vedic seers lived a life untouched by discord and imbalance. Indeed, one may rightly be struck by references to hardship and struggle that appear throughout the songs of the *Ṛgveda*. But, as we will see in this chapter, the effective and therefore powerful visionary poet was the one who was able to see and honor Ṛta despite the often fracturing nature of life in an uncertain world.

Drought and the resulting poverty seem to have been of particular concern to Vedic seers, as were disease and raids by neighboring people. Vedic poet-priests chanted verses of prayer as they performed rituals to the gods, in part, so that such misfortune might swerve from their way. They urged Agni, for example, to lighten the community's distress as that divine power ascended into the heavens in the form of smoke rising from the offertory fire: "lift yourself upward, driving poverty and famine far from us."[1] They pleaded to the Ādityas to "drive away disease and struggle, drive away evil, keep us ever distant from arrows, keep us away from famine."[2] One singer prayed to Indra for a plentiful and healthy harvest as well as her own fertility; that she also seems to ask that her father's head be replaced on his body suggests that she was familiar not only with violence but with different kinds of barrenness as well.[3]

Vedic seers envisioned harmful forces as demons, often as powers of deathly darkness and life-destroying drought. They found terror in the

Dānavas, the Rakṣasas, and the Yātudhānas, for example: demonic spirits who roamed in the darkness of the night and who worked to constrain the expansive powers of life. They feared Ahi, Aurṇavābha, and Vṛtra: malignant dragons who kept the water in the clouds from raining onto the land and flowing into the fields. They were frightened of Aśna and Arbuda and Ilībisa; of Kuṇāru, Kuyava, Kuśavā, and Cumuri; of Daśoni, Dṛbhīka, and Dhuni; of Namuci, Parṇaya, Pipra, Bṛsaya, Mṛga, and Margaya; of Vangṛda, Varcin, Vetasu, Viśvāc, and Vyaṁsa: all of whom (and others) Vedic poets regarded as evil spirits of the skies and earth who wished harm against the righteous people who struggled to feed and clothe and shelter their families and themselves. The poets' prayers to the gods to vanquish these demons form powerful and emotional verses. We might look, for instance, at *Ṛgveda* 7.104.3–5:

> O Indra, O Soma! Plunge the wicked ones deep into the depths.
> Yes! Cast them into the darkness that has no end,
> so that none of them may ever return here again!
> Your angry power has to prevail over them and conquer them.
> O Indra! O Soma! Together hurl down from the skies and from the earth
> your deadly, crushing thunderbolt
> onto those who speak evil.
> O Indra! O Soma! Thrust down from heaven
> fire-hot missiles that strike like stone,
> flames armed with fiery passion that never weaken with age.
> Yes! O Indra, O Soma! They should go there without a sound!

Is it any wonder that Vedic poets would describe the gods and goddesses with language of expansive, brilliant light; for what other than light defeats the constraints of darkness? Looking into the daytime's bright skies that had defeated the night's darkness, Vedic visionaries saw the gods and goddesses wearing brilliant clothing, carrying shining swords, and flying freely and unencumbered through the wide atmosphere on blazing chariots pulled by horses with fiery manes. With their bright arrows—flashing bolts of lightning—they punctured the dark clouds, freeing the rain to fall onto the dry earth. Of the Maruts (the "youthful ones"), one seer said:

> Free from taint or dark stain, the youthful ones said to me
> as they arrived boisterously with the birds at the break of day,
> "Praise them in this way, as you see them:
> 'You shine of your own power, you who decorate your chariots
> and bows, your swords and crowns and gold coins and broaches'!"[4]

It was not only the struggle with powerful, invisible demons of which Vedic poets sang; their songs refer not infrequently to bitter rivalries between people as well. Raids and invasions by others seem to have led, at times, to warfare; and—just as they invoked the deities to protect the community against the demons of darkness, disease, and drought—Vedic poets asked the gods and goddesses for help in gaining victory over opposing groups of people: the Bhalānas, the Dāsas, the Guṅgus, the Kīkaṭas, the Vṛṣākapis, and others.

We see in the *Ṛgveda* occasional verses and songs in praise of the weapons that keep the enemy at bay or drive them into oblivion. *Ṛgveda* 6.75 in its entirety is offered to the various weapons and implements of warfare, in a way similar to that in which other poets offer songs of praise to the deities. The bard extended that praise in remarkably poetic ways. In a set of effective similes, he likened an archer's bowstring to an amorous woman embracing her lover (the bow) and her child (the arrow):

> As one who yearns to say something,
> she repeatedly presses close to the ear,
> holding her beloved friend in her embrace.
> Strained by the bow, she whispers like a woman:
> this bowstring that saves us in our battle.
> Joining together, like a woman and her lover,
> these two who move like a young woman to her wedding
> should carry the arrow on their breast,
> like a mother holds her child.[5]

An arrowhead in Vedic India was made of deer horn, while the tail was fashioned of feathers bound together by a strap of leather. The poet described the arrow as a well-dressed and handsome girl:

> Her tooth is a deer,
> her dress made of eagle feathers bound with cowhide.
> She is launched forth; she flies onward.
> There: where the brave run outward in all directions;
> there, may the arrows protect us and give us shelter.[6]

He likened the glove that protected the arm from the sting of the bowstring to a crawling serpent and the handbrace as a loyal and protective friend:

> Like a snake it winds with its rings around the arm,
> repelling the friction of the string.
> So may the handbrace, so skilled in its responsibilities,
> manfully protect the man from all sides;[7]

and encouraged the arrow to perform its function:

> O arrow! Fly away,
> freed from the bowstring and sharpened by our prayer.
> Fly to the enemy; find your home in them;
> let not one be left living.[8]

The song ends with the poet's assertion that it is therefore finally his prayerful verses that keep him from harm:

> Whoever would kill us, be he unknown enemy or one of us:
> may the gods destroy him.
> My nearest and closest armor
> is my song![9]

Vedic poetic visionaries hoped therefore to protect their communities from the threat of the many malignant forces that endangered them. They did so, in part, by imploring the gods to strengthen their own visionary insight and ability to fashion effective prayers. Such prayers often took place in the context of the performance of ritual drama. We see representative evidence of this in these verses from a prayerful plea to Indra and Bṛhaspati (the Lord of Expansive Power or Lord of Prayer), *Ṛgveda* 9.97:

> 2ab. We long for the heavenly grace of the gods to protect us.
> O friends, may Bṛhaspati exalt us. . . .
>
> 3. I glorify Bṛhaspati, most high and gracious,
> with offerings and with praise.
> May the great verse divine reach Indra,
> the king of the divinely fashioned Holy Word.
>
> 4. May that most dearly beloved Bṛhaspati, he who brings all blessings,
> be seated by our altar.
> We wish for heroes and for prosperity;
> may he give them [to us] and carry us safely
> beyond the people who vex us. . . .
>
> 5c–7. Let us invoke Bṛhaspati, who has no foes,
> the clear-voiced god, the holy one of the households.
> Bring him here, this Lord of Expansive Power,
> his red-hued, powerful horses pulling as a team. . . .
> For he is bright and pure,

with a hundred wings and a sword of gold.
He is impetuous, winning the sunlight. . . .

9. O Bṛhaspati, this is your song of praise.
[This] prayer has been fashioned for the thunder-wielding
Indra.
Be pleased with our songs. Awaken our thoughts.
Destroy the godless and our enemy's malice.

These verses, and many others like them, suggest that life in Vedic India was difficult. Scarcity, disease, warfare: these and other death-dealing forces threatened the community from outside in and from inside out. One can almost hear in these songs the cry of the human heart searching for help as it faces a world that has been torn apart by disintegrating and deadening powers.

But we see a suggestion, too, that Vedic bards hoped that their very songs of praise to the gods would protect them in some way from those debilitating forces. "By this, our song, be strengthened," one of them sang to Agni, the god of fire who glows with brilliant light.[10] "Give life to our effective prayer and animate our thoughts," another prayed to the mighty celestial heroes, the Aśvins.[11] Still another proclaimed that "I have sung praises to Indra, the sustainer of this earth and heaven. This prayer of Viśvāmitra ensures the security of the people."[12] At times, Vedic songs suggest the idea that effective poetry offered to the gods brings worldly success and victory over enemies. "Truly, we poets call on you so that we may win wealth and power," reads one prayer. "In war people call on you."[13] Poetic verse in Vedic India served an almost magical function: its very utterance protected the poet and his community.

Furthermore, we see evidence of the idea that the visionary poet not only is able to understand the nature of the disintegrative powers that threaten the world but also through his or her song to elicit other forces that bring health and welfare. For example, in a song to Indra accompanied by an offering of the ambrosial *soma*, a seer pleads for the god to bring freedom from sorrow. His petitionary verses end with an assertion that such a vanquishing does, in some mysterious way, take place.

Most mighty, finder of the way!
Protect us from this utter confusion, from hunger and from evil words.
Comfort us with your grace,
with your discernible power of thought.
May your *soma* juice be poured.
Do not lose courage, O sons of Kali.

This darkening sorrow dissipates.
Yes! It vanishes of itself.[14]

The poet seems here to be proclaiming his realization that, despite and even within the often discordant uncertainties of existence, there is a mysterious and hidden force or structure of being that can defeat sorrow and thus heal the brokenness of life. "Somehow"—we can almost hear this and other Vedic poets say—"the world does fit and hold together, or at least we hope it does; it is sustained; it continues to exist." How it does so, they suggest, is a mystery. Life itself is a puzzle of sorts. In many ways, truth is a riddle.

THE POETIC CONTEST AND THE DISCERNMENT OF THE BRAHMAN

Throughout the *Ṛgveda* we therefore see passages that display a yearning to understand mysterious or hidden truths that Vedic sages seem to have felt established the patterns and directed the movements of the world as a whole. The hidden forces and structures that guided the ways of the universe beguiled these seers. Those sublime powers and laws perplexed, puzzled, and, at times, perhaps, frightened them. It also gave them their creative energy. We remember what one poet exclaimed while thinking of a river flowing into the ocean: "wondrous, everyone, is this mysterious statement: even though streams [continually] flow into it, the [amount of] water in the sea remains constant!"[15] Of course, the poet may simply have been noting the fact that the ocean does not get bigger, the way an engineer might think about the situation. Yet, doesn't his declaration suggest that he felt a deeper sense of puzzled and even reverential awe in front of the incomprehensible mystery of the cosmos as a whole? Furthermore, he held that his very statement about that mystery is itself "wondrous."[16] There is a structural and qualitative connection here between a hidden truth and the way that truth is expressed in words.

Responding to the often puzzling ways of the world they saw before them, Vedic poets came to contemplate within their own hearts the inner significance of those ways and then to express their intuition outwardly. Since the force holding the universe together was itself a riddle of sorts, the verbal expressions by which those visionary poets represented their understanding of that force often took the form of riddles and enigmas put to verse.

Much of the time those questions were presented in the context of the performance of sacred rituals; one poet-priest would intone these queries to others, perhaps originally as a way to challenge and plumb the level of their understanding of the significance of the rite itself. As an example, we might look at selected verses from *Atharvaveda* 10.7. Throughout these lines we see reference again and again to the mysterious unified world-self, the very being-ness of being itself, the universal "pillar" or "support" (*skambha*) that stands as the existential ground or foundation which supports all things in the universe.

1. In which of its limbs does *tapas* dwell?
In which of its limbs is Ṛta established?
Where is its solemn vow placed? Where is its faith?
In what limb is truth made firm?

2. From which of its limbs does the fire flame forth?
From which of its limbs does the wind blow?[17]
From which limb does the moon measure out,
when it measures the limb of the great *skambha?*

3. In which of its limbs does the earth reside?
In which of its limbs is placed the atmosphere?
In which of its limbs is the heaven set?
In which of its limbs is that which is beyond?

4. Toward what does the rising flame aspire?
Toward what does the wind eagerly blow?
On what do all of the turns of the compass converge?
Tell me about that support! What, please, is it? . . .

9. With how much of itself did it enter into that which exists?
How much of it lies in the future?
Into that single limb of which he made a thousand forms:
with how much of itself did the pillar there enter? . . .

11. Where *tapas*, striding forth, upholds the higher vow,
where Ṛta, and faith, and the waters,
and the Holy Word are established together:
tell me about that support! What, please, is it?

12. On whom is firmly set earth and heaven
and the atmosphere between; so too the fire,
the moon, the sun, and the wind, each in its own place:
tell me about that support! What, please, is it? . . .

37. How does the wind not cease to blow?
How does the mind not rest?
Why do the waters, seeking to reach truth,
never, ever stop flowing? . . .

39. To whom the gods continually bring tribute with hands and feet,
with speech and with hearing and with sight
unmeasured in the measuring forth:
tell me about that support! What, please, is it?

The entirety of *Ṛgveda* 1.164 similarly records a series of enigmas expressing the seer Dīrghatamas's sense that Vedic life is a riddle of sorts and presents insights into the nature of that riddle. "Who has seen him who has been born?" Dīrghatamas asks at one point. "[Who has] seen how the boneless one supports the bony? Where is the breath and blood and soul of the earth? Who can go to ask this of someone who truly knows?"[18] Admitting that he is "ignorant and uncomprehending," Dīrghatamas pleads, "I ask for understanding in this matter from the sages who know."[19]

What was Dīrghatamas talking about? Perhaps he was referring to the morning's sunrise, when the sun's shining rays looked to him like bony spikes. How was it, he may have wondered, that such a vital and powerful, brilliant form could apparently emerge from cold, dark, and lifeless earth? But then again he may have been thinking of a fire burning on the ground, perhaps the offertory fire that blazed in the ritual domain: the bony one is the spiked flame, the smoke rising from which holds the sky apart from the earth while at the same time spreading to the four cardinal directions; the boneless one that supports that flame might then be the solid ground underneath the hearth.

Dīrghatamas did not supply a ready or easy answer to his queries. Rather, he presented another enigma:

Bearing the three mothers and the three fathers, the One stands erect;
they never make him weary.
There, on the slope of heaven they speak together of Vāc
who knows all but does not move all.
Made of twelve spokes unweakened by the stretch of time
the wheel of Ṛta rolls around and around the heavens.
There, seven hundred and twenty sons
stand together in pairs, O Agni.[20]

Dīrghatamas's song suggests the idea that some visionaries truly saw sublime, transcendent, or otherwise hidden structures or forces while others could not, and that such vision allowed the seer to understand timeless truths. Dīrghatamas noted, for example, that people whose vision lacked clarity had described some of the deities as masculine when actually they are female and that one whose mind is clear enough to see this breaks the bonds of time to become "his father's father":

Truly, they are female, but people say to me that they are male.
He who has eyes can see this; the blind one does not understand.
The son who is a skillful poet has understood this.
He who truly comprehends it would be his father's father.[21]

In asking his enigmatic questions and other riddles, Dīrghatamas seems not to want a simple or direct answer. Rather, he wants to make a point: that underlying all phenomena in the world is a ubiquitous relationship of the One to the many. The One supports the six regions; the One stands upright and supports the three mothers and the three fathers: those who "have eyes" can see this underlying truth, while the "blind" do not understand.

Even when Dīrghatamas supplies a response to his own questions, his "answers" still veil—yet paradoxically also reveal—that same truth. In a subsequent verse in that same hymn we hear Dīrghatamas demand, possibly of another contestant:

Where, I ask you, is the farthest edge of the earth?
I ask you, where is the center of the universe?
What, I ask you, is this virile horse's semen?
Where, I ask, is the highest heaven, the home of Vāc?[22]

Perhaps having elicited no response from his competitors, Dīrghatamas then answered these questions himself:

This altar, here, is the earth's farthest limit.
This ritual ceremony is the center of the universe.
The *soma* is the virile horse's seed.
This priest is Vāc's home.[23]

In these verses Dīrghatamas answers an enigmatic question with an equally enigmatic response: that which is farthest away is actually right here. The edge is the center. Vāc's home in the highest heaven is to be found here, in the words spoken by the priest. Just as the One is identical to the many and the many are joined to the One, so too the different regions of the universe are so closely connected to each other that they all collapse, as it were, into the very moment at hand. Those with eyes to see and ears to hear would understand that the timeless truth is revealed right here and right now in the structure of the seer's mysterious verses themselves.

As we have already noted, this kind of verse was known in early Vedic India as a *bráhman*, a neuter word accented on the first syllable. Derived most likely from a verbal root meaning to "increase, expand, swell,"[24] the word *brahman* means roughly "possessed of the quality of expansiveness." A *brah-*

man was expansive in two ways. First, it gave voice to the mysterious force that holds the universe together. Second, it was an effective utterance; its mysterious, magical power extended into the world, carrying with it the power of transformation.

It is likely that Dīrghatamas presented these *brahmans* in the context of a competition or sacrificial symposium between poet-priests in which various visionaries challenged each other to understand the hidden forces and structures of being and to express their understanding in verbal form. Such a competition was known as a *sadhamāda*, literally, a "revel" or "drinking feast,"[25] for almost certainly the poets prepared for these contests in part by drinking the enrapturous *soma*, which inspired and transported the visionaries into an ecstasy of sorts. From this ecstatic perspective they were more able to see and understand hidden truths and connections that held the world together.

The *sadhamāda* was thus a verbal contest between visionaries who hoped to know, and then express, a *brahman*. That such a symposium was competitive in nature is indicated by the fact that Vedic songs sometimes refer to the *sadhamāda* as a chariot "race" or "battle."[26] Those contestants in the *sadhamāda* who could not discern the meaning of the *brahman* and then respond to that challenge in insightful and equally or even more enigmatic verses of their own must necessarily have remained silent. They lost the contest. Such less-insightful seers did not advance in the competition; they "are left behind because of their lack of visionary knowledge, while others emerge because of the power of language to which they give expression."[27]

The *sadhamāda* was of considerably more significance than merely verbal exercises undertaken at a festive revelry. They were a central part of the sacred ritual itself, for the competition between poets during the sacrificial symposium substituted, as it were, for the existential struggles that took place outside the ritual domain. One result of such competitions was that one poet was necessarily victorious over another—just as the divine forces of light and expansive life were hoped to be victorious over the demonic forces of darkness and death. This may be one reason why the poetic contests were called battles.

The mood of the *sadhamāda* may have been tense at times. We read that "two [contestants] debate the meaning of these [*brahmans*], sitting in the front and the back [of the symposium grounds], wondering: 'Which one of us who perform the offering will discern [the meaning of the *brahman*] . . . How many are the fires? How many are the suns? How many are the dawns, and how many, really, are the waters?' "[28]

The poet who could not "see" the *brahman* was eliminated from the competition. This was not an insignificant banishment. The person who could not see the *brahman* could not understand unseen and unstated connections between seemingly unrelated events or images, and one who could not see such connections could not be expected to see those that held the world together in general. Such a "blind" poet could not therefore sing the appropriate *brahman* during the rituals performed to help ensure the safety and well-being of that world. We will return to the importance of these rites in the following chapter. It is important to note for our present concern, however, that for an inadequate or unseeing visionary to be cast out of the poetic competition was analogous to his expulsion from the brilliant world of the gods. For such a would-be visionary, it was a defeat of the purpose of his very being.

This, in part, may explain much of the competitive imagery in many of the songs and verses of the *Ṛgveda*. Vedic poetry, in a sense, gave voice to the universal struggle between the various opposing powers that both threatened and sustained life in a fragile and broken world. The successful visionary was therefore the one who could see how all things in the universe in some way fit together despite what often seemed like their disjunctive discontinuity with each other, and could express that vision in words.

TO DISCERN THE "SPARKLING TREASURE WITHIN THE DARKNESS"

In giving voice to the *brahman* by means of verbal imagery, the Vedic poet in a sense aligned his formative, visionary imagination with that of the gods and goddesses themselves, for just as the gods brought hidden realities into the shimmering world of light and sonorous world of sound, so did Vedic poets bring forth previously unformed images from deep within their hearts. Readers will recall from the discussion in Chapter One that early Vedic sages regarded the objective world as a whole to be a mysterious artifact of the divine imagination, the artists being the gods and goddesses themselves. In fact, those deities were often regarded as poets: Soma, for example, and Agni, and Indra.[29]

It was also precisely the god's constructive ability that similarly characterized a hidden yet distinguishing subtle quality of human nature itself, namely, the inner power of the creative or poetic imagination. We remember that, according to one seer,

> it is Varuṇa who has placed
> lightning in the clouds, the sun in the heavens,
> ambrosia in the mountains, and
> effective imagination within hearts.[30]

The wording of this verse suggests the Vedic idea that the poetic imagination is an expression of the universal divine power of creativity itself. The creative force which gave rise to the cosmos as a whole is that, too, which gave rise to the poetic process. This being so, the verbal expressions that reflected that imagination were themselves understood to have a transformative effect in and on the world.[31]

In the Vedic world it was the poet, then, who understood and participated in the secrets of creation. Said to be wise, collected in thought, trembling with the inspiration of the gods, in an ecstatic state from which they could view the world from the immortals' perspective, Vedic visionaries came to see and thus know how the complicated world fit together. That vision was said to take place, not with the seer's physical eyes, but rather in the mind and heart, where images of otherwise invisible and untold truths were revealed, recognized, and clarified. The inwardly stirred and inspired poet—a "wise person"—formed mental images in his or her heart and mind and then expressed those images as verbal insights in the form of enigmatic verses, poetic songs, eulogies, and prayers.[32]

It was thus the visionary's revelatory imagination that allowed him or her to see meaning and significance in what would otherwise remain incomprehensible; and it was seer's linguistic imagination that allowed him or her to express that powerful understanding to others. Doing so, poets brought forth the secrets of the universe because they knew Ṛta.[33]

That which was hidden and mysterious, yet true and beautiful: it was this that fascinated the Vedic sages. As we see in these passages, the poets were understood somehow to see into and to penetrate aspects of being that would be unavailable to normal modes of perception, including that supreme mystery which links being and nonbeing. We see the idea, too, that such knowledge and understanding were somehow to be gained by coordinating the power of the mind with the wisdom of the heart.[34] The visionary saw the bond of being within nonbeing by means of an inner vision. The seer did not make up these verses. Vedic tradition holds that the truths the poets saw with their inner eye were eternal truths and thus not of human origin.[35] The songs they sang were therefore regarded as human articulations of the timeless and divine Word that gives rise to and sustains the universe. Nevertheless, as we will see toward the end of this chapter, their songs suggest that Vedic poets understood their speaking forth of a poem to be similar to the process by which a weaver weaves a fabric or a carpenter builds a chariot, that is, artfully, piece by piece, in a way in which everything fits together perfectly.

The effective poem was thus a verbal restatement or reconstruction of an eternal truth in a new, fresh, harmonious way. Such a newly formed verbal image was understood not only to please the gods' hearts but also to align the poet's imaginative vision with the universal process of creativity itself. The poet thereby joined the gods in a lineage of creative artistry.

As a Vedic invocatory prayer suggests,[36] the language consisting of such images gave verbal expression to the wonder of Ṛta itself:

> My word is firmly established in my mind!
> My mind is firmly established in my word!
> O manifest one, be manifest to me!
> Be for me the foundation of sacred, visionary knowledge;
> Do not let my sacred learning desert me.
> Thus meditating on what has been studied, I join nights and days.
> I will speak of Ṛta; I will speak of the true.
> May that protect me.
> May that protect the speaker; may that protect the speaker.
> Peace, Peace, Peace.

For Vedic seers, Ṛta was to be discerned and uttered forth, like "the wide splendors of the dawns reveal sparkling treasures covered in darkness."[37]

SEEING AS A WAY OF CREATIVE UNDERSTANDING

Readers will recall from the discussion in Chapter One that, looking into the world about them, Vedic poets seem to have been particularly intrigued by the mysterious play and display of light. In light, for them, resided the power of creation, for it was by means of light that objects came to emerge from the deep darkness and thus to appear from nonbeing into being.

The gods themselves were described as powerful forces who brought light to the world, thus bringing it into being.[38] For example, in the god Agni Vedic poets repeatedly recognized attributes of light: "here is all that all is lovely, here there is radiant splendor."[39] This, his power of "illumination," was further understood to give Agni the ability to "see" and thus to "know" all things.[40]

This description of Agni is not unique. Throughout their hymns in the *Ṛgveda*, Vedic poets describe the gods and goddesses in general as knowing all things, having eyes on all sides, many-eyed, and thus omniscient and all-knowing. Of Varuṇa, for example, one poet declared that "the divine being, the all-knowing Varuṇa, has firmly established the sky; he has measured off the dimensions of the earth."[41] Such a divine ability was said to include not only that of seeing into all dimensions of the universe but deep into the human heart as well. The realization that the deities could perceive inner forces is suggested by one visionary's proclamation that "vast, deep, undeceived and many-eyed, the Ādityas see the evil and good within; for all things, even what is most remote, are near to them."[42]

It was in fact their vision that, in part, allowed the gods to create the world to begin with. We remember *Ṛgveda* 10.81.2, regarding Viśvakarman: "How was it that the Maker of all Things, seeing all things, disclosed the heavens with his mighty power [and] produced the earth?" That they held this power of omniscience and creativity was due to the fact that the deities aligned themselves with the transcendent principle of Ṛta. Their vision was thus in harmony with that divine principle. "I bow to all of you mighty and far-seeing heroes," a seer intoned to the Viśvedevas, "to you, the charioteers of Ṛta and dwellers in the home of Ṛta."[43]

Vedic songs further present the idea not only that the gods create the world by seeing it, but also reveal themselves to human beings so that the latter can understand that very creation. Such is the sense of *Ṛgveda* 6.44.8, which holds that Indra, "gaining a great and wondrous name by means of sacred language," has "made his beautiful form apparent," that is, has revealed himself in order to be seen by those who sing his praises.

It is appropriate therefore that Vedic sages came to understand the gods' creation through a visionary experience. We are to remember here that sacred and sacralizing knowledge—*veda*—was understood to a large extent to have been gained through such vision. Their ability to see the gods and goddesses reflected in the objects and events of the world distinguished those sages from other people. Those with less visionary ability might have described the sparkling fire burning in the hearth, the dawn, the sun, the bright sky, lightning in the storm, and sparkling rivers in the valleys as, for example, *citra* ("sparkling, shimmering, beautiful"). Vedic seers, on the other hand, saw in those same objects reflections of the deities Agni, Uṣas, Sūrya, the Maruts, Indra, Sarasvatī, and other gods and goddesses of the shimmering pantheon. As one seer was to sing of the god Vena, "dressed in sweet clothing beautiful to gaze on: he, as light, produces forms that please us."[44] Seeing these deities, the sages' hearts were delighted.

In fact, the hidden gods' and goddesses' brilliance impressed the seers' hearts even more than it pleased their eyes or ears; for although they were said to reside within and be reflected by the objects of the world, those deities who gave life and being to all things could be seen only through the inner eye of insight or heard through the wisdom of the heart.

In the *Ṛgveda*, words denoting sight and the process of seeing therefore frequently suggest a comprehending of something as it truly is.[45] Similarly, Vedic sages described the experience of powers and events beyond the scope of normal human understanding with language denoting visual perception.[46] "The paths of the gods have been revealed to me!" one such visionary exclaimed, for example.[47] The poet thus came to see different realms of the spiritual cosmos that remained invisible to the normal eye. Furthermore, such knowledge allowed the visionary to see that those realms resided within the expansive space of the mind. In a song to Mitra and Varuṇa, gods who maintain normative and moral control over the universe by pervading all regions and thus strengthening them, the seer Viśvāmitra declared that, "having gone there in my mind, I saw the celestial spirits!"[48]

Their inner vision or imagination thus allowed the Vedic sages to come to see not only the sublime laws and structures that supported and directed the workings of the universe, but also the way in which the god's imaginative power actually brought forth that very universe. We see such an idea reflected in a short yet remarkable song, *Ṛgveda* 10.177, on the "Discernment of Delight." The verses tell of a bird and of a cowherder who move constantly along paths. The song apparently refers to the sun, which flies through the heavens like a bird and moves through the ever-changing clouds. At another level, however, the song implies that the bird and cowherder actually stand for the macrocosmic harmony and order of the universe, namely, Ṛta itself. It suggests, too, that the bird and cowherder signify that same artfulness at the microcosmic level, namely, as the inner light of insight or visionary understanding residing within the poet's heart:

1. Those with energetic inner vision
behold in their hearts and in their minds
the bird adorned with *māyā*.
Poets see him in the ocean's innermost depth;
the wise seek the trail of his rays.

2. The bird carries Vāc within his mind;
the divine spirit in the womb formerly uttered it.
In that seat of Ṛta the poets cherish this radiant,
divinely bright, inspired knowledge.

3. I saw that never-resting cowherder
coming and going on his paths.
Clothed in enwrapping waters that move here and there
he moves constantly through the worlds.

Seeing the hidden gods with their inner eye—a process which, as one poet put it, was one of "perceiving thought and light by means of the heart"[49]—Vedic sages then formed verbal images of those gods through their skill at using words, that is, through their illumined poetic imagination. The god of sacred speech, Bṛhaspati, is said to give "lucid words" to the poets,[50] who are described as "holding light in their mouths."[51] Those words then flew from their mouths like birds flying into the skies. When such insight came to him, one such poet proclaimed that "the light which has been placed in my heart" flew away.[52] That same seer praised Agni Vaiśvānara as the divine brilliance that shined within human visionary poets: "he is the immortal light among mortal beings."[53]

It is also because of the significance of light in the comprehension and celebration of divine realities that Vedic poets felt a special fondness for the early morning as the time most conducive to insight and visionary experience. One seer, for example, asked the goddess of the dawn to send "to us the charm of pleasing words" and to "impart inspired visions to us, as you rise."[54] Songs expressing that emergent, inner vision often were sung at the break of day, as is suggested by these lines from *Ṛgveda* 3.39:

> Sung forth and formed into the song of praise,
> this early awakening poetry sung at the sacrifice
> springs from the heart to Indra. . . .
> Born before daylight, auspicious, and
> dressed in beautiful white clothing:
> this, our ancient inspired poem of our forefathers,
> is recited periodically when the sacred functions are performed.[55]

According to this verse, the song that sprang from the poet's heart at the break of day as an inspired poem—a materialized thought[56]—was also sung by his ancestors when they performed rituals. We will return in later discussions to the paradox that the song was both new and old as well as to the important place the song holds in the enactment of ceremonial rites.

THE VEDIC SACRED "VISION"

Vedic poets thus came to know and express divine truths through a process they describe as a mode of seeing and which is closely and frequently associated with the experience of light. Their very contact with the gods took place through such "vision." Those poets spoke frequently of what they called *dhī*, a rich word that can be translated as "insight" or "enlightened ability to see hidden truths" or similar phrases that suggest the visionary's ability inwardly to perceive the sublime yet effective forces that direct the movements of the world and hold the universe together. But *dhī* included more than the passive ability to see the sacred. Through the power of such vision, Vedic poets also fashioned language which, in expressing those truths, allowed them to align themselves with those divine forces. The Vedic "vision" was therefore not only an experience of the gods and goddesses but also a means by which the poet established and sustained contact with the fundamental truths of the universe. Vedic poet-priests prayed to the deities for such vision. We just saw a translation of a phrase in which a Vedic poet used the word *dhī*, "inspired vision," in a prayer to the goddess of the dawn: "impart inspired visions to us as you rise."[57] Elsewhere, another asked the Aśvins to "give us inspired vision" as a way to protect the sacred community from misfortune.[58]

Moreover, as another poet's song to Agni suggests, such vision served as the means by which the gods approached the human community: "stretching the thread, follow the light of space; pay close attention to the paths of light that have been formed by *dhī*."[59] By this we are to understand that Agni is to travel across the wide expanses of space along the paths that are illuminated by the sun but have been made through the power of visionary insight. The poet does not say here just whose *dhī* made those paths. It may have been Agni's, or it may have been the poet's. It is also possible that this "vision" is a presence or process that exists independent of both the deity and the poet. It is the power of inspiration itself, a power on which both deities and wise humans draw and which they share.

The gods are described as *dhīra* ("wise") because they possess that very power of visionary insight. Indra, for instance, is addressed as a "wise seer,"[60] and Agni is praised as the "knowing one" who does not need to ask any questions of the otherwise confusing universe because he is *dhīra*.[61] Agni can see higher truths by looking into his own mind, where the preexisting power of the vision into those truths already resides.

As we will see shortly, human visionary poets, for their part, are said to be able to "fashion [sacred] language with their thoughts" because they, too, are sages who are "wise" or "insightful" (*dhīra*).[62] As a Vedic text notes, seers have access to a certain "skill" or "wisdom"—that is, to the indwelling "vision" or "imagination"—with which they formulate sacred speech.[63] But mere access to that vision was not enough. Vedic seers then had to cultivate and lovingly nourish that insight and express it in well-formed speech. That which is "revealed through love" is that "best and purest secret that had been hidden in mystery within them."[64] The poet expressed his or her clarified vision by presenting a "materialized thought" (*mati*) in the form of sacred verse and song. "O Indra," one poet prayed, "take pleasure in this, my praise; please help me and allow my materialized thought to thrive and increase."[65] That the poet's vision could wither and be in need of rejuvenation is suggested by such prayers as, "May Pūṣan, who moves all, restore fresh vigor; [may that god] revivify my vision."[66] One poet asked the All-gods to "fill this vision up, make it become swollen like a cow's udder filled with milk."[67]

The Vedic "vision" is at times associated with artists, who form their various artifacts after having perceived the model or plan of that work in their minds and then projecting it outward in physical form. In a song addressed to a deity who was to protect the faithful from evildoers, an Atharvan poet-priest asked, "He who as a skillful artisan put together your joints [like those] of a chariot through [the power of his] vision: go to him."[68] The artist fashions his or her work of art by duplicating in the external world the contours of an inward vision. A verse from the *Atharvaveda* describes those who build "chariots" (a reference, as we will see, to poets themselves: the "chariot" being the song that travels to the gods) as those "who possess vision, who are imaginative artists."[69]

It is artists' power of imagination that allows them to bring their intentions into reality, to make their images manifest. As for the Vedic poet, it was the imagination that converted thought into word; and it was through the expression of those words that the poet's intentions became real. This idea is represented, for example, in verse which states that, inspired "by [my] imagination, I honor Agni first,"[70] which suggests that the poet converts his inspiration into a verbal prayer. Uttering that prayer, he brings Agni's presence.

The poet was therefore a person who, by means of his or her cultivated insight, had the clearest and most enlivened access to an already existing yet perhaps unformed vision, a vision the contours and powers of which he or she shared with the deities. The poetic process itself was one in which that sublime model became solidified or materialized into distinct and audible physical sounds through a process of imagination. A verse describing insightful visionaries—"they who by means of vision led the origin of speech, or those who by means of the mind spoke forth sacred words"[71]—represents another important Vedic idea, namely, that the powerful imagination precedes not only speech but the mind itself, both of which are directed by that imaginative vision.[72]

IMAGINATION AND THE POWER OF REVELATORY LANGUAGE

The fundamental reality the visionary's words expressed—the universal Word itself—was understood to be timeless and infinite. Those poets who discerned the universal Word within what could otherwise be the confusing cacophony of existence advanced further in the assembly of seers and gained power and prestige in the Vedic community because their poetry carried the force of that universal truth. Because their songs gave voice to the timeless voice of the goddess Vāc, the language through which those songs were sung was understood to be similarly eternal in nature.

We find striking examples of the Vedic idea regarding the nature of the eternal and infinite Word and its relation to language itself in *Ṛgveda* 10.71, the "Hymn of Knowledge," which includes the following verses.[73]

1. O Bṛhaspati! When they [the seers] came forth
   to make firm the first beginning of language, assigning names,

their best and purest secret that had been hidden in mystery
within them
was revealed through love.

2. When the sages fashioned language with their thoughts,
filtering it like dried grain through a sieve,
friends recognized their friendship.
Auspicious beauty is set on their language.

3. They traced the path of language through ritual;
they found it embodied in the seers.
They held it and distributed it widely.
Together, the seven singers [the primordial seers] gave it praise.

4. Yet, many who look do not see language;
many who listen to do not hear it.
It reveals itself
like a loving and well-adorned wife to her husband. . . .

7. Though all of the friends are endowed with eyes and ears,
they are not equal in their flashes of insight.
Some are like ponds that are as deep as the mouth or shoulder,
while others resemble ponds deep enough to bathe in.

8. When the intuitions of the mind are given shape in the heart,
when those who know the *brahman* perform rites together
as friends,
some are left behind because of their lack of visionary
knowledge while
others emerge because of the *brahman* to which they give
expression.

9. Those who do not improve in any way, who do not know the
brahman,
who do not take part in the *soma* pressing,
who use language in an inappropriate way:
they weave on a warp of faulty thread, without true wisdom.

10. His friends rejoice when the friend emerges
glorious and victorious in the assembly.
He rids them of their error; he gives them nourishment.
He is presented for the prize.

11. One man carefully crafts the verses;
another sings a song in the Śakvarī meter.[74]
One—the one who knows the *brahman*—utters forth the

wisdom of being.
Another measures off the dimensions for the ritual ground.

According to this hymn, some true poets (*ṛṣis*, "seers," in verse 3) hear the eternal Word, while others cannot; for the Word—in a delightful phrase—"reveals itself like a loving and well-adorned wife to her husband." Those to whom she has revealed herself then form words of beauty by "filtering" her divine voice in their hearts and in their minds. Giving names to things by seeing their hidden essence through the revelatory power of love, poets sing the purified, sacred Word in the performance of sacred rituals, including those involving the *soma* offerings, a point to which we will return later in this chapter and in Chapter Four. Those who most purely revealed the eternal through their poetry—that is, those whose verbal images were most harmonious with it and therefore most reflective of the *brahman*—were understood to gain a kind of verbal victory over other lesser poets who, revealing language less purely, merely "weave on a warp of faulty thread, without true understanding."

It may be worth remembering at this point that the full title of the *Ṛgveda* as a whole is *Ṛgveda-Mantra-Saṁhitā*, the "collected *mantra*s of the *Ṛgveda,*" and that the word *mantra*, which literally means "an instrument of the mind," refers generally in this context to all the sacred syllables, words, verses, and songs of that collection. Sacred language gave verbal image to the eternal Word itself, which, in turn, revealed itself in those very images. Good poets were said to be able to see the eternal through the purity of their hearts and minds and then to produce their poems. Thus, the *mantra*s they sang in the assembly of seers gave expression to the eternal wisdom, that is, to the preexistent Word itself.

FUNCTIONS OF THE "MIND" AND "HEART"

We have read several passages from the *Ṛgveda* that reflect the related ideas that the mysteries of the sacred universe were somehow to be perceived in the "mind" (*manas*) and the "heart" (*hṛd*), and that it was in the mind and heart that the power of creativity resided and from which it was expressed. The first idea is stated explicitly while the second is implied. Given their importance, it is worth our attention to look more closely at the Vedic view regarding the functions of the mind and heart and their relationship to each other.[75]

The "Mind"

The etymological source of the word *manas*, "mind," returns to the verbal root *man-*, meaning to "think" or, better (as we will see), to "think in a productive way." In its narrowest sense, *manas* served as the abode for such intellectual functions as cognition and for sensual awareness. In a hymn to various deities, Atharvan singers listed a number of mental functions that warranted reverence and praise: "Would we pay worship to mind [*manas*], to thought, to insightful imagination, to intention, to mental prayer, to instruction, to vision."[76] All these different functions are generally subsumed by that of *manas*; for *manas*—a capability that was possessed by both deities and humans—was often associated with other related functions of sensual perception of some sort and with the knowledge gained from such awareness. Thus, a seer said this of a celestial horse who flies through the skies (perhaps an image of the sun): "I have seen the beauteous reins that guide you and which those who guard Ṛta keep in safety; with the *manas* I knew your spirit from afar."[77]

But the mind subsumed more than just the passive ability to perceive through the senses: it had an active and generative force of its own. It was the mind that admired and appreciated things, for example, as well as felt fear.[78] *Ṛgveda* 8.24.6, in which the poet asked Indra to "fulfill the desire and mind of him who sings your praise," suggests the idea that the *manas* could be gratified when its expectations were met. Indeed, in *manas* resided one's desire for specific ends. So, for example, we hear one poet say: "O Indra and Agni, longing for happiness, I looked within my mind for congenial spirits, or for [spiritual] brothers."[79] The very yearning for understanding itself contributed to inner vision. This same verse to Indra and Agni continues: "no one of the same mind except you is here with me, so I have fashioned this visionary insight for you."[80]

According to Vedic thought, then, the mind is the home of the capability to perceive the world through the senses. The mind also includes the ability to reflect on what has been perceived, and it searches for meaning and significance in the world it has come to know. The mind cognizes, discerns, interprets, and deliberates. That it is the place of inquiry and of the quest for the truth is suggested by one seer's query of his fellow "thoughtful sages to inquire within your minds: where did [the divine Artist] stand when he made all things?"[81] In the mind thus resides the transformative power of insight into the nature of the world, a power which then aligns the workings of the mind with the ways of that world. In *Ṛgveda* 7.90.5, we see the idea that *manas* is that function which understands the true nature of things and directs behavior accordingly: "shining brightly, with minds of truth, [the dawns] travel onward by means of the power of their will."

Two hymns too long to include here, *Ṛgveda* 10.57 and 10.58, suggest that the mind is the effective energy of life itself, a vital power that can separate from the physical body to travel far across the four quarters of the world, journey to the heavens and the deep oceans, visit the sun and the dawns, enter into plants, and go to the distant realms beyond the world: in short, the mind can go forth to "all that is now and is yet to be"[82] and thereby gain knowledge of things beyond the structures of time and space.

It is significant that at least one singer hoped to bring back the departed *manas* by means of the expressive power of the mind itself, specifically through the mentally formed words of the sacred hymns: "we call the *manas* back with the immortal elixir of our departed ancestors, yes, with the effective prayer of the fathers."[83] Verses from these hymns plead the *manas* to return so that "we may be with those who live"[84] and so that the dying person may again possess "effective wisdom, dexterous skill, and living energy."[85]

In its largest and most pertinent sense, the mind was thus considered to be the subtle or immaterial structure of being by which one knows that one was related in various ways to other beings and that, indeed, one knows that one even exists in the first place. Said differently, it is in the mind that the very sense of being alive resides. Accordingly, in Vedic thought the mind further refers not only to the perceptive and inquisitive power through which human beings come to know of their very existence and participate knowingly in that existence but also, more generally, to the "spirit" of life itself, and thus to the "living soul" or the "spiritual principle." To be *manasin* is to be "possessed of a soul." Such inward wisdom finds expression not only in one's thoughts, but also in one's speech and in the practice of contemplative meditation.[86]

The mind was understood to possess a transformative force that could effect change, bring about desired results, and establish a link between the human spirit and the gods. Just as the gods yoked their horses by means of their minds, thus empowering their journey through the skies,[87] so the poet skilled at the verbal imagination focused and controlled the effective power of his mind and through prayerful devotion directed its force toward the deities. "He who offers forth with his mind concentrated wins for himself a great benefactor," one seer assured his fellows in reference to the god Viṣṇu.[88] The poet's mind made such contact, in part, by inwardly forming verbal images of the divine and then pressing those images outward, "expressing" or "producing" or "sending" them forth as a chariot that traveled to the heavens in the form of sacred songs and hymns. Knowing that such an expression would establish contact with them, one seer offered his imaginative intuition to the gods: "Varuṇa and Mitra, may you anoint and make full the home of him who has fashioned this chariot for you in his mind, who makes this expression of insight rise upward, and sustains it."[89]

The Sanskrit verbal root *man-* thus connotes not only the ability to "think" but to "think in a creative or effective way," that is, to form expressive and effective connections not only with the gods and goddesses but with things unseen and as yet unknown. Such creative thought was understood to be intimately linked with the production of verbal images and thus with the verbal imagination. A verse composed of those verbal images—a sacred poem, a holy verse, a "prayer," if you will—was often known as a *mati*, literally, "that which is composed in the mind." The fact that the word *manas* is related through *man-* to the words *manu* and *manuṣya*, "man" or "mankind" and thus "human being," suggests the possibility that, in the Vedic world, the ability to think creatively—that is, to imagine—was understood to be the central distinguishing component of human nature.[90] To be truly human was to be *manīṣin*, "possessed of a thoughtful spirit," and thus "wise" or "spiritual" and, accordingly, "devout" and "pious."

The "Heart"

Vedic thinkers understood the heart (*hṛd*) in similar ways. Like the mind, the heart could see things that the eye could not. Addressing the god Soma, one seer noted that, "looking eagerly with their hearts," visionary poets "saw you flying like a bird up into the heavens."[91] Like the mind, the heart was the component of the human spirit by which one came in contact with the gods. Another sang to Agni: "I, a mortal being, remembering you with the mere heart, call to you who are immortal."[92] The heart thus enabled a human being to penetrate the world's deep mysteries or see into its hidden secrets. Speaking of visionary sages, Vasiṣṭha declared that "by the perceptions of the heart they penetrate into the mystery."[93]

But whereas the mind performed the more intellectual functions of cognition, discernment, volition, and deliberation, the heart served as the home of sincerity, emotional affection, trust, intuition, and spontaneity.[94] The gods were said to know when the sentiments expressed in the poet's words were true: "he sees the hearts within us," one noted of Agni, for example.[95] The gods and goddesses then revealed themselves to those poets who loved them in their hearts. "They [the poets] look upon you with longing in their heart," a bard sang of the god Vena, "as on a strong-winged bird that flies skyward."[96]

And it was in their hearts rather than their minds that the gods themselves heard and recognized that expressive poetry. Thus, one singer was to declare that "my songs of praise soar to Indra like envoys, carrying a well-thought expression put to words by my mind but touching his heart."[97] A god's heart was moved by such poetry in a way that was similar to the emotion a person feels when in the presence of the one he or she loves. Note, for example, this prayer to Agni:

> I sing this newest well-crafted song to him, the ancient one who
> loves it.
> May he hear our voice.
> May it come near his heart and stir it with love,
> as a loving, well-adorned wife embraces her husband.[98]

Vedic poets hoped that the gods not only would find delight in their verses but would also keep those songs with them. "May this hymn of praise rest in your heart," Vasiṣṭha sang to Varuṇa, for example, in *Ṛgveda* 7.86.8.

Vedic poets therefore composed or fashioned their thoughtful songs and poetic phrases in their hearts and then sent them off to the deities they praised. "Agni, with our song we bring you a gift fashioned in the heart," a seer proclaimed,[99] while another affirmed that "from my heart I bring forth a fair song to he who drinks the sweet honey, the *soma*-sprinkled Agni."[100] Similar sentiments find expression in these verses to Agni:

> May our most recent song of praise, born in the heart,
> reach him whose voice is as sweet as honey, even at his birth;
> to whom wise priests, human beings, offered tasty nourishment
> by means of this which they have created;[101]

in these from a song to the same god:

> To him we will send forth from the heart
> this well-fashioned song.
> Will he not understand it?[102]

and in the following lines to Indra:

> From the heart goes forth this mentally formed prayer,
> sung out loud, constructed by verses of praise.
> Please notice that which is given birth for you, O Indra
> the wakening song sung forth in the assembly.[103]

In some ways the mind and heart were the opposite of each other: the mind intellectually pondered and deliberately calculated the mysteries of the gods; the heart felt spontaneous, candid, or even undeliberated affection for them and trust in them. But the poet needed both mind and heart, for both had their distinctive purpose or effective force, and just as the power of the heart complemented that of the mind, the power of the mind augmented that of the heart. As one sage noted,

> The creative power of my will
> and the intuitions of my heart
> exert their effective force;
> they long with love and fly forth to all regions.
> No other source of comfort than these may be found.
> I direct my hopes and yearnings to the gods.[104]

But perhaps the heart, finally, was more important to the poet than the mind. This may have been what one visionary wished to imply when he noted that "when the intuitions of the mind are given shape in the heart . . . [successful poets] emerge because of the power of language to which they give expression."[105]

THE ROLE OF SOMA PAVAMĀNA

The mind and heart served as the places where the visionary poet's knowledge of the divine found its seat. Both were necessary, for the gods revealed themselves to both the mind and the heart. Smoothing and honing the rough edges of the eye's sometimes rather coarse perceptions, the mind explored, discovered, retrieved, or remembered the divine. Filtering and thus purifying what he had found by passing it through his mind, the seer then looked to the heart's wisdom for confirmation of the insights such clarified perceptions brought.[106]

We note here a suggestion of a ritual process of filtration or cleansing. Indeed, we remember that wise seers are said to have "fashioned language with their minds, filtering it like dried grain through a sieve," and that they "traced the path of language through ritual."[107]

The imagery here is reminiscent of the filtering of the juice of the *soma* plant for use in such centrally important Vedic sacred rites as the "Building of the Fire Altar" ceremony (the Agnicayana) and the "Drink of Power" ritual (the Vājapeya) so that offerings could be given to the deities, the correct performance of which was said to ensure health and abundance for the Vedic community.

The hymns of the *Ṛgveda* refer to *soma* as a plant that grows in the high mountains,[108] but whose true home was in the heavens, the realm of Ṛta itself: speaking of the *soma*, a seer noted, for example, that "the young and sacred mothers of Ṛta have sung forth praise; they cleanse the child of the heavens."[109] Vedic sacred narratives tell of a high-flying eagle who carries *soma* down to the earth,[110] where Vedic priests pressed it between stones or blocks of wood. They then filtered the liquid essence squeezed from the plant through the warp and weft of a clean woolen cloth, thus clarifying and purifying it.[111]

The essence of the pressed and clarified *soma* was known as *soma pavamāna* and described with terms suggesting resplendence, brightness, clarity, and a sparkling and beautiful brilliance.[112] The liquid extract, for example, was a "spring made of gold,"[113] whose "swift outpourings flow forth like the rays of the sun."[114]

Vedic poets described *soma pavamāna* as an energetic, restless elixir filled with the expansive power of life and being. One poet-priest put it this way: "more beauteous than the beautiful, this *soma* has clamored in the vat."[115] Carried by the god Agni to the skies along the rising pillar of smoke from the ritual fire into which priests had ceremonially poured it, the refined *soma* flowed across the vast regions of the universe like the currents of a river or flew through the heavens like a strong and many-voiced bird. Doing so, it distributed its vibrant brilliance and clarity throughout the divine realms, carrying with it the songs the priests had sung to the gods.[116] It found its way, finally, to the very top of the universe, the brilliant seat of Ṛta, whence it spread its bright rays across all that is. Singing to *soma pavamāna*, a seer declared that "at your birth you became great. You have found the light. You cover all things."[117]

The *soma* was especially welcomed by the deities in their celestial stations. Drinking that pure and resplendent power of life, the gods gained their own lustrous brilliance. It was from the *soma*, in fact, that the gods gained their very immortality. The refined *soma* was *amṛta*: ambrosia,[118] the nectar of the gods, the bright drop of life from which the divine universe gained its vitality and being.

The *soma* not only carried immortality to the gods; it was immortality itself: "that which is immortality, that is *soma*."[119] The splendor given to them by the *soma* allowed the gods—immortal forces of brightness and light—to bring the world of appearance into being. *Soma*, too, renewed that which had become deadened: as one Vedic visionary noted, *soma* "clothes the naked and heals the sick. The blind man sees and the lame man walks."[120]

In the *soma* thus resided the artful power of transformation and creativity itself. Hoping to please the gods and to ensure their continued vitality, Vedic priests offered the *soma* to the deities as they sang their hymns of praise. "Flow purely on your way, O *soma*, in the sweetest and most gladdening stream," one urged the divine nectar. "Flow onward with your elixir to the banquet of the mighty gods."[121] Another would similarly sing:

> Flow onward, O *soma*, in your own heavenly forms;
> flow, O sacred drop, poured into the cup and sieve.
> Brought forth by human beings and
> descending into Indra's throat with a roar,
> you made the sun climb into the heights.[122]

Drinking the *soma*, the gods were exhilarated, emboldened, and strengthened; hearing with newly expanded heart the songs of praise the Vedic poets sang to them, they rose from any lethargy they may have felt and swelled forth to engage any demonic forces that threatened to constrict or destroy the universe. "In the wild stimulation of this drink, Indra slays all the entrapping demons," we read. "The hero pours his blessings on us."[123]

Vedic priests worshiped the hidden essence of *soma pavamāna* as a god, Soma Pavamāna, or simply Soma, who stood in the same relationship to the physical extract as the god Agni did to the various forms of fire, namely, as sublime power hidden within manifest form. In addition to four hymns elsewhere, all 114 hymns of the ninth book of the *Ṛgveda* are dedicated to Soma Pavamāna,[124] as is the whole of the *Sāmaveda*. Soma Pavamāna was regarded as immortal—"here present this immortal god flies, like a bird upon her wings"[125]—and described with terms that, by now, should look familiar. He was "clear-sighted," for example, and thus "bright, radiant, splendid" but also "insightful, wise, cleverly creative." Other times he is described as "all-knowing," and characterized as being "one with energetic consciousness."[126] Soma thus possessed great creative skill: "because of your creative power you are most wise, O Soma, because of your dexterity you are skillful and all-knowing";[127] "squeezed forth for all to see and delighting the gods, the [holy] drop, the omniscient one, is mental power."[128]

As an agent of expansive vision and creative insight, Soma Pavamāna was regarded as a sagacious and skillful artist whose brilliant vision formed and integrated all things. He was, himself, a singing poet:

> You are the ocean, you, a singer, the all-knowing one:
> under your support lie the five regions of the world.
> You reach beyond the earth, beyond the heavens.
> O Pavamāna, the stars are yours, the sun is yours.[129]

Similar sentiments found voice in a singer's assertion that "Soma, the clear-sighted, skilled visionary and wise singer, is worshiped in the navel of heaven";[130] in another's declaration that "here is Soma, unbridled and energetic, all-powerful and bursting forth, made into a poetic and wise singer by means of his visionary awareness";[131] and in a third's "flow onward, O Soma, seer and singer, true of vision. You have become a poetic sage most appreciated by the gods."[132]

Soma's poetic vision not only enlivened the harmonious artfulness of the universe as a whole, but allowed the poets who sang his praises to share in that vision. "Let him find that which had been lost," one poet asked. "Let him push forward the man who [knows] Ṛta."[133] Others sang this:

> O holy drop!
> You are the master of ecstasies!
> You are the immortal god's favorite drink!
> Show us the way to success,
> as a friend to a friend.[134]

Throughout the *Ṛgveda* we see suggestions that perhaps Vedic seers themselves tasted *soma pavamāna* in which dwelled the god Soma in preparation for the poetic sessions. In a hymn to Soma, the Lord of Visions, a seer noted that "the drop that we have drunk has entered our hearts, an immortal inside mortals."[135] The effect of this elixir on these poets seems to have been similarly stimulating, even rapturous; for those who had inwardly enjoyed its flavor were said to break free from the limitations of the physical body and to enjoy the company of the gods. Having "bound me together in my limbs as a thong binds a chariot," one declared, "the drops I have drunk have set me free in wide space."[136] "Inflame me like a fire kindled by friction; make us see far," he asked of Soma, of whom he claimed that "when you penetrate inside, you will know no limits."[137] Such transport into the sublime was said not only to bring the poet into an intense personal awareness of and intimate relationship with the divine itself, but also to bring him to a state in which he was free of the mundane concerns of mortal existence and thus to the same immortality enjoyed by the gods.

Given the close association in Vedic thought between light and divinity, it is not surprising that the effect of *soma* on the poet's mind was typically described with images of intense or brilliant light. We see an example of this ecstatic transport into immortal brilliance in a seer's exhilarated proclamation[138] that

We have drunk the *soma*!
We have become immortal!
We have attained the light!
We have found the gods!

While it may be Indra's or Agni's,[139] the voice in *Ṛgveda* 10.119 may well also be that of the poet himself:

2. Like impetuous winds, the drinks I have drunk have lifted me up.
Have I not drunk the *soma*?

3. The drinks I have drunk have borne me upward, as speedy
horses pull a chariot.
Have I not drunk the *soma*?

4. The hymn has reached me, as a cow lows to meet her beloved calf.
Have I not drunk the *soma*?

5. As a wheelwright bends a chariot seat, so I turn the hymn
within my heart.
Have I not drunk the *soma*? . . .

8. In my vastness I have surpassed the heavens and all this
   wide earth.
   Have I not drunk the *soma*?

9. Yes! This wide earth I will place here, or perhaps there.
   Have I not drunk the *soma*? . . .

12. I am immense! Flying upward to the clouds, I am the greatest
    of the mighty!
    Have I not drunk the *soma*?

This ecstatic transport is vividly depicted in *Ṛgveda* 10.136, a song dedicated to the long-haired ascetic sages who, having enjoyed the drink, were said to experience the world in extraordinary ways, here represented by the vivid image of magical flight:

1. He with the long hair holds the fire, he holds the drink, he
   holds heaven and earth.
   He with the long hair is declared to be this light.

2. These sages, clothed by the wind, wear dirty tatters.
   Following the rush of the wind, they go where the gods have
   gone before.

3. "Exhilarated by asceticism, we have risen into the winds.
   Our physical bodies are all you mere mortals can see!"

4. He flies through the air, seeing all the various forms below.
   The sage has made himself a friend and associate to every god.

5. The stallion of the wind, the friend of the wind, and urged
   onward by the gods,
   the sage is at home in both the eastern and the western seas.

6. He moves like the heavenly spirits, like the beasts of the forests.
   He with the long hair, reading their minds, is a sweet and
   most delightful companion.

7. The wind has churned [his drink]. Kunaṁnamā has prepared it
   for him.
   He with the long hair drinks from the cup, sharing it with Rudra.

That the experience of ecstasy paradoxically but typically involved not only the expression of outwardly creative or expansive power is suggested by the fact that a word frequently used to describe the effect of the *soma*—the term *mada*, "exhilaration, rapture, inspiration"—is often associated in Vedic hymns with adjectives we can translate as "powerful," "vigorous," "mighty," "successful, victorious," and "speedy, direct."[140] But the word *mada* also implies an inner recognition of inherent and often unmanifest beauty. Thus, it often appears with such adjectives connoting shimmering beauty and a pleasing, delightful appearance.[141] In either case, the effect of the *soma* clarified the poet's mind. *Ṛgveda* 8.48.1 reads:

> Knowing that it inspires well-collected thought
> and joyous expansiveness to the extreme,
> I have savored the drink that everyone, both gods and mortals,
> seeks to obtain, calling it honey.

Such an extraordinary inward yet expansive experience allowed the visionary poet to penetrate the surface of things and to see with the inner eye into their true reality. Just as Mitra and Varuṇa were seen to move the sun through the heavens by means of their inner wisdom in accordance with Ṛta, so too the poet saw the inner significance of that sacred light by means of his visionary imagination:

> O Mitra and Varuṇa, just as you separated Ṛta from unholy chaos
> by means of your own mental dexterity and
> with your own wisdom's mental power,
> so, too, with our visionary insight we have seen
> the golden one in the seats wherein you live,
> not with our [normal] way of thinking or with our [physical] eyes,
> [but] through Soma's own eyes.[142]

Seeing the inner sublimity of the artful universe "through Soma's own eyes" (or "through the eyes that Soma gives")[143] and clarifying their vision in their minds, the poets then gained the skill to form words giving expression to their insights. "This sweet juice held the most powerful ability to bring joy," one proclaimed. "This stirs my voice when I have drunk it!"[144]

Soma inspired the poet and helped him gain the ecstasy he needed for his mind to be able to leave its normal, mundane concerns and to explore the sublime dimensions of the divine universe. (We are reminded of Viśvāmitra's declaration that "having gone there in my mind, I saw also celestial beings with windblown hair."[145]) Soma also enabled the poet to give voice to the insights gained through such extraordinary vision. Its inspirational quality was further understood to bring about an internal transformation within the poet himself such that the seer's own poetic ability improved or even became perfected. We see such an idea in the following selections from the prayerful hymn, *Ṛgveda* 9.4:

1. Win great fame and conquer,
O purifying Soma.
Make us more perfect!

2. Bring us the light—
the heavenly light—
and all things that make us happy.
Make us more perfect.

3. Strengthen our creative skill
and effective mental power.
Drive away our foes.
Make us more perfect. . . .

5. Through your own
effective wisdom and grace,
give us a share of the sun.
Make us more perfect.

6. Sustained and encouraged
by your effective wisdom and grace,
may we look long upon the sun.
Make us more perfect.

Through his "effective wisdom and grace," Soma imparted eloquent vision of the divine to the seer. But even Soma himself was not the original source of that insight. A verse in a song to the god Soma demonstrates the idea that the vision arises originally from Ṛta and is given to the seer through Soma's mediating gift: "the speaker [i.e, Soma, the giver], the lord of this song, the tongue of Ṛta, pours forth this pleasing honey."[146]

THE POET'S CREATIVE KINSHIP WITH THE GODS

Vedic poets were thus inspired and made "more perfect" in their visionary creativity by the god Soma, whom they not only revered as one who "grants poetic skill,"[147] but whom they also understood to be a divine visionary himself whose skill at poetic eloquence was due, in part, to his ability to clarify.[148] Soma clarified the experience of Ṛta and gave that pure vision to the seer. Soma is an

inspired poetic singer of the heavens
whose heart is wise, . . . [who]
sends us delightful poetic abilities.[149]

To at least one Vedic poet, Soma was a god "whose mind is that of a seer, who makes [human] seers, who wins the light of heaven, addressed by a thousand songs, a guide for inspired sages."[150]

Other gods and goddess besides Soma were regarded as cosmic poets. Indra, the most powerful and frequently praised god of the entire Vedic pantheon, was called an "imaginative seer,"[151] for example; and Agni, the centrally important god of fire and thus of light, was described as "one who sings forth"[152] and as a "skillfully creative singer."[153]

So, too, other gods besides Soma were honored as the source of the poetic imagination. One sage hoped, for instance, that Sarasvatī, the ebullient river goddess who came to be identified with the universal poetess Vāc, would inspire him and his fellow poets: "may Sarasvatī, sparkling with life, give us vision."[154] According to *Ṛgveda* 10.125, the "Song of the Goddess," selections of which follow, the muse was Vāc herself. Note in verse 5 that Vāc was reported not only to utter forth the Word but also to inspire visionary priests and poets:

1. I travel with the Rudras and the Vasus,
   I move with the Ādityas and all the gods.
   I hold aloft both Mitra and Varuṇa,
   Indra, and Agni, and the two Aśvins.

2. I hold aloft the swelling Soma
   I uphold Tvaṣṭṛ, Pūṣan, and Bhaga.
   I pour blessings on one who offers oblation,
   one who worships and presses the liquid.

3. I am the queen, the collector of treasures,
   the most wise, the first of those worthy of praise.
   The gods have set me in diverse places.
   I enter into and abide in many homes.

4. Whoever sees, whoever breathes, whoever hears spoken words:
   he gains his nourishment through me alone.
   He does not recognize me, yet he lives within me.
   Listen, everyone! What I say is worthy of faith!

5. It is I who announce and utter forth the Word
   celebrated by gods and humans alike.
   Him whom I love: him, I make swell in strength;
   him, I make a priest, a seer, a sage. . . .

7. At the summit of the universe I bring forth the father.
   My origin is in the [celestial] waters, in the [heavenly] ocean.

From there I spread into all creatures of the world.
I touch even the distant heaven with my forehead.

8. I breathe forth powerfully, like the wind;
even so, I hold together onto myself all things that exist.
I tower above this wide earth and above the high heavens,
so mighty am I in my power and brilliance.

Agni, the god of fire and thus of darkness-destroying light, was also particularly associated with enlightenment and therefore inspiration.[155] That brilliant deity is described, for example, as "one who makes a seer."[156] One poet noted this of Agni:

In response to our praise, O Agni,
release the insight to the trembling singer
by means of inspiration, as if through a channel.
Inspire us with a powerful thought which
you, O Honorable One, and all the gods will accept.
From you, O Agni, come gifts of poetic vision;
from you, insights; from you, effective hymns.[157]

Because the gods inspired human poets, those mortals could thereby come to know the gods. Indeed, many passages throughout the *Ṛgveda* imply that the poet comes in contact in some extraordinary way with a particular god or goddess or with the deities in general. Such familiarity would be suggested by *Ṛgveda* 10.136.4–7, which notes that having "share[d] the cup with Rudra" and "urged onward by the gods" the ecstatic and inspired sage has "made himself a friend and associate to every god." That poets and gods were friends is suggested, too, by a verse to Agni: "sharp-tipped, powerful, strong, of endless energy: Agni, he who knows the sublime song . . . has spoken to me this insight."[158]

This intimate relationship between the poet and the gods allowed the different human and divine parties to come to a sense of mutual recognition. The idea that the poet could know the gods found expression throughout the *Ṛgveda*, but is marked most succinctly perhaps by the proclamation that "We have attained the light! We have found the gods!"[159] That the gods could also come to know the poet is reflected in another's exclamation that "the gods will know me just as I am!"[160] We get a sense of the functional proximity shared by the poet and the gods in a plea to the Vedic visionary priest to "invite the Maruts from the heavens to come here, glorified with your poems" and to make that group of gods "happy with your song."[161]

That the poet and the gods shared an intimate relationship suggests that the poet was, in a way, a kindred spirit to the gods.[162] For, in the Vedic worldview, both gods and poets create things: the gods form the world; poets fashion poems. One might say that the difference between the human poet and the gods was not one of essential nature but rather one of degree: since the gods as *deva*s were more brilliant than the mortal poets, they were more visionary; and since they were more visionary their creative power was more obvious. One seer said as much when he noted that Soma sings out his vision of Ṛta more lucidly (or loudly, as it were) than did the human poet:

> Onward he flows, he who purifies himself:
> the king of everything that sees the sun
> has cried out loudly his knowledge of Ṛta,
> [a knowledge] that surpasses even that of the seer;
> he who is cleansed by the sun's arrowy beam,
> the father of creative thoughts
> whose poetic wisdom is beyond our reach.[163]

Just as the human seer here looked to Soma, the "father of creative thoughts," for productive energy, other poets yearning for understanding regarded their relationship to the gods in similarly familial terms. Bharadvāja Bārhaspatya, for example, regarded Agni as his "father" in the poetic lineage. Worried, perhaps, that he could not keep up with the other poets in composing the appropriate verses in the songs that tied together the Vedic ritual performance as threads bind a weaving, Bharadvāja admitted that

> I know neither warp nor woof,
> I know not which thread they weave when performing the rite.
> Whose son could indeed utter the words here
> better than his father nearby?
> Only this one understands both the warp and woof,
> and will speak correctly the words.
> He knows the thread, as does the protector of immortality
> who, though living here below, sees better than another.[164]

According to a later verse of that same hymn, Agni did indeed inspire the poet's fast-moving imagination: "a steady light has been established in order to be seen; among all things that fly, the mind is swiftest."[165]

The idea that a poet shares a filial relationship with the gods is represented by *Ṛgveda* 7.33.11, in which Vasiṣṭha's son describes his famous father as "the child of Mitra and Varuṇa, born into the world from the mind of Urvaśī." Elsewhere, Viśvāmitra was described as a "great seer" who was "born of the gods."[166] Kusīdin Kāṇva addressed the Viśvedevas by saying, "O bounteous gods, we share together the familial bond of brothers in the womb of the mother."[167]

Vedic tradition in general holds that visionary seers are of the same lineage as the gods.[168] It is in this context that the visionary could say that his true birthplace is in the bright heavens, where the sun spreads its beams:

> Where the seven rays shine forth:
> there my navel extends.
> Tṛta Āptya knows this well
> and praises our equal birth.[169]

That poetic lineage included the seer's ancestors as well:

> Dadhyac, the ancient Aṅgiras, Priyamedha, Kaṇva, Atri, Manu:
> these knew my birth. They and Manu knew my forefathers.
> Their long line reaches to the gods; in them is our origin.
> In their footstep I bow down with my mighty song of praise
> to Indra and Agni I bow with my song of praise.[170]

REVELATORY *VERSUS* CREATIVE POETRY

Much of our discussion in this chapter to this point has revolved around the idea that the poet saw sublime truths by means of the mind's eye or heard the divine Word deep within the wisdom of his or her heart. The gods were felt to have revealed these songs to the Vedic visionary. Having been open to that revelation, the true poet then verbally expressed that inner vision in the form of songs, eulogies, prayers, riddles, and admonitions. Therefore, although their poems were said to "spring forth like the *soma* from the filter,"[171] the vision given to the poet by the gods was not always understood to be a fabricated concept or new idea formed out of nothing. Rather, the poetic process revolved around the discovery or recovery of the same timeless truths the poet's own visionary ancestors had similarly come to see. According to one bard, for example, "we speak from the lineage of our fathers."[172]

Soma freed creative ideas that were already present within the poet's mind but needed to be brought to light. As one such seer pleaded to Soma while pressing the sacred plant, "Sending out your voice as the guide while they purify you, release the singer's imaginative thought, O Holy Drop."[173] Another related a similar notion when he declared that "when drunk, this drink raises my word, this has awakened the victorious inspired thought."[174]

Sometimes that process was described as a kind of drawing forth of the poem from inner to outer realms; this would be implied, for example, by the use of the verb *bhṛ*, to "bear," or to "carry," in such verses as these: "with my mind I bear forth these energetic songs of praise";[175] "carry forth your mental prayer as purest offering to Agni";[176] and "bring this visionary thought to Agni, who enlightens all and gives poetic insight."[177]

At other times, Vedic poets depicted the poetic process as one in which, overflowing with insight, the human heart spilled out that inner truth it had recognized, contemplated, and understood. "To you, O Agni," one sang, "we have poured forth our songs."[178]

The seer's poem thus gave human voice to eternal truths that, although known in the human heart, transcended normal human experiences and limitations. The poets did not actually create the poems themselves. They saw or heard them from the mysterious depths of timeless infinity. In a sense, theirs was not a creative imagination as much as it was a revelatory imagination. Vedic tradition regards the songs of the *Ṛgveda* to be *śruti*—"that which has been heard"—and characterizes them as not of human origin. This is also why they are considered to be perfect in expression and sacred in quality. Thus, tradition holds that these hymns and prayers constitute divine revelation and are not in any way to be altered.

Nevertheless, throughout the *Ṛgveda* we also see suggestions of a more creative rather than solely revelatory or expressive component to this poetry, for the poet is often said in some way to have "made" or "fashioned" his various forms of verbal expression.[179] Such seers were described as "they who with flowing Soma have made an expansive song."[180] The poet Bṛhaduktha, for example, was known as a "maker of a *brahman.*"[181] A similar term may be found in Vasiṣṭha Maitrāvaruṇi's invocation to Indra: "listen now to the effective songs we have made."[182] Sometimes that act of making the verse was put in explicitly creative terms, as in that latter seer's reference to his forefathers in his poetic lineage: "may your auspicious friendship be with us, O Indra, among all ancient and recent seers who as energetic poets have given birth to sacred hymns."[183]

The songs sung by the Vedic bards were indeed at times characterized as "new" or "newly formed." We see this, for example, in the vivid declaration that "I have given birth to this new hymn for Agni, the Falcon of the sky."[184] One poet noted that his song to Indra was not only full and worthy, but new: "for this Hero I have fashioned with my lips comprehensive and auspicious words without precedent."[185] Another spoke similarly of the work of the Vimada family of poets when he noted that "for you, O Indra, the Vimadas have given birth to a full and unprecedented laudatory song."[186] These lines certainly suggest that these particular poets regarded their poems as having been formed rather than discovered and that their verbal skill was essentially creative in force.

We may thus note a possible contradiction. On the one hand, the songs sung by Vedic poets and priests were said to be eternal and therefore uncreated. On the other hand, various passages suggest that those verses were "unprecedented" and have been formed by human beings. How are these two seemingly contradictory perspectives to be reconciled?

THE CONSTRUCTIVE NATURE OF VEDIC POETRY

We can answer this last question by pointing out that most of the time Vedic poets seem to have regarded their work as being more synthetic than strictly creative in nature. They thought of themselves as skilled, first, at penetrating into the mystery of being; second, at forming in their minds and hearts verbal images of those mysteries; third, at whittling and trimming those images, playing with them, shifting them from one context to another, separating them and rejoining them in ways that had not previously been done. This being the case, their songs were newly fashioned works of art; but the mysteries to which they gave expression were timeless and thus uncreated truths. It was in this way, then, that Vedic poets could speak of their recently formed hymns, and yet still hold the position that those same songs were eternal. That to which they gave voice—the pervasive and multivalent Word of the goddess Vāc; the effusive power of the *brahman*; or the timeless, harmonic, universal order of Ṛta—remained, as always, transcendent and uncreated.

Strictly speaking, sacred poetry in Vedic India was therefore more constructive than creative in nature. Vedic poets often described their work as similar to that undertaken by a sculptor carving a figure, for example, or a weaver weaving a fabric; for, in such instances, the artist takes what is given and shapes a new form out of it. "I have imagined a thought like a skilled workman [carves a piece of wood]," one poet said,[187] while another pleaded of Varuṇa, "let not my thread be severed while I weave the song, nor my work's sum be shattered before its time"[188] (the weaving imagery here is similar to that of a line from the *Atharvaveda:* "I know the finely drawn thread on which the creatures are woven; I know the thread of that very thread: therefore, I know the great *brahman*"[189]). Verbs used in poetic descriptions of this process typically suggest the idea that the poet constructed a poem artfully, piece by piece, in a way in which everything fits together perfectly. We might say that such poetry is a "fabricated" work; it is "woven" out of the fabric of previously existing, timeless language.

Sometimes that constructive process was described as a drawing forth of an insight that already lay within the human heart. Such would be the case, for example, in the acknowledgment that "O Indra and Agni, this noblest praise has been produced for you from my soul, like rain from a cloud."[190] (We might remember that rain lies inherent within a cloud before it falls from the sky.)

In at least one instance, the *Atharvaveda* likened the work of a poet to that of a farmer cultivating a field:

> The wise ones, the poets, harness the plows and,
> desiring blessedness, extend the several yokes toward the gods

Therefore, you must harness the plows, extend the yoke
and scatter the seed here in the fertile womb.[191]

The image here suggests the idea that, as a farmer turns and loosens hard soil to allow the earth's "fertile womb" to give birth to an abundant crop, so the poet reworks and cultivates his rough or inchoate insight to produce effective words.

In describing the constructive nature of their work, Vedic poets often made use of verbs based on *takṣ-*, a verbal root meaning to "carve" or "chisel" and thus "to form [an object] by means of carving or chiselling." Such an artistic act of chiselling would naturally be associated with that of planing a piece of wood and of binding wood together to "construct" or "fashion" a functional object of some sort. The poets spoke of their work as being similar to a carpenter who builds something, usually a chariot. Of the several instances in the *Ṛgveda* of this metaphor, mention need only be made of a few: "eager for blessings, human beings have formed this song for you, as a skilled craftsman constructs a chariot, so have they fashioned their bliss for you";[192] "may these prayers to the Aśvins be most pleasing: these which magnify their strength and which we have constructed like chariots. We have spoken forth our high reverence";[193] "with skill they made the smoothly running chariot; they formed the horses who bear Indra";[194] "as an artistic craftsman builds a chariot, so have I, a poet, fashioned this song for you [O Agni]."[195]

Images of both weaving and carpentry appear in these verses to Indra:

Accept, please, these prayerful songs being made—
the new ones we now make.
Seeking blessing, I have formed them
as a splendid and well-made robe,
as a skilled and knowing carpenter has made a chariot.[196]

At least one poet noted that the seer's formation of the hymn was not only a construction but an adornment: "we have prepared this song of praise for you, O Aśvins, and, like the Bhṛgus, have framed it as a chariot; we have dressed it as a bride to meet her groom."[197] The poet's words do not create something new; rather it added something attractive to that beauty which was already there.

These and other lines suggest the idea that such artistic work as fashioning a poem to please the gods was not without the poet's well-trained and sustained effort. The poet may not have created the poem out of nothing, but he or she did have to work at forming it into a work of art. Such is the sense in these verses to Indra:

> For him I send forth a song of praise,
> the way a builder makes a chariot for one who needs it.
> Honor be given to him who delights in our praise:
> a well-formed hymn that travels to all places.
> In order to please Indra and hoping for prosperity,
> I adorn my song with my words
> as if it were a [well-dressed] race horse.[198]

The image of the sacred song as race horse or chariot is consistent with the Vedic idea that the poetic imagination carries the human spirit to realms beyond the limits of everyday life. We should also keep in mind that the poetic competition in which these songs were first sung replaced other forms of rivalry and warfare between opposing people. An effective and powerful poem served the same function as a horse that wins the race or as a chariot that rolls over the enemy's territory. Perhaps this is why one poet noted that the songs of the seers are like the strong horses that pull the chariot to its goal: "to honor you I speak these honest songs to you; hoping for prosperity and fame, living human beings have formed them. May they win your favor, as a race horse reaches its goal."[199] In another hymn, one poet said the same thing of himself: "like a strong horse good at drawing [a chariot], I have imagined a thought."[200]

The final goal of that journey was, of course, the realm of the gods themselves. Just as a builder of a chariot would drive it to its new owner, so the poet sent his poem to the gods. "O mighty Indra, Gotama's son Nodhas has constructed this new prayer for you, the eternal and steady leader who yokes the strong horses. Emboldened by that song, may he come soon and early."[201] Another seer said that he has returned his song to the gods the way a shepherd returns sheep to their owner: "like a herdsman, I have brought you hymns of praise."[202]

THE ṚBHUS AS SEMIDIVINE ARTISTS

Vedic tradition holds that a particular class of primordial human artisans, the ancestral Ṛbhus, were so adept at forming "chariots"—sacred poetry—that they came to hold a force of imagination equivalent in ways to that of the gods. Some passages from the *Ṛgveda* suggest that the Ṛbhus had became more than human, as it were, and more like the gods and goddesses. Vedic tradition holds that the Ṛbhus had in fact gained "immortality" and lived in close proximity to the gods.

For an example of the idea that the Ṛbhus were semidivine artists, we may turn to the opening verses of *Ṛgveda* 3.60. We note in verse 2 that their creative artistry and miraculous power of transformation derived not only from the effective power of the mind but also from the force of poetic vision. We hear this of the Ṛbhus:

> 1. O human [poets]! Here by means of the mind,
> and here, through [spiritual] kinship and knowledge,
> [your visionary ancestors] the Usijs have learned these things
> from you,
> through which acts of *māyā* you have gained your share of the
> ritual offerings
> according to the plans to meet each need, O sons of Sudhanvan.
>
> 2. It was through these mighty powers—
> those with which you formed the chalices,
> the insight by which you drew the cow from within the hide,
> the mental power by which you fashioned the cream-colored
> horses:
> through these, O Ṛbhus, you gained your divinity.
>
> 3. The Ṛbhus have fully gained friendship with Indra.
> Grandsons of Manu, they began their journey as artists.
> Sudhanvan's sons have won immortality
> after they had worked with fitting diligence,
> skillfully with skillfulness.[203]

Similar ideas are reflected in the following verses from a song to the Ṛbhus, *Ṛgveda* 4.35. The "chalice" here probably refers to the cup that held the *soma pavamāna* but also therefore served to link the human and the divine worlds; as such, we may think of the chalice as an image of the poetic imagination. Such a cup was divided into four (perhaps the four Vedas) and distributed among the community of seers:

> 2. To us has come the Ṛbhus's bounteous gift,
> for here was drunk the well-pressed *soma*;
> for by well-formed expression and perfected skill
> as craftsmen you have made the single chalice into four.
>
> 3. You made the single chalice into four.
> You spoke these words and said, "O friend [Agni], have a taste!"
> Then, O spirited ones, O skillful Ṛbhus, you gained the path of
> immortality:
> the path [that leads] to the assembly of the gods.
>
> 8. You, by whose artistic skill have become like the gods,
> have alighted in heaven like eagles in a nest.

Grant us blessings, O children of Sudhanvan, O sons of strength.
You have become immortal!

Ṛgveda 4.36.4 records a similar expression of the idea that the primordial poets gained a place with the gods:

You have made what once was a single chalice into four,
and by the power of [your] insights
have brought forth the cow from the hide.
O spirited ones, O Ṛbhus,
you have attained immortality from the gods
through your willingness to serve.
That is to be glorified by you in song!

The story of the Ṛbhus thus expresses the Vedic idea that the imagination not only links the poet to the gods, but actually gives the poet the divine essence of immortality itself. It was in his poetry, then, that such a poet gained an impact on the world that was not limited by the constraints of time.

In an interesting verse, one seer implied that true poetic expression gained this immortal effect because it gave voice to Ṛta itself, that is, to the timeless, transcendent artfulness of the universe as a whole. Addressing the Ṛbhus, that seer proclaimed that

One of you has sung, "Most excellent are the waters [of Vāc's
    Word]!"
Another has said, "Agni is most excellent!"
Another has praised the lightning cloud to many.
[In any case], it was then that you shaped the chalices,
singing the words of Ṛta![204]

POETRY AND ṚTA

From the Vedic perspective, a truly sacred verse—a verbal revelation and expression of eternal truths—traveled in a full circle: visionary insight was given by the gods to the human poet, who in his mind and heart fashioned a poem; having been sung out loud, that poem both carried the poet's inner spirit back to the realm of the gods and gave the poem its immortal power.

In returning full circle to the divine realm, the inspired words that flowed from the poet's heart returned to the source of all that is, namely, to the original home of Ṛta itself. For, as we saw in an earlier part of this chapter, the creative word of the goddess Vāc—the voice of Ṛta—first flowed downward like a cascading waterfall from the heavenly realm of light. The image of nourishing rain falling from the sky is unmistakable. Hearing that sublime Word, Vedic poets then formed verses that gave it expression. The visionary was thus linked to Ṛta itself. Such an idea is suggested by *Ṛgveda* 7.34.1–2, which expresses the hope that the poets' "divine and brilliant imaginative song" will link people to the nourishing waters from which all things come:

> May our divine and brilliant
> imaginative song go forth,
> well-formed, like a prize-winning chariot.
> The waters listen as they flow along;
> they know the origin
> of heaven and earth.

In a song to Vena, the divine "Beloved One" embodied by the sun as it ascended into the heights, a Vedic visionary noted that, in knowing him—that is, in seeing the mysteries of the sublime as revealed by the morning sun as it moved through the heavenly waters of the sky—poets taste the sweetness of immortality. Rising with Vena through those celestial rivers to the realm of Ṛta, they return to the ordered and harmonious source of all that is.

> Rising to the high realm of Ṛta,[205]
> weavers [that is, poets] lick the sweets of deathlessness.
> Knowing his form [*rūpa*], inspired poets reached him;
> they joined in the buffalo's bellow.
> Going on the proper path, they climbed onto the [celestial]
> watercourse,
> for the ethereal spirit had found the immortal name.[206]

The phrase "the sweets of deathlessness" here likely refers to ambrosial drops of *soma pavamāna*, the essence of which, as we have seen, was often called "immortality." These lines represent the idea that Vedic poets who sang forth their vision in some way returned in their inspiration to the divine world of the gods and goddesses. But, as we saw in Chapter Two, even the deities were understood to have derived their power from a higher source, Ṛta, which gave rise to and encompassed even them. In an interesting verse, a seer noted that the god Soma embodied in the sweet elixir of life serves as the "tongue of Ṛta."[207] In other words, the inspiring master of visionary insight, the divine poet himself, gives voice to Ṛta, the unified and unifying source of all creative vision:

The trustworthy Speaker—
the master of visionary insight,
the tongue of Ṛta—
pours forth the pleasing honey.[208]

Their verses and songs thus suggest that Vedic poets understood the source of their creativity to be exactly the same as the source of the gods' creativity. From this perspective, the work of a human poet is analogous, even homologous, to the work of the gods; for just as, say, Viśvakarman constructs the world by putting together in a new way the many disparate elements of the once-unified Whole as a builder joins different pieces together to form a building, so a poet produces a poem by putting disparate verbal images together in an appropriate manner, "as a skilled and knowing carpenter builds a chariot."[209]

References to the construction and riding of chariots came, in fact, to represent not only the poetic process and the link between the visionary and the gods, but also Ṛta itself. It is "through the power of [his] radiance" that Agni, for example, "grasps the reins of Ṛta."[210] Agni, the "most active, is the expansive priest of the gods. He drives the chariot of Ṛta."[211] One poet implored Uṣas to "give us brilliant and sacred poetic skill, guided by the reins of Ṛta"; another sang to Pūṣan, "Come, bright god! Let us travel together: be our charioteer of Ṛta!"; a third likewise praised Varuṇa and Mitra: "thus, as the sun rises today, we think of you with songs; for you are the charioteers of Ṛta."[212]

According to Vedic thought, then, the visionary imagination was closely associated with Ṛta itself. We see this idea reflected in the following lines:

The worlds spread themselves out in front of the sun-finder
as he again uncovers the ambrosia each time.
When properly sung toward the drop,
the visionary song aligned with Ṛta gets louder,
like cows [low when released] onto the morning meadow.[213]

Understood to emerge from and to give voice to Ṛta, the poet's visionary song expressed truth itself and, accordingly, possessed transformative power. The song was "true" to the extent that it expressed Ṛta. In fact, in several instances, Ṛta is described as the "truth" that grounds and supports the songs themselves.[214]

Accordingly, Vedic poets were not to sing their songs for improper or deceitful reasons, particularly during the celebration of the important ritual ceremonies performed in order to keep the human community in harmony with the divine world. The singer of these verses from *Ṛgveda* 5.12, to Agni (the powerful "red steer" and reliable "protector of the seasons"), seems to have had in mind such evil magicians who had improperly won wealth and prestige:

1. To the mighty Agni—worthy of praise—
to Ṛta's leading steer, to the divine being,
I bring a poem—like well-rendered sacrificial fat to his mouth—
which goes toward the bull.

2. Watch over Ṛta, you—one who knows Ṛta;
open up the many streams of Ṛta.
I make use of no sorcery with violence or falsehood:
I hold high the red steer's artful order.

3. How have you, adhering to Ṛta by means of Ṛta,
come to know our newest song, O Agni?
The deity, the protector of the seasons, knows me;
I know neither the Lord nor he who has won this wealth.

4. Agni! Who was it, what bright helpers,
who—in concert with your enemy—won their blessings for them?
Who are they, Agni, who protect the abode of falsehood?
Who are they who guard the words of liars?

Agni! Which captor do you have for the deceiver?
Which shimmering protective spirits will carry away the prize?
Who are they who listen to the handiwork of lies?
Who are they who protect false words?

5. Your friends have turned them against you, Agni.
Once benign, they have become cruel.
They have deceived themselves with their own words,
speaking crooked words against the righteous.

6. He who maintains the red steer's Holy Order
honors you with homage, O Agni.
Spacious and prosperous is his home. May [only] the virtuous successor
of he who worships come to this place.

The poet has noted here, in verse 1, the importance of singing words in consonance with the harmony of the universe during the important ceremonial times in which gifts were offered to the gods. He also has affirmed in verse 2 that, in singing those powerful words, he has not used his visionary knowledge in a way that would destroy that harmony. But, in verses 4–5, he has expressed concern that there have indeed been deceitful singers who have bent the straight and righteous Word for their own selfish and unharmonious purposes, and that such deceit was a cruel act. In the final verse he reaffirmed the idea that the virtuous person is one who supports the harmony of Ṛta. These passages are consistent with others throughout the *Ṛgveda* that describe songs sung by Vedic priests as powerful words that oppose the unrighteous rival's expressions of *anṛta*.[215] They countered those "crooked" verses composed by a "wayward" and thus "evil" bard whose songs are "injurious"[216] to the truth.

Verses 1 and 6 from *Ṛgveda* 5.12 just translated, and many others we have read previously, thus suggest the idea that there is a close and effective connection between imaginative and artful poetry and the performance of sacrificial ritual drama. It is to Vedic ritual, and to the place of the imagination in that drama, that we now turn.

Chapter 4

The Priest as Artist: Universal Drama and the Liturgical Imagination

It was this ritual construction that the seers, our fathers, adopted
when, in the beginning, the sacrifice was first created.
With my mind's eye, I think I can see
those who first performed this sacrifice.

— Ṛgveda *10.130.6*

ṚTA AND COSMIC TRUTH, ṚTA AND CREATIVE FERVOR

Looking out over the earth's broad expanse, up into the skies and the heavens above them, Vedic poets saw a powerful and mysterious play of being. The sun rose in the morning seemingly out of nothing, emerging from the enveloping darkness, bringing form to a formless world and impelling sleeping creatures to begin the new day; the heavy clouds gathered and, punctured by lightning, dropped their rain onto the earth; as if following some invisible guide, cows returned from their pasture each day to be milked. Based on the principle of Ṛta, the world in all of its complexity revolved like a smoothly turning cosmic wheel.[1] When it was healthy, when it turned smoothly, the universe consisting of the three realms—the heavens, the sky, and the earth—was for these poets one of light and warmth, of nourishing waters, of plants and cattle and food: in short, of life and growth and vigor. It was a powerful and expansive universe. This, to these poets, was *sat*: the world of being, the world of reality. For these visionaries, the harmonious, expansive world of *sat* was *satya*: truth.

Vedic tradition also holds that those divine forces fashioned that world by drawing from within themselves an inward creative power described as a fervent, transformative heat, *tapas*. "Here, in the beginning," a representative text reads, "the Lord of Creatures was one only. He thought: 'How may I propagate?' He toiled arduously and enkindled *tapas*. He created fire from his mouth. Because he created fire from his mouth, fire is a consumer of food."[2] Another text suggests that the sun was produced from the unformed emptiness through the creative power of *tapas*: "truly, in the beginning this world was water, nothing but an ocean of water. The waters wished: 'How may we be propagated?' They toiled arduously and enkindled *tapas*. When they had become heated, a golden egg was produced."[3]

Vedic thinkers therefore closely associated Ṛta with *satya* and with *tapas*. An Atharvan poet noted, for example, that "the great *satya* and the powerful Ṛta sustain the earth."[4] While *Ṛgveda* 10.190 describes the creation of the world in this way:

> 1. Ṛta and *satya* were born from *tapas* inflamed to its height.
> From this was born the night, and
> from that arose the flowing waves of the sea.
>
> 2. From the same flowing waves of the sea was born the year
> which ordains the succession of nights and days,
> the lord of all that blinks the eye.
>
> 3. Then, in due order, the great creator formed the sun and moon.
> In order he formed heaven and earth
> and the regions of the atmosphere and of light.

Vedic visionaries were not naive. They saw an expansive and living universe, but they also saw the ubiquitous influence of the constraining forces of darkness, disease, misfortune, warfare, and death.[5] Tradition holds, however, that those who saw only these debilitating powers were unable finally to see how the universe in its entirety fit together in a meaningful way and that true visionaries could see Ṛta despite and perhaps even within the frequent distortions of *anṛta*.

Fashioned through the power of the gods' *tapas* and based on the patterns of Ṛta, the complicated world of *sat* was an immense symbiosis of being in which each and every thing in the world had its own particular function to perform within that harmonious order, so that the continuing working out of the cosmos would be ensured. The night gave way to the day and swelling waves billowed across the ocean because this was the true way, the way of truth. For them to do otherwise would be untrue not only to themselves but to the reality of which they were a part.

Thus, that which was true, *satya*, was that which was consonant with Ṛta. Conversely, that which was against Ṛta was thereby *asatya*, "untrue." Unharmonious, fracturing, or dissonant action was "false" to the integrity of the sacred cosmos. It constricted and trapped the expansive pulse of life and thereby led to darkness, to cold, to sterility; finally, to death: that is, to *asat*, "nonbeing." That which was debilitated or destroyed or deadened was characterized as *nirṛta* ("against or without *ṛta*"). One of the Vedic terms for such decay or destruction is *nirṛti*,[6] and the power of deathliness was embodied, in part, by the frightful demoness of that name, Nirṛti. The personification of destruction and of dissolution, Nirṛti was joined by other powerful Vedic demons like Vṛtra, the great dragon in the clouds whose coiled body trapped the life-giving rains; Vala, a cave-demon who trapped cattle deep in the mountains the way clouds imprison waters; and Mṛtyu, death personified.

A BACKGROUND IDEA: ALL THINGS HAVE AN ORDAINED PART TO PLAY IN THE UNIVERSAL DRAMA

Like all creatures in the world of *sat*, the deities had their own particular responsibility or obligation to the established ordinances of the universe. Said in Vedic terms, each had its *vrata*, that is, its own unique offering to or contract with the world. A deity's *vrata* was its solemn, holy vow to the established rule that guided the universe as a whole.[7] We remember *Ṛgveda* 4.13.2–3, from which we have already quoted in a previous chapter: "true to their *vrata*, Varuṇa and Mitra, the rulers of secure realms, raise the sun into the heavens. With unceasing consistency they impel Savitṛ to drive away the darkness." A Vedic seer described the gods Varuṇa and Mitra as "you who uphold the realm, the sphere of brightness, you who support the realm of the earth, O divine Ādityas. The immortal gods never harm your eternal *vratas*."[8] Describing the course of the night and morning, another said that "joined since ancient times, their paths remain unharmed; with mighty strength they preserve the immortal *vratas*."[9]

The gods' performance of their *vratas* helped maintain Ṛta. Vedic seers, in fact, saw a close connection between the two. Thus, for example, one seer was to say that, "praising the eternal Ṛta, these [gods] speak of Ṛta; following [their] *vrata*, they are the guardians of [their] *vrata*."[10]

The Vedic idea that one has a set of obligations to perform in order to contribute to the well-being of the universe is also represented by the concept of *dhāman*, a word referring to an "established rule" to which one is responsible. Accordingly, in the *Ṛgveda* we see verses in which a *dhāman* is associated with Ṛta, as in Agni's own reported declaration that "I have established many *dhāmans* based on Ṛta."[11]

As an obligation or set of responsibilities that contributes to the welfare of the world, a *vrata* or a *dhāman* was similar to what in Vedic India was characterized and known as *dharman*, meaning "that which upholds, supports, nourishes." In early Vedic texts *dharman* refers to an established or proper mode of conduct that supports or helps maintain the continuing health of the world. At times Vedic seers described action based on *dharman* as a pillar that props up the universe. According to one such visionary, for example, it was through Varuṇa's performance of his *dharman* that the sky was raised above the land, giving it room so that it could drop nourishing rains on the earth: "enveloping all that exists, wide and spacious, dropping honey, beautiful in form, heaven and earth . . . stand parted from each other by means of Varuṇa's *dharman*."[12] The Vedic idea of *dharman* stands as a precedent for the later idea of *dharma* as responsible, proper activity that supports the world, a key element of virtually all Indian religions.

The force and structure of *vrata, dhāman,* and *dharman* were grounded in or encompassed by the supreme principle that was Ṛta itself; for it was Ṛta that ordered, coordinated, and ordained those actions which supported harmony in the world. Anyone who acted in accordance with Ṛta was thereby true to the established ordinances. True to Ṛta, such a person performed one's established role in the world. Such a person was an actor of sorts, whose play was the universal drama itself. Actors performing this sacred drama thereby performed a cosmic liturgy. This liturgy was not regarded as merely symbolic drama. As we will see, Vedic thought holds that ritual helps sustain the world of truth and being in its struggle with the ravages of unreality, falsehood, and nonbeing.

SACRIFICE: HUMANITY'S FUNCTION IN THE UNIVERSE

Vedic thought holds that, like all creatures in the intricate divine ecology, human beings have their own responsibility to the harmoniously ordered yet fragile universe, for they, too, share the world of *sat* with the gods as well as with the powers of nature. Vedic seers referred to humanity in general as *manu*: the thoughtful one, the one who can imagine.[13] This word, too—"Manu"—was the name by which they knew the primordial ancestor of all human beings. Manu, the original person, is thus the image of human nature.[14] From the Vedic perspective, Manu's responsibility to the world is to honor and support the gods and to act in a way that attempts to reintegrate a disintegrated world.

This is to say that Manu's function was to perform sacrifices. The English word *sacrifice* ("to make holy"[15]) is the customary translation of the Sanskrit term *yajña*, a word built on the verbal root *yaj-*, meaning, to "consecrate, hallow, honor, offer." One of the verbs most frequently associated with *yajña* is *karoti*, "he makes." The verb *karoti* is related to the noun, *karman*: "action," specifically action that brings results. Sacrifice is beneficial *karman* par excellence; for, in honoring the gods and in offering them gifts and other forms of support, a sacrificer participates in the consecration of being itself, helping as he does so to make a better world not only for the gods but also thereby for the human community. To sacrifice is to make the divine universe stronger.

To sacrifice is therefore to express humanity's obligation to the world. The idea of *karman* is thus closely linked to that of *dharman*, the latter of which, as we have seen, refers to conduct that supports the integrity of the universe. In a verse to the god of fire embodied by the flame blazing on the ceremonial altar, one poet-priest sang, "O Agni, enkindled, worthy of songs of praise, the envoy of the gods, you cherish the established rites [*dharman*]";[16] another prayed to the same god, "I laud the wondrous Agni, the king of all that is, the guardian of the proper ritual performance [*dharman*]: may he hear!"[17]

The Vedic concept of *dharman* (and thus the later classical idea of *dharma*) is therefore closely associated not only with *karman* (and thus with the later concept of *karma*) but also with the experience of Ṛta, especially in the context of sanctifying action. In fact, Vedic seers used the word Ṛta to refer not only to the universal principle of harmony and order but also to the performance of sacred devotional rites.[18] Bharadvāja, for example, entreated the deities to "come quickly now, [you] who . . . visit our pious ritual performance [*ṛtasap*]."[19] The *Ṛgveda* also associates the performance of ceremonial action with poetic vision itself. Such connection is made explicit in Gṛtsamada's plea to Indra: "with you, O Indra, we have become energetic singers; may we offer honor with our poetic imagination and our performance of the sacred rite [*ṛtasap*]."[20]

Sacrifice lies at the very core of the Vedic worldview. Tradition holds that the universe itself has come about through the gods' own sacrifice and that all creatures owe their very being to such a divine offering. The idea that sacrifice forms and sustains the world finds expression in a Vedic sacred myth in which, once upon a time, the gods performed the *yajña* and that it was in fact through sacrifice that the deities gained the celestial world itself. According to the *Taittirīya Saṁhitā*, for example, it was through the "perfect performance of the sacrificial ritual that the gods proceeded to the heavenly realm."[21] We see a good example of this idea in the opening verses of a song from the *Atharvaveda*:

> By means of the *yajña* the gods sacrificed to the *yajña*.
> Those were the first *dharman*s
> These mighty ones gain the height of heaven
> where live the ancient, perfectible gods.
> Thus the sacrifice came to be; here, it revealed itself.

It gave birth to itself, and then increased again.
It became the lord and regent of the gods.
May it grant us blessings.[22]

According to this hymn, the priest asks that the human community follow the gods in the performance of the *yajña* and thus share in the divine world fashioned by the gods' own sacrifice:

Just as the gods made holy offerings to the gods with oblation,
to the immortal ones, with immortal mind,
may we too revel there, in the highest heaven.
May we gaze on it at the rising of the sun.[23]

The very fabric of the universe is woven by sacrifice—hallowed action—and it is through sacrifice that it is sustained, rejuvenated, and healed. The Vedic community could not feel complacent about *sat*, for truth and being were constantly threatened by the forces of falsehood and nonbeing. The world of *sat* could be overtaken by those deathly forces; there was no guarantee that the world would continue to exist forever. Life was fragile.

Vedic values hold that humanity has a particularly important role to play in such an uncertain world. Humankind could destroy itself; it could destroy the world; it could, indeed, destroy the gods themselves. Unless human beings acted in a way that honored the deities and the world they had fashioned, being would break up and dissolve into nonbeing. Having taken so much from it, human beings had to offer something back to the universe. They were to give gifts to the gods: songs of praise, declarations of thanksgiving, invigorating food. The latter sometimes took the form of a burnt offering of a valued sacrificial animal such as a horse, cow, goat, or sheep. More frequently it consisted of the offering to the sacred fire gifts of clarified butter and other milk products, honey, nuts, fruit, and seeds of grain, all of which symbolize and indeed embody the vital and generative power of life.

Other times the gift consisted of *soma pavamāna*. Agni carried this ambrosial nectar to the gods and goddesses in the upper regions of *sat* as he ascended in the form of smoke rising from the fire, like a bird taking flight into the heavens. Reaching the highest realms, those gifts of life refreshed the gods, whose light then increased: the sun rose in the morning, the moon became full again, the cold season turned to warmth. The deities returned the gift in the form of fertile rain, which nourished the earth below. The performance of the *yajña* therefore helped the members of the Vedic community struggling to live their lives on earth.

*Yajña*s were large, public ceremonies involving up to sixteen different priests and sometimes taking many days or longer to perform. The central component of virtually all such rites was the lighting, protecting, and nourishing of the sacred fire. The performance of the ritual was closely associated with sacred language itself, typically expressed in the *mantra*s voiced by the Vedic seers. In the *yajña*, therefore, sacred act was conjoined with sacred word. Indeed, in Vedic India, the performance of a *yajña* was inseparable from *śruti*, the verbal revelation of truth.[24] The language sung during the sacrifice was understood to be the expression of the goddess Vāc herself, the commands of whose divine voice held the universe together. As such, that language was described as *saṁskṛta* ("put together properly, well-formed") and thus as Sanskrit. Since Vedic times, Sanskrit has been regard as a perfected, powerfully effective, holy language.

SACRIFICE AS THE WEAVING OF A UNIVERSAL TAPESTRY

Vedic texts describe the performance of the hallowed ritual in cosmogonic and artistic terms. The world was viewed as an immense and intricate tapestry woven of various threads. Images of such cosmogonic weaving are as old as the *Ṛgveda* itself. They infuse, for example, *Ṛgveda* 10.130, which maintains that the performance of the sacrificial ritual not only integrates the universe but also, accordingly, aligns members of the human community with their visionary ancestors as well as with the gods themselves.

1. The *yajña* is a loom with threads drawn on all sides,
   stretched by a hundred and one sacred rituals.
   The fathers who have come this way weave the fabric.
   They sit by the loom, singing: "Weave lengthwise! Weave
   crosswise!"

2. Behold a man extends it; that man unbinds it:
   The man has spun it right up to the vault of heaven.
   Here are the pegs; they are driven into the place of worship.
   They made the Sāman hymns their weaving shuttles.

3. What was the model? What was the pattern? What was the
   connection?
   What was the anointing oil, and the boundary line?
   What was the hymn? What was the meter? What was the
   opening chant,
   when all the deities offered the god as the oblation?

4. Closely was the Gāyatrī meter conjoined with Agni;
   The Uṣṇih meter became one with Savitṛ;

Made brilliant by songs, Soma joined the Anuṣṭubh meter;
The Ḅrhati meter strengthened the voice of Bṛhaspati.

5. The Virāj meter adhered to Varuṇa and Mitra;
The Triṣṭubh meter was Indra's daily portion;
The Jagatī meter entered all of the gods together:
Thus, to this ritual construction human poets conform.

6. It was this ritual construction that the seers, our fathers, adopted when the sacrifice was first created in the beginning.
With my mind's eye, I think I can see
Those who first performed this sacrifice.

7. Well-versed in ritual and in meters, in hymns and in rules:
these were the seven godlike seers.
Envisioning the path tread by those of old,
the poets have taken the reins in their hands, like charioteers.

Weaving the sacrifice, Vedic priests were similar in a way to Vedic visionary poets, who wove the sacred verses used in those rites. "Let not my thread be severed while I weave the song," a poet-priest prayed to Varuṇa.[25] Another sang to Indra: "accept, please, these prayerful songs being made, the new ones we now make. Seeking blessing, I have formed them as a splendid and well-made robe."[26]

The priests' performance of the ritual was in this sense equivalent to the visionary seers' production of sacred poetry. Both were forms of the constructive imagination.

RITUAL AS A DRAMATIC IMAGE

In performing a *yajña* Vedic priests did what they could to weave the frayed fabric of being together, strengthening it as a way to stabilize an uncertain and even broken world. It is perhaps no coincidence that many of the verbs associated with the sacred and sacralizing drama are built on a Sanskrit verbal root meaning to "stand," "stabilize," or "make a station" for something.[27] A *yajña* helped "establish" or "reestablish" a meaningful world despite the threat of nonbeing and meaninglessness. Through it, the struggle between harmonious life and chaotic death could be performed through prescribed action within the confines of the dramatic stage. Because it could be enacted it could be controlled; for ritual is regularized and therefore ordered behavior.[28] What is more, the performance of a ritual—the stylized and well–governed giving-of-form to the competition between being and nonbeing—enabled the Vedic community to establish a realm or "world" (*loka*) of harmony and balance, or at least try to, within a context of what might often seem to be a frightful disharmony and imbalance of life.

As we will see in this chapter, the performance of a *yajña* presented a liturgical image of processes by which the whole world was understood to come into being and by which it was sustained. Furthermore, according to Vedic thought, sacrifice renewed the universe when it was threatened by decay and death. The Vedic sacrificial worldview revolves to a large extent around the hope that human society, too, could participate in that renewal of being. As the *Śatapatha Brāhmaṇa* asserts, "It is by the power of the ritual that the gods have brought to completion all of their various and appropriate undertakings. The sages have done likewise."[29] By means of ritual the Vedic community tried to live in consonance with the divine powers of life that give rise to and sustain the universe itself. We will recall from verses 6–7 of the song we just read, *Ṛgveda* 10.130, that such an alignment took place by means of the visionary imagination, which allowed the seer to conform to the ritual construction of the universe as a whole. From the Vedic perspective, the human attempt to stabilize a meaningful but fragile universe depended in part on the power of the ritual imagination.

THE DIVINE MODEL: THE SACRIFICE OF PURUṢA

In Chapter Two, we noted a Vedic idea that the world of multiplicity was formed as a result of the disintegration of a once-integrated Whole. We lingered on Dīrghatamas's vision of the goddess Vāc, whose universal Word descended "from the highest heaven" and came to be broken into "a thousand syllables, having become one-footed, two-footed, eight-footed, and nine-footed."[30] For Dīrghatamas, the world of multiplicity was thus in a sense a complicated poem uttered by the goddess herself. But the word for "footed" here connotes also the various rhythms and meters—the "feet"—of the verses sung during Vedic priests' performance of sacred rituals. Vāc's voice was expressed in the *yajña* itself. Sacrifice articulated the divine Word.

As we have seen in such hymns as *Atharvaveda* 7.5, Vedic thought holds that the world as a whole is formed through a divine sacrifice, for that song proclaims that the gods perform the *yajña*. In *Ṛgveda* 10.90, the "Hymn of Puruṣa," the world of multiplicity is said to result from a single god's offering of his own body in a cosmic sacrifice. Here, the poet envisioned the One, not as the universal goddess whose creative Word forms a thousand syllables, but rather as a single universal "Person" (*puruṣa*) who has "a thousand heads, a thousand eyes, and a thousand feet" (verse 1). According to this hymn, that unified body somehow became divided into the male and female principles, and then was sacrificially stretched apart (verse 6). Puruṣa's divine body was thereby dismembered. The various limbs of that broken form then became the many different parts of the physical, divine, and social world as a whole. The hymn is worth translating in its entirety:

1. Puruṣa has a thousand heads,
a thousand eyes, and a thousand feet.
He embraced the earth on all sides, and
reached beyond it the distance of ten fingers.

2. It is Puruṣa who is all that is,
all that ever was, and all that ever will be.
He is the lord of the immortal realms,
which he surpasses through ritual offerings of food.

3. Such is his greatness.
And yet, Puruṣa is even more than this!
All creatures comprise one-fourth of him:
three-fourths of him are the immortal in the heavens.

4. With his three-fourths Puruṣa ascended,
while the one-fourth remained here.
From this [fourth] he spread out in all directions,
into both animate and inanimate things.

5. From him was born the female,
and from the female was born the male.
When he was born, he extended
beyond the earth, both behind and in front.

6. When the gods spread out the sacrifice
with Puruṣa as the offering,
the springtime was the oil,
the summer the logs for the fire, and autumn the oblation.

7. They anointed Puruṣa, born at the beginning,
on the sacred ritual grass.
With his body the gods, the demigods, and the sages
performed the sacrifice.

8. From that sacrifice,
the dripping anointing oil was collected.
He formed the creatures of the air,
and of the forest, and of the village.

9. From this sacrifice, when it was completed,
were born the liturgical hymns and melodies.
From this were born the sacred rhythmic meters.
From this were born the liturgical formulas.

10. From this were born horses
[and] all creatures that have teeth in both jaws;

from this were born the breeds of cattle;
from this were born sheep and goats.

11. When they dismembered Puruṣa,
into how many parts did they arrange him?
What did they name his mouth? What were his two arms?
What are his thighs and his feet called?

12. His mouth became the priests.
His two arms were made into the warriors;
his thighs, the producers;
his feet, the workers.

13. The moon was born from his mind;
from his eye was born the sun.
Indra and Agni came from his mouth.
His vital breath became the wind.

14. From his navel arose the atmosphere;
from his head came the heavenly vault.
From his two feet came the earth,
and from his ear the cardinal directions of the sky.

According to this song, *Ṛgveda* 10.90, Puruṣa "embrace[s] the earth on all sides" and thus is "all that is," but also extends beyond that world the distance of ten figures. Perhaps this means that Puruṣa reaches his hands into infinity itself. It may also mean that Puruṣa lives deep within the poet's own heart, a space the width of ten fingers.[31] In either case, the poet also understood Puruṣa to extend into deathless eternity itself: while all mortal beings as well as inanimate objects in the world of time and space comprised one-fourth of his body, "three-fourths of him are the immortal in the heavens." Through Puruṣa's own sacrifice there is reality and truth to "all that is, all that ever was, and all that ever will be." His is the original, primordial, paradigmatic sacrifice. Puruṣa's self-sacrifice formed the world.

DEVELOPMENTS IN THE IDEA OF THE *BRAHMAN* (I): THE *BRAHMAN* AS THE TRANSFORMATIVE, UNIVERSAL POWER OF THE RITUAL

In telling of Purusa, the limbs of whose body form the universe, *Ṛgveda* 10.90 is consistent with Vedic thought in general, which holds that the world in its entirety emerges from and is ultimately is held together by a unified principle and power of being. Throughout the preceding pages we have stressed the idea of Ṛta as an example of just such a notion. In the previous chapter we also noted the Vedic idea of the *brahman*, which in its earliest instances referred to the enigmatic and at times puzzling yet effective power of the universal Word as it revealed itself to the Vedic visionary poets. As that Word, the *brahman* sustained all things.

Just as the transcendent, impersonal Ṛta was said to preexist the gods and thus to have no beginning, so too the *brahman* was described as "self-existing."[32] The *brahman* supported all of creation. It was through the *brahman* that "the earth was created, the heavens placed in the heights, the atmosphere aloft and the expanse across."[33] We have already noted that, according to one account in mythic form, the *brahman* was, in the beginning, the universal Whole before the emergence of multiplicity. It created the gods and placed them in their appropriate places and, having done so, ascended to the transcendent realm beyond. Having gone to the realm beyond, it descended again to these worlds by means of name-and-form so that "as far as there is name-and-form, that far, indeed, extends this [universe]."[34] Accordingly, the *brahman* was seen to be both the creative power and the manifest expression of that power.

Infusing the whole world and all things in it with its formative and sustaining power, the *brahman* was, like Ṛta, also associated with the goddess Vāc. Knowing the *brahman*, Vedic poets heard the words of Vāc. "Inspired sages, those with formative insight, those who know the *brahman*: they know the . . . parts into which Vāc was divided."[35] It was thus by means of the *brahman* that Vedic poets heard the divine voice of the universal artfulness of being.

And what allowed the seers to know the *brahman?* They did so by means of the effective power of *dhī*, the ability to envision otherwise hidden sublime forces and structures and subsequent skill to refine and express that vision with verbal images. The visionaries' imagination allowed them both to see and to give voice to the magical force of the *brahman.*

In fact, their verses and songs were understood to be expressions of the *brahman* itself. Expressing the *brahman,* the verses lent voice to Ṛta. This is why the songs of the *Ṛgveda* are described with such equivalent phrases as "swelling with Ṛta" and "expanding through the *brahman.*"[36] It is also why the truly effective verse, as an expression of the *brahman*, was said to "issue forth from the seat of Ṛta."[37]

By roughly the turn of the first millennium BCE, Vedic ritualists came to regard the *brahman* not only as the mystery that linked language to universal truth, but also as the hidden power and mechanism that gave efficacy to their ritual performances. Accordingly, the *brahman* came to be regarded as the force, expressed through the unifying power of the sacred word, that joined the human world with the world of the gods.

As the power of being itself, a divine and sustaining force, the *brahman* served as an inward protection against the forces of evil.[38] That it had the strength and endurance to do so is due to the fact that was understood to be imperishable, firm, and unmovable. The *brahman* was that mysterious force "by which the earth is created, the heavens are set in the heights, and the expansive atmosphere set aloft and across."[39] The gods possessed this power[40] and were strengthened by it.[41]

When performed properly, the ritual expressed the *brahman*. So, by performing the ritual, Vedic priests hoped to align themselves with that unified and effective power which joined together all things in the Vedic universe. In *Atharvaveda* 19.42, we see expression of the related ideas that within the apparent multiplicity of the ritual drama resides a single *brahman*, and that it was precisely the power of his imagination that allowed the priest to envision and invoke that unified power:

1. The *brahman* is the invocating priest; the *brahman* is the sacrificial offering;
   by the *brahman* are the sacrificial posts set in place.
   The officiating priest is born of the *brahman*;
   into the *brahman* is put the offering.

2. The *brahman* is the ladle dripping with clarified oil;
   by the *brahman* is the fire altar established.
   The *brahman* is the true essence of the sacrifice.
   The priests prepare the offering. Hail to the minister!

3. He who delivers from distress:
   to him I bring forward my mental prayer,
   unto him who rescues, and choosing his favor.
   O Indra, accept this gift! May the hopes of the giver be realized!

4. He who delivers from distress, the bull of the devout,
   he who shines forth, the first of the rituals, the child of the waters:
   O Aśvins, I invoke you with the formative power of imagination;
   with Indra, give me power like Indra's.

DEVELOPMENTS IN THE IDEA OF THE *BRAHMAN* (II): BRAHMAN AS THE UNIVERSAL GROUND OF BEING

In what was to become one of the most important developments in Vedic thought, Vedic philosopher-priests were to regard the *brahman*, not only as the unifying power or link by which the actions performed in the sacred ceremony had effect on the world as a whole, but also as the structure that held the entire universe together and on which that universe was established. One text describes it as the lumber from which the structures of heaven and earth are built.[42] For these thinkers, the *brahman* was the ontological ground of being itself. The *brahman*—we may now call it Brahman (capitalized and in roman script)—was the universal Absolute, the single, ultimate reality they saw standing behind and supporting all of the many and various things in the manifest world. This realization was to have profound influence on Vedic thought and practice, and thus on later Hinduism in general, especially in regards to the development of a contemplative spirituality.

We will return to this important development in Chapter Five. For now, we might note a text that presents the idea that it is Brahman on which all things in the universe rest and in which they find their being. The seers whose verses form *Atharvaveda* 10.8 described it as a universal pillar, *skambha*, which supports all things. This is a beautiful song, but it is too long to include in its entirety. Here are some of its verses:

1. Homage to that supreme Brahman who presides over all things—
that which already exists and
that which is yet to be—
and to whom alone belongs the heaven.

2. It is because of that pillar that
heaven and earth remain separate and fixed in place.
In him dwell everything that lives and breathes,
All that open and close the eye.

6. Though manifest, it is hidden and secret.
Its name is "Ancient." It is a great way of being.
On Skambha is formed this whole universe:
On it is established all that moves and breathes.

11. Whatever moves, whatever flies, whatever stands still;
whatever breathes, whatever does not breathe, whatever blinks the eye:
it is that which, though multiform, is concentrated into a single whole.
It sustains the world.

12. The infinite stretches in all directions.
The infinite and the finite share a common boundary.
The protector of the heavens alone can separate the two:
He who knows what is, and what is to become.

19. By means of truth he blazes aloft;
by sacred word he watches over what is near;

by living breath he breathes across [the world]:
the One on whom rests the Supreme.

24. A hundred, a thousand, tens of thousands, a hundred million:
countless are the forms of his own entered into him.
They die; he looks on.
Thus shines this god. Thus is he.

25. The One is smaller than a child;
the One is nearly invisible.
And yet this deity—she who is so dear to me[43]—
is vaster than the whole expansive universe!

27. You are woman. You are man.
You are boy, and young girl, too.
When old, you lean on a staff as you totter.
When born, you reveal your face in all directions.

28. He is their father, and also their son.
He is the largest and the smallest of them.
He is the one god, who has entered into the mind:
the firstborn, yet even now within the womb.

29. From fullness he spreads forth the full;
the full is poured with the full.
We would also want to know today
from whence that [fullness] is poured forth.

31. The deity, whose name is "Helpful," sits
enveloped by Ṛta.
It is because of her form that these trees
are green, and green the garland of flowers.

32. See! The marvelous wisdom of god!
Near though he is, one cannot leave him!
Near though he is, one cannot see him!
He neither dies nor grows old!

To the Vedic mind, Brahman was thus equivalent in many ways to Ṛta. Both supported and sustained the universe as a whole. Perhaps the fundamental difference between the two was that Ṛta was regarded as a *principle* of being, a dynamic cosmic order and truth that has always existed and that continues to drive the movements of the sacred universe, while Brahman was the unchanging foundation on which all things rest, the ontological beingness in which all things have their being. In the history of religious thought in

India, the idea of Brahman eventually supplanted and virtually replaced that of Ṛta. But it is worth noting that, in praising the harmony of Ṛta and the powerful presence of Brahman, Vedic seers expressed what they experienced as the highest truth: at the most ultimate of levels, reality is One.

DEVELOPMENTS IN THE IDEA OF THE *BRAHMAN* (III): THE VEDIC PRIEST AS *BRAHMIN*

Vedic thought held that human beings as well as the deities could come to know and possess the *brahman* and thus know Brahman. We see this assertion in these verses, also from *Atharvaveda* 10.8:

33. Words sent forth by the preexistent One
 tell things as they truly are.
 That place to which they travel, speaking,
 is called the great Brahman.

37. Who knows the finely drawn thread on which
 the creatures are woven;
 who knows the thread of that very thread:
 that person also knows the great Brahman.

38. I know the finely drawn thread on which
 the creatures are woven;
 I know the thread of that very thread:
 therefore, I know the great Brahman.

Vedic verses use the words *brahmán* ("one who possesses the *brahman*," a masculine word accented on the second syllable) and *brāhmaṇa* ("pertaining to the *brahman*") to describe a human being who knows this universal power and ground of being. The *Chāndogya Upaniṣad*, for example, holds that "one who knows the imperishable is a *brāhmaṇa*."[44]

The various similar words can be confusing: *bráhman, brahmán, brāhmaṇa*. For simplicity's sake, we may simply refer to the human being who knows the *brahman* as a brahmin, a word that most English-language dictionaries now include.

Knowing and thus possessing the power of the *brahman*, a brahmin was understood to make manifest to the human community the invisible, unified thread that binds the universe together.[45] The brahmin was therefore associated, even at times identified, with the cosmic *brahman*. At least one text is explicit in this regard: "the brahmin is indeed the *brahman*."[46] Vedic works place much emphasis on the brahmin's knowledge of the foundational structure on which the universe is built and the divine powers by which it is sustained.[47] Vedic society therefore stressed the importance of the brahmin's hearing and diligent study of the sacred Word. In fact, it is the goddess Vāc who is is said to make a person a brahmin.[48] Tradition holds that a true brahmin is distinguished from others by the extent and depth of his learning,[49] especially of the sacred and sacralizing knowledge embodied in Vedic literatures. Vedic texts describe the brahmin as being one who is "lustrous in sacred knowledge"[50] and as one who possessed "knowledge of all sacred things."[51]

The most important component of the brahmin's wisdom was of the nature, function, and performance of the sacrifice. As one who enacted that sacred and sacralizing drama for the benefit of the human community, a brahmin served as a Vedic "priest," a word commonly used to translate the term. One Vedic text describes such priests as "protectors of the *yajña* because they are well versed in the sacred Word [and] because they perform it [properly]."[52] So, too, that text says that brahmins are those "who have studied and teach the Veda; they promote the *yajña* since they perform it [properly and because] they produce it."[53] The brahmin's essence is said to have derived from the essence of the Vedas.[54] Accordingly, the brahmin—the "mind of the sacrifice"[55]—is "the living bearer of all that knowledge, of all that power."[56]

Vedic religion recognizes four general types of priest, each of which performed a different function in the various rituals with the help of specialized assistants. The *hotṛ*-priest ("one who offers") invoked the deities by singing appropriate verses of invitation, glorification, and praise. The *udgātṛ* ("one who sings out") knew the appropriate melodies with which to sing those verses. The *adhvaryu* ("one who knows the Adhvara," namely, the physical and mechanical aspects of the sacred drama) measured off and established the ritual domain, built the ceremonial altar, gathered the appropriate tools and implements, and so on.

The fourth was known as the *brahmán*. We have just seen this word in reference to the Vedic priesthood in general. But the meaning is more specific in the case of this fourth type of priest. By necessity, all priests were *brahmáns* because they possessed knowledge of the *bráhman*. We will refer to this fourth type as the "*brahman*-priest" as a way to distinguish him from the *hotṛ*, *udgātṛ*, and *adhvaryu*. The *brahman*-priest's function was different from those of the other three in that he watched silently over the entire drama to make sure that everything was done correctly. To do this he had to have complete knowledge of the structure and procedures of the sacred offering as a whole and of the ritual's relationship to the divine order of things. In a way, the *brahman*-priest inherited the Vedic seer's vision of the divine. But, whereas the visionary poet heard the Word and expressed it in poetic song, the *brahman*-priest presided over its liturgical enactment.

It is important to our present concern that, during the performance of the sacrifice, the *brahman*-priest was silent. Vedic tradition regarded that very silence to be as important to the ritual as was the other priests' chanting of mantras. Such silence was said to be "half of the sacrifice," for "the sacrifice has two tracks; one is by speech, the other by mind."[57] For the *brahman*-priest, the sacred ritual took place mentally, as it were.

The *brahman*-priest also protected the well-being and effective power of the sacrifice by providing an inward, silent continuity of sorts whenever there was a necessary break in the sacred action, that is to say, in those moments between different phases of the long and complicated ceremony.[58] The *brahman*-priest also performed expiatory rites whenever the other priests had unintentionally chanted a mantra incorrectly or erred in their own performance of the sacred drama. In performing these acts of reparation or atonement, the *brahman*-priest thus served as the "healer" when the sacrifice was fractured.[59]

His threefold responsibilities in the performance of the sacrifice—his silent watchfulness over the ceremony as a whole, his reparatory actions, and his maintenance of the rite's continuity at times of inactivity—point therefore to the *brahman*-priest's function as the "connection" that holds the sacrifice together. By means of his silence and knowing attentiveness, the *brahman*-priest thus "concentrates" the sacrifice within himself.[60] We will return in later discussions to an important legacy of the *brahman*-priest's inward, mental performance of the sacrifice and of the idea that the *brahman*-priest concentrates the sacrifice within his being when we look at the interiorization of the sacred world undertaken in the practice of meditation.

THE ROLE OF THE GOD AGNI

The deity most closely associated with the *brahman* as unifying force was the god of fire, Agni. Accordingly, it was primarily to Agni that Vedic brahmins turned in order to make contact with the universal power of being that linked all things, including the human and divine realms. The importance of Agni in Vedic religion cannot be overstated,[61] for Agni revealed the power of being and brought the human spirit in contact with the divine. "Among the gods, the *brahman* appeared by means of Agni," one text reads. "Therefore people wish for a place among the gods through Agni."[62] As we will see shortly, Agni was able to travel between the earth, sky, and heavens. Doing so, Agni—like the *brahman*—linked the three realms of the Vedic universe. Agni was in a sense the perfect intermediary whose movements joined the human and divine worlds.

This is to say that Agni was the perfect priest. "I will sing here to you, for grace, of the god Agni, for he is good to us," a Vedic ritual bard sang, "for he is true, whom our ancestors and the gods themselves enkindled. He is the invocatory priest with the melodious tongue, brilliant with the light of glorious rays."[63]

Agni is said to have come originally from the heavens,[64] where he was identified with the sun. Vedic priests invoked him as "the head of heaven" and as "the light of heaven that awakens the dawn."[65] Like the sun, Agni shined with lustrous brilliance[66] and, like the sun, dispelled darkness with his splendor.[67] True to his vows to the ordinances that held the universe together, he spread forth the sky: "when he came to life in the highest heaven, that Agni, the protector of the *vrata*s, performed his *vrata*s. Exceedingly wise, he measured out the atmosphere. He who is common to all people gained heaven by means of his power."[68]

Agni is also identified with the lightning in the stormclouds and thus with the sky, the middle region between the heavens and the earth. He is the "shining thunderer"[69] who "has the voice of the wind, the mighty roar of the thunder, and who clothes himself with the ocean [of the clouds]."[70]

Having been born in the heavens and moved through the skies, the god of fire is said to live with the human community on the earth, where he blazes in the domestic hearth and on the sacrificial altar. "He has been established in mankind's homes," one seer said of him, "fulfilling by means of Ṛta, he is a friend."[71] As the hearth fire he lives as "an immortal from ancient times, a Priest among mortals, the most delightful of the house."[72] Of all of the gods, Agni is nearest to people and is the human community's closest and most loyal ally. Of him, Vedic priests proclaimed, "We have in you the nearest friend of all, to help us serve the gods and in gaining wealth."[73]

Agni is therefore the god whom human priests invoke when they light the sacred flame. Receiving in his mouth the clarified butter and other offertory gifts the human priests have presented him as they place them in the fire, Agni then rises upward and, carried by the pillar of rising smoke, ascends back into his original home in the heavens. According to one seer, the "lord of the divine rites, a god who stand[s] upright, turning toward the gods: when the flame has sprung forth from the holy oil, the offertory fat, he yearns for [heaven] with his brilliance."[74] Another similarly noted that "bright flames that love the gods have mounted upward."[75] Agni "carr[ies] the sacrifice to heaven, to the gods."[76]

Agni thus moves in both directions through the three regions of the Vedic universe. He comes down, and he goes up.[77] Accordingly, Agni serves as a messenger between the human world and the realm of the gods. "Knowing thoroughly the paths of the gods," *Ṛgveda* 1.72.7 says of Agni, "you have come a tireless envoy and bearer of offerings."[78]

Agni therefore found praise as the divine priest par excellence. We see such an idea, for example, in the following song, *Ṛgveda* 1.1, which describes the god of fire—the ruler of the ritual ceremonies and radiant protector of Ṛta (verse 8)—as several different types of priest at one and the same time. Verse 1 describes him as a *puruhita*, a priest chosen by a family to perform a domestic ritual ceremony; an *ṛtvij*, a priest who performs the rituals at the appropriate time and season; and a *hotṛ*, the priest who chants invocations to the gods. In verse 2, he is remembered as being worthy of praise from past as well as present poets; in verse 6, he is said to be one of the Aṅgirases, a family of Vedic priests who traced their lineage to him; and verse 9 asks him to be available to his worshiper, "like a father to his son." (We might note, incidentally, that according to verse 5 he also possesses the power of poetic expression.)

1. I sing lauds to the god Agni—
the *purohita*, the *ṛtvij*, the *hotṛ*—
who brings the most blessings.

2. Agni is worthy of praise
by ancient as well as living seers;
he will bring the gods here.

3. Through Agni one may gain blessings,
growth day by day, and
glorious and most bountiful heroes.

4. O Agni! Only that offertory rite that
you encompass on all sides
truly goes to the gods.

5. The priest with a poet's powerful expression,
the true one, the most brilliant, the god:
may Agni come here with the gods.

6. Whatever blessing you would grant to one who worships you:
that truth, O Aṅgiras,
becomes your truth.

7. Day after day we come to you
who enlightens the darkness, O Agni,
bringing with us our prayerful vision:

8. to you, the ruler of the rituals,
the radiant protector of Ṛta,
who grows larger in your own home.

9. Be easy for us to approach,
like a father to his son.
Be with us, O Agni, for our happiness.

TWO REASONS WHY THE SACRIFICE IS TO BE REPEATED

We note in verse 7 of the song just quoted that the poet-priest sings, "day after day we come to you who enlightens the darkness, bringing with us our prayerful vision." The reason why such periodic sacred activity is undertaken lies at the center of the Vedic sacrificial worldview. In order to understand why this is so (and at the risk of overgeneralization), we may for our purposes at hand distinguish two essential components of that worldview and note the place ritual occupies in it.

One such component centers on the idea that ritual helps sustain the forces of life and being against those of death and nonbeing. This seems to be quite an old idea in the Vedic community, for it appears interlinearly in the earliest songs of the *Ṛgveda,* particularly those addressed to the martial sky gods of the Vedic pantheon (like Indra, for example, or the Maruts) who take part in a universal struggle between the forces of vitality and those of decay. The human community contributed to that struggle by offering strength to the gods either in the form of laudatory encouragement or by giving them gifts symbolizing the power of life. As we have noted, such gifts sometimes included the sacrificial offering of a valued animal. The most solemn ceremonies, however, included an offering into the sacrificial fire of the elixir of immortality itself, *soma*, which the gods and goddesses needed to fight the demons of death.

A second element of the Vedic sacrificial worldview revolves around the idea that, from another perspective, the universe had already fractured into a chaotic multiverse. We have already seen that, according to *Ṛgveda* 10.90, the world in all of its multiplicity was formed through the dismembering self-sacrifice of the once-whole Puruṣa. Later Vedic tradition holds that this dismemberment of God—now known generally as Prajāpati, the Lord of Creatures—had drawn the very life-force out of the divine body, which then lay broken and lifeless. Representing the human community, Vedic priests joined with the celestial beings in trying to put Prajāpati's body back together again. They did so by means of the sacrifice. Ritual drama liturgically reconstructed the divine body. This second key idea appears in later hymns of the *Ṛgveda* and comes to full expression in the Brāhmaṇas and revolves around a sacerdotal myth that tells of the primordial degradation of universal unity into the chaotic multiplicity of existence. According to this idea, it was precisely the ritual that reintegrated Prajāpati's broken body and thus reformed the cosmos as universe.

We turn our attention now to these two different but in some ways related ideas and to the role ritual plays in a world revolving around such views.

THE ROLE OF OFFERTORY RITUALS IN THE MAINTENANCE OF EXPANSIVE LIFE

We remember that, to the Vedic mind, the world characterized as *sat*—the world of expansive life and being—was constantly threatened by the forces of death and nonbeing, that is, of *asat*. This view found expression in both sacred narrative and ritual drama. It may be helpful to look first at the narrative version of this idea before turning to its ritual expression.

The Sacred Narrative: The Vital Struggle between the Forces of Life and the Powers of Death

To the Vedic poets whose songs comprise the earlier hymns of the *Ṛgveda*, the two primary opposing forces in the world—constructive powers and destructive powers—were personified by two opposing classes of spiritual beings, namely, the gods of expansive life and the demons who brought harm, disease, and death.

The forces of life were personified by the divine Ādityas; the powers of constraint and death, by the demonic Dānavas. The sons of the goddess Aditi (*a-diti*, "unfettered"), the Ādityas soared unencumbered across the expanses of the earth and through the light-filled skies and heavens, thus moving through the living and vital realm of *sat*.[79] As a group, the Ādityas were committed to freeing that which constrained the vitality of life, to releasing creatures to grow, and to liberating those who have been trapped. Theirs was thus the world of spacious, growing life unrestrained by death. The Ādityas were the primary protectors of the divine ordinances that regulated the movements of the universe.[80] Guided by their leader, the god Varuṇa, whose own *vrata* was to look over and protect the principle of Ṛta, the Ādityas were immortal, for they had access to the *soma*. They received this ambrosial nectar from human beings, who offered it to them as a gift by pouring it into the ritual fire.

Ṛgveda 10.72 notes the important role the Ādityas played in the establishment of the cosmos:

3. In the earliest age of the gods,
existence came forth from nonexistence.
Then, the cardinal directions were born
from the productive power.

7. O gods! When, like austere artists,
you expanded the world and all things in it,
you returned the sun to the realm of the day,
he who had been lying, hidden, beneath the ocean.

9. So, with her seven sons, Aditi
went forth to meet the earlier age.
She brought the sun to earth so that
he might spring to life, and die again.

The Dānavas were the opposite of the Ādityas. The sons of the demoness Danu, they haunted the dark realms under the earth where the sun never shined, where there was no life-giving rain, where there was no way to sustain life. Their commitment was to bondage, to inertia, to the constraint of expansion and imprisonment of vitality: in a word, to death. They had no *soma*; thus, they were mortal. Theirs was the realm of *asat*, of nonbeing, a bottomless chasm or abyss[81] in which there was no creative principle, and thus it was characterized as *anṛta*. Their leader was Vṛtra, the Encloser, depicted by Vedic poets as a demon-serpent whose coils entrapped and imprisoned the nourishing and powerful living forces that brought energy and growth to the world.

The struggle between the Ādityas and the Dānavas was therefore a battle between life and death. The antagonists' changing fortunes in this struggle found expression in the ebb and flow of light and thus of life, as represented by the diurnal rising and setting of the sun, the alternating lunar cycles, and the seasonal drying up and return of life. At sunrise, with the waxing moon, and with the lengthening days after the vernal equinox, the Ādityas defeated the Dānavas, whose dead bodies fell to the dark underworld. But new Dānavas were born rapidly and matured quickly to return to their struggle. Denizens of darkness, they prevailed during the nighttime, as well as that of the two-week period of the waning moon and throughout the dark months of the solar year.

An early Vedic myth appearing in various forms rather obliquely throughout the *Ṛgveda* holds that, in the beginning, the gods wanted to retrieve from darkness the diverse elements of nature and, from those many components, to form a universe based on order and harmony. The gods wanted to construct *satya* based on Ṛta. However, the demons had withheld those various components from the light, keeping them trapped within a dark and foreboding prison. According to one version of this myth, the demons had trapped the forces of life—represented as cows whose milk gave nourishment to the Vedic pastoral community—deep within an inescapable prison known as the Vala-cave. Then, drawing strength from the praises sung to him, Bṛhaspati, the Lord of the Expansive Power, burst open that deathly prison and freed the cows so that they could continue to give milk to the hungry world.

To Vedic philosopher-poets, such a freeing of expansive life from the binding inertia of nonbeing was directly associated with the realization of Ṛta from *anṛta*. Such was the case, for example, for the poet whose verses form *Ṛgveda* 10.67.1–4:

1. Our father has revealed this high visionary poem
consisting of seven parts and which has sprung forth from Ṛta.
Āyasya, who is known of all peoples, has given rise to a fourth
of it
as he recited his praise of Indra.

2. With correct insight, and singing properly of Ṛta, the sons
of heaven—
those in the legions of the Asura holding the status of inspired
poet—
were the first to think of the way to offer ceremonial gifts [to
the gods]
by making the Aṅgirases the path for the poet.

3. Supported by his friends [the Aṅgirases] who cried forth
like geese,
bursting the stony walls of the prison,
Bṛhaspati bellowed like thunder to the cows;
finding the tone, he sang loudly as a skilled one.

4. Below: through two openings; above: by one,
Bṛhaspati has driven those who were seeking light in the darkness
and who were hidden in the bonds of *anṛta*,
for he had opened the three [doors].

The cattle here are said to be stuck in falsehood, *anṛta*, and therefore in nonbeing, but to have been "seeking light in the darkness." Bṛhaspati freed them from that dark realm; it is likely that the reference in verse 4 to the three doors he opened (one "below" and two "above") refer to the tripartite sacred universe consisting of the earth, the sky, and the heavens.

For many Vedic visionaries it was not Bṛhaspati, but Indra, the king of the gods, who freed the forces of life from the snare of death. Indra's enemy here was Vṛtra, the demon who constricts life and who according to one widespread account of this event is said to have trapped the cattle in the Vala-cave. According to *Ṛgveda* 1.11.5:

O Lord of Thunder!
It was you who burst open the Vala-cave, bounteous in cattle.
The gods rushed to your side
and helped you overcome your terror!

In other versions of this key myth, the forces of life are represented, not by milk-giving cows but rather by the flowing waters. Vṛtra was said to have trapped these nourishing waters on the mountaintops within his own coiled body (the image here is that of a cloud that has not yet dropped its life-giving rain). Emboldened by *soma* and helped by Agni and the Maruts, Indra engaged Vṛtra in a furious battle. He slew the demon of death, whose body relaxed and released the flood of life.

References to both these and other versions of Indra's heroic defeat of Vṛtra appear frequently throughout the *Ṛgveda*. Perhaps the most explicit is in *Ṛgveda* 1.32, selections of which include the following verses. Note, in verse 3, that the heroic god was said to gain the strength to perform such a feat by drinking the pressed and clarified *soma* offered to him in the ritual:

1. Let me now proclaim the heroic acts of Indra,
those first deeds the wielder of the thunderbolt performed!
He killed the dragon and opened a channel for the waters;
he split the mountains' bellies.

2. He slew the dragon who lay on the mountain;
the divine sculptor, Tvaṣṭṛ, fashioned the bright thunderbolt
for him.
The waters [of life] flowed quickly and undeterred to the sea,
like lowing cattle.

3. Strong and forceful as a bull, he took the *soma* for himself:
three bowls of the elixir he drank from the ritual's pressing.
The generous one grabbed the lightning for his weapon
and killed the firstborn of the dragons.

4. O Indra! When you killed the firstborn of the dragons and
with your *māyā* overpowered the magic of the evil magicians,
then, at that moment, you brought forth the sun, the sky, and
the dawn.
Since then, you have found no enemy to overpower you.

11. They who had the son of Dānu, the dragon,
for their overlord and for their guard: they imprisoned the
waters
like the [evil] Paṇis had trapped the cows. When he slew Vṛtra
he opened up the waters' outlet, which had been closed.

Indra's defeat of Vṛtra and the subsequent release of the vital waters returned the world to life. According to the seer who sang another hymn, Indra, having restored the world to life, then "set the sun in the heavens, for all to see."[82]

The Sacred Drama: Ritual and the Periodic Rejuvenation of the Sacred World

According to Vedic thought, this restorative act did not take place just once. Indeed, Vedic thought saw such a renewal of the universe taking place on a periodic basis. From this perspective, the establishment of being is not a formation of a world ex nihilo, but a necessary revivification of the world that had been repeatedly captured by the demons of death. Furthermore, human beings contributed to that process. We see in the following verses from *Ṛgveda* 6.24 that Indra's renewal of life takes place on a daily, monthly, and yearly cycle, and that he gains his strength to confront and defeat Vṛtra from the force of the lauds sung to him during the performance of the ritual:

5. One act today, another act tomorrow:
in a moment, Indra makes being from nonbeing.
Here, we have Mitra, Varuṇa, and Pūṣan
to overcome the rival's wish.

6. By songs and offertory rites, O Indra,
they brought the waters from you, as if from a mountain ridge.
To you they came with these fine lauds,
fighting for the victory prize like horses rushing in a race,
O you who is attracted by the song.

7. This Indra, whom neither the months nor the autumn diminish
with age
nor the changing days enfeeble:
his body, now, is so very mighty; still, may it increase,
strengthened by laudatory hymns and songs of praise.

Given the notion that the gods brought forth and protected being (*sat*) from the dangers of nonbeing, and given the equivalence of *sat* with Ṛta, we may say therefore that the demons personified chaos while the gods embodied the harmonious dynamics of cosmic order. Accordingly, human beings who sang praises to the gods and offered them the *soma* and other life-sustaining gifts thereby aligned themselves with that cosmic order. Doing so, human beings ensured their place in the lap of Aditi and thus their immortality. Those who failed to do so were thereby against Ṛta: they fell with the Dānavas into the lap of Nirṛti and thus into dissolution, destruction, and death, that is, into nonbeing: *asat*.

Such dangers were particularly pertinent when cosmic darkness periodically threatened light and when cold challenged warmth. It was of central importance, then, that at these times of darkness and cold the Ādityas and other gods receive their *soma* so that they could continue in their struggle with the Dānavas. But they also were to receive those gifts during periods of light as well, for such offerings bolstered and sustained the powers of light in the struggle against darkness. This is one reason why the ritual offerings of *soma* and the performance of various fire ceremonies were so important; for it was through these offertory and light-giving rituals that the bright gods, the *deva*s, gained their strength to defeat the dark Dānavas.

So, for example, Vedic priests performed such rituals as the Oblation to Agni rite (the Agnihotra)[83] each morning and evening as a way to ensure the smooth transition between the darkness of night and the light of day; the New- and Full-Moon Offering (the Darśapūrṇamāsa-iṣṭi)[84] to join with and thereby gain some control over the similarly tenuous monthly transitions between waning and waxing lunar cycles; and the Four-Month rituals (Cāturmāsya)[85] at the beginning of each of the three Indian seasons (monsoon, dry season, and spring), which together constitute the annual cycle of life, death, and renewal. Hence, too, the importance of such rites as the Praise of Light, (Jyostiṣṭoma), a ceremony performed by one who was hopeful of gaining a place in heaven after death.

Since *soma* was understood to play a key role in the vision and establishment of universal order, many of the most important Vedic rites involved the ceremonial offering of the divine nectar to the gods: such performances were known generally as the Soma Ritual. Given the central cultural, mythological, and theological significance of light and of fire, most Vedic rites involved the lighting of various ritual flames. We have already mentioned the Agnihotra: others included specific rituals performed in the actual lighting and relighting of the fire.[86] As part of the Soma Ritual in general the priests would perform the Praise of Fire (Agniṣṭoma)[87] different varieties of which included the ritual Building of the Fire Altar (Agnicayana)[88]—the enactment of which took more than a full year—and the offering of *soma* in the Drink of Strength ceremony (Vājapeya).[89]

The elixir of immortality was pressed from the *soma* plant and filtered through woven cloth. Such nectar was ritually poured into the fire burning on the ceremonial altar, the smoke of which carried it to the gods in general and to Indra in particular. We might look at *Ṛgveda* 9.113 to get an idea of the mythic context and sacerdotal tone of the Soma Ritual:

1. May Indra, Vṛtra's killer, drink *soma* in the ritual bowl,
   gathering his virile power within himself
   in order to perform a great heroic act.
   O drop [of *soma*]! Flow for Indra's sake!

2. Purify yourself, O generous *soma* from the pressing bowl, O
   master of the regions.

Pressed with language that expresses Ṛta,
with faith, and with fervor.
O drop! Flow for Indra's sake!

4. Expressing Ṛta, brilliant by means of Ṛta;
You speak the truth, your acts are true.
You speak of faith, King Soma, as the priest prepares you.
O drop! Flow for Indra's sake!

5. The pressings of the great one—the truly mighty one—
merge together;
The pressed essences of him so full of essence join together
as you, the tan-colored one, purify yourself with the *brahman*.
O drop! Flow for Indra's sake!

7. Where the unfailing light shines,
in which world the sun is placed:
Place me in that immortal world beyond harm, O Purifier.
O drop! Flow for Indra's sake!

9. Where they move as they wish—
in the threefold sphere, in the third space of heaven,
in realms full of light: there, make me immortal.
O drop! Flow for Indra's sake!

This, then, was part of humanity's obligation to the universe as a whole: to offer gifts and to sing songs of praise to the gods, particularly at periodic moments of universal danger, namely, at those fragile times when the constricted chaos of death and nonbeing threatened to overcome the expansive and well-ordered cosmos of life and being.

Another part or perspective of Manu's responsibility was to contribute to the reintegration of a disintegrated universal harmony and a revivification of a deadened world. We turn now to that second view.

RITUAL AS THE DRAMATIC REINTEGRATION OF THE SACRED UNIVERSE

By singing praises to the deities and by offering them *soma* and other gifts of power and life, Vedic priests were understood to help give the brilliant and shining gods the strength they needed to continue their struggle against the demons of darkness and death. Accordingly, to the Vedic mind it was of paramount importance that such rituals continue to be performed.

For some Vedic thinkers, however, especially those whose mythic narratives and ritual instructions form the Brāhmaṇa texts, such disintegration had already in a sense taken place. For those holding this view, the ritual was necessary because it reintegrated what had become a multiverse; ritual transformed a fractured and disjunctive existence into a unified and harmonious whole.[90]

The Sacred Narrative: The Enervating Disintegration of the Divine Body

We have already read *Ṛgveda* 10.90, which tells of the single primordial Puruṣa, whose body is sacrificially pulled apart. From Puruṣa's dismembered body came the horses, cows, goats, sheep, and all other "creatures of the air, of the forest, and of the village." Similarly, the various members of Puruṣa's sacrificed body became the different parts of the physical, divine, and social worlds: his mouth, the gods Indra and Agni, as well as human priests; his mind, the moon; his eye, the sun; his breath, the wind; his feet, the earth. Society's protective soldiers came from Puruṣa's arms; its producers, from his legs; its manual workers, from his feet.

Other hymns substitute the names of other gods for Puruṣa. According to *Ṛgveda* 10.13.4, it was Bṛhaspati who was thus dismembered: "they sacrificed the Seer, Bṛhaspati; the lord of the dead delivered his own dear body."[91] Elsewhere, that sacrificed god is said to be Viśvarkarman.[92]

By the time of the Brāhmaṇa texts, that sacrificed deity was generally identified as Prajāpati, whose name means "Lord of Creatures."[93] Here, the dissemination of Prajāpati's once-whole body was a result of the god's self-sacrifice in order to give life to the world. The idea of the universality of Prajāpati's body is indicated by such assertions as *Śatapatha Brāhmaṇa* 5.1.3.11: "Prajāpati, indeed, is this all: these worlds and whatever there is here." This is a typical phrase in the Brāhmaṇas, one that is repeated in a number of variations throughout those texts. As we saw in Chapter One, Prajāpati—arduously practicing *tapas*—exploded his fervently heated solitary "self" (*ātman*) outward, the many different yet broken parts becoming the divine, aerial, and terrestrial worlds as well as the gods who lived therein.

While this dismemberment created the many worlds, the dissemination of Prajāpati's self also dispersed his vital inner heat. Drained of his life-force, his body lay broken and disjointed. According to the *Śatapatha Brāhmaṇa*,

> This Prajāpati . . . has emitted all things, both those that breathe as well as those that do not breathe, both gods and humans. Having emitted all existing things, he was emptied [of his life-force]. He was afraid of death.[94]

In such a world there could be no cohesive and integrating principle of being. Thus, there could be no true life, no "firm foundation," because there would be no effective link between the many distinct objects.[95]

> Prajāpati produced the creatures. Having produced those creatures . . . he became broken. When broken, his vital breath left from within; when broken, his living energy left from within: they having left him, he collapsed. . . . Truly, there was no firm foundation whatever for anything here.[96]

That which had once been universe in which all things were related to all others in an interconnected unity was now a fractured multiverse in which the many creatures existed in a disconnected or unconnected plurality. Rather than forming an ordered and living cosmos, Prajāpati's dismemberment produced a disordered and deadened chaos.[97] He yearned to be made whole again:

> Having created the creatures . . . he fell to pieces. Having fallen to pieces, the vital air went out of him. When it had gone out of him the gods left him. He said to Agni: "Put me back together again!"[98]

Wishing to bring order to the world of fragmented existence, the gods then decided to help re-member Prajāpati's dismembered body. Our passage from the *Śatapatha Brāhmaṇa* continues:

> The gods then said, "Truly, other than this there is no established foundation. Let us therefore put him together, our father Prajāpati; in him we will become firmly established."[99]

The narrative goes on to say that the gods then gathered together food, the sun (Prajāpati's living energy), the wind (his vital breath), and the recollected elements of the god's dismembered form in the fire. We might say that the gods enkindled a form of *tapas*, the power of which refashioned Prajāpati's enervated body. When

> thus heated, the fire rose around him. That same vital breath which had left him from within returned, and they put it back into him. They put back into him his living energy that had left him.[100] They put back into him the food that had flowed out from him. Having constructed him entirely and completely, they stood him upright; thus, because they stood him upright, he is these worlds.[101]

While Prajāpati's sacrificial dismemberment gave rise to the world's constituent elements, the gods' reconstructive activity rejoined those fractured and disjointed elements and thereby re-formed the universe as an actual, firm reality. The gods' activity fashioned cosmic reality out of chaotic existence. But this new cosmos was a reconstruction of the original but disseminated divine body; in a sense, it was a ritually constructed counterform or "image" of the original body of god.

The Sacred Drama: Ritual as an Image of the Reconstituted Divine Body

Vedic ritual texts expound on the meaning of the ritual actions in the context of such reintegrative cosmogonic events. The Brāhmaṇas assert the idea that the physical world thus constructed by the gods was homologous to the reunified divine body:

> This [earthly] world is [now] truly his firm foundation. Whatever fire there is in this world is his inward breath. The atmosphere is his body; whatever winds there may be, they are his body's vital breath. The sky is his head, the sun and moon are his eyes. . . . Now, that same firm foundation which the gods thus put together is here, even to today, and will be so even hereafter.[102]

The enclosure marked off for the performance of the ritual was itself regarded as homologous in structure to Prajāpati's body. We will return to this idea in the next section; but we might note for the moment that—in reference to various fires the priests lit within the sacred space—Vedic ritual texts maintain, for example, that "the offertory fire is his head, [while] . . . his trunk is the area between the fire brought from the domestic hearth and the offertory fire."[103]

Because cosmic structures and divine events were duplicated and enacted within the confines of the ritual domain itself, that ceremonial space was homologous to the sacred universe as a whole. Furthermore, since all components of the universe were said to be connected to all others because they were all of the single body of Prajāpati, then any activity performed within the ritual domain was understood to be linked with the movements of the universe by means of those metaphysical connections and correspondences. So, for example, "this [earthly] world is, in truth, his domestic hearth, so whatever fire there is in this world [of the ritual] is, to him, a fire in his home hearth. This [ritual domain] is indeed his [Prajāpati's] own self."[104]

Thus, the Vedic ritual ground was identified as Prajāpati's body and the priests' actions were identified with the gods' reconstructive acts. Referring to the construction of the five-tiered altar on which the offertory fire burned, a Vedic ritual text asserts that

> it was five parts of his body that fell apart: his hair, skin, internal organs, bone, and marrow. These are the five layers [of the fire altar]. Therefore, when [the priest] constructs the five layers [of the altar he] constructs [Prajāpati].[105]

Referring to a pot of offertory food that was to be warmed, a shield to be worn, and the fire to be stoked, that text similarly notes that

> the same Prajāpati who became broken is this very fire we now build [on the altar]. That very fire pan over there which lies empty before being heated is just like Prajāpati as he lay collapsed, the vital air and living energy having drained out of him and the food having flowed from him. . . .
>
> He [the priest] warms it [the empty pot] on the fire, just as the gods once warmed him [Prajāpati]. When the fire rises around it, thus heating it, then that same vital breath which went out from him comes back to him, and he [the priest] puts it back into him [Prajāpati]; when he places the gold plate [near the fire] and wears it, he puts in him [Prajāpati] the living energy that had left him; when he puts kindling sticks [into the fire] he puts into him [Prajāpati] that very food which had flowed out of him.[106]

The priests' performances thus were not only *identified with* those of the gods; they were structurally *identical to* those divine acts. If the priests did not periodically perform the reconstructive ritual, Prajāpati's ritually reconstituted body would fall apart again and the universe would revert to a state of disjointed chaos. It is because of this identity that

> he [the priest] puts them [the kindling-sticks] on [the fire] in the evening and in the morning; for [at Prajāpati's collapse], both morning food and evening food flowed out of him. These same acts should be performed for a whole year, . . . unless he wants to see our father Prajāpati being torn apart![107]

Just as the properly performed ritual actions undertaken by Vedic priests were seen to be identical in function to the cosmogonic work of the gods, so, too, the sacred songs those priests sang while performing the ritual were homologous in function to the cosmogonic Word of the goddess, Vāc. Singing that divine poetry by means of their human voices as they kindled the ceremonial fire, the priests returned the vital "breath" (*prāṇa*) to the exhausted Prajāpati and thereby revived the Lord of Creatures. Referring, for example, to the *anuṣṭubh* meter,[108] the *Śatapatha Brāhmaṇa* holds that

> the *anuṣṭubh* is Vāc. Therefore, it is the two forms of language: the divine and the human, the loud and the soft. . . . Taking the form of breath, the fire goes along with it [that is, accompanied by the singing of the meter, the life-force returns to Prajāpati]. . . . Truly, he who knows this constructs for himself the whole of language, the whole life-force, the whole self [of Prajāpati].[109]

In these passages we see expression of an important Vedic idea regarding the nature of the creative process in general. True creativity, from this perspective, consists of two necessary stages: one of differentiation and particularization of being, which releases the different components of being from their constricted bondage to each other; the next, of the sacerdotal reintegration and harmonious relinking of those components in service of the larger whole. The first stage establishes existence, albeit chaotic existence. The second stage constructs cosmos out of this chaos.

IMAGES IN THE STAGING OF THE RITUAL: THE STAGE AS "PERSON," THE "MIND" AS "BIRD"

The sanctified ground or ritual enclosure on which Vedic ceremonies were performed often took the shape of a man (*puruṣa*) and was identified as Prajāpati's body. Such a delineation of sacred space resulted from the Vedic priest's act of drawing or projecting from his mind an image of that integrated body, measuring its dimensions, and then drawing those measurements on the ground. The sacrificial rite performed on that ground is then also described as the "man." Thus, we read, for example, that

> the *yajña* is the man. The *yajña* is the man because it is a man who spreads [its dimensions]. Being spread, it is formed in the same measurements as the man [who performs the rite]. This is why the *yajña* is the man.[110]

The ritual stage is therefore a projected image of a human body. This representation forms first in the priest's mind; the pattern thus imagined is then drawn outward and measured onto the ground in a corresponding shape. This imaginative process is made explicit in the following lines, which maintain that the altar

> should measure the distance of the outstretched arms . . . for that is the size of a man, and it should be the size of a man. . . . Let him make it as long as he thinks proper in his own mind.[111]

Such a process in which the priest imagines a human-shaped form and then draws that form outward from within his mind and lays it down on the ground in front of him is at times described in terms of birth. The head of that figure is pointed to the east, thus aligning the newly created form with the rising sun.

As an example we might point to a set of lessons regarding the ceremony accompanying the construction of the fire altar, the Agnicayana rite, part of which includes a subritual in which Vedic priests enact Agni's bringing forth of the sun at the dawn.[112] According to the *Śatapatha Brāhmaṇa*,

> preparing to build *agni* [that is, the fire altar], he [the priest] gathers him [Agni] within his self: for it is from within his own self that he makes him to be born, and one's source determines who one is. . . . He then sings the Song of Truth for, as the gods have said, "Let us make the truth his mouth: thereby we will become the truth, truth will turn onto us, and our hopes in performing the ceremony will come true." . . .
>
> He then places a lotus leaf in the center of the site. The lotus leaf is a womb. Thus he places a womb [from which Agni may be born] on the site. . . . Then he places a gold plate on [the ground]. This gold plate is the distant sun that shines on all creatures here on earth. . . .
>
> He then projects onto the ground [the shape of] a person. This is Prajāpati. This is Agni. This is the officiating priest. He is made of gold, for gold is light and fire is light; gold is immortality and fire is immortality. It is [in the shape of] a man, for Prajāpati is the man.
>
> He projects [the figure of a person onto the ground as if he were] on his back. . . . He projects his head toward the east, for [it is with the head toward the east] that this fire altar is constructed.[113]

Ritual texts instruct the priests to construct the shape of a person out of various ritual implements. Such a construction could become quite complicated and exact. To get a sense of this detail it is worth reading at some length a passage from the *Āpastamba Śrauta Sūtra*:

> The three offertory vessels form the head. . . . He [the officiating priest] should put two milk pots on the sides so as to form the ears. He should lay down either two pieces of gold or two spoons for clarified butter on the two sides in order to form the eyes. He should lay down two spoons in order to form the two nostrils; the ladle holding the holy water in order to form the mouth; the jar of clarified butter, the neck; the two stirring sticks to form the collarbones on each side; the pincers to form the two shoulders; the two ladles for offering the rice cakes to form the two arms; the stake toward the east to form the ribs; two fans to form the two

> flanks; a third fan in the middle to form the chest; a ladle in the center to form the stomach, within which he should place everything made of cord in order to form the intestines. He should place the hoe to the north in order to make the buttocks; two pegs on the side to make the form of the two thighs, with a third in the middle to make the penis. On two sides he place potsherds holding rice cakes to form the two heels.
>
> He should dust [various parts] with the remainder of the rice flour to form the nerves and should scatter [wood chips] to form the muscles. He should cover the various parts with grass and wedges of incense to form the skin and, with his hand turned downward, should sprinkle over everything curds mixed with honey to form the blood.[114]

Various passages from the Brāhmaṇa texts teach that the eastern altar on which the offertory fire burns is to be constructed in the shape of a bird. Perhaps this is because, just as the morning sun ascends from the horizon into the heavens, so too birds fly from the earthly to the aerial realms. Similarly, offerings poured into the offertory fire on the bird-shaped altar travel with the rising smoke through the skies and heavens, linking all parts of the universe. The chants and songs the priests sing are also envisioned to be birds, for they, too, rise forth from the mouth of the singer into the celestial and heavenly realms. Prajāpati himself is said to have seen and then sung those songs. We read that

> Prajāpati wished to come to these worlds. He saw this bird-like body, the fire altar. He formed it and thereby gained this [earthly] world. He saw another bird-like body, namely, the Great-Rite chant. He formed it and thereby gained the air. He saw a third bird-like body, the Great Song. He formed it and thereby gained the heavens.[115]

The gods in general are said once upon a time to have sung those chants, too, and thus to have gained their place in the divine worlds. In a passage regarding the performance of the Śatarudriya ceremony we hear why it is that the priests sing the various songs around the bird-shaped altar as they undertake their prescribed activities. Again, it is worth quoting at length:

> Why does he [the priest] sing hymns around it [the altar]? [It is because] the gods at one time wished, "May we make this body of ours boneless and immortal." They said, "Meditate on this: how can we make this body boneless and immortal?" They said, "Contemplate!" by which they meant, "Look for a layer [of bricks that form the altar]. Seek the way in which we may make this body of ours boneless and immortal."
>
> While contemplating, they saw those hymns and sang them around [the altar]; by means of [those songs] they made that body of

> theirs boneless and immortal. Similarly, the performer of the ritual makes that body of his boneless and immortal when he sings the hymns around [the altar]. He sings it on every side [of the altar]. . . .
>
> First, he sings the Gāyatrī hymn, for the Gāyatrī meter is Agni. He thereby makes Agni his head, and he makes that head boneless and immortal.
>
> At the right wing [he sings] the Rathantara hymn, for the Rathantara is this [earth] and this [earth] is the most essential of these realms because in her are contained the essence of all things. . . . He thereby makes this [earth] the right wing, and that right wing he thus makes boneless and immortal.
>
> At the left wing [he sings] the Bṛhat hymn, for the Bṛhat is without doubt the sky and the sky is the most expansive [of all the worlds]. He thereby makes the sky [Agni's] left wing, and that left wing he thus makes boneless and immortal.
>
> On the body [he sings] the Vāmadevya hymn, for the Vāmadevya is the breath, and the breath is wind, and [the god of] the wind, truly, is the self of all the gods. He thereby makes wind his body, and that body he thus makes boneless and immortal.
>
> Near the tail [he sings] the Yajñāyañiya hymn, for the Yajñāyajñiya is the moon, for whenever a solemn offering is completed the essence of its oblations flies up to [the moon]. Because offering after offering flies up to him, the moon is the Yajñayañiya. He thereby makes the moon [Agni's] tail, and that tail he thus makes boneless and immortal.
>
> He then sings the Heart-of-Prajāpati hymn, for the heart is the sun, for the sun is round and smooth, just as the heart is round and smooth. . . . He thereby makes the sun [Agni's] heart, and that heart he thus makes boneless and immortal.[116]

Let us step back for a moment to summarize. We see descriptions in these passages of a ritual stage in the shape of a human body, at the head of which stands the altar. The altar is in the shape of a bird. It is significant for our purposes that the fire altar in the shape of a bird and which stands as the place where gifts are offered to the gods is said to be the *mind* in that body. "Now, with regard to the [body] of this self, the fire altar is the mind."[117]

These passages suggest the idea, then, that the ritual stage and the various implements and places within it were themselves "products" or "drawings forth" of the sacerdotal imagination—"for it is from within his own self that he makes it [the fire altar] be born."[118] The priest then projects that inward image outward,[119] onto the ground. Furthermore, we see that it was the "mind" in that dramatically formed image—the bird-shaped fire altar—that carried the gifts from the human world to that of the gods in the heavens.

It was the dramatic imagination, then, that thus formed and linked together the divine body, the way a bird by means of flight joins the earthly and the aerial worlds.

RITUAL AS CREATIVE IMAGINATION: THE LITURGICAL ESTABLISHMENT OF LIFE IN THE HEAVENLY WORLD

Vedic ritual thus allowed its performers to align themselves with the structures and powers of the sacred universe itself. Such an alignment allowed the ritual to be an efficacious expression of cosmogonic power. The primordial agonistic act of creation to which the earlier Vedic songs gave verbal image was filled with uncertainty and danger, for darkness could conquer light just as light could dispel darkness: the demons of the darkness were just as powerful as were the bright deities. But, just as through their imagination Vedic visionaries were able to see through the confusion and understand the riddle of the cosmos, so too Vedic priests in their enactment of the ritual participated in the ordering and structuring of the universe as a whole. The ritual was a microcosmic version of the macrocosm.

Accordingly, from the Vedic point of view, not only was knowledge of the correct performance of the ritual equivalent to knowledge of the structure and workings of the universe itself, but because of the structural connection that linked microcosm and macrocosm, actions performed in the ritual affected the movements of the universe as a whole.[120] Because of the metaphysical and causative bond between cosmic realms, the gods were bound to defeat the demons if the priests performed the ritual drama properly. The ritual took the danger out of the universe by controlling its chances; it gave structure to the chaos of existence.

From this perspective, the ritual no longer merely presented a dramatic image of cosmic order; it created that order itself. The ritual had the power to form functional reality out of mere existence.

It is not surprising therefore that Brāhmaṇa texts at times suggest the idea that some of those performances were in fact more creative than reconstructive. Some of the most important Vedic rituals involved performances in which the priests were said not only to revivify Prajāpati's body, but also by means of those ceremonies to fashion new states of being described as not previously existing. In these instances, the sacrifice created a new "realm" or "world"—*loka*—either for the priests or, more commonly, for its patron.[121]

The word *loka* originally referred to an open place (as in a deep jungle) in which one could see the light of day,[122] and thus to a secure and expansive space.[123] It is not difficult to see how this sense of the word could lead to the idea of a place or state of being in which one emerged from existential darkness into light or from the uncertain world of human existence to the divine world of the gods. We are reminded here of the basic meaning of the Sanskrit word *veda*, which referred in part to the seer's visionary knowledge of divine truths embodied in the deities' luminous forms. The *Pañcaviṁśa Brāhmaṇa* presents the effect of such knowledge when it asserts that "he who, knowing this [and] performs [the rite] attains the luminous, pure world."[124] Within the confines of the ritual domain the priests and patrons replayed the very acts that the gods performed in the larger universe; thus, just as the universe as a whole was formed by the sacrifice of Prajāpati, so new states of being were constructed for the patron by the performance of the ritual's symbolic sacrificial drama.

To reside in a *loka* was therefore not only to live in a place of safety but also to live where one could see things the way they truly are. In other words, to establish a *loka* was to form a systematic and meaningful "world" in which one's actions make sense in the larger universe; it is to *locate* oneself in a cosmos, to find a *locus* of being within the chaos of existence. This establishment of a meaningful world resulted from the poet's ability to see the divine and the priest's ability to give dramatic form to that vision. Both the poet in his poem and the priest therefore gave image to the divine. Furthermore, priests who dramatically enacted the dismembering and re-membering of the cosmic body thereby participated in the cosmogonic ordering of the universe itself. But they could not participate in that order if they did not themselves act in an ordered way. Therefore, their ordered ritual activity not only embodied Ṛta; it *was* Ṛta. From the Vedic perspective, sacrifice constructed, supported, and in a sense created a vital world.

Sometimes those new states of being were described in terms of the patron's winning this-worldly abundance, wealth, and long life: "You will have a firm grounding in this world," the ritual's patron is assured.[125] Sometimes they were said to exist in the celestial realm. In an exposition on the Soma Ritual one text declares that the sacrificer "gains the world of heaven."[126] We see references to both in another work, which asserts that through his support of the Agnihotra rite the patron gains benefits both in "this world" and in "yonder world," the latter of which is described in the same passage as the "world of heaven."[127]

THE SACRIFICIAL MOVEMENT TOWARD THE INNER SELF

If the priest mentally projected the shape of a person's body onto the sacred ritual domain, the opposite was also true in Vedic religion: practitioners introjected the structures and movements of the ritual drama into their own minds and incorporated them into their own bodies. In the former case, the ritual was the externalization of the body and mind. In the latter, the body and mind were the home of an internalized ritual. Here, Vedic religious adepts in a sense personalized the dynamics of a world that depended on humanity's continued performance of hallowed or sanctifying action.

To these priests and others, the true sacrifice took place not only in the outer world, but also within the individual human spirit itself. This was no insignificant development in Vedic thought and practice, for it established the trajectory that was to lead to the realization articulated most forcefully in the Upaniṣads (more on these texts in the following chapter): that divinity is to be found, finally, within the eternal nature of the soul residing deep within the human being. As we will see, though, this inward movement has its origins, in part, in the ideology and practice of the sacrifice itself.

Prajāpati's Victory over Death within His "Self"

This internalization of the sacrifice began, perhaps, with the Vedic idea that the whole world is in fact God's body. As we have seen, the Brāhmaṇas tend to identify this deity as Prajāpati, the universal Lord of Creatures. And, as we have noted, those texts also say that this divine body is threatened by deathly forces or becomes drained of its life-force through its own self-sacrifice. In giving Prajāpati his body again by means of the ritual, Vedic priests themselves embodied and therefore controlled in dramatic form the struggle between the forces of life and being against the powers of death and nonbeing. Whether it served to rejuvenate the sacred universe or to reintegrate a disintegrated world, sacrifice therefore attempted to regularize and thereby control the mutual contradictions of being and nonbeing.[128] The *yajña* supported *satya* against a*satya*—truth against untruth—and thus buttressed Ṛta against the ravages of *anṛta*. When properly performed, sacrifice made a "firm foundation" where otherwise there was none.

The *yajña* was the universe in miniature: in it played all the forces and dynamics that pulled the world apart and, more important, put that world back together again. What used to be the weapons used in the unpredictable external struggle between the opposing forces of life and death came to be the different components of the regularized and routinized liturgy. The "weapons of the sacrifice" were in fact the various chants intoned by the *udgatṛ*-priest, the verses sung by the *hotṛ*-priest, and the actions performed by the *adhvaryu*-priest, respectively: "at that time the 'weapons of the sacrifice' were the same as these 'weapons' [used] nowadays. . . . What is chanted, what is recited and what is being acted, that was Prajāpati's armor."[129]

The *Jaiminīya Brāhmaṇa* recounts a relevant story in the context of the Soma Ritual. Here, Prajāpati, the universal Lord of Creatures, and Mṛtyu, the personification of death, are said to struggle against each other in the sacrificial arena for years and years, neither being able to overpower the other, for the two "were equally strong; as much as the one had, so much had the other. For a long time, during many years, they tried to defeat each other without a decision being reached." Finally, Prajāpati had a decisive vision of the symbolic and numerical equivalences among the sacred meters, melodies, and innumerable verses available to him as well as of the way these equivalences could be used as various "weapons" in his struggle against Death. Mṛtryu could not envision those connections and lost his ability to control those very weapons. With the force of this vision Prajāpati then overpowered Mṛtyu and banished him to a distant part of the sacrificial stage. There Death remained, enervated, "his *soma* wasted away."[130]

We should note two elements of this sacerdotal narrative. First, Prajāpati gains victory over Mṛtyu due to his vision of the unifying structures and forces that support and drive the world, a vision that Death does not share. Second, the Lord of Creatures defeats Death, not by expelling him from the sacrificial arena, but rather by sending him to a far corner of that domain, for Mṛtyu could merely attack Prajāpati again if he were allowed to leave the domain without being subdued. In other words, Prajāpati overpowers Death by keeping Mṛtyu within the Lord of Creatures' own sanctified world. Death loses his autonomy, but not his being.

Furthermore, we remember from previous discussions that the sacrificial domain is said to be Prajāpati's body. Accordingly, Prajāpati's self (*ātman*) now envelops and subsumes Death. Therefore, Prajāpati is, at one and the same time, both sacrificer and sacrificial oblation, victorious deity and defeated demon, the force of life and the power of death. He is the monistic deity who has subsumed all things into his now-reunified *ātman*. To repeat: "Prajāpati, indeed, is this all: these worlds, and whatever there is here."[131] From this perspective, there is nothing that is not Prajāpati.[132]

The "Sacrifice in the Body"

Since the various areas and components of the ritual were said to be the different parts of Prajāpati's body, then in laying out the dimensions of the ceremonial ground, placing the appropriate ritual implements in their proper place, and undertaking the prescribed activities in which all of those various components fit together properly, Vedic priests thereby liturgically re-membered God's dismembered body. They established the stage in which Prajāpati could incorporate and thus defeat Mṛtyu. The *yajña* was thus a dramatic microcosm of the universe as a whole. Understood from this perspective, the supreme deity whose body forms the universe is not only represented by sacrifice; that divine body is none other than sacrifice itself. As the Brāhmaṇas repeatedly note, *prajāpati vai yajñaḥ*: "Prajāpati is the sacrifice."[133]

As we have seen, the shape of the ritual stage on which the sacrifice was performed was an image of the human form. In a process that reflects the continuing miniaturization of the cosmic body, Vedic thinkers came to feel that the true sacrificial ritual actually took place within the human body itself. Accordingly, the Brāhmaṇas maintain not only that "Prajāpati is the sacrifice" but also repeatedly assert *puruṣo vai yajñaḥ*: "the sacrifice is man."[134]

Vedic teachers whose lessons formed the Upaniṣads were then to point out the equivalence between the sacrifice and an individual person's particular existence. The *Chāndogya Upaniṣad* holds that

> truly, a person is himself the sacrifice. His first twenty-four years correspond to the [*yajña*'s] morning offerings, for the Gāyatrī meter in which the morning chants are sung consists of twenty-four syllables. . . .
>
> His next forty-four years correspond to the noontime offerings, for the Triṣṭubh meter in which the midday chants are sung consists of forty-four syllables. . . .
>
> His next forty-four years correspond to the [*yajña*'s] third offering, for the Jagatī meter with which the third libations are offered consists of forty-four syllables.[135]

The fact that the number of years totals 112 should not distract us here. The point is that Vedic philosophers of the ritual saw a connection between the structure of the sacred drama and the structure of life itself. So, similarly, the performer and various components of the external sacrificial rite (the ritual's patron, his wife, the priests, the *soma* bowls, and so on) were said to be the various parts of an individual person's own physical and mental being. So, for example, one text outlines the various components of that "sacrifice in the body":

> Of this sacrifice in the body performed with the sacrificial post and holder, who is the sacrificer? Who is his wife? Who are the priests? Who watches over everything? What are the bowls [for the *soma*]? What are the gifts? What is the altar? . . .
>
> Of this sacrifice in the body performed with a sacrificial post and holder, the self is the sacrificer, intelligence is his wife, the Vedas are the priests, the ego is the underpriest and the mind is the head priest. . . . The body is the main altar, the nose is the northern altar, the skull is the bowl.[136]

Vedic teachers taught that the individual person's own inner being was the true sacrificial arena; it was in the inward soul residing deep within the human heart where one searched for the knowledge of the *brahman* that linked the divine and human worlds. A life infused with the discipline necessary to such an inward search is known as *brahmacārya* (literally, "moving in the *brahman*," or "abiding in the truth"). An early suggestion of such an idea appears in the *Chāndogya Upaniṣad*:

> What people call "the sacrifice" is really the disciplined life of a seeker of sacred knowledge [*brahmacārya*]. It is only through *brahmacārya* that one who thus knows gains the [heavenly] world. What people call the "sacrificial offering" is really *brahmacārya*, for it is only through *brahmacārya* that one gains the self [*ātman*].
>
> And what people call "the long sacrificial performance" is really *brahmacārya*. It is only through *brahmacārya* that one gains the protection of the real self. What people call the [ritual's] "vow of silence" is really *brahmacārya*, for it is only through finding the self through *brahmacārya* that one truly meditates.
>
> And what people call the "practice of [ritual] fasting" is really *brahmacārya*, for the self that one finds by the disciplined life of a student of sacred knowledge does not perish.[137]

The Vedic tradition thus came to maintain the idea that the whole of one's physical, mental, and spiritual life is to be understood as sacrifice. One's very being is to be regarded as a sacred offering to the gods. In reference to the Agnihotra, one of the most important of all Vedic ritual ceremonies, the *Kauṣītaki-Brāhmaṇa Upaniṣad* says this: "it is called the 'Inner Agnihotra.'"[138]

The "Five Great Sacrifices"

The idea that all of one's life could and should be lived as an offering to the gods made the practice of such discipline available to others besides Vedic priests who performed the large public ceremonies. Not everybody could perform or sponsor a full *yajña*, but everybody could burn just one stick in a small flame, thereby honoring and thanking the gods in a more private and personal way. One may not be able to feed everyone in the kingdom, as a responsible king would, but one could feed and care for injured and forsaken animals or other living creatures in the world and give a small morsel of food to another human being. One may not have been able to find and press the *soma*, but one could offer a cup of water to soothe the ancestor's thirst. One may not have been able to memorize the entire Vedic canon of sacred songs, but one could recite just one verse a day.

Accordingly, Vedic tradition came to recognize five forms of personal offering or sacrifice to be performed by individual householders in their own homes for the benefit of the larger universe as a whole. They were understood to inspire feelings of appreciation and devotion to the gods, to allow one to express one's loving memory of deceased family members, to encourage and give form to compassion, tolerance, and kindness toward all beings in the world.

Vedic tradition identifies these as the Five Great Sacrifices, which are said to be "like the great sacrificial sessions" themselves.[139] Terms describing them vary slightly. A typical list appears in the *Taittirīya Āraṇyaka*, which identifies them as the offering to the gods, the offering to the ancestors, the offering to animals and other living creatures, the offering to fellow people, and the offering of one's study of sacred truths.[140]

Whereas the large public sacrifices were performed on an episodic or periodic basis—at the installation of the king, for example, or at the new or full moon—these personal offerings were to be performed constantly and throughout one's lifetime. According to the *Āśvalāyana Gṛhya Sūtra*, they were to be performed every day,[141] a lesson also taught in the *Śatapatha Brāhmaṇa*, which holds that such sacrificial acts are to be performed "day by day."[142]

In performing the offering to animals (*bhūtayajña*), the householder does not offer food to the fire, but places it on the ground, which has been wiped clean and sprinkled with water. The offering usually takes the form of rice pressed into small balls. Such a gift is to be offered to all animals, even those normally shunned.[143] A later text influenced by such ideas holds that such gifts are to be given to dogs, crows, and insects as well as to animals suffering from disease, and that one "who thus honors all beings on a daily basis goes on a straight path in a resplendent body to the highest dwelling place."[144]

The typical setting for the practice of the sacrifice to one's fellow human beings (*manuṣyayajña*) is the proper reception and treatment of visitors in one's home. The guest is to be offered food until he is no longer hungry, a light to lead him through the darkness, and a bath in which to clean and cool his body. The *Taittirīya Upaniṣad* teaches that one is to "be one to whom a guest is a god"[145] and "not [to] turn away anybody from your residence; that will be the rule."[146]

The offering to the ancestors (*pitṛyajña*) typically takes the form of the solemn daily offering of various types of food and drink—grains, rice, water, milk, fruit, and so on—in loving memory of those deceased family members.[147] Later Hindu tradition was to hold that the offering may also be performed by inviting at least one brahmin for dinner.[148]

The Vedic practice of the personal sacrifice to the gods (*devayajña*) consists of offering food or "at least a small stick" to a fire[149] while chanting the names of the gods or of one god in particular. Some texts influenced by Vedic thought use the word *homa* almost synonymously with *devayajña*,[150] for in the performance of a *homa* one offers clarified butter to a fire while chanting the divine names. The gods and goddesses so honored are the same as those praised in the large public *yajña*s. According to the *Āśvalāyana Gṛhya Sūtra*, for example, those deities include Agni, Prajāpati, Soma, Indra, Heaven and Earth, Dhanvantari, the Viśvedevas, and Brahman.[151] The Vedic practice of *devayajña* stands as a precedent of sorts for the later Hindu practice of *pūjā*, in which an individual worshiper honors an iconic or aniconic image of a deity (such as a sculpture or a painting or a geometrical figure) by placing in front of it flower petals, fruit, seeds, clarified butter, and other symbols of vitality and life.

The offering of one's study of sacred scriptures consists of the daily recitation and contemplation of texts from the Vedic canon. It is described as *brahmayajña*, "offering to the *brahman*," and as *svādhyāya*, "study by oneself" or "self-reflection." The two words seem to be nearly synonymous: in fact, one text holds that "*brahmayajña* is *svādhyāya*."[152] The practice includes that of *japa*, that is, of repeating Vedic mantras quietly to oneself. Various texts are identified with different components of the larger, public ritual. For example, according to the *Śatapatha Brāhmaṇa*, passages from the *Ṛgveda* serve the same function as the milk offerings to the gods; those from the *Yajurveda* are equivalent to the offerings of clarified butter; those from the *Sāmaveda* serve the same function as the *soma* offerings; and those from the *Atharvaveda* serve the same function as the offerings of animal fat.[153] Similarly, the different spoons with which the offerings are poured into the large public fire are identified as various components of the individual person: "in the *brahmajayña* the *juhū*-spoon is one's speech, the *upabhṛt*-spoon is the mind, the *dhrūva*-spoon is the eye, the *sruva*-spoon is mental power."[154]

The quiet recitation of these and other lessons is then said to be "offerings of honey to the gods [otherwise given in the external ritual]; knowing this, whoever practices *svādhyāya* on a daily basis . . . satisfies the gods with honey offerings. Because they are satisfied, they satisfy him [by giving him] security, vital breath, seed, his whole self, and all auspicious blessings. Rivers of clarified butter and rivers of honey flow to the Fathers, as their familiar drink."[155]

Vedic tradition holds that the practice of *brahmayajña* or *svādhyāya* is to be undertaken by oneself in a quiet place some distance from public activity, often in a forest. There, the person is to sit down by himself in a clean place with his legs crossed over each other, wash his hands and face, touch his head, eyes, nostrils, ears, and heart, and quietly recite and contemplate Vedic passages.[156] If for some reason one is not able to leave the village for the forest, then one may

> perform *brahmayajña* by turning the Veda over in his mind in the village itself by day or even by night; or if he cannot seat himself, then he may perform the *brahmayajña* even standing or lying down, since the principle purpose is to recite the Veda.[157]

According to the *Āśvalayana Gṛhya Sūtra*, one should undertake the practice of *svādhyāya* while gazing at the horizon or even by closing one's eyes in such a way (as one scholar has summarized) that "one feels that one can concentrate one's mind."[158]

Performing *brahmayajña*, the practitioner thus effectively performs the sacrificial offering by means of the contemplative imagination. Such a mental sacrifice is said to bring even more desirable results than does the performance of the large public rite. According to the *Śatapatha Brāhmaṇa*, the

> end of the [*brahmayajña*] is heaven. And, truly, no matter how great is the world he gains by supporting [the public ritual], three times and more of this earth and all of its wealth—an imperishable world—does he gain: he who, knowing this, contemplates his lesson day by day. Therefore, let him contemplate his daily lesson.[159]

Vedic tradition holds that the solitary reflection on Vedic texts, quiet recitation and chanting of sacred scriptures, and other practices associated with *brahmayajña* and *svādhyāya* were not to be taken lightly. There was much to know and understand; for, as one text says, the Vedas are endless in scope.[160] Furthermore, tradition holds that the content of one's study is to include more than the verses from the four Vedas.[161] Another holds that the day that a true brahmin ceases to practice *svādhyāya* is the day the sun, moon, and stars cease to move through the sky.[162]

Performing *brahmayajña* and the others of the Five Great Sacrifices, a person thereby both personalized and internalized the power and effect of the large public offerings. The fact that, of these five, *brahmayajña* garners the most attention from Vedic thinkers and teachers indicates that the Vedic tradition holds much respect for the deep contemplation of sacred truths and inward performance of the sacrifice.

The "Sacrifice in the Mind"

The contemplative strain of Vedic thought thus came to shift its attention away from the forces and dynamics that were once considered to take place in the external world; for, just as the priest saw Prajāpati's "self" (*ātman*) to be found in outward sacrifice, so too the meditator experienced God's *ātman* residing deep within his own innermost being.

Some Vedic thinkers came to teach that all the deities of which Vedic poets sang actually resided within the creative power of the mind itself. Accordingly, such teachers held that the true sacrifice was a performance undertaken by the imagination.

We have just noted an expression of such an idea in the practice of *svādhyāya*, part of which involves the use of the mind as the instrument through which honor and respect are given to the gods. Suggestions of such an idea appear occasionally in the Brāhmaṇa literatures, which taught that the oblation to the as-yet formless Prajāpati should be performed silently.[163]

That the workings of the mind plays a central part in the performance of the sacrifice is indicated, too, by the admonition given to the priests as they construct the various levels or layers of the altar while performing the Agnicayana ceremony. Each layer represents a different aspect of the sacred world populated by the deities. The instructions play on the linguistic similarity between the verb translated here as *meditate* and the word *layers*:

> Now, the gods said, "Meditate! [*cetayadhvam*]." Undoubtedly, they meant to say, "Seek a layer [of the sacred world represented by the layers of the altar]." Because they saw them while meditating, they are called "layers [*citayaḥ*]."[164]

The mental performance of the sacrifice also recalls the role the *brahman*-priest performs in large public rituals. We remember from an earlier discussion that according to Vedic thought "the sacrifice has two tracks; one is by speech, the other by mind."[165] The mental function was embodied by the *brahman*-priest, whose responsibility to the *yajña* was, in part, to watch silently over the performance of the ritual. Vedic teachings hold that a person who sacrifices with words only is "injured" by doing so, for speaking words only one omits the other essential sacrificial track, namely, that of the "mind."[166]

Of these two functions, the *brahman*-priest "performs one with his mind; the *hotṛ*, *adhvaryu*, and *udgātṛ* [perform] the other by speech." But, having performed an offering by speech only, a sacrificer

> is injured. Just as a one-footed person walking or as a one-wheeled chariot moving is injured, just so his offering is injured. When the sacrifice is injured, the sacrificer is injured. . . . But if the *brahman*-priest does not speak . . . they [thus] perform it both ways and neither [the sac-

rificer nor the priest] is injured. As a two-footed person walking or as a two-wheeled chariot moving is well supported, even so is his offering well-supported.[167]

The *yajña* therefore took place not only on the ritual stage but also in the *brahman*-priest's mind. Given the fact that the *brahman*-priest served as the "healer" of the sacrifice, it could be said that the *brahman*-priest's mental sacrifice was of paramount importance to the *yajña* as a whole. One of the most influential of Vedic teachers is reported to have taught that it was through the *brahman*-priest's mind that the sacrificer gains the infinite realm. In a sacrificial symposium attended by many learned Vedic priests, the sage Yājñavalkya is reported to have been asked a number of questions by a priest about the *yajña*, its procedures, and its rewards. Part of the dialogue includes this exchange:

> "Yājñavalkya," asked [Aśvala], with how many divine powers does the *brahman*-priest . . . protect the *yajña* today?"
>
> "With one," [Yājñavalkya replied.]
>
> "Which is that one?"
>
> "The mind, alone," [Yājñavalkya said.] "Truly, the mind is infinite. Infinite are the All-gods. He gains an infinite world thereby."[168]

By the latter part of the Vedic Period and into the Classical Period of Hinduism, that inner discipline came to be known as *mānasayajña*, the "ceremonial rite performed within the mind," which could be practiced by contemplatives other than the silent priest overseeing the performance of the external ritual. Furthermore, just as the public *yajña* was said to establish or locate the ritual's patron in a new, heavenly *loka* of light and fulfillment, so too the practice of meditation was understood to establish the contemplative seeker in a state of timeless, infinite, and expansive wholeness unfettered by the constraints of time and space and unbuffeted by the wavering vicissitudes of life and death.

The outward, visionary experience and the ideology of the ritual thus both lead in Vedic thought to a contemplative movement inward, for the entire sacred world—including all the gods and other universal forces of life—were seen to dwell within the human spirit. As the *Jaiminīya Upaniṣad Brāhmaṇa* says, "all the gods are within me,"[169] a realization that is also expressed succinctly in the *Brahma Upaniṣad*:

> In the heart reside all the gods; in it are established the vital breaths.
> In the heart are life and light. . . .
> [All this] stands within the heart,
> in the sparkling of consciousness.[170]

The inward realization of sacred truths stands as the culmination of the Vedic religious experience. Such a realization is said to take place through the disciplined practice of meditation. In the following chapter we look more closely, then, at the structure and power of the contemplative imagination, which sees light and life and divinity itself as residing in the heart, "in the sparkling of consciousness."

Chapter 5

The Inward Seer: The Liberating Power of the Contemplative Imagination

That which is nonthought [yet] which stands in the midst of thought, the unthinkable, supreme mystery!: thereupon let one concentrate his thought. . . . One sees Brahman through meditation.

— Maitrī Upaniṣad *6.19–20*

The form of that One is not to be seen.
No one sees it with the eyes.
Only one who has opened the heart,
the thoughts, and the mind [may see it].

— Mahānārāyaṇa Upaniṣad *1.11*

Keeping his neck and body straight and his mouth closed, a wise person should meditate unwaveringly on the center of his heart. . . . His mind calm, he should see with his [mind's] eye the ambrosia flowing there.

— Varāha Upaniṣad *5.31–32*

THE INDWELLING PRESENCE OF DIVINITY

The interiorization of the sacred sacrifice is consistent with a trajectory in Vedic religious sensibilities in general. The earliest of Vedic literatures tend to describe the deities as living in the external world, particularly within the forces of nature and in the drama of the sacred ritual. Through the years, however, Vedic philosophers and teachers came to hold that the human engagement with the divine took place not only by seeing and hearing it outwardly but also by knowing it within the structures and dynamics of the human spirit itself. Vedic texts speak of a mysterious indwelling of the holy, an infusion of the divine in the world of form. A relatively early verse from the Saṁhitā literatures asserts, for example, that the gods "enter into this world through their hidden natures."[1] A somewhat later verse from the Saṁhitā literatures represents the Vedic experience that such an indwelling includes, especially, the human being: "having made the mortal their home," it reads, "the gods entered into man."[2] Elsewhere it is said that the deities, "needing a place in which to establish ourselves," entered into the human being, "each according to its proper place."[3] And a lesson from a still somewhat later work presents the idea that it is the light of consciousness itself shining in the heart that stands as the deities' central abode: "in the heart reside all the gods. . . . [All of this] stands within the heart, in the sparkling of consciousness."[4]

"LIKE A TORTOISE DRAWING IN ITS LIMBS, THE *YOGĪ* ENCLOSES THE MIND WITHIN THE HEART"

Both the ritual interiorization of the sacred universe and the experiential realization that the divine world resides in the structure and power of consciousness arose out of and lent support to an important, some would say culminating, development in Vedic religion. We refer here to the spiritual practice of contemplative meditation.

The practice of meditation has its ritual precedent in the fact, for example, that Vedic priests are instructed to contemplate inwardly the nature of the divine while they outwardly construct the ceremonial altar. Similarly, as we have seen, the *brahman*-priest was to perform the entire *yajña* in his mind. We remember, too, that Vedic ritual texts teach that Prajāpati's reconstituted self (*ātman*) dwells within all things in the sacred universe, and that, accordingly, the divine self resides deep within the human being. As we hear the Vedic teacher proclaim in *Chāndogya Upaniṣad* 8.3.3, "Prajāpati is the heart."

Vedic sages therefore came to teach that one could come to know and experience the divine by turning one's attention inward. Teachers who led their students in this manner tended to reside in quiet forest retreats beyond the reach of the town or city, where their students could live with them in relative solitude while they practiced various spiritual disciplines. It is likely that the Vedic lessons recorded in the Āraṇyakas ("forest teachings") dating from roughly 900–600 BCE were first given by teachers to their students in such settings. Religious tradition in India influenced by Vedic thought came to hold that such a seeker must first have fulfilled all of his responsibilities to his family and to society before moving to the forest retreat, where he was to live in austere simplicity.

Such an anchorite was known as a *vānaprastha*, a word sometimes translated as "forest-hermit" or "forest-dweller." Ideally, the *vānaprastha* was to eat only fruits, roots, and vegetables growing in the forest; wear only a deerskin or shirt made of bark or *kuśa*-grass; live a restrained and disciplined life at all times; and be friendly and compassionate to all creatures. He was to keep a fire burning at all times so that he could continue to perform by himself such Vedic ceremonial offerings as the Agnihotra, the New- and Full-Moon Sacrifice, and the Four-Month Rite.[5]

Having retired to the forest, the *vānaprastha* was also to continue the personal practice of the Five Great Sacrifices to which we made reference toward the end of the previous chapter. He was to be dedicated in his quiet and solitary study of the Veda, which he was to chant quietly to himself.[6] Before performing *brahmayajña* and other specifically contemplative techniques, the student was to find a clean place on the ground, where he was to fashion a seat made of sweet *darbha*-grass on which he would sit facing the east with his legs crossed.[7] Such a setting and posture was said to be conducive to inward reflection and meditation.

Foreshadowing developments in later Yogic and Tantric spiritual practices in which the adept meditator was to sit quietly and, with great discipline, control and focus the mind, a Vedic text dating to roughly the fifth century BCE instructs the seeker in this way:

> Holding one's body steady
> with the three upper parts straight,
> and bringing the senses and the mind into the heart,
> a wise person should cross over all of the rivers of anxiety
> with the boat of the *brahman*.
> Having controlled one's breathing here [in the body]
> and stilling one's movements . . .
> let one restrain the mind without distraction,
> the way a chariot is yoked to wild horses.
> One should practice meditation in a hidden retreat protected from
> the wind,
> a clean and level place that is free from pebbles, fire, and gravel,
> near the sound of water and other features,
> conducive to thought, and pleasing to the eye.[8]

According to another text the workings of the mind are to be enfolded into the deeper and more sublime heart. The contemplative does this, in part, by closing his eyes and mouth ("shutting the doors") and slowly calming the breathing by inwardly pronouncing the *Praṇava*, the sacred syllable *oṁ*:

> Like a tortoise drawing in its limbs,
> [the contemplative] encloses the mind within the heart.
> Slowly pronouncing the twelve sounds[9]
> within the syllable *oṁ*
> he fills his whole body with one breath
> and shuts all of its doors.[10]

Sitting quietly in this way, the contemplative practiced inner disciplines. The senses were muted; mantras were chanted silently; the mind was stilled. Meditation in this manner presented the setting in which the contemplative could worship the divine presence within. We read, for example that

> Choosing a posture such as the lotus position,
> or whatever else may please him . . .
> controlling the mind at all times,
> the wise should meditate
> continuously on the syllable *oṁ*,
> enthroning the highest god in their hearts.[11]

The practice of meditation was undertaken by people other than *vānaprasthas*. Meditation came to be practiced by people who had not necessarily left their homes to live in the forests, for this spiritual discipline came to be seen as an effective way inwardly to know and experience the splendor of divinity, no matter what the external setting may be.

In this chapter we will look into the role of meditation in the Vedic context, noting as we do so the function the imagination holds in the Vedic spiritual seeker's coming to experience and understand the nature of the Absolute.

THE UPANIṢADS

Our primary sources will be the set of teachings known collectively as the Upaniṣads, the most influential of which can be dated from roughly the seventh century BCE to around the rise of the Common Era. The word *upaniṣad* initially referred to a mystic teaching given by a Vedic sage to a person who ponders issues pertaining to the religious and spiritual life. Sometimes those lessons took place in the context of speculative symposia.[12] Used in this sense, the word *upaniṣad* is therefore similar in a way to the term *brahmodya*, the latter we recall referring to a particular form of theological discourse in which philosopher-priests performing a Vedic ritual ask each other sets of questions regarding the hidden significance of various aspects of the ceremonial drama.[13] By extension, the word *upaniṣad* is therefore similar to the early

Vedic use of the word *brahman*: both refer to an effective phrase or verbal image, the understanding of which is said to transform the questioner's comprehension of the forces and structures that hold the sacred world together.

The word *upaniṣad* is more commonly associated, however, with lessons Vedic sages gave to individual spiritual seekers practicing intense contemplation and meditation under the sage's guidance in the teacher's home or in quiet meditation retreats in the forest.[14] Used in this way, an *upaniṣad* is a particularly powerful and enlightening teaching given in an intimate setting by a compassionate teacher to a truly earnest student sitting close by.[15] These lessons were collected and honored by the Vedic community as the Upaniṣads, a term we may now use in reference to that particular genre of Vedic sacred teachings.[16]

Indian religious traditions based on Vedic sensibilities have come to regard the Upaniṣads as *vedānta*, that is, as the "end" (*anta*) of the Veda. They are the "end of the Veda" in two ways. Of less importance—or at least less universally accepted—is that, according to some traditions of Vedic thought, they form the closure to the Vedic canon. More important, though, they are the "end" of the Veda in the sense that they are said to reveal the "intended purpose" or "hidden significance" of the Veda as a whole. Tradition holds that it is in the Upaniṣads where the "real meaning" of Vedic visionary experience and sacrificial action is revealed. The *Chāndogya Upaniṣad* typifies this position in proclaiming that the Upaniṣads give the nectarean essence of the Vedas: "these [teachings] are the very essence of the essences, for the essences are the Vedas, and these are their essence. Furthermore, they are the immortal nectar of the nectars, for the nectars are the Vedas, and these are their nectar."[17]

What, from the point of view presented by those Vedic sages whose lessons form the Upaniṣads, is the true significance of the Vedic songs and ritual practices? The answer to this question is, of course, complicated. We might summarize it by saying this: from the perspective offered by the Upaniṣads, the intended purpose or hidden meaning of both these forms of religious experience and expression reveals and leads to the underlying sacred unity of being. Both are revelations of what is said to be the single, eternal World-Soul or "Self" that abides within all creatures. Upaniṣadic teachers hold that, because it dwells within the human heart, this universal Self is known most perfectly and fully through the process of inward contemplation. If the patron of the Vedic sacrifice intoned the plea, "From the unreal lead me to the real. From the darkness, lead me to the light. From death, lead me to immortality,"[18] the teachers whose lessons form the Upaniṣads taught that the Absolute is known inwardly, "through knowledge, through contemplative fervor, and through meditation."[19]

Accordingly, Upaniṣadic teachers in general were less interested in proclaiming the wonders of the objective world than they were in exploring the mysterious depth of the inner world. Similarly, for them, the outward performance of the sacred ritual was not as effective in the engagement with divinity as was the recognition of eternal truths and taste of sublime states in the inward realm. This idea is represented by such teachings as a lesson from a late Upaniṣad, which holds that the contemplative sage has no need for "ritual baths, nor periodic rites, nor [external] deity, nor location, nor sacred space, nor [outward] worship."[20] For Upaniṣadic teachers, the true intended purpose of the Veda, *vedānta*, was none other than the awareness and direct experience of the unified and unifying, sublime power and structure of being—Brahman—which, though remaining hidden, infuses and supports all things. For them, the hidden significance of the Veda was that it revealed the presence of the universal Self, Ātman. Another of the late Upaniṣads declares that "the highest Brahman, which is all forms, which is the supreme reality of the universe, which is the most subtle of the subtle and which is eternal, is nothing but the Self. You are only That."[21]

As we will see, like the Vedic seer's outward experience of the gods and goddesses and like the priest's enactment of sacred processes on the ceremonial stage, the contemplative's inward experience of the divinity of being includes the use of the mind and imagination. But we will also see that, according to Upaniṣadic teachings, the complete and liberating experience of the divine requires the mind's ability to fold itself into the more encompassing domain of the heart and, finally, to transcend even its own power of imagination.

THE YEARNING FOR AN ABIDING DIVINE SPLENDOR

We begin our discussion by asking: Why would Vedic sages look inward into their own minds and hearts through the process of contemplation and meditation when, to their visionary ancestors, the external world seemed to be so filled with the presence of the gods? Part of the reason for such a turn inward lies in a shift in which Vedic sages came to understand the nature of the outer world, including the divine world in the heavens, and of their relationship to that world.

We remember that, according to early Vedic thought, the universe consisted of three realms.[22] There was the earth, on which human beings lived their lives. This was a realm of constant change in which beings were born, lived their lives, and eventually died. This was a realm of light and beauty, to be sure, but also of struggle and doubt and pain. While it was a world of light and life, it was also a world of recurring darkness and of ever-present and recurring death.

Above the earth was the region of the sky, the realm of the many and splendid gods and goddesses whose imaginative brilliance shined forth as the moon and the stars at night, the dawn on the eastern horizon, lightning in the clouds, and the powerful but invisible wind that blew unhindered across the wide expanse. But this, too, was a world of change. Sometimes that change was spectacular, as in the sudden display of thunderbolts from a darkened cloud. Other times, it was rhythmic and balanced, as in the return of the goddess Uṣas each morning as the glowing sunrise or in the waxing and waning of the moon as it coursed through the month. Despite its grandeur and beauty, the realm of the sky was also one in which creatures—divine creatures, in this case—came into being and then disappeared. It, too, was a world in which light not only overcame darkness, but darkness also overcame the light.

The sky was known as *antarikṣa*, the "middle region," for above it was yet another, third realm that was full of radiance. This was a heavenly region where the sun never set and thus one of unceasing light, *svar*. Vedic visionaries therefore described it as *svarga* ("moving in light"). According to the early Vedic religious worldview, in this realm (in this *loka*) were none of the fluctuations and changes of earthly life. There was no death here.

It was for the transcendent *svargaloka*, then, that the Vedic heart yearned. Accordingly, it was toward this realm of unfailing light that Vedic poets directed their liturgical songs. As one prayed:

> O Pavamāna, place me in that deathless and undecaying world
> on which the light of heaven is set
> and unchanging brilliance ever shines. . . .
> In that realm where they freely go where they wish;
> in the third region, in the heaven of heavens;
> where lucid words are made of light:
> make me immortal.
> In that realm of eager longing and strong desire . . .
> make me immortal. . . .
> In that realm where happiness and delights, joys and felicities,
> come together and
> where longings are fulfilled:
> make me immortal.[23]

For Vedic poets, heaven was thus a light-filled realm in which all one's yearnings were met. The ecstasy given by the elixir of immortality, *soma pavamāna*, gave the poet-priest a foretaste of this divine world.[24] Heaven was a realm in which there was no fear due to the uncontrollable, changing nature of life as it is normally experienced. Said differently, heaven was a place in which the negative aspects of life were themselves negated; thus, it was not only a realm of brilliant light and vigorous life, but also of the absence of darkness and death. We see such imagery in one poet's plea: "O Pavamāna, place me in the world in which heaven is established, where the light is inexhaustible; [place me] in the endless, deathless world."[25]

But within this early Vedic cosmological perspective we see increasing indications of the idea that even heaven underwent change and thus included the possibility of death. The phrase from the hymn just quoted—"in the third region, in the heaven of heavens"—suggests the possibility that even within the third realm there are lower and higher heavens. If so, then there would be different degrees of light and life even in those celestial realms. This implies that, just as there are different amounts of happiness on earth, so too there are varying degrees of contentment in the heavens. If this is the case, then heaven, *svargaloka*, is like earth, only brighter.

Later Vedic sages came to feel that heaven was simply part of the cosmos it shared with the sky and earth. Like the two other regions, heaven was still a realm in a world of fear and doubt arising from constant change. The happiness one experienced in such a world would therefore not be a true, unconditioned bliss—what later philosophers influenced by Vedic thought would call *ānanda*—because it could come to an end.

Over the years, Vedic philosophers thus came to wonder about the location and nature of heaven and the means by which the correct performance of the sacred ritual drama carried one to it. It was probably apparent to anybody watching such a ceremony that neither the priest nor the ritual patron was lifted into the skies while undertaking such a performance. What did it mean, then, to say that the ritual carried one to the realm where there is no death?

This very question stands as the impetus of a reported conversation dating to roughly the eighth century BCE between the Vedic sage Yājñavalkya and Aśvala, a *hotṛ*-priest (we read part of the conversation toward the end of the previous chapter). The setting was a theological symposium sponsored by King Janaka of Videha, which Janaka had invited many learned brahmins from the Kuru and Pāñcāla clans to attend. The king had expressed his interest in knowing which of these many brahmins was the wisest.[26] When it became clear that Yājñavalkya was this person, Aśvala began to challenge that sage with a series of questions. Here is some more of that exchange:

> "Yājñavalkya," asked [Aśvala], "since everything here [in this world] is overtaken by death, by what means is one who performs a *yajña* completely liberated from the reach of death? . . . Since everything here is overtaken by day and night . . . by which means is one who performs a *yajña* liberated from the reach of day and night? . . . Since everything

here is overtaken by the bright and dark fortnights, by what means is one who performs a *yajña* liberated from the reach of the bright and dark fortnights?"[27]

Continuing to question Yājñavalkya, Aśvala wondered just how it was that the person performing the sacred rite actually ascends into heaven, since the sky has no steps on which to climb:

> "Since this atmosphere does not give a foothold, as it were, by what means of ascent does a one who offers the sacrifice climb into the heavenly world?"

Yājñavalkya responded to Aśvala in a way that is consistent with the interiorization of the Vedic sacrifice in general. He replied by saying:

> "By means of the mind," [he said]. . . . This is liberation. This is complete liberation."[28]

In responding to Aśvala in the way he did, Yājñavalkya presented the idea that it was through the mind rather than through outward means that one "ascends" into the heavens. What is more, he taught that this inward movement itself leads to "liberation" (*mukti*)—even "complete liberation" (*atimukti*)—from the pervasive reach of death.

Another Upaniṣad, this one dating to roughly the fifth century CE, similarly teaches the ideas that the true offering to the divine takes place within one's inner being and that one gains freedom from the vicissitudes of life and death by turning one's attention inward, where one comes to know and experience the eternal Self itself. The setting is more mythic than that of the disputation between Yājñavalkya and Aśvala in King Janaka's court. The teacher is Yama, whom Vedic tradition regards as the first being to have died and to have journeyed to the realm of the dead. Yama therefore knows the constraints of mortality. But he also knows the way in which one can be free of those constraints. The seeker is Naciketas ("one who does not know"), a young boy who was sent to Yama's deathly realm by his angry father, who was impatient with Naciketas's pointed and insightful questions regarding the efficacy of the outwardly performed ritual. According to Yama:

> Seeking life eternal, a wise person
> turned his gaze inward and saw the [divine] Self within.
> The [spiritually] immature seek outward pleasures;
> they walk into the snare of widespread death.
> But wise people, knowing life eternal,
> seek not the changeless among those things which change.[29]

For Upaniṣadic teachers, heaven was therefore neither a place nor a time, because places and times are susceptible to the degradations of change and transformation. Rather, for these sages, heaven was a state of being or mode of consciousness that remains firm in an abiding constancy and in which there is unconditioned celebration of being in its unalloyed perfection, without the fear and sorrow occasioned by the constraints of spatial and temporal existence. Like their visionary counterparts, Vedic contemplatives described heaven as a state or mode in which all negativities were themselves negated. As Naciketas was to proclaim to Yama:

> In the world of heaven there is no fear whatsoever.
> You, O Lord of Death, are not there.
> There, one does not dread old age.
> Transcending both hunger and thirst, and leaving sorrow behind,
> one rejoices in the world of heaven.[30]

Consistent with Vedic ideologies centered on the interiorization of the sacrifice that was said to "lead to heaven," Upaniṣadic teachers as a whole taught their students that the divine powers and structures otherwise experienced in the outer world could be known in the inner world as well. One of the earliest of the Upaniṣads, the *Chāndogya Upaniṣad* (ca. eighth century BCE), notes the equivalence of the transcendent light of the sun blazing in the highest realms with that of an inner, immanent fire burning deep within one's being:

> Now, that light which shines higher even than the heavens and onto the back of all creatures and on the backs of all things; [that light] which shines in the highest worlds, than which there is no higher: truly, that is the same as this light which is here within the person.[31]

The idea that the sacred flame burns within also finds expression in Yama's lessons to Naciketas, as recorded in the *Kaṭha Upaniṣad*. Uncertain of the true meaning and significance of the sacred offering to the divine fire, Naciketas asks his teacher:

> You know the fire [ceremony] that leads to heaven.
> Describe it to me, one who is full of faith.
> How do those who live in heaven gain the nature of immortality?[32]

Yama responds to Naciketas by noting that

> I do indeed know well that fire which leads to heaven
> and will describe it to you. Listen to me attentively.

The attainment of the timeless world as well as its firm establishment: know that as abiding in the cave of the heart.[33]

THE VEDIC REALIZATION OF THE UNITY OF THE ABSOLUTE

The inward trajectory of revelation accompanies another fundamentally important Vedic theological position that certainly must have emerged from Vedic teachers' own experiential realization. This is the idea that within the apparent multiciplicity of being, there is only one true ultimate reality known by many names and reflected by the contours of countless physical forms. We remember—to pick just one example from the earlier Vedic literatures—Dīrghatamas's assertion that the many gods are simply different names of a single divine reality he called simply the One.[34] Upaniṣadic teachers were to note that it is this single divine presence that dwells within all things: "the subtlest of the subtle, the greatest of the great, he abides as the Self dwelling in the heart of this creation. . . . From him arise the seas and mountains; from him run the rivers of all sorts; from him arise all plants and saps, while he arose as the [universal] indwelling Self. . . . He has entered all the worlds. The Lord of Creatures becomes one with all beings."[35]

The indwelling Absolute was not an object to be known among other objects, for it was the source of all objects, without which they would have no possibility of existence. The *Kaṭha Upaniṣad* is typical of Upaniṣadic thought in general when it says that it is "has no sound or touch, no form, no taste, no smell."[36] But the Upaniṣads also teach that this ultimate reality is unconstrained by the forces of time. The many *beings* in the world may die, but *Being* itself never ceases to be. Recognizing the vital presence of this truth deep within their own innermost being, Upaniṣadic sages experienced what they described as immortality of sorts. As the *Kaṭha Upaniṣad* says, "it has no beginning and no end. It does not decay. It is eternal. Discerning it, firmly established and beyond the immense, one is freed from the jaws of death!"[37]

The Realization of the Unity of Brahman and Ātman

We recall from our discussion in Chapter Three a development in the Vedic idea of the *brahman*. The word originally referred to an enigmatic verse that gives voice to the mysterious structure and force that holds the world together. Later, it came to refer not only to the verbal expression but to that unifying yet hidden truth those powerful words express. And then over the years Vedic philosopher-sages came to regard Brahman as the pervasive and timeless ground of being. For them, Brahman was the one, ultimate reality residing eternally hidden within and as all manifest being: "that from which all creatures are born, that by which, when born, they live, that into which, when departing, they enter."[38] Just as Vedic poets described the transcendent Ṛta as existing before the gods and thus having no beginning, so too Vedic thinkers described Brahman as "self-existing" and thus as uncreated.[39] It was by means of Brahman that "the earth was created, the heavens placed in the heights, the atmosphere aloft, and the expanse across."[40]

Later Vedic teachers therefore taught that, since all the gods and goddesses are different names for the One, and if that unified Absolute was Brahman, then all the deities were various forms of Brahman. Yājñavalkya made this point in another conversation recorded in the *Bṛhadāraṇyaka Upaniṣad.* Part of that conversation (in edited form) runs like this:

> Vidagdha Śākalya asked him: "How many gods are there, Yājñavalkya?"
> "Three hundred and thirty-three."
> "Yes, but how many gods are there really, Yājñavalkya?"
> "Thirty-three."
> "Yes, but how many gods are there really, Yājñavalkya?"
> "Six."
> "Yes, but how many gods are there really, Yājñavalkya?"
> "Three."
> "Yes, but how many gods are there really, Yājñavalkya?"
> "Two."
> "Yes, but how many gods are there really, Yājñavalkya?"
> "One and a half."
> "Yes, but how many gods are there really, Yājñavalkya?"
> "One."

To Vidagdha's final question, "Which is that one god?" Yājñavalkya replied, "He is the breath of life. He is Brahman. He is what they call 'That.' "[41]

Using particularly theological language,Vedic priests whose insights form the Brāhmaṇas had earlier called this common beingness residing within all beings the "self" (*ātman*) of Prajājapti. We remember the declaration that, having defeated the power of death and thus of nonbeing through the force of the sacred sacrifice, Prajāpati's *ātman* came to encompass all things, including death itself. "Prajāpati is this all," the priest proclaims: he is all of "these worlds, and whatever there is here."[42] Then, through the interiorization of the sacrifice and related hallowed actions, Vedic priestly sages came to recognize Prajāpati's *ātman*—now the sole Self of the universe—residing deep within the human being itself. Accordingly, they were to teach not only that "Prajāpati is the sacrifice" and that "the sacrifice is man" but also, as one texts says, "Prajāpati is the heart. It is the Absolute. It is the universe. . . . One who knows this goes to heaven."[43] Another similarly declares that "truly, the Self [*ātman*] dwells in the heart. . . . One who knows this enters into the heavenly realm day by day."[44]

Vedic teachers whose lessons form the Upaniṣads referred to this universal Self in a more ontological manner: it is ultimate reality itself, without which there can be no particular existence. Hidden, it nevertheless abides within all things, "like butter in cream."[45] Accordingly, this Self, this Ātman, is identical in many ways to Brahman: the universal power and structure gives rise to and supports all things. It is the transcendent and yet imminent, unconditioned ground of being on which all conditioned things are utterly contingent.

The interiorization of the unified power that sustains the entire universe is not to be understood as a miniaturization or diminution of the sacred. Rather, it is consistent with the idea that the universal Self resides within all things and is therefore an affirmation of the ubiquity of the sacred. As one text says—and the ideas presented here are quite representative—the divine Self infuses and sustains all that is:

> There is one power that lies hidden within all creatures.
> All-pervasive, he is the inward self of all beings.
> He is the controller of all actions.
> He resides in all beings.
> He is the inner witness.
> He is autonomous, conscious, and free of attributes.[46]

Texts from Indian religious traditions influenced by the idea were at times to state this lesson quite poetically, as is the case in these lines from the *Brahmabindu Upaniṣad*:

> There is only a single Being-Self.
> It lives in each and every being.
> Uniform, yet multiform,
> it appears like the [reflections of the single] moon
> in [the many ripples of] a pond.
>
> [Think of] the empty space enclosed by a jar.
> When the jar is broken into pieces,
> the jar alone breaks, not the space.
> Life is like the jar.
>
> All [manifest] forms are like the jar.
> They constantly break into pieces.
> When gone, they are unaware.
> Yet, he is aware, eternally.[47]

A passage from the *Chāndogya Upaniṣad*, a key Vedic text, expresses similar sentiments and presents similar images. According to this lesson, though, the fullness of Brahman resides finally in the space of the heart:

> Truly, what is called Brahman
> is the same as that space outside a person.
> Truly, that space which is outside a person is
> the same as that which is inside the person,
> and that space which is inside a person is
> the same which is inside the heart.
> That is fullness. That is the unchanging.
> One who knows this
> invariably gains full prosperity and
> unwavering happiness.[48]

Noting the equivalence of outer and inner sacred reality, but emphasizing the immediate presence of the Absolute within the heart, Upaniṣadic teachers were to present to their students a lesson that has reverberated throughout Indian spirituality for nearly three millennia: the sublime essence of the World-Soul is identical to the sublime essence of the inner Self residing within all beings. Nowhere, perhaps, is this realization stated more concisely than in the *Bṛhadāraṇyaka Upaniṣad*, which asserts: "Truly, this Ātman is Brahman!"[49]

The *Chāndogya Upaniṣad* makes this point quite vividly:

> This is the Self within my heart: smaller than a grain of rice, or a corn of barley, or a mustard seed, or a grain of millet, or the kernel of a grain of millet. This is the Self within my heart: more vast than the earth, more vast than the atmosphere, more vast than the heavens, more vast than all these worlds. . . . This is Ātman within my heart. This is Brahman.[50]

Using the term *puruṣa* ("person") to refer to this ultimate reality, the *Bṛhadāraṇyaka Upaniṣad* associates the universal Self not only with light and the heart, but also with the mind:

> This Puruṣa who consists of mind is of the nature of light and lives within the heart, [small] like a grain of rice or barley. And yet this same [Person] is the controller of the universe, the lord of the universe. He rules over all that is.[51]

Realization of the identity of Ātman and Brahman is said to lead to freedom from the redundant cycles of life and to a healing of the fracture that separates the human soul from the universe in which it lives. As the *Adhyātma Upaniṣad* proclaims: "he is a free person who, in his wisdom, sees no difference between the Self and Brahman, and between Brahman and the universe!"[52]

Teachings regarding the essential identity of Brahman and Ātman and the value of inward contemplation in coming to know that ultimate reality find sustained and repeated expression in the Upaniṣads as a whole. It is worth quoting from several of those works. The *Muṇḍaka Upaniṣad*, for example, holds that

> Enthroned behind an excellent, golden veil
> sits Brahman, untainted and undivided.
> Brilliant, it is the light of lights.
> One who knows Ātman, knows it.[53]
>
> It shines forth: vast, transcendent, of unthinkable form,
> and yet more minute than the minute.
> For those who behold it, it is farther than the far
> yet here, near at hand, set in the cave of the heart.[54]

The *Kaṭha Upaniṣad* similarly teaches that

> the sole controller, the inner Self of all beings
> who makes his one form into many:
> to the wise who see him abiding within the soul,
> to them and to no one else is timeless peace.[55]
>
> . . . The sun does not shine there, nor the moon, nor the stars.
> Lightning does not shine there, much less this earthly fire.
> [But] because of him, as he shines forth, does everything shine.
> This whole world is illumined by his light![56]

The Self is described as the divine breath of life within all creatures,[57] and as the single subject residing within all objects.[58] Abiding within all things, the universal Self dwells within the human spirit as well. In its interior aspect, the Self is that hidden, mysterious inner wisdom of being that directs and pervades the workings of the body, "right up to the hair and tips of the fingernails."[59]

Upaniṣadic sages thus came to teach the identity of the Absolute with the imperishable Self that girded and enfolded a person's very own existence. In a well-known conversation recounted in the *Chāndogya Upaniṣad*, the sage Uddālaka Āruṇi repeatedly teaches his son Śvetaketu, "That which is the subtle essence [of all things]: the whole world has that for its Self. That is the true, that is the Self. You are That!"[60]

True to Vedic imagery, the home of the Self is said to be in the warmth and expansive wisdom of the heart, which later Vedic religious teachers regard as the hub of the sacred universe. As one lesson says, quite succinctly, *hṛdi hy eṣa ātmā*: "Truly, in the heart resides the universal Self."[61]

The Identity of the Inner Being and the Supreme Deity

Drawing on the idea that the Absolute resides within all beings, Upaniṣadic teachers taught their students that the truth and power they were to seek within their own hearts was not only the unified ground of being but also a personal Lord (*īśa, īśāna, prabhu,* and so on) who ruled powerfully yet benevolently over all things. Some of those teachers described this universal monarch as the supreme deity himself or herself. The sages who taught the lessons forming the *Īśā Upaniṣad*, for example, describe the Absolute both as the universal Self and the Lord. According to them, a seeker finds that Lord by seeing through and rejecting the apparent plurality of the external world and looking instead at the underlying unity of being:

> One is to enfold this whole universe into the Lord:
> everything that lives in this world!
> If you renounce [attachment to external pleaures]
> you will truly enjoy [the Lord]. . . .
>
> [The Self] moves. It moves not.
> It is far. It is near.
> It is within all things,
> and yet it is outside all.
>
> One who regards all beings
> as within the Self
> and the Self as within all beings
> never turns away from him.
>
> For one in whom all beings have become
> none other than the Self of the knower:
> then what delusion, or what sorrow
> can possibly befall that one who sees the unity![62]

The *Śvetāśvatara Upaniṣad* describes the Absolute as the single source and foundation of the universe itself. That Upaniṣad also says that it through the One's divine grace that the sage receives the wisdom to know this:

> The One—who himself has no color—
> by the manifest exercise of his transformative power [*śakti-yoga*]

distributes the many colors in his hidden purpose,
into whom the universe is gathered in the beginning
and dissolves in the end:
may he endow us with clear understanding!

Truly, the fire is that, the sun is that;
the wind is that, and the moon is also that.
Truly, the bright one is that, the *brahman* is that.
The waters are that, and Prajāpati is that.[63]

The *Subāla Upaniṣad* presents the idea that the universal Self permeates, but is not permeated by, all things:

> In the hidden place within the body there lives the eternal One. The earth is his body; he moves in the earth, but the earth knows him not. The waters are his body; he moves in the waters, but the waters know him not. Light is his body; he moves in the light, but the light knows him not. . . . He alone is the indwelling spirit within all being, free from all stain: the One, the divine. . . . The wise see the Self, of incomprehensible form, radiant, autonomous, pure . . . residing in the hidden place, immortal, shining with bliss.[64]

Having noted that "the one god hidden within all things, all-pervading, the inner self of all beings, the overseer of all activity, abiding in all beings, the witness, the observer," the *Śvetāśvatara Upaniṣad* asserts that "the wise who perceive him as abiding within themselves: they and no others have eternal happiness."[65] Furthermore, for the teachers whose lessons form that Upaniṣad, the lord is a divine magician or artist of sorts (*māyin*) who mentally fashions the world as a whole through the power of his *māyā*:

One should know that the world is [a result] of *māyā*,
and that the Great Lord is the *māyin*!
This whole world is pervaded
by beings that are part of him.[66]

According to those teachers, such divine artistry emerges from and expresses God's benevolence—the Great Lord (Maheśvara) mentioned in this last passage is subsequently identified as the Benevolent One (Śiva), and that, knowing this, one attains unending peace:

The One who rules each and every source,
in whom this whole universe comes together and dissolves,

> the Lord, the bestower of blessings, God, the adorable:
> by discerning him, one goes forever to this peace. . . .
> More minute than the minute, in the midst of confusion
> the creator of all, of many forms,
> the one embracer of all things:
> by knowing him as the Benevolent One, one attains peace forever. . . .
> By knowing him as the Benevolent One, he who is hidden in all
> things,
> like the exceedingly fine cream that rises from clarified butter:
> by knowing God, one is liberated from all fetters.[67]

The *Śvetāśvatara Upaniṣad* notes that the same Lord who rules the universe lives within the individual spirit as well. Because he is "framed by the heart and known through insight," recognition of this divine Lord takes place in those inner realms.

> By him, the Person, is this whole universe filled:
> beyond whom there is nothing, beneath whom there is nothing,
> smaller than whom there is nothing, larger than whom there is nothing.
> the One stands like a tree planted firmly in heaven. . . .
> A person the size of a thumb is the Self,
> ever seated in the heart of creatures.
> The Lord of Knowledge is framed by the heart
> and [known through] insight.
> They who know this become immortal.[68]

Later sectarian Upaniṣads continue this identification of the Absolute with a supreme deity. Some teachers follow the *Śvetāśvatara Upaniṣad* in urging their students to know the Lord as Rudra or Śiva.[69] For others, that supreme deity is Viṣṇu.[70] For still others—notably those aligned with the Śākta Tantric tradition, which worships God as divine feminine power[71]—the Absolute is not the universal Lord but rather the universal Lady, as it were. The *Tripurā Upaniṣad*, for example, praises her as "the abode of all, deathless, ancient, great, [and] the principal cause of the greatness of the gods." She is "the Joyous, the Proud, the Auspicious, and the Prosperous. And she is the Beautiful and the Pure One; the Modest, the Intelligent, the Satisfied, the Desired, the Thriving, the Wealthy, Lalitā [the Lovely]." She is the "Mother of the Universe."[72] The *Bahvṛcā Upaniṣad* says this of her:

> She alone is Ātman. . . . She is Brahman. . . . The texts have said that "Thou art That" and "This Ātman is Brahman" and "I am Brahman" and

> "Brahman alone am I." But She who is contemplated as "That which I Am" . . . is the Beautiful Great Goddess of the Three Cities, the Virgin, the Mother, the Lady of the Universe.[73]

DHĪ, DHYĀNA, AND *DHĪRA*: VISIONARY INSIGHT, DISCIPLINED MEDITATION, AND THE WISE SAGE

Vedic teachings hold that, since the universal, divine Self dwells within the heart, the way to experience and recognize divinity is to turn one's attention inward in a process of contemplative meditation. Because of the association of light and divinity, it is consistent that the contemplative seeking vision of the divine might at first, while meditating, see various forms of inner light:

> Fog, smoke, sun, fire, wind,
> fireflies, lightning, a crystal, a moon:
> these are the preliminary forms,
> which produce the manifestation of Brahman
> in the practice of disciplined meditation [*yoga*].[74]

The experience of an inward light is similarly described in this way:

> Here are its [increasingly bright] signs: first, it is seen to look like a star. Then it looks like a dazzling diamond. Then, it looks like the full moon; then, like the brilliance of nine gems; then, like the fullness of the mid-day sun; then, like the flame of Agni. One sees all of these, in order.[75]

The contemplative process leading to this inner vision of the universal Self involves and requires the use of the imagination, if we understand "imagination" to be that mental faculty which forms and perceives images. As we will see, the Self is said to be of the nature of consciousness itself. Accordingly, the contemplative process involves not only the opening of the heart to what Vedic religious sensibilities hold to be the reality of the divine, but also the disciplined use of the imaginative mind, which stands as a pivotal link in the formative, transformative, and reformative power of universal consciousness.

In previous chapters we have noted at some length the functions of the heart and mind in the recognition of the divine. We might note as an aside that the word *citra* ("sparkling, shimmering, beautiful")—a word used to describe not only the brilliance of fire, the bright daytime sky, lightning in the storm, the twinkling stars, the sun, and the shimmering rivers but also the bright deities Agni, Indra, the Maruts, the Nakṣatras, Uṣas, Sūrya, Sarasvatī, and others of the Vedic pantheon—is related to the word *cit*, meaning "thought, spirit, consciousness."[76] Such linguistic connection suggests a philosophical one as well: the light of divinity that is perceived inwardly characterizes the nature of that consciousness which enables such perception. Accordingly, the term *cit*, and others like it, suggests the idea that the process of revelation involves the intuitive experience of an inner light reflected in the sparkle of consciousness itself.

The Vedic idea that the experience of divine power in the outer world is closely associated with the cultivation of inward vision finds expression in what is perhaps the most frequently recited verse in all Vedic literatures over the past three thousand years. This is *Ṛgveda* 3.62.10, a prayer attributed to the sage Viśvāmitra in the twenty-four-syllabled Gāyatrī meter and offered to the god Savitṛ, a bright deity typically associated with the early rays of the rising sun whose name also implies the creative impulse in general.[77] This prayer, which has come to be known both as "the Gāyatrī" and as "the Sāvitrī," is still sung today at the dawn, a particularly auspicious time for inward contemplation:

> We meditate on the glorious splendor of the Arouser divine:
> may he himself illumine our inner vision!

The verb translated in this last verse as "meditate" (*dhīmahi*) and the noun rendered "inner vision" (*dhī*) both derive from the verbal root *dhī-*,[78] the meaning of which, as we have seen in Chapter Three, centers on the notion of a transformative and powerful intuitive vision into the hidden but powerful forces that sustain and direct the movements of the universe as a whole. By means of *dhī*, Vedic poets were said to see the acts of the gods and goddesses within the universal principle of Ṛta and to construct verbal images of that divine artistry in the form of poems, songs, and riddles. As we have seen, according to the *Ṛgveda*, a *dhīra* (a related word) was a visionary or insightful, and thus "wise," poet. For example, *Ṛgveda* 10.71.2 describes such seers as "wise visionaries [*dhīra*] who have fashioned sacred speech by means of the mind." The Upaniṣadic sage was also regarded as a *dhīra*, as in the *Muṇḍaka Upaniṣad*'s statement regarding the wise person's ability to see the imperishable unity of the Absolute: "timeless, pervading all things, present everywhere, superbly sublime: that is the imperishable which wise people [*dhīra*] see to be the source of all beings."[79]

We have seen these words before, of course. The gods themselves were described as *dhīra*s. They were insightful or wise because they were skilled in visionary imagination. "O Indra," one bard sang. "You are splendid! You are a *dhīra*. Mighty in mental power and skilled in visionary imagination, may you strengthen us, too, with such might, O Lord of Power."[80] And poets prayed to the gods for the gift of imaginative vision, *dhī*. Singing to the goddess of poetic eloquence, another pleaded, "May Sarasvatī, sparkling with life, give us *dhī*!"[81] The cultivation and expression of *dhī* therefore constituted a major form of the Vedic visionary imagination.

The Sanskrit verbal root *dhī-* also gave rise by means of its variant *dhyā-* to the noun *dhyāna*, which we might justly translate as "meditation." It is not unusual to find the word *dhyāna* associated in Vedic texts with the term *yoga*,[82] which connotes a unifying process by which the world experienced as broken multiverse comes to be experienced as an integrated universe. The word *yoga* refers also to those spiritual techniques that lead to such a healing return to the unity of being. The compound *dhyāna-yoga* thus stands for the "spiritual practice of meditation" that leads to an awareness of the unified divine Self which girds and embraces all that is.

THE LIBERATING POWER OF MEDITATION

In teaching the value of *dhyāna*, Upaniṣadic teachers thus expressed their conviction that the Absolute which dwells within may indeed be known, and that such vision takes place through inward vision. Such vision is said to lead ultimately to the recognition of the eternal nature of the Absolute and thus to complete freedom from the repetitive cycles of existence. The *Mahā Upaniṣad* holds that "one who by means of inward vision, held steady and clear, rises above any experience of duality: that one merits the title 'Liberated while Living.'"[83] Similarly, the *Brahmavidyā Upaniṣad* teaches that one's *dhī* allows one to experience the transcendent reality of the Absolute and thus to be free from the constraints of temporal existence: "one in whose inward vision [*dhī*] Brahman resides is suitable for gaining deathlessness."[84]

The cultivation of such inner vision requires diligence and fervent contemplative discipline (*tapas*). Drawing on various similes to describe the divine presence as a subtle essence within manifest form, part of the *Śvetāsvatara Upaniṣad* notes the relationship between knowledge of the Self and the cultivation of *tapas*:

> As oil in sesame seeds, as butter in cream,
> as water in river beds,[85] as fire in friction sticks,
> so is the Self held within one's own soul,
> if one looks for it with truthfulness and with *tapas*.
>
> The Self which pervades all things,
> as butter lies within milk,
> which is the root of Self-knowledge and *tapas*:
> that is the supreme mystic teaching of Brahman![86]

That same work likens the *yogī*'s practice of meditation to the releasing of the hidden fire lying dormant within wood by diligently applying friction to a stick. The imagery here suggests that such contemplative practice constituted in part the *yogī*'s *tapas*. We read that

> the eternal one that rests in the Self should be known; for truly there is nothing higher than this to be known. . . . Just as the form of fire is not visible when latent in its source, but may be found over and over again by use of friction, so . . . by practicing the friction of *dhyāna* one may see the divine, hidden, as it were.[87]

The practice of meditation required the *yogī*'s diligence. As the *Tejobindu Upaniṣad* admits,

> difficult to master, difficult to attain,
> difficult to perceive, difficult to establish,
> difficult to practice, is this *dhyāna*,
> even for the solitary and wise.[88]

While difficult to practice, such discipline was said to be worth the effort. The *Śvetāśvatara Upaniṣad* notes that it is precisely through contemplative meditation that one comes to know the Absolute:

> Those who were skilled in the practice of meditation [*dhyāna-yoga*] saw the autonomous power of the divine, hidden within its own qualities. He is the One who rules over the origins of all things.[89]

The *Muṇḍaka Upaniṣad* teaches that

> [Knowledge of] this Self cannot be attained by one without strength,
> nor through carelessness, nor through false austerity.
> However, one who has knowledge and who strives by these means:
> his *ātman* enters the abode of Brahman.
>
> Seers who are fulfilled in their knowledge—
> they who have disciplined and prepared themselves and
> who are dispassionate and serene—
> when they have attained him
> they gain the omnipresent wholeness:
> joined to the Self, the wise enter into the All itself.
>
> Truly, one who knows that supreme Brahman becomes that
> Brahman. . . .

> [Such a] one goes beyond sorrow; such a one goes beyond evil.
> Freed from the knots [that close] the cave of the heart,
> one becomes immortal![90]

Despite its need for diligent practice, Upaniṣadic seekers undertook such discipline because of their yearning to know the "vast, transcendent," timeless truth that "shines forth . . . here, near at hand, in the secret place of the heart."[91]

Hence the value of inward contemplation and meditation. Referring to the physical body (a "lotus bloom with nine doorways, encircled by three strands")[92] as the abode of the hidden, sublime Self, the *Atharvaveda* holds that:

> the lotus bloom with nine doorways, encircled by three strands;
> what a wondrous marvel—the Self—
> lies within it! It is of this that
> the knowers of Brahman have knowledge.
>
> He who knows the Self as wise, immortal, self-existent,
> full of fresh sap, fully complete, free of desire;
> knowing that wise, never-aging, eternally youthful Self,
> one has no fear of death.[93]

Upaniṣadic sages taught their students to find the universal Absolute by turning their attention in tranquility and with reverence toward the Self, the home of divinity itself. As the teachers of the *Chāndogya Upaniṣad* declared,

> truly, this whole world is Brahman, from which one comes forth, into which one dissolves, and in which one breathes. Tranquil, let one meditate on it. . . . [Let one meditate on] him who consists of mind, whose body is the breath of life, whose thought is truth, whose soul is space, enveloping all actions, enveloping all yearnings, enveloping all odors, enveloping all tastes, encompassing the whole world, silent, and without worry.[94]

The Upaniṣads teach that the contemplative experience of the Self within frees the seeker from the vicissitudes of life as it is experienced outwardly. According to the *Kaṭha Upaniṣad*,

> he who is difficult to see, hidden in the cave of the heart,
> dwelling in the mysterious depths, primeval:
> by seeing God, an insight gained through inner contemplation,
> the wise person leaves [the fluctuations of] joy and sorrow behind.[95]

The *Maitrī Upaniṣad* vividly notes that the realization of Brahman and thus of the immortality of the Self takes place in a sharpened, attentive mind, and that such realization leads one not only from an experience of darkness to one of powerful light, but to a realization of the eternal nature of the Absolute itself:

> Now, as it has been said, "The body is a bow." The arrow is [the sacred syllable] *oṁ*. The mind is its point. Darkness is the mark. Having pierced through darkness, one goes to what is not enveloped in darkness. Having pierced through what is thus enveloped, one sees him, who sparkles like a wheel of fire, the color of the sun, full of power, the Brahman beyond darkness: that which shines in the distant sun and also in the moon, in fire, in lightning: truly, having seen him, one goes to immortality.[96]

We are to remember that the "immortality" of which these texts speak is not so much the destruction of death as it is the conscious incorporation of the reality of death within the whole of one's being. Just as Prajāpati, whose *ātman* is the soul of the universe, defeats Death by knowing the hidden correspondences that unite all being, so too the meditating sage sees the unity of all being and thus is released from sorrow brought on by death. The *yogī* is said to understand the identity of the universal power of life and immortality, for since the power of life lies deep within all beings, that power is not extinguished with the dissolution of any particular body. Listening to the inner voice of divinity itself, the teachers of the *Kauṣītaki Upaniṣad* hear: "I am the breath of life. I am the wise Self. As such, meditate on me as the life-force. Meditate on me as immortality."[97] Thus knowing the identity of Ātman and Brahman, that meditating sage knows the bliss of liberation.

THE ABSOLUTE AS CONSCIOUSNESS

The adept practice of meditation was thus understood in Vedic India to bring the seeker to an awareness of the eternal and unchanging World-Soul and of its essential unity with the bond of being itself. Both this realization of the existential integrity of being and the discipline that leads to this unifying awareness constitute *yoga*, the joining together of that which has apparently been separated. Such reunion with the timeless and infinite ground of being led the *yogī* to freedom from the constraining and fracturous cycles of constant becoming. Such is part of the message of this lesson from the *Śvetāśvatara Upaniṣad*:

> As a mirror clouded by dust
> shines brilliantly when it has been cleaned,
> the embodied one—upon seeing the nature of Ātman—
> becomes integrated, of fulfilled purpose, and liberated from sorrow.
> When one who is integrated beholds, as if by [the light of] a lamp,
> the essence of Brahman by seeing the essence of the soul as
> unborn, abiding, free of all [limiting] characteristics:
> by knowing God, [such a] one is released from all fetters.
> Truly, he is the god who pervades all regions.
> He is the firstborn, and yet he is within the womb. . . .
> The god who is in fire, who is in water,
> who has entered into the whole world,
> who is in plants, who is in trees:
> to that god be adoration, yes, be adoration![98]

Here we have an image of the *yogī*'s return to his eternal source. Knowing the Self, the "one who is integrated" (*yukta*) knows that timeless truth which enfolds and supports his very being; and, knowing that truth, he knows that divine reality which gives rise to all beings, including fire and water and plants and trees.

According to Upaniṣadic thought, such recognition of the divine takes place through the practice of *dhyāna*, which the *Maṇḍalabrāhmaṇa Upaniṣad* defines as "the contemplation of the unity of consciousness within all bodies."[99] The *Aitareya Upaniṣad* maintains that the whole world is founded on a universal Consciousness, which it identifies as Brahman itself. It teaches that this Consciousness is to be discovered within the functions of the mind and heart; hence, again, the importance of inward contemplation:

> That which is heart, this mind: that is Consciousness. [Consciousness] is perception, acuity, intelligence, wisdom, insight, steadfastness, thought, thoughtfulness, impulse, memory, conception, the power of the will, the breath of life, passion, control. Truly, all these are names for Consciousness.
>
> It is Brahmā, it is Indra, it is Prajāpati. It is all of these gods. It is the five gross elements of being: earth, wind, space, water, and light. . . . It is horses, cows, people, elephants; whatever is alive, whether moving or flying or remaining still. All of this is guided by Consciousness. The world is guided by Consciousness. Consciousness is its foundation. Brahman is Consciousness.[100]

The Upaniṣads in general describe such universal Consciousness as the supreme knowledge and truth that puts this entire universe together and keeps it from falling apart. As we have already seen, they also say that such wisdom not only supports the world as a whole but lies within the heart as well. In this regard the *Taittirīya Upaniṣad* says that

> one who knows Brahman reaches the supreme [state of being]. As to this, the following has been declared: one who knows Brahman as truth, as knowledge, and infinity,[101] abiding in the cave of the heart and in the highest heaven—he realizes all desires, along with Brahman, the Intelligent One.[102]

A later Upaniṣad, the *Varāha Upaniṣad*, makes a similar point but from a theistic perspective. The teacher is said to be God himself:

> Concentrating on Consciousness as unwavering, meditate on my abode in your heart. . . . All that is conscious in the universe is actually [a reflection] of absolute Consciousness. This universe is absolute Consciousness only. You are Consciousness. I am Consciousness. Meditate on the world as Consciousness.[103]

THE PLACE OF THE MIND IN THE MULTILAYERED METAPHYSICS OF BEING

Turning inward, the contemplative returned his awareness to Ātman which, as the abiding Absolute, stands as the unified source of all that is. In this return to the ontological ground of being, we therefore see the reverse of the emanational process of becoming to which we have made several references in previous chapters. Before we discuss the importance of this return to the unity of being, it might be helpful to step back for a moment to review this idea from the perspective of the Upaniṣads.

The Emanational Process

The *Muṇḍaka Upaniṣad* presents a pertinent passage in this regard. It offers various similes to describe the emergence of multiplicity from the unified Brahman:

> Just as a spider emits and draws in [its thread],
> just as plants sprout forth from the earth,
> just as hair grows on a living person's head,
> so, everything here arises from the Imperishable.
>
> By *tapas* Brahman expands forth.
> From that, food is produced;

from food: life-breath, mind, truth,
the worlds, sacred action, immortality.

He who is all-knowing and all-wise,
whose *tapas* is made of knowledge:
From him is produced that which is expansive here:
food and name-and-form.[104]

The underlying idea here is that the material cosmos is a many-faceted product of the transformations of the unified Brahman. Such an idea is made more explicit by the *Mahānārāyaṇa Upaniṣad*, which says this:

The subtlest of the subtle and the greatest of the great,
He lives as the Self in the heart of the creation.
Through God's grace one sees him:
autonomous and free from sorrow, the Lord, the Great One. . . .
Out of him come the oceans and all of the mountains.
Out of him come all types of rivers.
Out of him come all plants and all juices.[105]
He arose as the Self dwelling within.
There is not now, nor was there ever, any
created being higher than him.
He has entered into all the worlds.
The Lord of Creatures becomes one with all beings.[106]

The Upaniṣads as a whole agree that the objective world has no reality independent of Brahman. The *Maitrī Upaniṣad* describes the Self as the sun, the many rays shining forth from which then form all the different aspects and objects of being.[107] The various deities, the sacred songs and their meters, the seasons, the heavenly bodies: all things are said to be emanations from the one universal Soul, into which they return again.

The Upaniṣads in general envision a hierarchy of sorts within this emanation. Those components of being that are closer to the source are purer and more sublime than those that are farther away. Perhaps a metaphor from the natural realm will help elucidate this idea: although it is all essentially the same thing, light that is closer to the sun is brighter and stronger than light that is at some distance.

The imagery in this metaphor is not so different from images we see in Vedic ritual texts, which describe the way in which the priest and ritual patron may "ascend to heaven," that is, to the highest realm of bright and unwavering light. Upaniṣadic teachers might well reverse this metaphor's spatial imagery. To them, the light shines deep within one's inward being. The closer to that light something is, the closer it is to the abiding truth itself. Being farther from the heart, the external, changing, objective world experienced through the senses is therefore less sublime—and less real—than the unchanging truth residing within.

The Manifest and Subtle Layers of the Body

Some of the Upaniṣads therefore describe the human being as consisting of different layers or sheaths; the outward coverings are more physical and material in nature than the inner, more sublime layers. The classic example of this idea appears in the *Taittirīya Upaniṣad*, which refers to five such sheaths comprising the human person. The text identifies Brahman as "the real, as knowledge, and as the infinite" and maintains that a person can know Brahman as "established in the cave of the heart and in the highest heaven."[108] It also teaches that this sublime reality, which it also calls Ātman, takes increasingly more physical form as it becomes the many forces, objects, and creatures of the universe. Since the most material component of one's being is one's physical body, the gross body is therefore the farthest removed from the sublime Brahman/Ātman. That outermost, physical layer derives from and depends on food; therefore, the material body is known as the "person made of the essence of food." The Upaniṣad states that

> truly, from this Ātman arose ether; from ether, air; from air, fire; from fire, water; from water, the earth; from the earth, plants; from plants, food; and from food, the person. This, truly, is the person made of the essence of food.[109]

Beneath or within this outer body, however, are increasingly subtle and therefore sublime bodies. The next, more inward level of the self is the more rarified body, which "consists of the breath of life."

> Truly, other than and within that body consisting of the essence of food is the self that consists of the breath of life. . . . With this vital breath breathe the gods, as do humans and all of the animals. Breath is the life of beings. Therefore, it is called the life of all things.[110]

Within and more subtle than the vital body is the self that "consists of thought," and within that mental body is the self that "consists of understanding":

> Truly, other than and within that self [of life] is one that consists of thought. By that this [vital body] is filled. . . . Truly, other than and

> within that self which consists of thought is the self which consists of understanding. By that is this [mental body] filled. . . . It is understanding that directs the sacrifice and also [other hallowed] actions. All of the gods adore understanding as the oldest Brahman. If one knows Brahman as understanding and does not diverge from it, then one leaves [any] wickedness in his body and attains all for which one yearns. Truly, [the physical body in which we live in] this [life] is the embodied self of the former, [mental body].[111]

These four layers—the material body, the breath body, the mental body, and the body consisting of wisdom and understanding—comprise the four outer sheaths of the Self, the outer layers being increasingly grosser forms of the inner layers. At the center lies a fifth body. This the teachers of the *Taittirīya Upaniṣad* describe as the "self that consists of bliss." The innermost of the five sheaths, the body of bliss is the most sublime and the closest to the heart, the original and thus true home of Brahman. It is described as having the different limbs of a human form:

> Truly, other than and within that self which consists of understanding is the self which consists of bliss. By that is this [body of understanding] filled. It has the shape of a human being, and according to that shape it has pleasure as its head; delight as its right side; extreme delight as its left side; bliss as its body; and Brahman as its lower part, the foundation.[112]

The teachers of the *Taittirīya Upaniṣad* thus taught that the physical body is a manifest coagulation—an "image," if you will—of the more subtle mind, and that the mind is a manifestation or image of a preexisting wisdom. Wisdom itself is a vessel into which an even more sublime and unalloyed joy, *ānanda*, is poured. This unconditioned bliss, *ānanda*, characterizes the nature of Brahman in its purest state.

Because the physical body is "filled" by the mental body, the patterns and intentions of one's thoughts are therefore of signal importance to the quality of one's life in the physical world. One's outer experience is determined by the quality of one's imagination. Similarly, that mind which turns its attention inward will find its own source in the timeless bliss of the divine Self itself. Hence, again, the importance of inward contemplation.

The Manifold and Unified Modes of Awareness

If the Upaniṣads speak of different sheaths of the Self, they also speak of different modes of awareness. Just as the Ātman becomes "incarnate in bodily form"[113] through a series of progressively less sublime and more material layers, so too that unified Self—the "light within the heart"[114]—emanates into increasingly manifest, visible states.[115] Modes of consciousness that are most aware of multiplicity in the world are therefore farther away from those that abide in a deeper unity of being within that apparent diversity.

Upaniṣadic teachers found a key example of this layering of consciousness in the difference between waking consciousness and dream sleep, and between dreaming awareness and dreamless sleep. In waking consciousness one is aware of the many different objects of the external world and assumes that they are quite real. But those external objects disappear to one who has entered into sleep. Said differently, as one falls asleep one enfolds the objects of the outer world into one's inner world, and then mentally constructs or projects a new world out of that inward material. The *Bṛhadāraṇyaka Upaniṣad* notes that, when one falls asleep,

> one takes along the material of this all-encompassing world and breaks it apart oneself. [Then], through one's own brightness, through one's own light, one builds it up again as one sleeps. In that state, a person becomes self-illuminated. Here there are no chariots, nor [beasts] yoked to them, nor roads. One projects chariots, [beasts] yoked to them, and roads. Here there are no joys, no pleasures, no delights. But one projects joys, pleasures, delights. Here there are no pools of water, no lotus ponds, no rivers. But one projects pools of water, lotus ponds, rivers. For one is indeed a creator.[116]

As a creator of forms, a dreaming person is like a god:

> Traveling aloft and below while in the state of sleep,
> the deity makes many forms for himself:
> now enjoying pleasures with women, as it were;
> now laughing, as it were, or even beholding frightful sights.[117]

Aware of those apparently objective forms, the dreamer nevertheless remains unaware of the inner subject who creates them: "everyone sees their own sporting ground, but the Self no one ever sees!"[118]

Our Upaniṣad notes that, having created and lived in this world fashioned by the mind, the sleeping person then becomes tired from all this activity and seeks a state of being in which there is calmness and rest. Enfolding even the projected images of the dream into himself, he then enters into a dreamless sleep. Here, the sleeping person lives in a state in which there is no longer any objective world whatsoever. Dreamless sleep is therefore closest to the realm of the vital, unchanging, and abiding Self. One is no longer aware of being chased by an elephant or of falling into a well or of being a god or a king—for "this is imagined through ignorance"—and one is therefore free from all craving, free from all taints, free from fear.[119] Free from this multiplicity of being, one lives in a state of complete unity. Yājñavalkya made this point quite poetically:

> As, when in the embrace of his beloved wife,
> a man knows nothing within or without,
> so too this person, when in the embrace of the wise Self,
> knows nothing without or within.
> Truly, that is his [true] form in which his yearning is fulfilled,
> in which the Self is his yearning,
> in which he is free of desire, free of sorrow.[120]

Even though the objects of knowledge disappear, the unified Knower itself remains:

> Even though here [in the state of dreamless sleep] one does not know, truly, one is nevertheless still knowing; for there is no cessation of the knowing of a knower because of the imperishability [of the Knower. Whatever one may know] is therefore not a second [object other than oneself], for there is nothing else that is separate from one that one could know.[121]

For Yājñavalkya the unified state of dreamless sleep was therefore closest to the state of the abiding, integrated, ultimate reality. In such a state, "one becomes like an ocean, unified, a seer beyond duality. This is the world of Brahman!"[122]

Yājñavalkya presents an idea that foreshadows some later Hindu theologies, especially the nondual theologies of Kashmir Shaivism, which hold that divine Consciousness expands and contracts in an unfettered and free pulsating movement between wholeness and multiplicity within the singularity of the One. Here, he teaches that a person moves among these three modes of awareness:

> Having enjoyed deep sleep, having roamed about and seen good and bad [things], one returns again in the way that one came to the place from which one started, to dreaming sleep. Whatever one sees there, one is not followed by it, for such a person is free from all attachments. . . . Having enjoyed the dreaming state, having roamed about and seen good and evil [things], one returns again in the way one came to the place from which one started, to waking consciousness. Whatever

> one sees there, one is not followed by it, for such a person is free from all attachments. . . . [And] having enjoyed waking consciousness, . . . one returns again in the way one came to the place from which one started, to dreaming sleep.[123]

Some Upaniṣadic sages told of still another deeper or more transcendent and encompassing mode of awareness than even dreamless sleep. They called this simply the "fourth" state (*caturtha, turya*, and especially *turīya*). Perhaps they worried that their students would mistakenly think that Brahman is in some way unconscious, as is a sleeper while in deep sleep. These teachers regarded the fourth state as one in which all of the many and diverse objects of the manifold world merge into a unity of being—just as they do at the level of deep sleep—but taught that this takes place, not in a state of unconsciousness, but rather in an abiding, perfect, and always-wakeful supreme Consciousness.

The *Māṇḍūkya Upaniṣad* mentions this fourth state in the context of a discussion of the significance of the mantra *auṁ* (= *oṁ*). It calls the waking state Vaiśvānara ("common to all people"), perhaps because people in this state share a common world. Dream sleep is Taijasa, perhaps because it has the Self as its transformative light (*tejas*). Dreamless sleep is Prājña, perhaps because it is in this state that one is closest to the divine wisdom (*prajñā*) of the Self.[124] The waking state is associated with the phoneme *a* in the syllable *auṁ*; dream sleep is connected with second component, *u*; and deep sleep is the sound *ṁ*. But, just as there is the encompassing silence from which all three physical sounds emerge, so too the three states of awareness emerge out of the transcendent state of Turīya. This unmanifest silence frames and grounds the manifest elements of the syllable *auṁ*. It is identical to the Self. According to that text, such silence

> has no elements; it has no [worldly] effects; it is that into which the world resolves. It is benevolent, nondual. Therefore, the syllable *auṁ* is the very Ātman itself. One who thus knows, enters the Self with his self.[125]

The *Māṇḍūkya Upaniṣad* specifically identifies that silent ground of being, the universal Self, with the fourth level of Consciousness:

> It is not that which cognizes inward [objects]; not that which cognizes outward [objects]; not that which cognizes both [inward and outward objects]. . . . Unseen, ungraspable, having no distinctive marks, unthinkable, beyond description, the essence of the knowledge of the one Self, that into which the world resolves, peaceful, benign, nondual: [on this] they meditate as the Fourth. He is the Self. He should be discerned.[126]

The Role of the Mind in the Determination of One's World

If the Upaniṣads hold that there are gradations in the various manifest and subtle layers of the body, and if they teach that mental awareness plays out at different levels of consciousness, so too they maintain that the mind resides within a certain metaphysical hierarchy of being. This is, in part, the message presented by these lines from the *Kaṭha Upaniṣad*:

> Higher than the objects of the senses is the mind.
> Higher than the mind is awakened intelligence.
> Higher than the intellect is the great self.
> Higher than the great self is the unmanifest.
> Higher than the unmanifest is the Person.
> Higher than the Person there is nothing at all.
> That is the end. That is the highest goal.[127]

According to this line of thought, the sublime and unified Person of the universe devolves, as it were, into the increasingly gross forms of the world experienced by the senses. It first becomes the unmanifest, which then becomes the manifest great self, which then becomes intelligence, which becomes mind, which becomes the senses and the object of the senses.[128]

We must note the important place of the mind (*manas*) and the awakened intelligence (*buddhi*) in this scheme.[129] The mind is a more sublime form of the sensual world but is itself a grosser embodiment or crystallization of a more sublime intelligence. But our text notes that even such an awakened intelligence is a grosser form or crystallization of the great self.

Viewed from this perspective, the world apparently experienced by the senses has in fact been determined by the quality of the mind. The mind forms images and then projects them outward, where they appear as the objects of the world. The process is reminiscent of the gods' *māyā*, in which the deities formed images in their minds and then drew them onto space to fashion the world of objects.[130]

The nature of this process means that if a person's mind is filled with the dark thickness of ignorance, he projects solid and substantial forms outward onto the emptiness of space. These gross forms he then perceives to be the objects of the world. Not knowing that his mind has in fact given them their form, he takes them to be real. Taking them to be real, he lives in a world of constant change in which creatures apparently come into being and struggle through the constant changes and alternations of life. For such a thick and dense mind, the world as it is experienced through the senses is thus one of *saṁsāra*: the "turning wheel of existence," the cycle of suffering as one moves from one unfulfilled life to another.

If it is pure and clear, however, the *yogī*'s mind will form only brilliant and light-filled images. He then may do one of two things with those images. He may project them outward and thus come to see the many shimmering deities enlivening the objective world. Or, he may turn his mind back to its even purer and more clarified source, the awakened intelligence, which in turn reflects the unbroken brilliance of the supreme Person, who is none other than the divine Self.

The mind thus serves as the pivotal link between the eternal Ātman and the world of change as it is experienced by the senses. It is the mind, therefore, which establishes a person's state of being. As the *Tripurātāpanī Upaniṣad* teaches,

> The mind alone is the cause
> of bondage and of freedom.
> Bondage is clinging to objects;
> a mind withdrawn from them leads to freedom.[131]

Similarly, the *Muṇḍaka Upaniṣad* says,

> Whatever world a person of purified nature imagines
> and whatever wishes he may desire:
> that world and those desires he attains.
> This is why he who desires happiness
> should adore the knower of Ātman.[132]

If the mind looks outward to the sensory world of changing objects, it dissipates its purity and moves farther away from the sublime truth that stands at its source. On the other hand, if the mind focuses its attention on the more subtle and therefore more real intelligence, it will turn back toward that imperishable truth. It is in this light that we can read this passage from the *Yogakuṇḍalī Upaniṣad*:

> Keeping the mind in the midst of transformative power [*śakti*], and *śakti* in the midst of mind, one should look into the mind by means of the mind. . . . The mind alone is the seed, the source of creation and of preservation. It is only through the mind that this seed is produced, like curd is produced from milk;[133]

or these lines, from the *Chāndogya Upaniṣad*:

> Truly, this whole world is Brahman, from which one comes forth, as that into which he will dissolve, and in which he breathes. One should

meditate on it in tranquility. Truly, now, a person consists of [the mind's] ability to determine [one's world]. According to the mind's effective power of intention in this world, so he becomes when he leaves hence.[134]

It is thus the imagination that allows a person to know the universal Self. Before it can do so, however, it must gain control over the unruly senses. The *Kaṭha Upaniṣad* describes a meditating sage with the use of a vivid metaphor. His body is a chariot in which rides a king. His mind is the driver; his senses, the powerful horses that pull the chariot.

Know the Ātman as the lord of the chariot,
and, truly, the body as the chariot.
Know the awakened intellect as the chariot driver,
and the mind, truly, as the reins.

The senses, they say, are the horses;
the objects of sense, the roads [along which they run].
That which is associated with the body, the senses and the mind
wise people call "the enjoyer."

One has no understanding,
whose mind is not constantly held in control,
his senses are unrestrained,
his senses are uncontrolled,
as wild horses are for an [untrained] charioteer.

However, one who has understanding,
whose mind is constantly controlled,
his senses are restrained,
as well-trained are horses for a [skillful] charioteer.[135]

We have in this metaphor an image of a powerful process that can either lead to fulfillment or in which the seeker can become lost. The mind must control the senses or the seeker will never reach his goal.

The *Kaṭha Upaniṣad* continues to say that the person who has no control over his mind does not reach his goal but returns again to the entrapping cycle of *saṁsāra*. On the other hand, one who has controlled one's mind and has gained understanding reaches the end of one's journey, the timeless "supreme realm of the All-Pervading One":

Indeed, one who has no understanding,
who has no control over his mind, is ever unclear.

> He reaches not the goal [of his journey],
> but comes back again to *saṁsāra.*
>
> However, one who has understanding,
> who has control over his mind, is ever clear.
> He reaches the end [of his journey]
> from which there is no rebirth.
>
> One who has understanding,
> who harnesses with his mind the team of his senses:
> that person reaches the goal of the journey,
> the supreme realm of the All-Pervading One [Viṣṇu].[136]

The *yogī* with the clear and purified mind thus sees all beings, including himself, as images of the universal Self. He thus lives in a constant revelation of the divine and no longer regards himself as a separate being, disjoined from the rest of the universe. Such is the meaning of this passage from the *Adhyātma Upaniṣad*:

> The Unborn One ever lives in the cave [of the heart] within the body. . . . Through the practice of meditation, wise people should abandon the concept of "I" and "mine" in the body and in the senses, which are not really Ātman. Having known himself as an embodiment of the Self, the witness of the awakened intelligence and of its activities, one should ever think "I am That" [*So 'ham*]. . . . Thus, one should see Ātman as pervading all things and as existing autonomously by itself. Brahman is self-contained. Viṣṇu is Ātman. Rudra is Ātman. Indra is Ātman. This whole universe is Ātman; there is nothing but Ātman.[137]

That text continues to teach that

> he is a perfected being [*siddha*] who knows the Ātman himself by means of his own mind, who has known the identity of his soul with the changeless Self [of the universe].[138]

The Upaniṣads suggest that the recognition of the source of his being brings to the *yogī* an experience of an undying truth, which is described as one of immortality. At times, the Upaniṣads make use of striking spatial imagery reminiscent of the ritualist's ascent to heaven to depict the seeker's return to the Absolute. Such is the case, for example, in *Aitareya Upaniṣad* 3.4, which tells of the sage Vāmadeva, who, having cultivated his inner wisdom, soared upward from this world by means of the wise Self. He enjoyed all wishes in the heavenly world. He became immortal. Yes, he became immortal!

IMAGINATION AND CONTEMPLATIVE VISION

Throughout the Upaniṣads we note the idea that the infinite and eternal Brahman is somehow to be "seen" within the structure of one's own being, and that such inward vision brings an experience of abiding tranquility. "The Eternal in the transient, the Intelligence in the intelligence, the One among the many," the *Kaṭha Upaniṣad* teaches, "to the wise who see him as dwelling in the soul: to them is eternal peace."[139] Such recognition takes place through a clarified consciousness that has subsumed and controlled the outward senses. According to the *Muṇḍaka Upaniṣad*:

> The sublime Ātman is to be known only through that consciousness
> into which the five senses have been enfolded.
> The mind of all beings is pervaded by the senses.
> [Therefore,] when it is purified, the Ātman shines forth.[140]

The Upaniṣads describe the human body as the dwelling place of the soul. The *Chāndogya Upaniṣad* speaks of the body as the "city of Brahman," much as other religious traditions speak of the body as the "temple of God." It also describes the heart, in which contemplative inner vision takes place, as a small house or a lotus flower in that city of Brahman, and includes a set of teachings regarding the nature of the lotus of the heart:

> Within this city of Brahman is an abode, a small lotus flower. Within that is a small space. What is within that space: that should be sought; for, truly, that is what one should yearn to understand. . . .
>
> Truly, as far as the space of this [universe] extends, that far extends the space within the heart. Within it are held both heaven and earth, both fire and air, both sun and moon, lightning and the stars. Whatever there is of him [in the outer world] and whatever there is not: all of that is held within [the heart]. . . .
>
> [The lotus of the heart] does not age with old age and does not die at the death [of the body]. That, [and not the body], is the true city of Brahman. The Self is free from taint, free from old age, free from death, free from sorrow, free from hunger and thirst. Its yearnings are for the Real; its thoughts are for the Real. . . .
>
> Just as, in this [earthly realm] the world one earns through activity perishes, even so there [in the heavenly realm] the world earned [by

> the merit gained from performing external sacrifices] perishes. Those who depart [this world] without having found the Self and those yearnings for the Real: for them there is no liberation in any of the worlds. But those who depart having found the Self and those yearnings for the Real: for them there is liberation in all of the worlds. . . .
>
> Truly, the Self abides in the heart. Knowing this, the [wise person] enters daily into the heavenly world. The Self is the immortal, the fearless. That is Brahman. The name of Brahman is Truth.[141]

It is thus to the heart that Upaniṣadic sages instructed their students to direct their contemplative imagination, for it is in the heart that the "brilliant seed" (*tejobindu*) of the Self is firmly planted. We see, for instance, that

> the highest meditation should be on the *tejobindu*,
> the Self of the universe, which is seated in the heart:
> the size of an atom, peaceful, quiet
> both manifold and subtle, as well as neither of these.
> That alone should be the meditation of the sages
> as well as of ordinary people.
> [Such meditation] is full of difficulty and is far from easy.
> [The Self] is difficult to perceive and difficult to attain.
> It is the imperishable one, the liberated one [*mukta*].[142]

Practicing *dhyāna* and related disciplines, the seeker is to envision divine forces and truths within the heart. This inward vision relies on the meditator's cultivation of ascetic fervor (*tapas*), which leads to a certain "warming" (*tapana*) of the contemplative spirit. A number of the sectarian Upaniṣads direct their students to such practices. Drawing on its Śākta heritage, the *Tripurātāpanī Upaniṣad*, for example, instructs the meditator to "enthrone in the heart the supreme knowledge, the Goddess," and to

> meditate on the goddess Mahālakṣmī in the heart. Her face smiling, she is beautiful and undeniably attractive: she is the great Māyā. Wearing three earrings she sits on a three-tiered seat and dwells in the ineffable, sacred place, the throne of auspicious beauty. . . . Meditate on her through the great *yoga* of contemplation.[143]

Several of the Upaniṣads maintain that the heart stands as the axis of a wheel of sorts, the spokes of which are depicted as channels or streams of energy that distribute the life-force throughout the body. We see expression of such an idea in the *Praśna Upaniṣad*:

> In the heart, truly resides the Ātman. Here, there are the one hundred and one channels. From each one comes one hundred smaller channels. From each one of these come 72,000 channels rushing [with energy]. Within them courses the diffused breath.[144]

Similar imagery appears in the *Muṇḍaka Upaniṣad*:

> Firmly established, thriving and revealed in the cave of the heart:
> such is the great foundation. . . .
> Where the arteries of the body are brought together
> like spokes at the hub of a wheel:
> there, within it [the Ātman] lives; there it reveals itself.
> *Oṁ*! Meditate in this way on the Ātman.[145]

The vital force, *prāṇa*, is said to enter and leave the body through the process of breathing, without which there can be no life. It is literally, therefore, the life-breath itself. It has different forms: the breath that stays in the body even after one has exhaled and that gives life to the heart; the inhalation and downward breath, which distributes energy to the lower parts of the body; the suffusive breath, which carries life throughout the body; the balanced breath between inhalation and exhalation, which brings vitality to the body's midregion; and exhalation, the rising breath, which lifts the energy of life upward toward the head.[146]

Sitting in meditative absorption, the seeker envisions within the heart not only the whole world but also the many gods and goddesses and directs the *prāṇa* in the direction of those deities. The soul is said to reside quietly, as if asleep but yet constantly awake, in the center of that vital system. A passage from the *Subāla Upaniṣad* represents such a vision. Although rather long, it is worth quoting at some length.

> In the middle of the heart is a fleshy, red lump. In it a small, fine white lotus blooms, spreading its petals in different directions, like the red lotus. There are ten openings in the heart. In them are established the vital breaths. When [the contemplative meditator] is yoked to the life-breath he sees many and various rivers and towns. When yoked to the suffusive breath he sees gods and visionary sages. When yoked to the downward breath he sees the heavenly nymphs, spirits, and angels. When yoked to the upward breath he sees the world of heaven and the gods Skandha, Jayanta, and others. When yoked to the balanced breath he sees the heavenly world and treasures of all sorts. . . .
>
> These [ten openings of the heart] branch out into ten branches of ten each [held by] an invisible sheath. Out of each one of these branch

> the 72,000 channels. In these the Ātman seems to dream and causes various sounds to be heard [by the *yogī*]. In a second invisible sheath the soul experiences dreams, yet nevertheless sees this world and the other world and comprehends all sounds. This is a state of serenity [and clear] perception; in it the vital breath protects the [physical] body.
>
> The branched channels course with blue, yellow, yellow-green, and white fluids. Manifest channels called "speedy" one-thousandth as thick as a strand of hair dwell in a sheath within the small, fine white lotus, which has bloomed like the red lotus, with its petals spreading in all directions. In the space of the heart sitting in the middle of the sheath, the divine Self rests. . . . Its form is one of radiance and immortality. . . . It rules all things. It is a radiant and immortal form.[147]

Three main channels, or *nāḍīs*, are said to run up and down the spine. Of these the *suṣumnā nāḍī* stands in the center, straight—like a pillar, or sacrificial post, or world-axis. Around the *suṣumnā* wind the *īḍā nāḍī* and the *piṅgalā nāḍī*, forming a helix through which the vital breaths course.

Some of the later Upaniṣads, especially those reflecting Śaiva and Śākta influences, also teach that the supreme Consciousness that resides in all things is to be regarded as a transformative power, *kuṇḍalinī*. Contemplatives imagine this power in the form of a young lotus stalk or as the fertile serpent, Kuṇḍalinī, sleeping at the bottom of the spinal column, whence the *suṣumnā*, *īḍā*, and the *piṅgalā nāḍīs* emerge from a single bulb. The *Yogakuṇḍalī Upaniṣad* describes Kuṇḍalinī in this way:

> The transformative power [*śakti*], named Kuṇḍalinī,
> shines like the stem of a lotus.
> Like a serpent, coiled upon herself,
> she holds her tail in her mouth.
> She lies, resting and half asleep,
> at the base of the body.[148]

Fed by the nourishment provided to her in the form of the vital breath directed her way by the disciplined meditator's *tapas*, Kuṇḍalinī wakes and, uncoiling, climbs upward through several energy centers or "wheels" (*cakras*) of different shapes and colors envisioned along the spine. She begins at the bottom of the spine and climbs through a *cakra* located at the level of the sexual organ, then pierces one at the level of the navel, then ascends through one at the heart, then one at the throat, followed by one between the eyebrows, and finally reaches a glorious diamond-colored *cakra* in the form of a thousand-petalled lotus (*sahasrāra*) envisioned above the top of the head.[149]

Traditions vary regarding the number and characteristics of these *cakras*. The *Saubhāgyalakṣmī Upaniṣad*, for example, teaches that there are nine rather than the more commonly recognized seven such "wheels" or centers of consciousness.[150] But in all cases the texts teach the idea that consciousness moves through and can be directed toward these different modes of awareness.

As she climbs through the different levels of consciousness, Kuṇḍalinī ascends from a world of slumber and ignorance through the *cakras*, finally gaining the realm of transcendental knowledge at the resplendent *sahasrāra cakra* above the head. At each level the contemplative envisions and subsequently experiences different deities, shapes, and colors and hears various sublime sounds.

Sometimes those forms are imagined within the body, in which case they constitute a contemplative vision the *Maṇḍalabrāhmaṇa Upaniṣad*, for example, teaches is "to be seen inwardly." Other times such a contemplative vision is "to be seen outwardly" and appears as objective forms in the external world. Still other times they are a combination of the two, and thus "to be seen in between" the outer and inner worlds.[151]

Descriptions of Kuṇḍalinī's ascent vary somewhat from text to text. But these variations are minor and rather technical in nature. Throughout these works, however, we see references to brilliant and shimmering visual imagery. For example, this is how the *Maṇḍalabrāhmaṇa Upaniṣad* describes the experience of consciousness as it passes, for instance, through the *cakra* situated at the forehead. Here, the contemplative envisions a form in the shape of a star between the two eyebrows.

> In the middle of the two eyebrows [one imagines] Tāraka, which—being Brahman—is of the spiritual resplendence of Being, Consciousness, and Bliss. One sees it by means of three types of contemplative vision [namely, the visualization of images to be seen inwardly, outwardly, and in between]. . . . It has the radiance of the sun. Kuṇḍalinī shines in the middle of it, like thousands of millions of bolts of lightning and as fine as the stalk of a young lotus.[152]

The text distinguishes the content of the three types of contemplative vision:

> When focused on it while practicing visualization of images to be seen inwardly, the mind sees a blue light between the eyes, as it did also in the heart. In the practice of visualization of images to be seen outwardly one sees the color blue, then indigo, then brilliant red, then yellow and orange-red colors in the space in front of his nose. Then he is a *yogī*.
>
> When he sees sparkling lights the size of twelve fingers above his head he attains the state of ambrosia. In the practice of visualization of

images to be seen in between, he sees the various colors of the morning, as if he [were watching] the sun, the moon, and the fire join together in the previously empty space. Then he comes to have their nature [of light].[153]

Our passage from the *Maṇḍalabrāhmaṇa Upaniṣad* then reviews the stages through which one moves as one cultivates these three forms of contemplative vision. Such practice is said to lead to what, following Yogic tradition, the text calls *śāmbhavī-mudrā*, a meditative state in which one is so deeply immersed in the universal Self that all one sees is the inward divinity, even though one keeps one's eyes open and thus appears to be looking at external objects.

> By practicing contemplative vision, [the *yogī*] sees a sparkling light in the shape of an endless sphere. This alone is Brahman. This is Truth, Consciousness, and Bliss. When the mind is absorbed in the bliss thus produced, then *śāmbhavī-mudrā* takes place. She, alone, is called "Khecarī." By practicing [*śāmbhavī-mudrā*], one gains firmness of mind.[154]

The body itself is sometimes described as a temple in which the divine flame burns, like the sacred fire that blazes and rises from an altar. The *Yogaśikhā Upaniṣad* offers a number of metaphors to represent the idea that the body serves as the place where the contemplative inwardly worships the divine. It speaks of a temple supported by one pillar and three posts, that is, the spinal column and the *suṣumnā*, *iḍā*, and *piṅgalā nāḍīs*. It has nine doorways and serves as the home for five deities. These are probably the nine openings in the body (eyes, ears, nostrils, mouth, and places of evacuation) and the five senses, respectively.

> Upon one pillar and three posts,
> with nine doorways and having five deities,
> stands a temple. It is the body.
> In it one should seek the highest.
>
> There, a sun blazes
> surrounded by rays like flame.
> In its center is a fire
> that burns like the wick of a lamp.
>
> As large as is its pointed flame,
> that large is the highest divinity therein.
> Practicing yoga constantly,
> the *yogī* penetrates the sun.

> Then, he goes upward in a spiralling manner
> through the *suṣumnā*'s shining door.
> Piercing the top of the head,
> he finally sees the highest one.[155]

Practicing such meditation, the contemplative sage is said to gain a vision of the divine that brings an experience of the Self immersed in ambrosia. The *Varāha Upaniṣad* asserts that,

> keeping his neck and body straight and his mouth closed, a wise person should meditate unwaveringly on the tip of his nose, in the center of his heart, and in the middle of the seed [within the heart]. His mind calm, he should see with his [mind's] eye the ambrosia flowing there. . . . He should envision the Ātman as the Resplendent Goddess and as being bathed in ambrosia. . . . What is thought of by the mind is accomplished by the mind itself.[156]

THE SACRIFICE OF THE IMAGINATION IN THE RETURN TO THE ABSOLUTE

Practicing contemplative meditation, the Upaniṣadic *yogī* becomes firmly established in the ambrosial nectar of the divine, an experience that is closely associated with inner light. For Upaniṣadic teachers and their students, the sacred cosmos has thus shifted from the outer to the inner world. True and effective contact with the deities and other divine forces therefore takes place, not only by means of the external *yajña*, but also within the human spirit itself. The contemplative meditator does not have to offer sacrificial gifts to the fire burning on the ritual altar. Rather, one directs one's breath of life to the base of the spine as an offering to the divine power dwelling there. Then, just as the external offerings of *soma pavamāna* and other gifts of life are carried to the bright skies and brilliant heavens by the god Agni as he rises from the sacrificial altar in the form of smoke, so too the vital life-force rises upward along the *suṣumnā nāḍī* through the various levels of consciousness, finally reaching the splendid thousand-petalled lotus that blossoms above the head. The human body has become analogous to the entire sacred universe. In it reside all the gods, in it stands the sacrificial fire altar, through it climbs the offertory pillar of fire, throughout it shines the expansive and illuminating power of light that remains undefeated by any inner darkness. Even the dissolution of the physical body has no sway over that universal power of life. The meditator's contemplative fervor, *tapas*, subsumes the forces of darkness and death within the unwavering brilliance and vitality of the universal and unified Self.

That which was "higher" in the Vedic metaphysics of being was also "deeper" within the Self. We remember the *Chāndogya Upaniṣad*'s assertion that the "light which shines higher even than the heavens . . . is the same as this light which is here within the person."[157] This spatial homology applies to the structure and function of the mind and imagination as well. We remember the passage from the *Kaṭha Upaniṣad* quoted earlier which holds that

> Higher than the objects of the senses is the mind.
> Higher than the mind is awakened intelligence.
> Higher than the awakened intelligence is the great self.[158]

Drawing on such perspectives as that presented by the *Taittirīya Upaniṣad*—which, as we have seen, teaches that the self consists of different layers, the outermost being the least real, the innermost being the "body consisting of bliss" and identified as the universal Self itself—we would be consistent with Vedic thought if we were to restate the above lesson in this way:

> Deeper than the objects of the senses is the mind.
> Deeper than the mind is awakened intelligence.
> Deeper than the awakened intelligence is the great self.

The mind thus stands as a pivot of sorts. It can direct its attention and energy outward, thereby entrapping the human spirit in the ephemeral and transient manifold world of multiplicity; this is the world the Upaniṣads characterize as *saṁsāra.* Or the mind can turn its attention around and direct its energy deeper, toward its unified, sublime source. This latter, inward movement frees one from the frustrations, disappointments, and pain of *saṁsāra.* Such a turn of the mind leads finally to liberation.

In order for one to know the divine Self within, the mind must necessarily reverse the metaphysical emanation of being. This means that, in returning to that which is "higher" or "deeper" the mind must transcend itself. It must surrender to the divine Self. It must offer or sacrifice itself in its return to its divine source. Teaching the mental reversal of the emanation of being in favor of a return to the divine source, the *Kaṭha Upaniṣad* holds that

> the wise person [*dhīra*] should surrender his words to his mind,
> and the [mind] he should surrender to the knowing self.
> He should surrender the knowing self to the great self, and
> he should surrender that to the peaceful self.[159]

The "sacrifice in the mind," we noted at the end of the previous chapter, therefore includes the "sacrifice of the mind" as well. Turning on its pivot away from its own mentally formed world, the mind thus becomes the sacrificial offering itself.

The *Śvetāśvatara Upaniṣad* similarly notes that

> by meditating on the one god, by union with him, and
> by increasingly entering into his being, there is, finally,
> cessation of the imaginary world
> formed by the fluctuations of the mind.[160]

A related idea appears in the *Śāṇḍilya Upaniṣad*:

> Centering his mind on an image to be seen inwardly . . . with eyes half-closed and with a firm mind . . . one becomes aware of that which is of the form of light, that which is free of all external [qualities], that which is luminous: the supreme truth, the sublime. . . . Placing the mind in the middle of the divine power [*śakti*] and the divine power in the midst of the mind, and looking on the mind with the mind, be happy! Just as camphor is subsumed by fire and salt is dissolved in water, so too the mind becomes absorbed in the truth.[161]

In this regard, the *Amṛtabindu Upaniṣad* speaks of the contemplative process of *dhāraṇā*, which is the steady "maintaining" of one's inward concentration and one of the eight practices of classical yogic discipline. "When one sinks the mind, the organ of imagination, into the Self, and thus remains firmly attached to the Self," this Upaniṣad teaches, "that is known as *dhāraṇā*."[162]

Drawing on such ideas and practices, the Upaniṣads in general note two forms of meditation, depending on just what the contemplative places his or her focused awareness. In one type, the mind directs its attention toward images and forms. In the other type, the mind is empty of such images but concentrates, instead, on the formless Self. "Meditation [*dhyāna*] is of two kinds," the *Śāṇḍilya Upaniṣad* reads: "that with qualities and that without qualities. 'With qualities' is the contemplation on a form, 'without qualities' on the reality of the Self."[163] According to the *Maṇḍalabrāhmaṇa Upaniṣad*, the latter is a more advanced form than the former. It takes place in a mode of awareness that is deeper than the level of the mind: "understand that there are two types of meditation [*yoga*] by means of the division into 'earlier' and 'later.' . . . the later is without the use of the mind."[164]

This state (*bhāva*) in which the mind has dissolved itself into the encompassing reality of the Self is sometimes known as *unmanī-bhāva*. At the literal level, the word *unmanī* means "absence of mind," but here it more properly refers to that state of awareness which transcends the mind itself. The *unmanī*-state is associated with the process of *laya*, or "absorption into the Absolute." Thus, for example, the *Maṇḍalabrāhmaṇa Upaniṣad* says that

> the mind which is influenced by the objects of the world is set for bondage; that [mind] which is not influenced by these is suitable for liberation. Therefore, the whole world becomes an object of the mind's activity. Yet, when it is without support and well-ripened in the *unmanī*-state, the same mental activity becomes worthy of absorption [into the Absolute].[165]

Since according to Vedic thought the heart lies deeper within the Self than does the mind, the mind surrendering itself to the divine Self surrenders, first, to the heart. As the *Tripurātāpanī Upaniṣad* states,

> free of attachment to objects and
> enveloped in the heart,
> the mind ceases to be the mind.
> This is the supreme state.
> Control the mind until it becomes quiet within the heart.
> This is knowledge. This is meditation.[166]

Practicing contemplative meditation, the Upaniṣadic *yogī* uses the transformative power of the imagination to offer the mind to the heart, and then to the Self. Offering itself to the Self, it dissolves into bliss. The *Maitrī Upaniṣad* notes that

> when the mind has been dissolved
> and there is the bliss whose only witness is the Self:
> that is Brahman, the immortal, the radiant!
> That is the way! Truly, that is the [real] world![167]

A subsequent passage from that same Upaniṣad is worth quoting at some length:

> Just as fire without fuel becomes extinguished in its own source,
> so, too, is the mind quieted in its own source
> when its activities have ceased.
>
> When a seeker's mind is quieted in its own source
> he is no longer misled by the objects of the senses, which are
> deceptive and determined by past actions.

For, truly, *saṁsāra* is just one's own thought.
It should be clarified, therefore, with great effort.
This is the eternal secret: whatever one thinks, that one becomes!

It is only by means of a peaceful mind
that a person is rid of good and evil deeds.
With a serene soul, abiding in the soul, a person gains unending bliss.

If the mind were as firmly fixed on Brahman
as it usually is attached to the objects of the senses,
who, then, would not be released from bondage?

The mind has been said to be of two kinds: the pure and the impure.
It becomes impure when associated with desire;
it is pure when it is freed from desire.

When a person—having made his mind perfectly steady,
free from distraction and laziness—
enters into that state beyond the mind:
then he attains the supreme abode!

The mind must be controlled until it is subsumed by the heart.
This, truly, is knowledge. This is freedom.
The rest is nothing but the string of knots [that bind the soul].

The bliss of a mind whose stains are washed away through
concentration
and which has entered the Self
can never be expressed in words!
One must experience it in one's inner being.[168]

The *Brahma Upaniṣad* holds that the contemplative's realization of that universal Self, the fullness of which cannot be imagined by the mind, is the very purpose of Upanṣadic teachings as a whole:

That from which words turn back
along with the mind, without reaching it:
that is the bliss of the living spirit.
Knowing this, the awakened one is free.
Like butter hidden in cream,
based in self-knowledge and in discipline,
the all-pervading Ātman
is the final goal of the mystic teaching regarding the Brahman.[169]

The power of the imagination to create its own world thus also allows it to turn away from that very world and to redirect itself back to the Self that gives it its very being. The mind thus imagines itself out of a fractured and splayed world and thus out of *saṁsāric* existence itself. By sacrificing itself, however, the mind returns to its eternal and infinite source, the universal Self. Such a return to the blissful Absolute constitutes, not the death of the imagination, but rather its fulfillment.

Chapter 6

Religious Functions of the Imagination

It is now time to turn our attention to a summary of the specifically religious functions of the imagination in Vedic thought and practice. In previous pages we have discussed separately the nature and role of the imagination in poetic inspiration and expression, in the performance of sacred drama, and in the ideology and practice of meditation. Poetry, ritual, and contemplative vision are closely connected to each other in Vedic religion; what pertains to one therefore pertains to the others as well. In this chapter we will look at three different functions of the imagination reflected in each of these forms of expression. We will review the way the imagination serves to (i) fashion a world where previously there was none, (ii) reveal the essential harmony of being that girds the world thus created, and (iii) reunify and thus revitalize that world when it has become disjointed, broken, or meaningless. These, then, are three types of imagination in Vedic religion: the creative imagination, the revelatory imagination, and the reunitive or cosmogonic imagination.

Each of these three functions involves and complements each of the others. But they are also distinct from one another. The creative and cosmogonic functions of the imagination may at first seem to be the same, and in some ways they are. But in other ways, from the Vedic perspective, they are quite different from each other. Creation may involve a chaotic process of the particularization of the many through the apparent dismemberment of the One. Cosmogony, on the other hand, is the reestablishment or recognition of a meaningful, unified cosmos out of that empirical chaos.[1] Creation often leads to a fractured multiverse; cosmogony returns that multiverse to an ordered and harmonious universe. The difference between the two is most marked in the ritual context,[2] but given the close relationship among ritual drama, poetic vision, and contemplative meditation, such a distinction between creation and cosmogony may be found elsewhere in the Vedic imagination as well.

In serving creative, revelatory, and cosmogonic functions, the imagination, from the Vedic perspective, gives expression to the mysterious workings of Ṛta, the unified and harmonious artfulness of being of which all things are reflected images. Vedic priests tended to identify that principle with the *brahman*, the prayerful word and effective mechanism by which ritual activities had an effect on the world and by which ceremonially formed new worlds came into being. Upaniṣadic sages regarded the Brahman as the expansive and all-encompassing ground of being, the ontological Absolute, and saw its identity with the Ātman, the universal subject residing within all of the many objects of the world.

Because the later Vedic understanding of Brahman and thus of Ātman is closely associated with the early Vedic concept of Ṛta, we can say that Vedic sensibilities as a whole revolved around the cultivated awareness and energetic expression of the universal artfulness of being. Vedic seers were said to understand this foundational truth and to recognize it even within the often threatening, confusing, and discouraging alternations and discontinuities of life. They did so through the various powers of the imagination, broadly defined. Seeing and expressing such a harmonious power and truth, the imagination returned a world experienced as fractured or deadened multiverse into a world as vital universe, that is, as a unified system in which the many and different parts reflect the artful integrity of the whole. The imagination thus served a fundamentally religious role.

In the following pages we will return to Vedic texts as we review these types and functions of the imagination in Vedic India. We will be looking at many of the passages from a different angle this time, as we point out the way they reflect Vedic ideas regarding the creative, revelatory, and cosmogonic imagination. This chapter concludes with the presentation of the idea that, in Vedic India, the imagination served as *religion* itself.

THE CREATIVE IMAGINATION

To the early Vedic mind, the complicated, often wondrous, and deeply mysterious world experienced in time and space could not have existed without the brilliant artistry of the many gods and goddesses. For it was these luminous powers who built the many and diverse objects of the world. The bright and shining *deva*s and *devī*s—the brilliant, divine forces: the splendid gods and goddesses themselves—brought the world into existence from the depths of nonexistence.

The deities were understood to perform such wondrous artistry by first envisioning images of the world in their minds and then bringing the world into being and supporting it through the mysterious formative power of their imagination. One seer sang this of the god Soma:

> This sage who is skilled in visionary imagination
> has measured out the six wide realms
> in which no beings are excluded.
> This, yes this, is he who has made the width of the earth
> and the high heights of the heavens.
> He formed the nectar in the three sparkling rivers.
> Soma supports the wide atmosphere.[3]

Another visionary sang this of a god he did not name:

> Well-established in the world, he was a skillful artist;
> he who formed these twins, heaven and earth.
> Skilled in visionary imagination, with his power
> he joined together both realms, spacious and deep,
> well-formed, and unsupported.[4]

As we have seen, Vedic poets used many terms to refer to such imaginative creativity. We might mention only *māyā*, which in early Vedic texts referred, not to a misleading or dangerous "illusion" (as it does in later Indian philosophy), but rather to the gods' mysterious mental ability to form dimensional realities where once there was nothing.

In reference specifically to the latter term, we might remember these verses in a song of praise to the god Varuṇa:

> He has encompassed the night and,
> with his wondrous *māyā*,
> has formed the mornings.
> He is transcendently beautiful![5]

or these to Varuṇa and Mitra:

> Mitra and Varuṇa! Your voice refreshes.
> The thunderer sends forth
> a wondrous, mighty sound.
> With their *māyā* the Maruts
> easily dress themselves with clouds:
> you cause the ruddy, spotless cloud to rain.[6]

The gods created the many objects of the world, in part, by forming images of those objects in their minds, then "measuring" those mental images, and finally projecting those measurements onto the emptiness of nonbeing. For an analogy, we might think of the way in which an architect produces an architectural plan. He or she first thinks of the shape and dimensions of a building—*plans* its design—and then draws that plan outward, finally to give it form as the plan one reads on a blueprint. The difference here is that the Vedic gods not only envisioned the world-plan in their minds and projected it outward, but also subsequently entered into and dwelled within that plan, giving the objective world its vitality and movement. Such was their creative imagination. We read in the *Ṛgveda* that,

> entering into this world through their hidden natures,
> [the gods] adorned the regions for [Indra's] control.
> Measuring with rulers, they fixed the wide expanses
> and separated and secured the immense worlds.[7]

Referring to the artistry of what it regards as the supreme deity, the *Śvetāśvatara Upaniṣad* teaches:

> The past, the future, and all that the Vedas declare:
> all of this the image-maker [*māyin*] sends forth out of this;
> and in this the other is held by *māyā*.
> Know, then, that the material world is [a result of] *māyā*,
> and that the Great Lord is the image-maker.
> This whole world is filled with beings that are parts of him.[8]

This process in which the divine imagination expands from within the deity's mind suggests one of a creative emanation of sorts in which the content of that imagination flows outward, creating and sustaining the manifest world as it does so. This is consistent with a Vedic idea that holds that the world as a whole is created through the expansive emanation of divinity itself. Because Vedic thought regards all the deities to be different expressions or names of a single ultimate reality, such an emanation is that by which the sublime One becomes the manifest many. We see evidence of this larger idea in songs recounting the creative expansion of a single, divine Word into the various realms, forming and supporting the many and different beings throughout the sacred universe. Indeed, Vedic thought holds that even the deities are born of this universal Word. "The Word is infinite, immense, transcendent of all this," the *Taittirīya Brāhmaṇa* declares. "The gods, the celestial spirits, human beings, and animals: all of these live in the Word. In the Word all of the worlds find their foundation."[9] According to the *Pañcaviṁśā Brāhmaṇa*,

> in the beginning was only the lord of the universe. His Word was with him. This Word was his associate. He contemplated to himself. Then he said: "I will give forth this Word so that she may produce and bring into being all of this world."[10]

The link between the energetic divine imagination and the divine Word is made explicit in the following passage from the *Śatapatha Brāhmaṇa*:

> In the beginning this universe was neither being nor nonbeing. Indeed, in the beginning this universe both existed and did not exist: only Mind was there. . . . Strictly speaking, this Mind neither existed nor did not exist. . . . This Mind wished to become manifest. That Mind then fashioned the Word. This Word, when so formed, wished to become manifest, more apparent, more physical. It sought after a self. It practiced intense meditation and assumed substance. It then beheld the thirty-six thousand fires of its own self, composed of the Word and formed by the Word. . . . That Word created the Breath of life.[11]

To Vedic poets, the universal Word was spoken by the goddess Vāc, who resided in the light-filled realm above the highest heaven. Descending into the various realms below, like the many raindrops that fall from a single cloud, Vāc broke into many syllables and rhythms, each forming an aspect of the divine, natural, and human worlds. In one hymn from the *Ṛgveda*, the goddess herself declares:

> At the summit of the universe I bring forth the Father.
> My origin is in the [celestial] waters, in the [heavenly] ocean.
> From there I spread into all creatures of the world.
> I touch even the distant heaven with my forehead.
> I breathe forth powerfully, like the wind;
> even so, I hold together onto myself all things that exist.
> I tower above this wide earth and above the high heavens,
> so mighty am I in my power and brilliance.[12]

Listening to the universal rhythms and melodies of life in the wondrous but mysterious world about them, Vedic poets heard the voice of Vāc herself. They did so inwardly, that is, when the power of the divine had "entered into" and thus "inspired" them. The following verses from the "Song of the Goddess" (the "Devī Sūkta") recall Vāc's own words:

> I enter into and abide in many homes
> Whoever sees, whoever breathes, whoever hears spoken words:

he gains his nourishment through me alone.
He does not recognize me, yet he lives within me.
Listen, everyone! What I say is worthy of faith!
It is I who announce and utter forth the Word
celebrated by gods and humans alike.
Him whom I love: him, I make swell in strength;
him, I make a priest, a seer, a sage.[13]

As the universal poetess whose voice formed all things, the goddess Vāc was associated with other images of the divine as creator: Tvaṣṭṛ, the Fashioner, for example; or Dhātṛ, the Ordainer; Viśvakarman, the All-maker, the architect of the universe; and Bṛhaspti (or Brahmaṇaspati), the Lord of the Expansive Power. Vedic songs note that such creativity took fervent energy, or *tapas*:

From *tapas* came cosmic order and truth;
thence was born the mysterious night;
and thence the [universal] ocean with its swelling waves.
From that ocean with its waves was born the year,
which orders the passage of nights and days
and which controls all things that blink the eyes.
Then, as previously, did the Ordainer fashion
the sun and moon, heaven and earth,
the sky and the realm of light.[14]

Because of their creative ability, and because creation itself gave voice to the divine Word, the gods and goddesses were often described as brilliant or thoughtful poets. Soma, for, example, found praise from Vedic visionaries as "an inspired poetic sage of the heavens whose heart is wise"[15] and as a "poetic singer who brings all to light."[16] Agni, the god of fire and thus of light, received similar adulation as a "skillfully creative poet."[17]

The idea that divine poetry was a form of creativity is suggested by the following verses, in which the seer describes Varuṇa as a "most poetic god." Varuṇa's artistry was an expression of his mysterious and wondrous creative power—his *māyā*—through which he fills the seas, brings rainclouds to the sky, guides the sun as it moves through the heavens, and places imagination itself within the human spirit:

It is Varuṇa who
    put milk into cows and
    mighty speed into horses, and has
woven the air between the tree branches.

It is Varuṇa who
has placed lightening in the clouds,
the sun in the heavens,
soma in the mountains, and
effective imagination within hearts.[18]

Other gods were said to have inspired the Vedic poets as well. We recall that Soma, for example, found praise as a deity "whose mind is that of a seer, who makes [human] seers, who wins the light of heaven, addressed by a thousand songs, a guide for inspired sages."[19] Of Indra, one poet proclaimed:

Indra! Mighty in mental power and skilled in visionary imagination:
you are splendid!
Strengthen us, too,
with such power, O Lord of Power.[20]

Inspired by the gods, Vedic poets entered into a filial relationship of sorts with those creative powers. A faithful visionary noted that "they who hear [Agni's] word fulfill his wish, like sons obey their father's request."[21] One of the Vedic seers, Viśvāmitra, is described as being "born of the gods."[22] The artistic descendants of the gods, with whom they shared an intimate familial relationship, Vedic poets in general were "images" of the gods formed of the deities' own creative imaginations. The Vedic poet Vasiṣṭha, for example, is remembered as "the child of Mitra and Varuṇa, born into the world from the mind of Urvaśī."[23]

Hearing the sublime Word that gave rise to all things and inspired by the gods, Vedic poets filtered that divine sound through their hearts and minds and then gave it verbal image in the form of poetic song. Their hymns were therefore utterances from the human heart that gave imaginative voice to the transcendent and powerfully creative Word itself. The words and rhythms of their songs were said to be in effective harmony with each other and therefore pleasing to the gods. An effective poem—one that touched the gods' hearts—was to be fresh, sparkling, well-formed,[24] and sung forth with a spontaneity reminiscent of a sudden shower bursting from a cloud.[25]

The human poet was similar in a sense to the gods, for both exhibited a creative brilliance of sorts: the bright deities fashioned the luminous world, the ingenious poet fashioned a sparkling poem. Both processes demanded creative energy. We remember that two of the terms referring to a Vedic poet were *vipra* and *vipascit*, both of which connote a vibrant inner fervor or inspired consciousness that gave rise to poetic expression. It should not be surprising that images of light infuse descriptions of the poetic process itself. Visionary poets were said to have "light within the heart that leads to poetic thought"[26] and to "hold light in their mouths;"[27] their songs were "lucid words."[28]

That such poems thus formed were understood to be new creations is demonstrated by such verses as "I have given birth to this new hymn for Agni, the Falcon of the sky."[29] Vedic poets described their verses as without precedent. Thus, one family of poets is said to "have given birth to a full and unprecedented song of praise" to Indra, for example,[30] while another seer asked for Indra's favor by pointing out that "for this hero I have fashioned with my lips comprehensive and auspicious words that have no precedent."[31]

The power of imaginative creativity resided in more than just the gods and the visionary poets. In their own way, Vedic priests also expressed such an ability. We recall that the shape of the ritual stage was established in the image of the divine cosmic person, Puruṣa. Puruṣa's "head" faced east, his two "arms" stretched to the north and south; the fire altar was placed at his "forehead." Vedic priests mentally conceived of such a shape and then projected it outward and drew it on the ground. In this way, the manner in which the priests established the sacred ritual domain is reminiscent of the way the gods with the power of their *māyā* imagined the forms of the objective world, then drew those images outward into the dimensions of time and space. Such a process is suggested by the *Śatapatha Brāhmaṇa*, which notes that the ritual altar

> should measure the distance of the outstretched arms . . . for that is the size of a man, and it should be the size of a man. . . . Let him make it as long as he thinks proper in his own mind.[32]

Elsewhere, that same text says that

> he [the priest] then projects onto the ground [the shape of] a man. This is Prajāpati. This is Agni. This is the officiating priest. He is made of gold, for gold is light and fire is light; gold is immortality and fire is immortality. It is [in the shape of] a man, for Prajāpati is the man[33]

and that

> he projects [him onto the ground as if he were] on his back. . . . He projects him with his head toward the east, for [it is with the head toward the east] that this fire altar is constructed.[34]

The sacralizing actions the priests undertook within the reduplicated and miniaturized "body" of God were performative and imaginative in nature: performative, because they gave active form to the divine; imaginative, because they gave dramatic image to it.

Those imaginative ritual performances can be said, in part, to have been creative in function. This is because the rituals performed within the ceremonial body of Puruṣa were said to establish or make firm a world (*loka*); typical language notes that such sanctifying activity is undertaken in order to "gain firm foundation."[35] Like Vedic poems, such a foundation was often described as being without precedent, *apūrva*. Such a ritually formed *loka* was therefore a new creation.

Sometimes the *loka* formed by the ritual existed here in "this world." Other times, it was somewhere else, in "yonder world," specifically "in the heavenly realm." In either case, the founding or grounding of that world was an establishment of a "place"—a *locus*, if you will (a word related to the Sanskrit *loka*)—in which gods and humans lived in harmony with each other. Whether "here" or "there" in the heavenly realm, a *loka* was a bright world in which all things fit together properly. It was a world of created order fashioned within and despite the disharmony and chaos of life as it was normally lived.

The divine world was established or made firm to large extent by means of the offering of gifts of light and life to the gods and goddesses. Over the years, the priests whose lessons form the Brāhmaṇas came to teach that the true offertory sacrifice actually took place within an individual's own life processes and physical body. Thus, just as the ritual domain served as the reconstructed body of Prajāpati and the arena for that deity's defeat of Mṛtyu (Death), so too the human body came to be seen as the real locus of such transformative events. Those teachers thus taught the importance of the "sacrifice within the body." According to the *Śatapatha Brāhmaṇa*:

> Preparing to build Agni [that is, the fire altar], the priest gathers him [Agni] within himself: for it is from within his own self that he makes him to be born, and one's source determines who one is.[36]

The Vedic contemplative philosophers whose lessons form the Upaniṣads were then to teach that the sacred powers and contours of the divine cosmos as a whole were to be recognized within the human mind and heart. "In the heart are all the gods," the *Brahma Upaniṣad* asserts. "In it, too, are the vital breaths. In the heart is life and light. . . . [All of this universe] stands within the heart, in the sparkling of consciousness."[37] Therefore, just as Vedic poets understood the creative powers to be the brilliant gods and goddesses of the sacred cosmos, Upaniṣadic teachers regarded them as the light of divine consciousness itself. As the *Aitareya Upaniṣad* notes,

> that which is heart, this mind: that is consciousness. . . . That [consciousness] is Brahmā. It is Indra. It is Prajāpati. It is all these gods. It is the five gross elements: earth, wind, space, water, and light. . . . It is

> horses, cows, people, elephants; whatever is alive, whether moving or flying or remaining still. All this is guided by consciousness. The world is guided by consciousness. Consciousness is its foundation.[38]

Vedic philosophers came to teach that the world of objects perceived to have independent external existence were, in fact, determined by images held in the mind. We remember the lesson from the *Taittirīya Upaniṣad*, which holds that the physical body is "filled" or "suffused" by the mind[39] in the sense that the mind fashions and permeates the body, just as the mind is filled by the power of wisdom, which itself is suffused by the bliss of the soul.[40]

The *Varāha Upaniṣad* notes that the consciousness residing within the power of the meditator's own imagination is a reflection of the divine consciousness that has formed the universe as a whole.

> This whole universe is brought into being through the transformations of consciousness alone. It is only through the transformations of consciousness that the universe becomes manifest. . . . All that is conscious in the universe is actually [a reflection] of absolute Consciousness. This universe is absolute Consciousness only. You are Consciousness. I am Consciousness. Meditate on the world as Consciousness.[41]

THE REVELATORY IMAGINATION

From the Vedic perspective, then, the many objects of the world experienced by the senses are diverse images of consciousness itself. In other words, the sparkling and shimmering sensual world is an *imaginary* world. This is not necessarily to say that it is invalid or untrue. It is to say, however, that it is a contingent world: its very existence depends on the creative power of the imagination.

Being contingent on the imagination, the objects of the world experienced by the senses both veil and reveal their source. On the one hand, all things in the world have their own particular and unique identity or, in Vedic terms, their own "name-and-form" (*nāma-rūpa*). On the other hand, all the various "names" in the world ultimately derive from and give voice to one divine Name that was none other than the single and unified divine Word itself. Similarly, according to the Vedic understanding, any manifest form reflects or embodies a transcendent model. Thus, for example, the true form of any particular fire (*agni*) is the divine shape of the god Agni who, though hidden, resides wherever there is a fire of any sort.

An object in the world of manifest form was thus seen to be a display or embodiment of a divine "counterform" (*pratirūpa*). The objective world thus consisted of phenomenal images of divine, noumenal forces. As one seer was to sing of Indra,

The counterform of every form,
his form is to be seen in all things.
By means of his *māyā* Indra moves in various forms.[42]

For Vedic visionaries the physical and moral world itself thus constituted a revelation of the divine, for it gave form to the many powerful deities who had brought it into existence. Such a revelation was not apparent to everyone. Only those who had opened their hearts to the reality of the divine could see and hear its presence. Let's revisit the imagery one visionary poet used when singing of the goddess Vāc to describe such a revelation:

Many who look do not see Vāc;
many who listen do not hear her.
She reveals herself
like a loving and well-adorned wife to her husband.
Though all of the friends are endowed with eyes and ears,
they are not equal in their degree of insight.
Some are like ponds that are as deep as the mouth or shoulder,
while others resemble ponds deep enough to bathe in.[43]

But, we recall from Chapter Two, the metaphysics get somewhat complicated. The physical and moral world reflect the power and directing presence of the gods; but on what model do the gods base their own imaginative creativity? Such a quandary seems to have driven a seer's query of the Maruts:

O Maruts!
By whose power of mind,
by whose image,
do you extend forth your measure?[44]

Vedic thought holds that, just as the world gave image to the creative presence of the gods, so too the many and various personalities of the gods reflected a timeless and unified principle of harmony and balance that preceded even them. This primordial, beginningless, and universal principle was, of course, Ṛta. Put in more ontological terms, it was the unified and unifying truth—the "One"—which gave rise to and supported all things in their wondrous diversity and complexity. Vedic philosopher-poets variously honored the One as the smoothly turning wheel on which the universe turned; as the universal Word, the voice of which gives rise to all things; as the cosmic Person; as the universal pillar that supports all things; and as Brahman, the expansive power that grounded and linked everything in the sacred universe.[45]

The Vedic visionary poet who not only could see the invisible form of the gods and goddesses and hear the sublime sound of the deities' ineffable names could thereby also come to know that those same divine powers were themselves images of Ṛta. To such an extraordinary seer, the world (populated not only by humans and deities but by the myriad other creatures and mysterious forces of nature as well) revealed the universal artfulness of being as a whole. As one seer exclaimed, "The paths of the gods have been revealed to me!"[46]

The gods and goddesses, and therefore Ṛta, could not be seen or heard with the normal eye and ear. The divine was recognized by the heart. "My eye is opened, this light shines on me that is placed in my heart," one visionary bard sang,"[47] while another proclaimed of his fellow poets, "By the perceptions of the heart they penetrate into the mystery."[48] Such visionary knowledge derived from the poet's *dhī*, that is, from the seer's revelatory imagination.

The heart's intuitions were then filtered through the mind in a manner similar to the way the ambrosial *soma pavamāna* was clarified by pressing it through cloth before being offered to the gods. As one seer declared, "Wise seers fashioned the Word with their minds, filtering it . . . through a sieve."[49] The mind then made verbal images of those clarified insights in the form of lucid verses and songs, which Vedic poets sang in praise of the deities. One asked this of Varuṇa and Mitra: "May you anoint and make full the home of him who has fashioned this [verse] for you in his mind and who makes this expression of insight rise upward and sustains it."[50]

It was thus the mind and heart wherein resided the power of such imaginative vision. Revelatory vision itself was often said to have been given to the poet by the gods. Thus inspired, the poet set out to fashion a song in response to that gift. As one such seer sang to Agni,

> In response to our praise, O Agni,
> release the insight to the trembling singer
> by means of inspiration, as if through a channel.
> Inspire us with a powerful thought of which you,
> O honorable one, and all the gods approve.
> From you, O Agni, come poetic gifts;
> from you, insights; from you, effective hymns.[51]

Here, the imagination does not create a new sacred song. Rather, it discovers or receives a song that already exists, the understanding of which has been given to the poet by the gods. "Release the insight to the trembling singer by means of inspiration," our seer prayed. "From you come poetic gifts; from you come insights; from you come effective hymns." Sacred poets are believed to have "heard" (*śruta*) the sacred verses from the depths of eternity.

This is partly why their songs are described as Śruti, that is, as "revelation" (*śruti*: "that which has been heard").

In this, its function of discovery, the poet's *dhī*—we can say "visionary imagination"—thus served to reveal timeless truths. Understood from this perspective, the imagination therefore was not so much creative as it was revelatory in nature.

Ṛgveda 1.164 notes the relationship between the process of revelation and the Vedic priests' coming to know the proper songs to sing during the performance of the ritual.[52] We have made frequent reference to that hymn in earlier discussions. In that song, the visionary sang these lines in reference to the goddess Vāc, whom he described as a buffalo cow whose resonant low in the highest heaven descends like a waterfall, forming the different poetic meters that comprise the flowing waters of existence:

> The buffalo cow lowed,
> producing the tumultuous, chaotic floods.
> She who is in the highest heaven has a thousand syllables,
> having become one-footed, two-footed, eight-footed, and nine-footed.
>
> It is from her whence
> the four cardinal directions
> derive their being.
> It is from her whence
> flow the immortal waters.
> It is from her whence
> the universe assumes life.
>
> From a distance I saw the rising smoke
> spread equally above here and below there.
> The heroes ritually offered the ox: these were the first ordinances.
> The three long-haired ones appear at the proper moment.
> Throughout the year's course
> one of them consumes,
> one looks over the universe with his powers,
> and of one of them the rushing effect is visible but not his form.[53]

According to this vision, Vāc's lowing voice became the many and different "one-footed, two-footed, eight-footed, and nine-footed" meters of the sacred songs. That universal voice was also said to bring about the diversity of being, for it had become the "thousand syllables" that descended into the "tumultuous, chaotic floods" of existence as a whole. In other words, Vāc's voice created the multiplicity of life in its totality. But she is also said to have given the universal syllable by which what is potentially a befuddling chaos could be ordered: that sacred syllable resulted, for example, in the establishment of the "four cardinal directions" that gave order to space.

The seer reports that the "heroes ritually offered the ox" and that "these were the first ordinances." He did not name these heroes; but the "long-haired" ones of the next verse suggest either the celestial Ādityas, whose flowing hair flies behind them as they soar through the skies, or the gods Agni, Sūrya, and Vāyu, who are described elsewhere in similar terms.[54] In any case, for that visionary, these deities seem to have been the first to perform the ritual ceremonies that gave structure and vitality to the world.

Earlier verses of that hymn suggest that these heros learned the ritual from Agni, the "structured one" who rises from the "unstructured one" and that, with this knowledge, they "weave" the rite's organizing "threads":

> Who saw the unstructured one when the unstructured one bore
> him? . . .
> Ignorant and uncomprehending, I ask in my mind
> about the footprints the gods set down at that time.
> The [divine] poets stretched forth the seven threads
> to weave the warp and woof [of the ritual].[55]

We are to remember that elsewhere the *Ṛgveda* describes Agni as the "firstborn of Ṛta."[56] We are also to note that it was in his mind that the seer inquired about the procedures ("footprints") by which the gods performed the first ritual. Other verses of *Ṛgveda* 1.164, too numerous to quote here, note that it was by means of the gods' first performance of the ritual that the sun was produced;[57] others state that the repeated performance of the rite ensures that the sun will rise each morning.[58]

In this hymn we therefore get a glimpse of the early Vedic understanding of the relationship among the creative imagination, the process of revelation, and the origin of the sacred ritual. First, Vāc formed the various and diverse objects of the world. Those many things remained in a chaotic state until organized by means of the goddess's unifying syllable, which she taught to the "firstborn of Ṛta," namely, Agni. Agni then revealed that holy syllable to the gods, who performed the first rites. The visionary saw those gods in his mind. Singing forth that sublime knowledge in the form of poetic verse, he gave the priests of the Vedic community the sacralizing knowledge by which they, too, could perform the daily and seasonal rituals that helped ensure the universe's continued health and safety.

Thus, the proper procedures by which to perform the world-sustaining ritual were revealed to the human community by means of the visionary imagination.

Like the seer and priest, the Vedic contemplative sage also experienced such a revelatory vision of the One within the heart and mind. As the *Mahānārāyaṇa Upaniṣad* reminds us,

> The form of that One is not to be seen.
> No one sees it with the eyes.
> Only he who has opened his heart,
> his thoughts, and his mind [may see it].[59]

Whereas the seers and priests tended to locate the One in the "seat of Ṛta"—sometimes described as in the highest heavens, where the light never ceased to shine, or in the fire burning on the ritual altar—Upaniṣadic sages beheld that unified ground of being deep within their very own being, where it dwelled as the universal Self, Ātman. Invisible, it nevertheless supported and enveloped one's essential being as a whole. Neither tainted nor degraded by the contours and pressures of time, it was eternal, changeless, and pure. Suggestion of the Vedic realization of the identity of Brahman and Ātman appears in such verses as these, from the *Chāndogya Upaniṣad*:

> Now, that light which shines higher even than the heavens and onto the back of all creatures and on the backs of all things; [that light] which shines in the highest worlds, than which there is no higher: truly, that is the same as this light which is here within the person[60]

and finds explicit expression in these teachings from the *Muṇḍaka Upaniṣad*:

> Enthroned behind an excellent, golden veil
> sits Brahman, untainted and undivided.
> Brilliant, it is the light of lights.
> One who knows Ātman knows it[61]

and from the *Kaṭha Upaniṣad*:

> The sole controller, the inner Self of all beings
> who makes his one form into many:
> to the wise who see him abiding within the soul,
> to them and to no one else is timeless peace.[62]

Like their poetic forebears, Upaniṣadic sages were described as *dhīra*, "wise." They were wise because they were *insightful*: they had turned their sight inward; they had cultivated their powerful inward vision.

That inward vision gained through the practice of contemplation, *dhyāna*, allowed the *yogī* to understand that the essence of one's Ātman was identical to the essence of Brahman, the very beingness of being itself. Though invisible, that supreme Self of the universe could be "seen" within all things, as taught by *Muṇḍaka Upaniṣad* 1.1.6:

> Timeless, pervading all things,
> present everywhere, superbly sublime:
> That is the imperishable, which
> wise people see to be the source of beings.

Upaniṣadic teachers felt that the divine was more manifest in the constancy of the timeless, inner Self than in the ephemeral nature of the world outside. Therefore, they instructed their meditating students to look inward to see that universal Self. As the *Kaṭha Upaniṣad* notes,

> Seeking life eternal, a wise person
> beheld the soul with his gaze turned inward.
> The immature seek outward pleasures;
> they walk into the snare of widespread death.
> But the wise, knowing life eternal,
> seek not the changeless among those things that change.[63]

Since it was eternal, the Self thus envisioned could not in any sense be created. It could, however, be discovered. We remember this lesson from the *Muṇḍaka Upaniṣad*:

> Enthroned behind an excellent, golden veil
> sits the Brahman, untainted and undivided.
> Brilliant, it is the light of lights.
> He who knows the Ātman, knows it.[64]

In these texts we see the idea that, through contemplation, the wise sage discovered the divine source deep within his own being. The sage's empirical self came to see the eternal and infinite Self, which is the source and essence of all that is. Such a beholding constituted a revelation of the divine.

At times, this process was an active revelation in the sense that the vision of the divine resulted, not so much from the seeker's own specific efforts, but from the grace of the infinite Self within. According to the *Kaṭha Upaniṣad*:

> More minute than the smallest atom yet greater than the great
> is the Self set in the cave of the heart of the creature.
> He who is without the active will beholds him

and becomes free of sorrow,
when through the grace of the Creator
he beholds the greatness of the Self. . . .
This Self cannot be gained through instruction,
nor through intellectual reasoning, nor even through much learning.
He is to be gained only by the one whom he chooses.
To such a person that Self reveals his own nature.[65]

THE COSMOGONIC IMAGINATION AND THE RETURN TO WHOLENESS

These two aspects of the imagination, the creative and the revelatory, may seem at first to contradict each other; for the process of creation implies the emergence of something new, while that of revelation suggests the discovery of what is already present.

The resolution of this apparent contradiction resides in the fact that, from the Vedic perspective, truly effective poetry, ritual drama, and contemplative meditation are constructive in nature. Drawing on different elements of the apparent chaos of being, the imagination builds a world that has meaning and significance. The imagination fashions wholeness out of what otherwise may be experienced as brokenness. Furthermore, in constructing cosmos from chaos, the imagination serves what is nothing short of a cosmogonic function.

To understand why this is so we will recall various images of the primordial unity of being somehow breaking apart, the various pieces of the once-unified but now broken whole becoming the many and different components of the world. For example, we noted from the Brāhmaṇa literatures a theme in which Prajāpati produces the world by splitting his body into many parts in a sacrificial dismemberment that left his very life-force depleted. According to the *Śatapatha Brāhmaṇa*,

> Prajāpati produced the creatures. Having produced those creatures . . . he became broken. When broken, his vital breath left from within; when broken, his living energy left from within; they having left him, he collapsed. . . . Truly, there was no firm foundation for anything there.[66]

The idea presented here is that existence as a whole consists of a chaos created by the excessive differentiation of being. Life in such an existence is thus one of brokenness, fear, and uncertainty due to its lack of vitality and solidity.

Visionary sages in the Vedic community saw things differently. During moments of inspiration, they seem to have seen in the world around them, not merely a random collection of unconnected objects, but rather images of the gods and goddesses who imaginatively brought those objects into being in the first place. That such visionaries could see and hear the various deities who remained invisible and silent to others was due to their ability to open their hearts to the divine presence. Having done so, those poets formed verbal images in their minds of those heartfelt intuitions. The images thus produced were the poetic songs themselves, which the poets sang in praise of those same gods and goddesses their hearts had come to see. In a song offered to Indra, for example, one poet affirmed that "from the heart goes forth this mentally formed prayer, sung out loud, constructed by verses of praise."[67]

The poet fashioned a poem artfully, word by word, phrase by phrase, in a way in which disparate elements fit together properly as a whole. Here, the imagination discovers what is already there and reworks it in a fresh way. The poet gathered together disparate images and put them together in a new manner, the way a carpenter constructs a new chariot by putting together different pieces of wood that already exist. Similarly, the poet was like a tailor who takes existing thread and weaves it into the warp and woof of a newly formed fabric. The poet took an already beautiful and enticing vision and added the finishing touch, the way a bride's attendants will dress her with flowers and jewelry. As a farmer loosens soil so that already existing seeds can take root and grow into new, healthy plants, so too the poet turned and cultivated his rough and still immature insight in order to produce mature songs. The imagination in its totality is therefore a constructive imagination.

The constructive nature of the poetic imagination is suggested in the *Ṛgveda* by such verses as the following, which make use of these very similes. The first set is to Indra:

> Please accept these prayerful songs being made,
> the new ones we now make.
> Seeking blessing, I have formed them
> as a splendid and well-made robe,
> like a skilled and knowing carpenter has fashioned a chariot.[68]

The second is to the Aśvins:

> We have prepared this song of praise for you, O Aśvins,
> and, like the Bhṛgus, have framed it as a chariot;
> we have dressed it as a bride to meet her groom.[69]

Another, from the *Atharvaveda*, instructs aspiring seers in this way:

> The wise one, the poets, harness the plows and
> extend the yokes toward the gods. . . .

You must therefore harness the plows,
extend the yokes, and scatter the seed here
in the fertile womb.[70]

Other passages we have read suggest the idea that Vedic poets heard the sublime Word in their hearts and filtered them through their minds. They then carved and reshaped them, nursed them, moved them about, adorned them, separated them, and put them back together again in a different arrangement.

The poet's initial vision was like the light moisture held by an ephemeral mist. His or her fervent inward endeavor condensed and gave shape to that inchoate vision. Gaining substance, the songs made up of those many droplets sprang from the poet's soul "like rain from a cloud."[71]

Sung out loud, the poem was then said to fly outward and upward into the heavens, like a flying chariot soaring into the skies. One seer noted that

The creative power of my will and the intuitions of my heart
exert their effective force;
they long with love and fly forth to all regions.
No other source of comfort than these may be found.
I direct my hopes and yearnings to the gods.[72]

Returning to the skies through the force of the poet's imagination, the many words of the poetic songs pleased the gods' hearts and returned to their unified source in the highest heavens, namely, to the realm of the universal poetess, the divine Vāc herself.

It was the Vedic poet, then, who listened to the many disconnected syllables of the "tumultuous, chaotic flood" of existence and, putting them together in new and original ways, reconstructed Vāc's primordial and once-unified Word, which stood as their source. Doing so, the poet transformed chaos into order. The poetic imagination therefore served a cosmogonic function.

In this, its cosmogonic function, the poet's imagination was similar to that of the gods. We might repeat these lines to Mitra and Varuṇa from the *Ṛgveda*:

O Mitra and Varuṇa, just as you separated Ṛta from unholy chaos
by means of your own mental dexterity and
with your own wisdom's mental power,
so, too, with our visionary insight
we have seen the golden one
in the seats wherein you live,
not with our [normal] way of thinking or with our [physical] eyes,
but through the eyes which *soma* gives us.[73]

The Vedic priest's sacerdotal imagination served a similarly reconstructive purpose. The Vedic sacrificial worldview centered to large extent on the idea that, while the dismemberment of Puruṣa's or Prajāpati's universal form did indeed give rise to the many things of the world, it did so at the expense of the integrity of the primordial wholeness itself. But then, in imagining the shape of Prajāpati's body in their minds and then projecting that mental image outward onto the ritual stage in the form of a single and whole person whose various limbs are all properly in place, Vedic priests liturgically reunified God's body. The *Śatapatha Brāhmaṇa* therefore notes that the ritual stage "is indeed [Prajāpti's] own self!"[74]

Ceremonially placing various ritual implements in their proper place, Vedic priests put the various parts of Prajāpati's broken body back together again. We remember an expression of this idea in the following instructions from the *Śatapatha Brāhmaṇa*:

> The same Prajāpati who became broken is this very fire we now build [on the altar]. That very firepan over there which lies empty before being heated up is just like Prajāpati as he lay collapsed, the vital air and living energy having drained out of him and the food having flowed from him.
>
> He [the priest] warms it [the empty pot] on the fire, just as the gods once warmed him [Prajāpati]. When the fire rises around it, thus heating it, then that same vital breath which went out from him comes back to him, and he [the priest] puts it back into him [Prajāpati]; when he places the gold plate [near the fire] and wears it, he puts in [Prajāpati] the living energy which had left him; when he puts kindling sticks [into the fire] he puts into [Prajāpati] that very food which had flowed out of him.[75]

Activities undertaken by means of the ritual imagination thus healed the brokenness of life. The Brāhmaṇas speak of such activities as restorative of universal vitality as a whole. A contemporary scholar has written that the ritual reconstruction of Prajāpati's body involved "collecting together the luminous energy and life essence of all the emitted creatures, thereby simultaneously reuniting the dispersed creation into a reconstituted unity and reinvigorating Prajāpati who is that unity."[76]

Vedic priests participated in the reunification of the sacred cosmos. Upaniṣadic sages, for their part, came to see that this unity had never truly been broken. For them, the one Self of the universe stood eternally and unwaveringly within all of the many apparently different things in the world. We have read these lines from the *Brahmabindhu Upaniṣad*:

> There is only a single Being-Self.
> It lives in each and every being.

Uniform, yet multiform,
it appears like the [reflection of the single] moon
in [the many ripples of] a pond.[77]

The great insight of the Upaniṣads, then, was that the foundation of one's own particular being residing within one's own soul was identical to the expansive, single Self which gives rise to and supports the universe as a whole.

According to the Upaniṣads, people have somehow forgotten or become blind to the essential and invaluable Self, which resides within. In their ignorance they pursue ephemeral pleasures in the world of objects that never fully satisfy. The *Kaṭha Upaniṣad* is quite forceful in this regard:

The pleasant is one thing; the good is [quite] another.
Both, of different aim, bind a person.
Of these two, it is well for him who grabs hold of the good,
for he who chooses the pleasant is never fulfilled.

Dwelling in the midst of ignorance,
impressed with their own wisdom and thinking themselves wise,
deluded fools run here and there
like blind people led by someone who is himself blind.[78]

Upaniṣadic sages therefore taught their students to turn their attention away from the vagaries and uncertainties of the outside world to concentrate instead on the realities of the inner world, to know the Knower rather than the known. Such inward attention necessarily involved the control of the mind's tendency to wander. This is the lesson of the *Śvetāśvatara Upaniṣad*:

Holding one's body steady with the three upper parts straight,
and bringing the senses and the mind into the heart,
a wise person should cross over all the rivers of anxiety
with the boat of the *brahman.*

Having controlled one's breathing here [in the body] . . .
let one restrain the mind without distraction,
the way a chariot is yoked to wild horses.
One should practice meditation in a hidden retreat.[79]

Practicing meditation, the contemplative formed mental images of divine realities "to be seen within" (*antarlakṣya*). Such an inward imagination allowed the contemplative to become absorbed in the divine presence. At times, that vision consisted of the many and various deities once regarded as living in the external world but now known to reside within the contemplative's own being. As an example of such vision we remember the *Subāla Upaniṣad*'s lesson that

> in the middle of the heart is a fleshy, red lump. In it a small, fine white lotus blooms, spreading its petals in different directions. There are ten openings in the heart. In them reside the vital breaths. When [the contemplative] is yoked . . . to the downward breath he sees the heavenly nymphs, spirits, and angels. When yoked to the upward breath he sees the world of heaven and the gods Skandha, Jayanta, and others. When yoked to the balanced breath he sees the heavenly world and treasures of all sorts.[80]

Sometimes that vision is of only one form of the divine, as in the case of the following instructions from the *Varāha Upaniṣad.*

> Keeping his neck and body straight and his mouth closed, a wise person should meditate unwaveringly on [the Ātman] . . . in the middle of the seed [within the heart]. His mind calm, he should see with his [mental] eyes the nectar flowing there. . . . He should meditate on the Ātman as the resplendent goddess [Śrī] and as being bathed in nectar.[81]

That vision is sometimes said to become increasingly bright. We will recall the *Maṇḍalabrāhmaṇa Upaniṣad*'s notice that

> by practicing inward vision, he sees a sparkling light in the shape of in endless sphere. This alone is Brahman. . . . Here are its signs. First, it is seen to look like a star. Then it looks like a dazzling diamond. Then, it looks like the full moon; then, like the brilliance of nine gems; then, like the fullness of the midday sun; then, like the flame of Agni. All these he sees, in order.[82]

Sometimes that vision was of a geometrical shape. Here is how the *Maṇḍalabrāhmaṇa Upaniṣad* describes one such practice:

> [One imagines] a star in the middle of the two eyebrows. Being Brahman, it is of the spiritual resplendence of absolute Truth, Consciousness and Bliss. One sees it by means of three types of inner vision. . . . It has the radiance of the sun.[83]

At the deepest levels, however, the contemplative saw only divine splendor. In this regard we will recall the following passage:

> Centering his mind on an inward image . . . with eyes half-closed and with a firm mind . . . one becomes aware of that which is of the form of light, that which is free of all external [qualities], that which is luminous: the supreme truth, the sublime. . . . Just as camphor is subsumed by fire and salt is dissolved in water, so too the mind becomes absorbed in the truth.[84]

In such an absorbed, inner vision, the contemplative seeker of truth abandoned his attachment to the multiform world of objects known through the physical senses. Through the technique of *dhyāna* that *yogī* came instead to recognize the formless, divine presence already living within the soul.

Like the Vedic poet who heard the eternal voice of the goddess Vāc in the many rhythms of life and, gathering together diverse words in a new and fresh way, sang songs that returned to their heavenly source; like the Vedic priest who collected the different parts of Prajāpati's broken body and, gathering them together, ritually refashioned that fractured form into a single body once again: so, too, the Vedic contemplative converted an existence dominated by alienation and fear into one filled with the realization of the timeless and infinite Brahman, which stands as the sole foundation of all that is. Knowing the Absolute, the *yogī* was free from the cycles of disappointment and death.

Such is the power of the constructive imagination, which returned the poet, priest, and contemplative to an experience of universal wholeness. The return to wholeness was a conversion to the integrity of being, an integrity in which the alternations of existence, particularly of life and death, lost their power. The constructive imagination, which subsumed death within the integrity of being as a whole, led finally to an experience of immortality. Thus, the poet could sing,[85]

> O Pavamāna, place me in the deathless and undecaying world
> on which the light of heaven is set
> and unchanging brilliance ever shines. . . .
> In the third region, the heaven of heavens,
> where lucid words are made of light:
> make me immortal;

the ritualist could proclaim,[86]

> He who knows [the ritual] thus gains victory over repeated death. Death has no hold over him;

and the contemplative could rejoice in saying,[87]

Truly, he who knows that supreme Brahman
becomes that Brahman. . . .
He goes beyond sorrow; he goes beyond evil.
Freed from the knots that bind the secret place [of the heart],
he becomes immortal!

Both in scope and in function, the constructive imagination thus encompasses the creative and revelatory imagination. True, the imagination forms new "worlds" for the poet, priest, and contemplative; that is, it gives those specialists a new way of seeing things (we remember the original meaning of the word *loka*, "world," which referred to a place where one could see clearly). But it does so by rearranging, recognizing, responding to, retrieving, or returning to that divine and preexisting truth which—though hidden, perhaps—is already present. The imagination allows such a recognition and a return because it reveals what was experienced as the truth itself. Such revelation takes place within the sensitive and appreciative heart and is given articulate verbal, dramatic, and contemplative image by the discerning and articulate mind. But revelation must lead to transformation if it is to be of any effect in one's life. The constructive imagination transforms insight into realization.

RELIGION AND THE RETURN TO UNITY

We might notice the number of words beginning with the prefix *re-* in the preceding paragraph: the imagination served to recognize, reveal, respond to, rearrange, retrieve, and return to divine truths. Though they are English words, the language here is consistent with an important idea in Vedic thought.

As we have seen in virtually all the Vedic texts from which we have read in the preceding chapters, Vedic seers recognized in the universe about them suggestions of a metaphysical pulse or cycle of being that resonates in the existential rhythms of life in the human world. Said briefly, that pulse reverberates like this: in the beginning is the One. Then, in a procreative yet fracturous process of differentiation, the One becomes the many, which at once veil and reveal their unified source. Finally, in a (re)constructive process that heals the brokenness of being, the many return to the One.

Throughout each of its stages, the whole process by which one comes to know the harmony of the One within the often dissonant clamor of the many involves the power of the imagination. It is through the imagination that the world comes into existence. It is through the imagination that such a world is seen to have meaning and significance. And it is through the imagination that one comes to know one's significant place in that meaningful cosmos.

Because of its reunitive function, we could find no better term in English to describe this process than the word *religion*. Although its derivation remains somewhat uncertain, most likely the word comes to us from the Latin *religiō*, which refers to the bond that links the gods and the human community. The term *religiō* itself probably comes from the Latin *relig(āre)*, from *re-*: "back, again," and *lig-*: to "tie, bind." The term *religion* literally refers, then, to a process of "relinking" something that was once joined but has somehow become broken or separated.

If we transfer the literal meaning of the English word *religion* to the Vedic context, we may say that "religion" is that process which relinks the human spirit with the divine truths or with ultimate reality itself, with which it once was in some way joined. From the Vedic perspective, that eternal universal principle and unified ground of being nevertheless still lie within the befuddling complexity and swirling changes of the objective world as it is experienced by the senses. We see in Vedic thought the idea that the world as normally experienced is not truly an integrated whole. Rather, it is a disintegrated chaos in which the many creatures live their lives dissociated not only from each other but also from their unified, creative source.

Existence in the world of multiplicity was seen as one of fear, competition, and loss. Such existence may have been soothed occasionally by the fleeting victory over a rival or the passing gratification of one's pleasures and wishes. But, just as the night followed the day, such momentary clarity soon dissolved once again into confusion. The demons resumed their struggle with the gods; the creatures formed by Prajāpati's broken body turned on one another and "ate each other';'[88] foolish people seeking happiness in the objective world "walked into the snare of widespread death."[89]

Life in such a world was characterized by brokenness and doubt. According to one seer, even the lonely sun in the sky questioned the meaning of its own existence. Noting that "alone, he has risen," that poet then heard the sun admit that "'I do not know just what this is that I am!'"[90] In a like manner, the Upaniṣadic seeker pondered the meaning of his life with the haunting cry, "Who am I?"[91]

The sages of the Vedic community, however, saw things differently. The visionary pierced the troubling mysteries of that confusing world by means of his ability to see the gods and goddesses hidden within all things. Opening his heart and mind to the presence of the divine, the inspired poet heard the sublime Word within the very cacophony of existence. Replacing together the many dissonant syllables of that chaotic noise in a new and fresh way, the bard formed verbal images and sang those prayerful songs to the hidden deities. Their words soared "upward into the heavens" like "birds of golden hue."[92]

It is significant that Vedic sages referred to such imaginative utterances as *satya*, "true," because they were *ṛtavāk*;[93] they were "artful words" because they gave voice to Ṛta. Those verbal images returned to their original home with the gods. One poet told the gods that he has returned his song to them like a shepherd returns lost sheep to their owner: "like a herdsman, I have brought you hymns of praise."[94] Their original home was said to be beyond the structures of time and space. As Vena Bhārgava sang:[95]

> Rising to the high realm of Ṛta,
> bands of poets lick the sweet tastes of deathlessness.
> Knowing [its formless] form, poets longed to meet [it].

In sending their songs to the "high realm of Ṛta," poets thus came to live in intimacy with the gods and goddesses; for, as one was to sing, "The gods will know me just as I am!"[96] If the deities came to know the poets, poets likewise came to know those divine artists: "We have attained the light!" they exclaimed. "We have found the gods!"[97]

We note, again, suggestions here of a circular or pulsating process. The dynamics of creation begin when Vāc utters forth her divine Word, which is then refracted as the personalities of the various gods and goddesses of the Vedic pantheon, who therefore serve as diverse images of that universal artfulness. The deities then form the world in their own image, through the process of divine imagination. But to normal eyes the world thus created is a broken world, a multiverse of unconnected objects. It was the poet who, through his ability to hear the single and ineffable divine Word within all manifest names, could see through this fracturous and dissipated multiverse and know, instead, its truth as a universe in which all things fit together in an interconnected totality; and it was the poet who then formed and sang forth verbal images of that unified truth.

According to Brāhmaṇa literatures, the Vedic priest who knew the correct words to sing during the ritual similarly "returned" to the transcendent and timeless realm of the One that gave rise to all the multiplicity in the world. As we recall, the *Śatapatha Brāhmaṇa* tells of the *brahman*'s creating the many gods and having them rise into the heavens above, where it joined them in those eternal realms. Descending then into the celestial, atmospheric, and finally earthly realms again, the *brahman* became the many names and forms of the manifest world.[98] The visionary priest who truly understands those various names and forms thereby truly understands Brahman itself.[99]

> Truly, these [name-and-form] are therefore the two great forces of *brahman*. Therefore, he who knows these two great forces of the *brahman* becomes himself a great force.
>
> Truly, these are indeed the two great manifestations of the *brahman*. Therefore, he who knows these two great manifestations of the *brahman* himself becomes a great manifestation. . . .

> In the beginning, even the gods were mortal. It was only when they came to possess [knowledge of] the *brahman* that they became immortal. Therefore, when he [the priest] offers a libation to the mind—form being mind, since it is by means of the mind that one recognizes form—he thus obtains form. And when he offers a libation to the Word—name being the Word since it is by means of the Word that he is able to speak names—he thus obtains Name. Truly, as far as this whole [universe] reaches: all this he obtains. And since the Whole is imperishable, he thus gains undying merit and the immortal world.

Like that of the poet's songs, the force of the ritualist's sacralizing drama returned finally to that celestial harmony from which it originally came:

> By effective power of the ritual offering founded in the highest realm, and established in universal harmony by means of universal harmony, [our ancestral fathers], though mortal themselves, gained immortal places in those higher regions that so firmly support the heavens.[100]

The Āraṇyakas present other images of the return to universal wholeness. Thus, just as the Vedic poet helped put the original and unutterable Word back together again, so too the Vedic priest helped put Prajāpati's broken body back together again. Establishing the sacred space of the ritual stage in the image of the divine Person, Vedic priests thus imaginatively re-membered the dismembered body of God. Doing so, they helped Prajāpati regain his "self" (*ātman*). As the *Taittirīya Āraṇyaka* proclaims, "That very Prajāpati, having dissipated himself, reentered it with his *ātman*!"[101] Doing so, the priest reformed a world of harmony from the chaos of existence. Joining the lineage of the gods, who themselves had gained a sense of identity and purpose by performing the ritual, the priests similarly established a meaningful world by performing that same ritual.

Like the Vedic priest who ritually re-membered Prajāpati's dismembered body, the contemplative sage similarly "remembered" the divine Self. He did so by means of his inner vision—his "insight"—gained through the process of contemplative inner vision. Envisioning the gods deep within his own heart, he reversed the fragmenting process by which the imagination formed the many and diverse apparent objects of the external world. Refining that inward vision, he came to see that even the many gods and goddesses residing within his own heart were reflections of the single and unifying Brahman. The inner and the outer world thus came to be reunited through the meditator's insight into the essential unity of being. As the *Maitrī Upaniṣad* says,

He who dwells within the fire,
he who dwells within the heart,
who dwells within the sun:
He is One.
Truly, the person who knows this
attains the oneness of the One.[102]

The contemplative vision allowed the meditator to know the universal Self—ultimate reality itself—as *sarva*: the "All," the "universe" in its wondrous complexity yet sublime integrity. The *Muṇḍaka Upaniṣad* teaches that

He who has knowledge and who
strives by means [of strength, attentiveness, and austerity]:
his Ātman enters the abode of Brahman.
Having attained him, the visionaries who are fulfilled in their
  knowledge—
they who have disciplined and prepared themselves and
who are dispassionate and serene;
having attained the omnipresent wholeness that is everywhere:
joined to the soul, the wise enter the All itself.[103]

Thus realizing the fundamental identity of Ātman and Brahman, and of Brahman and the All, the Upaniṣadic visionary sage could answer the plaintive cry—"Who am I?"[104]—with the powerful affirmation, *aham brahmāsmi*: "I am Brahman!"[105]

Such an affirmation was not an expression of megalomania. For the "I" which stands as the subject of such a realization is not a particular creature that experiences the world through the dimensions of time and space and under the controlling laws of causation. Rather, the "I" here is that infinite and timeless unified Subject that subsumes and gives rise, not only to the world as object, but also to "you" and "me" as temporal and spatial embodiments of that Presence. The "I" of the phrase "I am Brahman" cannot be limited to any particular objective form. Perhaps this is why the sage Yājñavalkya was so careful to repeat over and over again that the Absolute is *neti neti*: "not this, not that."[106] The Self is "not this" and "not that" because the single Subject of the universe is within *all* things. The Self is paradoxically everything and nothing at once. Therefore, Upaniṣadic sages do not contradict themselves when they say that the Self is "not this, not that" while also teaching that the Self subsumes and embraces all things. If one text can say that Brahman is revealed in all forms, as the *Chāndogya Upaniṣad* does in this passage:

> Encompassing all works, encompassing all desires, encompassing all fragrances, encompassing this whole world, the silent, the unmoved: this is the Self of mine within the heart. This is Brahman.[107]

another can say this:

> [Like] the sharp razor's edge, difficult to tread,
> this difficult path is this: so poets declare.
> What is without sound, without touch, without form, imperishable;
> similarly, [what is] without taste, abiding, without fragrance,
> without beginning, without end, higher than the great, constant:
> By discerning That, one is liberated from the jaws of death.[108]

According to another text,

> That person who remains awake even while sleepers sleep
> and fashions all desires: that, truly, is the pure.
> That is Brahman.
> That, indeed, is the immortal: on it rest all worlds.
> None can transcend it.
> In truth, this [Self] is That![109]

Because it is the timeless essence standing as the foundation of all forms, the Absolute itself in a sense has no form. One therefore cannot behold the Absolute with one's normal way of seeing things:

> Neither above, nor across,
> nor in the middle has one held him.
> There is no image of him
> whose name is Great Glory.
> His form is not to be seen.
> No one sees him with the eye.
> Those who, in their heart and mind,
> know him as abiding in the heart:
> they become immortal.[110]

The teachers whose lessons form the *Bahvṛcā Upaniṣad* preferred to speak of the One Self as the universal Goddess:

> She alone is Ātman. . . . She is Brahman. . . . It has been declared that "Brahman is consciousness" and that "I am Brahman." The texts have said that "Thou art That," and "This Ātman is Brahman," and "I am

> Brahman," and "Brahman alone am I." But She who is contemplated as "That which I Am" . . . is the beautiful great Goddess . . . the Virgin, the Mother, the Lady of the Universe.[111]

The visionary who thus proclaims "I am Brahman" is not really saying "I am God." Rather, he or she is declaring that "God is I." From the Vedic perspective, there is only one Self who can truly be known as "I." That is the eternal and infinite Self of the universe.

One of Vedic India's greatest insights, then, was that the source of people's longing to know ultimate reality was in fact that very reality itself. The very fact that the human heart yearned to know the divine at all was in itself a reflection or expression of the presence of the divinity within the heart itself. The Self reveals itself precisely in the means by which one looked for it: the truth resided not only in the finding, but also in the means by which one seeks.

IMAGINATION AS RELIGION

We return now to the English term, *religion*: "that which relinks." Religion is literally a reunitive process. It is that means by which the broken world becomes whole again. As a process undertaken by human beings, religion involves practices, techniques, and disciplines. There are no words in the Vedic literatures that translate the English *religion* literally. Such terms as *vrata*—"action undertaken as an expression of one's responsibility to the whole, obligation"—suggest the moral dimension of religion. Later Hindu traditions were to teach the central importance of *dharma*, a classical Sanskrit word derived from the Vedic *dharman* and which means literally "that which supports" the whole. Those later traditions were also to maintain the importance of *sādhana*: "disciplined action that leads to fulfillment," that is, "that which perfects and completes" the whole.

But the terms *vrata*, *dharma* and *sādhana* do not, of themselves, imply the specifically restorative or reunitive sense of the English word *religion*. Perhaps the closest Sanskrit word signifying both the reunitive process and the techniques which drive that process would be *yoga*, a term that was to gain much prestige in subsequent Hindu traditions. Translated broadly, *yoga* refers to a method, technique, means, or manner by which a goal is attained. In this sense, *yoga* is disciplined activity expressing an effective process. More specifically, *yoga* refers to the disciplined performance of some sort that leads to a suitable and fitting "bringing together" of two or more things. The word *yoga* derives from a Sanskrit verbal root that means "fasten together." (Its closest English cognate is the word *yoke*, but it is also related to the word *join*.) We saw a related word (*yukta*: "joined to") in a line recently quoted from the Upaniṣads, *dhīrā yuktātmānas sarvam evāviśanti*: "joined to the Self, the wise enter the All itself."[112]

The process of *yoga* involves the bringing back together of what once was united and has somehow become divided. *Yoga* allows a healing of that which has become fractured; a remerging of that which has become broken; a converging of that which has become divergent; a returning to consonance of that which has become dissonant. In other words, *yoga* is a "[re-] linking;" *yoga* is *religion.*

As we have seen, in the Vedic world the imagination itself serves a similarly reintegrative function. The whole chain of creation, revelation, and cosmogonic reunification performed by the divine and human imagination was thus essentially a *religious* process. The gods and goddesses—brilliant artists—created the wondrous and mysterious miracles of existence through the power of the divine imagination. The imagination allowed visionary poets to see the deities' hidden form and to hear their sublime words and to fashion pleasing songs of praise in their honor. Doing so, they joined the lineage of the gods and ultimately rejoined them in the highest heavens. It was through the ritual imagination that Vedic priests ceremonially reconstructed the broken body of God and returned the divine soul to that fractured form. They also (re)joined the divine lineage. So, too, it was through the imagination that the contemplative sage came to know the fulfilling presence of the eternal and infinite within his or her heart. Doing so, such a inner seer relinked his or her own being with the very Beingness of the universe as a whole.

Faced with the multiplicity of being and thus the possible fracture and brokenness of life, the imagination envisioned and revitalized a world that had become disintegrated and deadened. It saw meaning in what otherwise was meaningless; shimmering light from within the deep darkness; wholeness within brokenness; the possibility of extraordinary sublimity despite the sometimes difficult struggles of life in a complicated world. It did so because it could see how things were connected, as it were; that is to say, it could envision how things fit together, or potentially could fit together. The imagination saw unity within multiplicity. It saw order within or behind or despite chaos. In fact, it often was in the most discordant or debilitating experiences that the imagination saw into the deeper significance of life as a whole. Even in the uncertainty of existence, even in the changes and transformations of life, even in the ubiquity of death, the imagination saw or sought to see reflections of a deeper, unified, and unifying harmony of being. Doing so, the imagination served a fundamentally religious function.

In the Vedic world, the imagination therefore functions as *religion*; for in seeing and expressing hidden truths within the apparent chaos of life, the imagination relinks the human spirit to the Absolute, and thus to the wondrous mystery of the artful universe itself. The effect of such a *religious* process in which the human spirit returns to its sublime source seems to be quite powerful. Describing the realization of the immediacy of the "inner Self of all things, the one Controller who makes his one form manifest in many ways," Vedic sages declare that "This is it! This is the highest, ineffable bliss."[113]

Notes

PREFACE

1. I am aware that, to some, the attempt by a Westerner to define and explain the Veda may sound presumptuous. In recent years a number of scholars have openly questioned the intentions of Western scholarship on Indian thought and argued that it is ripe with what has come to be known as Orientalism. According to these critics, Western scholars have taken it upon themselves to "represent" Eastern thought, but in doing so have actually superimposed Western ideas and values of colonial domination onto the East and thereby deprived the East of its own authentic self-understanding. The founding voice of such criticism is that of Edward Said, who in his book *Orientalism* (New York: Vintage, 1979) argues that European scholars have not really tried to understand the East; rather, they have prescribed the way in which the people of the Orient are to understand themselves. The Orientalist's assumption, according to Said, is that (quoting Karl Marx) "they cannot represent themselves; they must be represented" (see the opening epigraph to Said's *Orientalism*). Said is particularly critical of philology, which according to him reflects a Western ideology of domination and in which he sees "an unmistakable aura of power" (p. 132). Another critic, Ronald Inden, maintains that the "Orientalist constructions of India" have taken from Indians "the power to represent themselves" and thus fostered in Indians a sense of alienation (see Inden, "Orientalist Constructions of India," *Modern Asian Studies* 29 [1986], pp. 401–46, esp. p. 402). Similarly, Sheldon Pollack has argued that the study of India by Western scholars has had less to do with India than with forces of domination and control (see Pollack, "Deep Orientalism?: Notes on Sanskrit and Power beyond the Raj," in *Orientalism and the Postcolonial Predicament: Perspectives on South Asia*, edited by Carol A. Breckenridge and Peter van der Veer [Philadelphia: University of Pennsylvania Press, 1993], pp. 76–133).

I offer my interpretation here with humility, respect, and appreciation. I hope that my work does not encourage in Indians a sense of "alienation." I also tend to feel that, in the anti-Orientalist critique of Western scholarship, there is a danger of what Wilhelm Halbfass calls "reverse Eurocentrism." If "the West has imposed its methods of research, its values and modes of orientation, its categories of understanding . . . upon the Indian tradition and alienated the Indians from what they really were and are," Halbfass has written, "it now takes the liberty to remove such superimpositions, to release the Indians into their authentic selfhood, to restore their epistemic and axiological sovereignty. This self-abrogation of Eurocentrism is at the same time its ultimate affirmation." See Halbfass, *Tradition and Reflection: Explorations in Indian Thought* (Albany: State University of New York Press, 1991), p. 12.

INTRODUCTION

1. For an argument on the Veda as the foundation of Hinduism, see Brian K. Smith, *Reflections on Resemblance, Ritual and Religion* (New York: Oxford University Press, 1989), pp. 3–29. Smith argues that "Hinduism is the religion of those humans who create, perpetuate, and transform traditions with legitimizing reference to the authority of the Veda" (pp. 13–14). For a lively discussion of the way in which the Veda has been used to serve various aesthetic, social, cultural, and political purposes, see the various articles in *Authority, Anxiety, and Canon: Essays in Vedic Interpretation*, edited by Laurie L. Patton (Albany: State University of New York Press, 1994). On the legacy of and attitudes toward the Veda in classical Indian philosophical schools, see Wilhelm Halbfass, *Tradition and Reflection: Explorations in Indian Thought* (Albany: State University of New York Press, 1991), pp. 23–50.

2. The phrase *encompassing whole* here translates the Sanskrit *sarva*, which may otherwise be translated as "everything together" or "the All." For discussion of the idea of *sarva*, see Jan Gonda, "Reflections on *Sarva*- in Vedic Texts," *Indian Linguistics* 16 (November 1955), pp. 53–71. By referring to the idea of a "multiverse" here, I am trying to represent the Vedic experience of a chaotic world characterized by an unbridled, fragmented multiplicity (*bahutva*) and discordant unrelated variety (*nānātva*). Such a world is *pṛthak*, that is, characterized by what Smith calls an "excess of differentiation." For discussion of these latter concepts, see Smith, *Reflections on Resemblance, Ritual and Religion*, p. 52.

3. Scholarship tends to hold that the etymology of the word *ṛta* returns to the Indo-European **ar-* , which, in its transitive forms, meant "fit together, unite," and in its transitive forms, "be fit, be proper." See Julius Pokorny, *Indogermanisches etymologisches Wörterbuch*, 2 volumes (Bern: A. Francke, 1959), volume 1, p. 55. Other Sanskrit words said to be derived from the same Indo-European root include the adverb *aram*, "suitably, properly, fitting," and the noun *ara*, which in the *Ṛgveda* refers to the spoke of a wheel, that is, that which holds a spinning wheel together. (The asterisk that precedes an Indo-European verbal root indicates that such a form has been reconstructed by applying linguistic laws in reverse. Thus, the Indo-European **ar-* does not appear in any texts; it has been extrapolated from evidence provided by the variety of Indo-European languages.)

4. So, for example, Heinrich Lüders has translated one of the meanings of *ṛta* in German as *Wahrheit*. See Lüders, *Varuṇa und das Ṛta*, volume 2 of *Varuṇa* (Göttingen: Vandenhoeck & Ruprecht, 1959), pp. 415-20. Such a translation is appropriate, especially given the fact that Vedic texts use the word's antonym, *anṛta* ("falsehood, lie"), almost interchangeably with *asatya*, "untrue," and often associate *anṛta* with such terms as *druh* (which as a noun means "injurer" or "foe," and as an adjective means "injurious, harmful, hostile, fiendish"), *vṛjina* ("crooked" and thus "not true" and "deceitful, false"), and *yātu* ("wayward" and thus "wicked, demonic"). If Ṛta is the normative principle of order that organizes and supports reality as a whole, then *anṛta* characterizes the chaos that fractures or destroys that universal order.

5. The linguistic link between the Indo-European **ar-* and the Sanskrit *ṛta* lies in the Sanskrit verbal root *ṛ-*, which means "go in a fitting manner" or "move smoothly." Viewed from this perspective, Ṛta is thus a principle of harmony in which all things move together smoothly and support each other in a fitting manner.

6. For etymologies of these English words derived from the Indo-European **ar-*, see *The American Heritage Dictionary of the English Language*, edited by William Morris (Boston: Houghton Mifflin, 1981), p. 1506.

7. Maurice Bloomfield felt so strongly about this that he wrote that the notion of Ṛta is "unquestionably the best conception that has been elaborated by" the Vedic tradition. See Bloomfield, *The Religion of the Veda* (New York: G. P. Putnam's Sons, 1908), p. 126.

8. The derivations of the Sanskrit *veda* and the English *wise, wisdom, idea, vision, view,* and *wit* all return finally to the Indo-European **weid-*, to "see." See Morris, ed., *The American Heritage Dictionary of the English Language*, p. 1548, and Pokorny, *Indogermanisches etymologisches Wörterbuch*, p. 1125, under *u(e)di-*.

9. The Indo-European **weid-* led to the Sanskrit verbal root *vid-*, meaning to "know, perceive, understand" and thus to "experience, make known, teach." We see a similar reference to a special kind of wisdom derived from such an ability in the meaning of a number of classical Sanskrit nouns and adjectives linguistically related to *veda* through the verbal root *vid-*. Such words include *vitti*, understanding, consciousness; *vidyā*, knowledge, learning, scholarship, philosophy, practical art; *vidu*, intelligent; *vidura*, knowing, clever, skilled; *vidvala*, clever, artful; and *vidvas*, a learned person, sage.

10. Of many examples, see *Māṇḍūkya Upaniṣad* 9–12; *Maitrī Upaniṣad* 6.17.

11. See *Ṛgveda* 3.61.7.

12. See *Ṛgveda* 5.63.6.

13. See Jan Gonda, *Four Studies in the Language of the Veda* (s'Gravenhage: Mouton, 1959), pp. 129, 133.

14. See Sāyaṇa's commentary on *Ṛgveda* 1.144.1, 3.27.7, 5.30.6, and 5.63.6. The term *śakti* does not appear in the *Ṛgveda*, although the verbal root *śak-*, to "be able," stands as the basis of a number of words.

15. Otto Böhtlingk and Rudolf Roth translated *māyā* as "Kunst, ausserordentliches Vermögen, Wunderkraft" (art, extraordinary ability, wondrous power). See Böhtlingk and Roth, *Sanskrit-Wörterbuch*, 7 volumes (Petrograd: Kaiserlichen Akademie der Wissenschaften, 1868), volume 5, p. 732. Sir Monier Monier-Williams rendered the word as "art, wisdom, extraordinary or supernatural power." See Monier-Williams, *A Sanskrit-English Dictionary* (Oxford: Clarendon Press, 1899; reprint edition, 1974), p. 811.

16. See, for example, *Ṛgveda* 3.20.3, which describes the many forms of the god of fire as "possessing *māyā*."

17. *Ṛgveda* 1.144.1.

18. The word translated as "hymn" here would usually be the Sanskrit *sūkta* ("that which has been eloquently sung"). When such a song was directed or offered to any particular deity it would also at times be known variously as *arka* (a "brilliant song of praise"), *ukta* ("that which has been put to voice"), *gīr* ("invocatory words in verse"). Such panegyric eulogies would also known by the related words *stuti*, *stotra*, and *stoma* ("celebratory song of praise, laud"). There were thus in Vedic India different types and functions of what we might call the sacred "hymn." In addition, Vedic poets referred to particular compositions as *vacas* and *chandas*—terms that can be translated roughly as "poetic utterance" and "pleasing chant," respectively. For discussion on the particular meaning of similar terms pertaining to the Vedic "hymn," see Paul Thieme, "Brahman," *Zeitschrift für der Deutschen Morgenländischen Gesellschaft* (Leipzig) 102 (1952), pp. 91-129.

19. Some Vedic traditions count 1,017 rather than 1,028 hymns in the *Ṛgveda*. The eleven hymns that constitute the difference form what has come to be known as the *Vālakhilya*. (Sāyaṇa did not interpret these hymns.) Those traditions that divide the *Ṛgveda* into ten books either do not count the *Vālakhilya* as part of the *Ṛgveda* proper, or append them to the *Ṛgveda* as a supplement of sorts. Some insert them after 8.48. Traditions that divide the *Ṛgveda* into eight books, on the other hand, do include those hymns. References in the following pages to hymns from the *Vālakhilya* will be so noted.

20. For discussions on the history of the Sanskrit language, see Louis Renou, *Histoire de la langue sanskrite* (Lyon: Editions IAC, 1956); Thomas Burrow, *The Sanskrit Language*, second edition (London: Faber and Faber, 1965).

21. For discussion of these hymns, see S. S. Bhawe, *The Soma Hymns of the Ṛgveda* (Baroda: University of Baroda, 1957–62).

22. See, for example, *Ṛgveda* 8.59.6 (*Vālakhilya*): "What in ancient times you, Indra and Varuṇa, gave the seers—revelation [*śruta*: literally, "that which has been heard"], thoughtful expression, and power of song, as well as places that the wise made, weaving the sacrifice—these I have seen through my spirit's fervent energy." Vedic texts, the content of which is believed to have been "heard" from the depths of eternity, are characterized therefore as *Śruti* ("revealed truth").

23. According to traditional Vedic exegetical thought, such truths are *apauruṣeya*, "not of human origin." The term *apauruṣeya* itself does not appear in the Vedic canon. We see it first in literatures of the Purva Mīmāṁsā, an orthodox Vedic philosophical tradition that sought to understand and explain the nature of the Veda as verbal revelation.

24. *Kaṭha Upaniṣad* 3.15.

25. These *Śruti* literatures (for the meaning of the word *Śruti*, see note 22) are to be distinguished from other authoritative religious texts in the Vedic tradition classed generally as *Smṛti*, "that which has been remembered." The latter literatures are so described because they consist of lessons fashioned by human teachers and memorized by their students. The *Smṛti* literatures consist of many and various sets of instructions and philosophical interpretations of Vedic teachings: the six *Vedāṅga*s ("ancillary texts"), which taught Vedic priests how to understand the Veda by establishing the proper pronunciation of its words,its meters and chants, the meaning and grammar of its language, and contours of the astrological and sacerdotal sciences; the *Sūtra* texts dealing with both public and domestic ritual practices; the *Śāstra*s (law books); the *Itihāsa*s (epic stories, primarily the *Mahābhārata* and *Rāmāyāṇa*); the *Purāṇa*s (encyclopedic collections of sacred myths); and the various *Nītiśāstras* (political treatises and teachings regarding morals and ethics).

26. With the exception of occasional references to interpretations given by Sāyaṇa, a fourteenth-century CE commentator on the Veda, the textual sources for the discussion in this book are all canonical texts. Given a more limited topic and scope, it would be appropriate to have included some discussion in this book of the ways in which the Vedic commentarial tradition has regarded the Veda. Indeed, some recent studies—one thinks, for example, of those presented in *Texts in Context: Traditional Hermeneutics in South Asia*, edited by Jeffrey R. Timm (Albany: State University of New York Press, 1992)—argue that Indian religious sensibilities can be fully understood only if one takes into account the various perspectives of its indigenous commentators. Students interested in a summary of the ways in which different commentators (*bhāṣyakāra*s, and other terms) from the Yājñika, Aitihāsika, Nairukta, Parivrājaka, Naidāna, and other schools of interpretation have approached the Veda should consult Ram Gopal, *The History and Principles of Vedic Interpretation* (New Delhi: Concept Publishing, 1983).

27. See my discussion of the "Hymn of Puruṣa" (*Ṛgveda* 10.90) in Chapter Four.

28. I refer to the descent of the unified sacred "Word" (Vāc) as it (she) falls from the heavens, breaking into many "syllables" as it (she) does so, thereby forming the world of multiplicity. Reference to this idea appears throughout the following pages. For a succinct summary, see Chapter Two.

29. According to an older Vedic myth, the expansive forces of life, personified by the free-flying demigods, the Ādityas, must constantly struggle against the constricting powers of death, personified by the demonic Dānavas. For discussion, see Chapter Three.

30. Jan Heesterman, *The Broken World of Sacrifice: An Essay in Ancient Indian Ritual* (Chicago: University of Chicago Press, 1993), p. 3.

31. Heesterman has argued this point at some length in his *The Broken World of Sacrifice*, especially pp. 7–85.

32. *Atharvaveda* 17.1.9.

33. *Atharvaveda* 10.7.10.

34. *Ṛgveda* 10.129.4.

35. Willard Johnson makes this point in his *Poetry and Speculation of the Ṛg Veda* (Berkeley and Los Angeles: University of California Press, 1980); see also Johnson, "On the Ṛg Vedic Riddle of the Two Birds in the Fig Tree (RV 1.164.20–22) and the Discovery of the Vedic Speculative Symposium," *Journal of the American Oriental Society* 96, number 2 (April–June 1976), pp. 248–58.

36. In saying this, I make a point that is similar in some ways to one made by Antonio T. de Nicolás. Drawing on concepts formalized by Edmund Husserl's phenomenology, de Nicolás has concluded that the seers of the *Ṛgveda* present a certain purpose or "intentionality" of consciousness and expression, namely, to order in a conscious way the structures of experience and to act in a dynamic way that is in keeping with such structures. According to de Nicolás, such an ordering of experience constitutes the construction of Vedic discourse, that is, of an "intentional life." De Nicolás sees in the *Ṛgveda* evidence of an "intentional life" consisting of four such structures of discourse, or "languages": the language of nonexistence (*asat*), the language of existence (*sat*), the language of images and sacrifice (*yajña*), and the language of embodied (*ṛta*) vision (*dhīḥ*). The four "dimensions" of the Vedic intentional life outlined by de Nicolás are similar in some ways to the poetic and ritual aspects of the Vedic world I discuss in Chapters Three and Four, below. We overlap most in regards to what de Nicolás calls the "language of embodied vision." My approach is different from his, however, in that, whereas he concentrates on the linguistic nature of visionary knowledge, I focus my attention on the visionary background of linguistic expression. See Antonio T. de Nicolás, *Meditations through the Ṛgveda: Four Dimensional Man* (Stony Brook, N.Y.: Nicolas Hays, Ltd., 1976), pp. 77–88 and 89–177. For related discussion, see de Nicolás, *Avatāra: The Humanization of Philosophy through the Bhagavad Gītā* (New York: Nicolas Hays, Ltd., 1976), pp. 344–49.

37. The derivation of the word *religion* returns to the Latin *re-ligāre*, to bind back together.

CHAPTER ONE

1. Relevant Sanskrit terms here would include *sahas* (translated here as "energy"), *ojas* ("glimmering creative power"), *varcas* ("splendor"), and *jyoti* ("sparkling light"). For discussion of such terms as *sahas, ojas*, and *varcas*, see Jan

Gonda, *Ancient-Indian ojas, Latin *augos and the Indo-European nouns in -es-/-os* (Utrecht: N. V. A. Oosthoek's Uitgevers Mij., 1952); Gonda, *Some Observations on the Relations between "Gods" and "Powers" in the Veda a propos of the Phrase 'Sūnuḥ Sahasaḥ'* ('s-Gravenhage: Mouton, 1957).

2. Compare the following, regarding the experience of light in Islam: "It is the divine light which brings things out from the darkness of nothing. . . . [T]o be visible signifies to exist; now, just as shadow adds nothing to the light, things are real only to the extent that they share in the light of Being." See Titus Burckhardt, *Art of Islam: Language and Meaning* (Westerhan, England: World of Islam Festival Trust, 1976), p. 77.

3. The wording and central idea of this sentence are similar to a passage in Raimundo Panikkar, *The Vedic Experience: Mantramañjarī* (Berkeley and Los Angeles: University of California Press, 1977), p. 314. Panikkar writes that the Vedic revelation is one of *līlā* ("play"), a later, classical Sanskrit word that does not appear in the Vedic texts themselves.

4. Namely, **deiw-* to "shine." See Morris, ed., *The American Heritage Dictionary of the English Language*, p. 1511; Pokorny, *Indogermanisches etymologisches Wörterbuch*, 2 volumes (Berne: A. Francke, 1956), volume 1, p. 183, under *dei-*.

5. In fact, like the Sanskrit *deva*, the English words *divine* and *deity* also derive from the Indo-European **deiw-*.

6. By saying that the Sanskrit word *deva* ("deity") derives from an Indo-European verbal root meaning to "shine," I seem to come close to restating Max Müller's theories regarding solar mythology and the linguistic origin of religion. I do not wish to imply a full endorsement of those theories, although they do seem to me to remain pertinent to some extent even a century after he first presented them and despite the rather harsh criticism they received from a number of scholars. This is not the place to revisit those theories at any length. A brief summary of them might, however, be appropriate.

Drawing on ideas presented by Franz Bopp, who in the early nineteenth century set out to demonstrate the common structure of Indo-European languages and thus prepared the stage for the development of the idea that all those languages derive from a common source, Müller came to feel that the names of the various deities from the Indo-European world were related to each other. The Indian god Varuṇa was equivalent to the Greek Uranos, for example, or the Indian gandharvas to the Roman centaurs. He felt that the major Indo-European deities were all personifications of solar and atmospheric phenomena. He was particularly intrigued by the apparent Indo-European fondness for deities of the dawn (Uṣas in India, Eos in Greece, and so on) and the revelatory and inspirational effect the emerging morning light had on the poetic heart and mythmaking imagination. But he saw in the gods personifications of other forces of nature as well: "Nearly all the leading deities of the Veda bear the unmistakable traces of their physical character. Their very names tell us that they were all in the beginning names of the great phenomena of nature, of fire, water, rain and storm, of sun and moon, of heaven and earth" (*Three Lectures on the Vedanta Philosophy* [London: Longmans, Green and Co., 1898], p. 25). For Müller, what originally were merely terms describing natural phenomena came to signify divine powers: *nomina* became *numina*. In other words, it was what Müller called a "disease of language" that gave rise to the gods and goddesses of the various Indo-European pantheons. Most obvious, to him, were the parallel names for the celestial male deity, "Sky Father": *Dyaus pitar* in India, *Zeuz pater* in Greece, *Jupiter* in Rome. "These words," he wrote, "are not mere words . . . but the oldest prayer of mankind" (*Introduction to the Science of Religion* [London: Longmans, Green and Co., 1897], p. 107). He felt that this was not so different from contemporary uses of language and its relationship to cosmic sensibilities. "What we call the Morning, the ancient[s] . . . called the Sun or the Dawn. . . . Why, every time we say 'Good morning,' we commit a solar myth" (*India: What Can It Teach Us? A Course of Lectures Delivered before the University of Cambridge* [London: Longmans, Green and Co., 1883], p. 216).

Similarly, the many and various myths of the Indo-European world, Müller felt, told of natural phenomena in personal form. Drawing on their own sensual experiences to describe such natural processes, the earliest Indo-European peoples spoke, not of the sun "rising in the morning" (the way we might metaphorically describe it), but rather as the "father" in the sky "chasing," or "pushing," or "kissing" his "daughter."

Müller's ideas regarding the solar and linguistic source of Indo-European mythology in general and in Vedic Indian mythology in particular caused much excitement in intellectual circles during his time. But they were not universally accepted. The anthropologist Andrew Lang was especially critical of Müller's ideas. Lang felt that the belief in divine spirits reflected a stage in the evolution of the human mind in which there was no sharp distinction perceived between the human and natural worlds. For Lang and his students, mythic narratives did not reflect a mythopoetic "disease of language" as much as they represented worldviews based on totemism, animism, and fetishism.

For more on Müller's ideas, see his *Natural Religion* (London: Longmans, Green and Co., 1892); *Contributions to the Science of Mythology*, 2 volumes (London: Longmans, Green and Co., 1897); *Lectures on the Origin and Growth of Religion* (London: Longmans, Green and Co., 1880); *Chips from a German Workshop*, 4 volumes (New York: Charles Scribner and Co., 1869). For discussions of his thought, see Johannes H. Voiqt, *Max Müller, The Man and His Ideas* (Calcutta: Firma K. L. Mukhopadhyay, 1967); Richard M. Dorson, "The Eclipse of Solar Mythology," in Thomas A. Sebeok, ed., *Myth: A Symposium* (Bloomington: Indiana University Press, 1958), pp. 25–63; Eric J. Sharpe, *Comparative Religion: A History* (New York: Charles Scribner's Sons, 1975), pp. 35–46; Jan de Vries, *Perspectives in the History of Religions*, translated by Kees W. Bolle (Berkeley: University of California Press, 1977), pp. 86–90.

7. *Ṛgveda* 8.28.1. See also 1.139.11, which refers to eleven celestial, eleven terrestrial, and three atmospheric deities.

8. *Ṛgveda* 10.52.6.

9. *Ṛgveda* 10.51.3.

10. *Ṛgveda* 10.127.1.

11. *Ṛgveda* 4.19.7.

12. *Ṛgveda* 1.32.1–2.

13. *Ṛgveda* 10.168.1.

14. Analysis of Vedic mythology often has revolved around the relationship of the gods to the natural elements. Mention has already been made in a previous note to F. Max Müller's theories regarding the solar nature of much Vedic religious imagery. Reference could also be made in this regard to Abel Bergaigne's *La réligion védique d'aprés les hymnes du Rig-Veda*, 3 volumes (Paris: F. Vieweg, 1878–83), translated by V. G. Parenjpe as *Abel Bergaigne's Vedic Religion*, 4 volumes bound together (Delhi: Motilal Banarsidass, 1979). Bergaigne's study concentrates especially on celestial and atmospheric imagery in Vedic myth, with a particular interest in the deities' gender. Recent Vedic scholarship has also stressed elements of Vedic religion that are not so closely aligned with the relationship between divinity and nature. For example, in a study on the Vedic deities known as the Ādityas—custodians more of the moral rather than of the natural order—Joel P. Brereton protests what he calls "the one-sided characterization—or rather caricature—of Vedic religion as merely 'nature worship.' The Vedic poets do express wonder and awe before the processes of nature, but this is far from all that they express." See Brereton, *The Ṛgvedic Ādityas*, American Oriental series, volume 63 (New Haven, Conn.: American Oriental Society, 1981), p. 328.

15. *Ṛgveda* 3.38.2.

16. *Ṛgveda* 1.68.5.

17. *Ṛgveda* 2.8.3–4.

18. *Ṛgveda* 5.8.5.

19. *Ṛgveda* 5.80.5.

20. The same Indo-European root **stā-*, "stand," which is the origin of the Latin *ex-sistere* and thus the English *exist*, serves as the basis for the Sanskrit verbal root *sthā-*, "stand, stay, station," on which are built such verbs as *anuṣṭhā-*, "perform, carry through"; *upasthā-*, "be present"; *prasthā-*, "arise, proceed, advance"; *pratiṣṭhā-*, "establish, found, make stable"; *saṁsthā-*, "bring to fulfillment, complete, accomplish". It also stands as the foundation of the Sanskrit noun *sthāna*, "ground, place, abode".

21. The words *established* and *stabilized* in this sentence are also related through the Indo-European **stā-* and thus to the Sanskrit *sthā-*.

22. *Ṛgveda* 3.38.2–3.

23. *Ṛgveda* 2.13.7.

24. *Ṛgveda* 6.17.6–7.

25. *Ṛgveda* 7.34.20.

26. See *Ṛgveda* 1.112.5.

27. For numerous examples of such feats performed by the Aśvins, see *Ṛgveda* 1.112 and 1.116–1.120.

28. *Ṛgveda* 3.61.7.

29. "Woven the air between the tree branches" translates *vaneṣu vy antarikṣaṁ tatāna*, which might more literally be rendered, "[he] spread out the atmosphere in the trees."

30. That is, lightning in the clouds.

31. In stating that it is Varuṇa who prevents the oceans from overflowing with all of the waters from the many rivers, verse 6 here supplies a response of sorts to the sentiment expressed elsewhere (*Ṛgveda* 5.47.5): "Wondrous, everyone, is this statement: even though rivers continually flow into it, the amount of water in the sea remains constant!"

32. The phrase *inner power* (verse 5) translates *svadhā*.

33. *Aitareya Brāhmaṇa* 5.32.

34. On *tapas* and related ideas, see Chauncy Blair, *Heat in the Rig Veda and Atharva Veda* (New Haven, Conn.: American Oriental Society, 1961); David Knipe, *In the Image of Fire: Vedic Experiences of Heat* (New Delhi: Motilal Banarsidass, 1975); Uma Vesci, *Heat and Sacrifice in the Vedas* (New Delhi: Motilal Banarsidass, 1985); Walter O. Kaelber, *Tapta Mārga: Asceticism and Initiation in Vedic India* (Albany: State University of New York Press, 1989).

35. *Ṛgveda* 10.129.3.

36. *Ṛgveda* 10.129.3c–4b.

37. The creative process itself, the means by which something comes into being, was known in Vedic Sanskrit by various terms. Many are built around the verbal root *bhū-* ("become, arise, come into existence") and many connote not only a sense of emergent being and thereby firmness and integrity but also of the attainment of prominence and thus of distinction, power, and authority: thus, *udbhū-*, "rise, come forth, spring up"; *prabhū-*, "emerge, become visible"; *vibhū-*, "expand, become manifest, appear, pervade"; *saṁbhū-*, "develop, come to completion, occur." As a noun, the word *bhū* refers to the earth itself (as do *bhūman* and *bhūmī*), which suggests the idea that the earth is real not simply because it has always been real, but because it has come to exist, to have been "built." (The English word *built* actually is related to *bhū* through the Indo-European **bheu-*, to "grow" and thus to "be.") Many other words signifying the creative process derive from the verbal root *kṛ-*, "make, produce, bring about, perform, realize," and thus carry a sense of an effective action that forms or constructs something. Readers will recognize the root in the word *karman*, which refers to the process of forming something through one's intentional actions, particularly, in the early Vedic context, the gods' and priests' dramatic construction of the world through

ritual performance. While, of course, different prefixes modify those verbs (*samākṛ-*, "bring together, arrange, construct"; *parikṛ-*, "embellish, adorn"; *prakṛ-* "put into effect, work out, execute"), various words built on this verbal root appear throughout the *Ṛgveda*, particularly when associated with acts of the gods and goddesses: the deities are described as those who in some way have made the various objects of the world, and indeed the world as a whole.

38. *Ṛgveda* 10.82.2.

39. *Ṛgveda* 3.38.2.

40. *Ṛgveda* 4.56.3.

41. *Ṛgveda* 6.7.3b–4.

42. *Ṛgveda* 1.62.12.

43. The term *kratu* is sometimes syntactically associated with the word *dakṣa*, which as a noun means "dexterity" and as an adjective means "dexterous." Other adjectives in the same constellation of meaning denoting imaginative skill include *apas*, "skilled in artistry," and *iśira*, "vigorous, quick." Those referring to shimmering brilliance include *dyumat*, "bright, shining," and thus "divine"; *bhadra*, "splendid"; *mayobhū*, "delightful."

44. These phrases all translate the Sanskrit *vibhu*.

45. See, for example, 10.84.6, which describes the god Manyu as possesed of the highest or most might of strength, *ābhūti*.

46. *Ṛgveda* 1.165.10. Indra's "all-pervading power" here translates *vibhu*.

47. We might mention here also the words *medhā* (a wise, mental formulation or construction), and *pracetas* (effective wisdom, creative consciousness), both of which imply the ability to give manifest form to what has been planned and designed within the mind.

48. Paul Regnaud was therefore correct in pointing out the important function of the divine imagination to bring the content of the gods' ideas into reality: "Les dieux (*devas*), en tant que lumineux ou lucides, sont intelligents, penseurs, et imaginatifs, et comme tels ils figurent et réalisent leurs conceptions" ("The gods, to the extent that they are luminous or lucid, are intelligent, thoughtful, and imaginative, and as such they give form to their ideas and bring them into existence"). See Regnaud, "La *māyā* et le pouvoir créateur des divinités védiques," *Revue de l'Histoire des Religions* (1885), p. 237.

49. *Ṛgveda* 3.61.7.

50. *Ṛgveda* 5.85.6.

51. In his analysis of *Ṛgveda* 5.30.6, the influential classical commentator on the Vedas, Sāyaṇa (1320–87), characterized *māyā* as *śakti*, the "power to accomplish."

In other places, as in his comment on *Ṛgveda* 1.144.1, Sāyaṇa characterizes *māyayā* ("by means of *māyā*") as *prajñayā* ("by means of wisdom"). See also Sāyaṇa's comment on *Ṛgveda* 5.63.3.

52. Examples would include *āmā-*, "build, construct"; *upamā-*, "put together"; *nimā-*, "shape, form"; *parimā-*, "fashion"; *pramā-*, "make, build, construct"; *vimā-*, "arrange"; *sammā-*, "put together."

53. For etymological discussion, see Jan Gonda, "The 'Original' Sense and Etymology of Skt. *Māyā*," in *Four Studies in the Language of the Veda* (s'Gravenhage: Mouton, 1959), pp. 119–94. See also Panikkar, *Mantramañjarī*, p. 507n.

54. See, for example, *Ṛgveda* 3.20.3, regarding the many forms of Agni.

55. *Ṛgveda* 2.17.5.

56. For studies on Vedic concepts of beauty, see Pramod Chandra Ray, *Theory of Oriental Beauty (with Special Reference to Ṛg Veda)* (Sambalpur: First Orissa Sanskrit Conference, 1974); P. S. Sastri, "The Rigvedic Theory of Beauty," *Proceedings and Transactions of the All-India Oriental Conference, Twelfth Session, Benares Hindu University, 1954–44*, edited by A. S. Altekar (Benares: Benares Hindu University, 1946), pp. 232–39.

57. For example, the Sanskrit adjective *darśata*, which literally means "visible" (from *dṛś-*, to "see, behold"), can be translated as "striking (to) the eye" and therefore as "beautiful." The general connotation of terms derived from *dṛś-*, often with the prefix *su-* ("good, excellent, well, very, right") appended to them, establishes the basis for some of the later classical Sanskrit vocabulary of beauty. Thus, for example, *sudṛk, susaṁdṛk, sudarśata, sudrśa, sudṛśika*. Similarly, *darśaneya* and *dṛśīka*, both of which literally mean "worthy to be seen," imply an attractive beauty.

58. *Candra*, for instance, can be translated as "beautiful" or "lovely" (from *can-*, to "be pleasing") but more specifically means "glittering, shimmering" and thus "brilliant" and "divine." A related term, *cāru*, describes that which is "pleasing" to the eye, thus, "pleasant," and thereby "delightful" and "beautiful." As a noun, *caru* means not only "beauty" but also sensual "delight." Similarly, *rukma* can be translated as "beauty" but more exactly means "golden splendor" or "brightness"; the adjective *bhadra* means "holy" or "sacred" in appearance but literally denotes a "glowing" or "shining" quality; and *śrī* refers to a quality of "splendor" or of "resplendence" and thus to an ethereal or sublime beauty.

59. *Ṛgveda* 8.41.3–4. According to Sāyaṇa, the "three dawns" are the morning, noontime, and evening. If so, then the phrase *the dawn* refers in general to the sun in its various forms.

60. *Ṛgveda* 10.88.6–7.

61. *Ṛgveda* 10.121.9.

62. *Ṛgveda* 1.72.10.

63. *Ṛgveda* 1.188.6.

64. *Ṛgveda* 10.70.9.

65. *Ṛgveda* 5.82.6.

66. *Ṛgveda* 1.123.11. For related discussion, see Ray, *Theory of Oriental Beauty*, pp. 31ff.

67. The etymologies of both the Sanskrit *vāc* and the English *voice* return finally to the Indo-European *wekw-*, to "speak." See Morris, ed., *The American Heritage Dictionary*, p. 1548; Pokorny, *Indogermanische etymologische Wörterbuch*, p. 1135 under *u̯eksu̯*.

68. The idea and wording of this sentence are similar to a passage by Klaus Klostermaier in his "The Creative Function of the Word," in *"Language" in Indian Philosophy and Religion*, edited by Harold G. Coward, SR Supplements 5 ([Toronto?]: Corporation Canadienne des Sciences Religieuses/Canadian Corporation for Studies in Religion, 1978), p. 5.

69. Compare *Psalm* 33.6 (Revised Standard Version): "By the word of the Lord were the heavens made; and all the host of them by the breath of his mouth"; and *Genesis* 1.3: "And God said, 'Let there be light'; and there was light."

70. *Ṛgveda* 10.125.7–8.

71. *Ṛgveda* 1.164.41–42.

72. See *Ṛgveda* 1.153.3.

73. See *Ṛgveda* 10.63.3.

74. *Ṛgveda* 4.33.8.

75. *Atharvaveda* 13.5.21 (Paippalāda recension). Reference to this verse comes from Jan Gonda, *Pūṣan and Sarasvatī* (Amsterdam: North Holland Publishing Co., 1985), p. 42.

76. Known also as Brahmaṇaspati and later as Vācaspati, the "Lord of the Sacred Word," Bṛhaspati's name derives from the word *pati*, "protector, lord," joined to a word built on the verbal root *bṛh-*, the latter of which means, essentially, to "swell, expand, grow." A related adjective, *bṛhat*, characterizes something that possesses the quality of expansive power and thus is vast or lofty and, not coincidentally, both bright and clear as well as effusive and loud. That which was *bṛhat* was not only great, powerful, or sublime but also associated with the expression or revelation of that which is great, powerful, or sublime.

77. *Ṛgveda* 1.164.49.

78. The word *saras* may come from the Sanskrit stem *sṛ-*, which means to "flow." Some scholars see in her name the verbal root *svṛ-*, to "make a sound" or to

"resound." See, for example, Ragunath Airi, *Concept of Sarasvatī* (Delhi: Munshiram Manoharlal, 1977), pp. 125–28, an English version of a Sanskrit paper published by Gurukul Kangri University in *Gurukul Patrika* (October–November, 1970), pp. 116–20.

79. See *Vājasaneyi-Saṁhitā* 20.55, 20.65, 21.34; *Maitrāyaṇi-Saṁhitā* 3.11.23; *Kāṭhaka-Saṁhitā* 38.8; *Taittirīya-Brāhmaṇa* 2.6.12.1.

80. See *Ṛgveda* 5.43.11, 6.61.11, 7.96.1, and 9.95.2, respectively.

81. See *Ṛgveda* 6.49.7 and 7.95.2, respectively.

82. *Ṛgveda* 2.41.16.

83. See *Ṛgveda* 1.3.10.

84. *Ṛgveda* 10.17.10.

85. *Ṛgveda* 1.3.11.

86. *Ṛgveda* 2.3.8.

87. This association appears most frequently in the many *āprī* (propitiatory) hymns of the Vedic corpus.

88. For further discussion, see Gonda, *Pūṣan and Sarasvatī*, pp. 17–29.

89. See *Ṛgveda* 2.41.18, 6.61.9.

90. *Ṛgveda* 1.3.11.

91. See *Vājasaneyi-Saṁhitā* 9.30.

92. *Śatapatha Brāhmaṇa* 5.2.2.13.

93. See, for example, *Śatapatha Brāhmaṇa* 5.3.4.25; *Kāṭhaka-Saṁhitā* 14.9, 208.17; *Maitrāyaṇī-Saṁhitā* 1.11.9, 1.170.21.

94. *Ṛgveda* 1.164.39.

95. *Ṛgveda* 10.125.8.

96. *Ṛgveda* 1.164.10.

97. *Ṛgveda* 1.164.12. W. Norman Brown has suggested that since the sun dies every evening it is mortal, and therefore cannot live in the realm of the truly immortal. See Rosane Rocher, ed., *India and Indology: Selected Articles by W. Norman Brown* (Delhi: Motilal Banarsidass, 1978), pp. 74–75, a reprint of Brown's "The Creative Role of the Goddess Vāc in the Ṛg Veda," in *Pratidanam: Indian, Iranian and Indo-European Studies Presented to F. B. J. Kuiper* (The Hague: Mouton, 1968), pp. 393–97.

98. Brown makes these two points as well. See "Vāc in the Ṛg Veda," p. 76.

CHAPTER TWO

1. *Ṛgveda* 6.44.14.

2. *Ṛgveda* 3.53.8.

3. *Ṛgveda* 2.17.5.

4. *Ṛgveda* 1.165.10.

5. The word is based on the verbal root *rūp-*, to "exhibit" or "display."

6. Namely, *mā-*, to "measure."

7. It may be of interest in this regard to note that a Vedic etymological relative and near-synonym for *rūpa*, the word *varpas,* also means "form" in the sense of "artifice" or "image," but carries the connotation of "assumed form" or "phantom."

8. See *Ṛgveda* 9.10.6.

9. *Ṛgveda* 10.85.16. Reference and Sanskrit text in Jan Gonda, *The Vision of the Vedic Poets* (Berlin: Mouton, 1963; reprint edition, Delhi: Munshiram Manoharlal, 1984), pp. 34–35.

10. *Ṛgveda* 6.47.18. Sanskrit terms here are: *pratirūpa* ("counterform"), *rūparūpa* ("every form"), *rūpa* ("form"), and *pururūpa* ("various forms").

11. *Ṛgveda* 10.130.3. "Model" here renders *pramā*; "image" translates *pratimā*.

12. *Ṛgveda* 1.39.1.

13. See *Ṛgveda* 10.81.4.

14. *Ṛgveda* 10.121.7. The "golden embryo" here (*hiraṇyagarbha*) could also refer to the round sun rising on the eastern horizon, or it could refer to the ritual hearth fire into which sacrificial oblations are offered.

15. *Ṛgveda* 10.82.5.

16. *Ṛgveda* 10.82.7.

17. H. D. Velankar, *Ṛg Veda Maṇḍala VII* (Bombay: Bharatiya Vidya Bhavan, 1963), p. v.

18. *Ṛtayuj-* and similar terms.

19. *Ṛtajā, ṛta ājāta, ṛtaprajāta, ṛtapravīta*, and so on.

20. See *Ṛgveda* 4.51.5, 6.39.4, 6.48.5, and 1.65.5, respectively.

21. That Varuṇa is the Āditya, par excellence, is suggested by such verses as *Ṛgveda* 7.36.6, which refers to "Varuṇa, with the Ādityas."

22. For an extensive study of this god, see Heinrich Lüders, *Varuṇa*, 2 volumes (Göttingen: Vandenhoeck and Ruprecht, 1959): volume 1: *Varuṇa und das Wasser*; volume 2: *Varuṇa und das Ṛta*.

23. "We bring you to mind with sacred hymns" translates *vo . . . manāmahe sūktaiḥ*.

24. As we saw in the Introduction (note 3), other Sanskrit terms derive from the same verbal root. In this regard we may also mention *ṛtu*, which refers to the smoothly running cyclical passage of time marked by the seasons. *Ṛgveda* 1.15 mentions *ṛtu*, "season" in the sense of the "proper time to perform the ritual." The hymn personifies the concept as the god Ṛtu and as various "deities of the season" (*ṛtudevatāḥ*), namely, Indra (verses 1, 5), the Maruts (verse 2), Tvaṣṭṛ (verse 3), Agni (verses 4, 12), Mitra and Varuṇa (verse 5), Agni as Wealth-giver (verses 7–10), and the Aśvins (verse 11). On *ṛtu* in the Veda in general, see V. Raghavan, *Ṛtu in Sanskrit Literature* (Delhi: Shri Lal Bahadur Shastri Kendriya Sanskrit Vidyapeeth, 1972), pp. 1–9.

25. See, for example, 8.22.7 (*ṛtasya pathibhiḥ*), 9.73.6 (*ṛtasya panthāṁ*), 10.133.6 (*ṛtasya pathā*), and 10.5.4 (*ṛtasya vartanayaḥ*).

26. *Ṛgveda* 9.113.4.

27. *Ṛgveda* 1.145.5.

28. *Ṛgveda* 1.105.12.

29. *Ṛgveda* 4.42.4.

30. *Ṛgveda* 2.13.7.

31. Ibid.

32. *Ṛgveda* 3.61.7.

33. *Ṛgveda* 1.23.5.

34. *Ṛgveda* 6.51.1.

35. *Ṛgveda* 10.8.3.

36. *Ṛgveda* 4.5.1.8.

37. *Ṛgveda* 5.15.2.

38. See, for example, *Ṛgveda* 1.65.10, 6.7.1, 4.40.5, 6.48.5, 1.70.7.

39. The Sanskrit here is *sahojā* (see *Ṛgveda* 1.58.1), *sahaskṛta* (see *Ṛgveda* 3.27.10, 8.44.11), *sahasā jāyamānaḥ* (see *Ṛgveda* 1.96.1, 6.44.22).

40. See also *Atharvaveda* 18.14–18.

41. *Ṛgveda* 10.154.4–5.

42. *Ṛgveda* 7.66.2. The phrases "exceedingly dexterous" and "dexterity as [their] father" render *sudakṣa* and *dakṣapitṛ*, respectively. The metaphor of filial relationship between a "power" and a "god," as in *dakṣapitṛ,* is a typical way in which the Vedic poets point out a god's essential nature. For extended discussion of this theme, see Jan Gonda, *Some Observations on the Relations between "Gods" and "Powers" in the Veda a propos of the Phrase 'Sūnuḥ Sahasaḥ'* ('s-Gravenhage: Mouton, 1957).

43. See, for example, *Ṛgveda* 2.23.17, 7.64.2, 10.66.4, respectively, which speak of the "great order," *mahat ṛtam*. See also 5.68.1, 6.13.2, 1.75.5, which speak of the "expansive order" or "mighty order," *bṛhat ṛtam*. Textual references here come from Lüders, *Varuṇa*, volume 2, pp. 580–83.

44. *Satya, tapas, ojas,* and *sahas,* respectively.

45. See Chapter One, above.

46. The philosophical insight regarding such a process came to be known in classical India as *sṛṣṭividyā*, or "knowledge about the emanation" of being.

47. *Ṛgveda* 3.38.4.

48. *Śatapatha Brāhmaṇa* 11.2.3.1–3.

49. For studies, comments, and further bibliographies on this hymn, see Paul Deussen, "Das Einheitslied des Dīrghatamas, Ṛigv. 1.164," in *Allgemeine Geschichte der Philosophie* 1.1 (Leipzig: Brockhaus, 1920), pp. 105–19; C. Kunhan Raja, *Asya Vāmasya Hymn (The Riddle of the Universe) Ṛgveda 1.164, with the Commentaries of Sāyaṇa and Ātmānanda* (Madras: Ganesh and Co., 1956); C. Kunhan Raja, *Poet-Philosophers of the Ṛgveda, Vedic and Pre-Vedic* (Madras: Ganesh and Co., 1963), pp. 1–49; V. S. Agrawala, *The Thousand-Syllabled Speech*, part 1: *Vision in Long Darkness* (Varanasi: Vedāraṇyaka Ashram, 1963); W. Norman Brown, "Agni, Sun, Sacrifice and Vāc: A Sacerdotal Ode by Dīrghatamas (Rig Veda 1.164)," *Journal of the American Oriental Society* 88 (1988), pp. 199–218; reprinted as "Dīrghatamas's Vision of Creation," in *India and Indology*, edited by Rosane Rocher (Delhi: Motilal Banarsidass, 1978), pp. 53–83; Wendy Doniger O'Flaherty, *The Rig Veda: An Anthology* (Harmondsworth: Penguin Books, 1981), pp. 71–83, 307–8.

50. See also *Ṛgveda* 1.35.6 and 7.87.5. W. Norman Brown believes the "six regions" refer to the terrestrial and heavenly worlds, each of which consists of three parts. See Brown, "Dīrghatamas's Vision of Creation," pp. 58 and 66.

51. *Ṛgveda* 10.125.7–8.

52. *Ṛgveda* 1.164.42.

53. This sentence is a close paraphrase of one by Maryla Falk, who writes of a Vedic ideology that "hinges on the idea that before the beginning of things, before the manifestation of multiplicity, all rūpas were one rūpa, *viz.* the unmanifest shape of the universal *Puruṣa*, and all *nāmas* were one nāma, *viz.* the unuttered universal Vāc." See Falk, *Nāma-rūpa and Dharma-rūpa: Origin and Aspects of an Ancient Indian Conception* (Calcutta: University of Calcutta, 1943), p. 2.

CHAPTER THREE

1. *Ṛgveda* 3.7.2.

2. *Ṛgveda* 8.18.10.

3. See *Ṛgveda* 8.91.5–6: "O Indra, make three places sprout again, these of which I speak—my father's head, his planted field, and this part [of my body] below my waist. Make all these grow crops of hair . . . this planted field of ours, my body, and my father's head." The hymn will appear as *Ṛgveda* 8.80 in those editions which do not include the Vālakhilya.

4. *Ṛgveda* 5.53.3–4.

5. *Ṛgveda* 6.75.3–5.

6. *Ṛgveda* 6.75.11.

7. *Ṛgveda* 6.75.14.

8. *Ṛgveda* 6.75.16.

9. *Ṛgveda* 6.75.19.

10. *Ṛgveda* 1.31.18.

11. *Ṛgveda* 8.35.16.

12. *Ṛgveda* 3.53.12.

13. *Ṛgveda* 6.46.1.

14. *Ṛgveda* 8.66.14–15 (8.55.14–15 in editions without the Vālakhilya).

15. *Ṛgveda* 5.47.5.

16. "Statement" renders *nivacana*; "wondrous" translates *vapu.*

17. "The wind" here translates *mātariśvan* (see also verse 4), whom the influential Vedic commentator, Sāyaṇa, elsewhere interpreted to refer to Vāyu, the god of the wind. See Sāyaṇa's commentary on *Ṛgveda* 1.93.6.

18. *Ṛgveda* 1.164.4.

19. *Ṛgveda* 1.164.6.

20. *Ṛgveda* 1.164.10.

21. *Ṛgveda* 1.164.16.

22. *Ṛgveda* 1.164.34.

23. *Ṛgveda* 1.164.35.

24. Namely, *bṛh-*, "grow larger."

25. See, for example, *Ṛgveda* 10.88.17.

26. "Race" here translates *āji*; see, for example, *Ṛgveda* 10.61.1. "Battle" represents *pṛtanā*: see, for instance, *Ṛgveda* 1.152.7. For a similar point, see Willard Johnson, *Poetry and Speculation of the Ṛg Veda* (Los Angeles and Berkeley: University of California Press, 1980), p. 7.

27. According to *Ṛgveda* 10.71.8. For further discussion of *Ṛgveda* 10.71, see below.

28. *Ṛgveda* 10.88.17.

29. See, for example, *Ṛgveda* 1.12.6 and 6.7.7 (which describe Agni as a poet), 9.86.29 (Soma), and 5.29.1 (Indra).

30. *Ṛgveda* 5.85.2c–d.

31. For a discussion of this idea, see Ellison Banks Findly, "*Mántra kaviśastá*: Speech as Performative in the Ṛgveda" in *Understanding Mantra*, edited by Harvey P. Alper (Albany: State University of New York, 1989), pp. 15–47.

32. The Sanskrit for various phrases in this paragraph would be *sumedhas* ("collected in thought"); *vipra* ("trembling with inspiration, inwardly stirred, inspired poet"); *dhīra* ("wise person"); *manman* ("mental images"); *hṛd* and *manas* ("heart" and "mind"); *dhīti, maniṣā, mati* ("verbal insight"). For similar discussion, see Findly, ibid., p. 24.

33. "Secrets" here translates *ninya*; "know Ṛta" renders *ṛtajñā*.

34. See the discussion on the role of the mind and heart below. See also *Ṛgveda* 1.62.2, 1.67.4, 1.105.15, 1.171.2, 1.182.8, 2.23.2, 3.39.1.

35. Vedic tradition in general but especially the Pūrva Mīmāṁsā school of Vedic interpretation holds that the words of the Veda are *apauruṣeya*, "not of human origin."

36. This is the invocation for the *Aitareya Upaniṣad* and several of the Śākta Upaniṣads, namely, the *Tripurā, Bahvṛcā, Sarasvatīrahasyā,* and *Saubhāgyalakṣmī Upaniṣads*.

37. *Ṛgveda* 1.123.6.

38. We will remember that the word *deva*, "divinity" or "divine power," derives from the verbal root *div-*, to "shine."

39. *Ṛgveda* 10.124.6.

40. Agni is described as *viśvavedas*, "all-knowing" (see, for example, *Ṛgveda* 1.12.1), an adjective and epithet derived finally from *vid-*, to "know [by seeing]."

41. *Ṛgveda* 8.42.1.

42. *Ṛgveda* 2.27.3.

43. *Ṛgveda* 6.51.9.

44. *Ṛgveda* 10.123.7c–d.

45. The most common verbal root with this triple sense would be *dṛś-*, to "see, behold." So, for example, the Sanskrit adjective *darśata*, "visible," can be translated as "striking to the eye" and therefore as "beautiful." But the word also implied for Vedic poets not only a sense of viewing a pleasant sight, but also of seeing into a hidden or sublime mystery. When joined by various preverbs, *dṛś-* assumes a number of related but slightly different meanings, each significant to our point at hand: *anudṛś-*, for example, literally means to "become perceived" but also means to "become known by the mind" and thus to "comprehend the truth." *Apadṛś-* similarly means "to become visible" but refers to that process by which one comes to "grasp the truth." *Pratidṛś-*, to "appear" or "seem," can be translated as "be known as true," while *vidṛś-*, to "be seen clearly," can rightly be understood to mean to "discern" and thus to "know" or to "understand."

46. In addition to *dṛś-*, such verbs would include *paś-* and *cakṣ-*, both of which translate literally as to "see" or to "have in one's vision."

47. *Ṛgveda* 7.76.2.

48. *Ṛgveda* 3.35.5–6.

49. *Ṛgveda* 3.26.8.

50. See *Ṛgveda* 10.98.2–3.

51. *Ṛgveda* 10.67.10.

52. *Ṛgveda* 6.9.6.

53. *Ṛgveda* 6.9.5.

54. *Ṛgveda* 7.79.5.

55. *Ṛgveda* 3.39.1–2.

56. The phrases *inspired poem* and *materialized thought* both translate *mati.*

57. *Ṛgveda* 7.79.5.

58. *Atharvaveda* 6.4.3.

59. *Ṛgveda* 10.53.6.

60. *Ṛgveda* 5.21.1. "Wise seer" translates *ṛṣir . . . dhīraḥ.*

61. See *Ṛgveda* 1.145.1–2.

62. *Ṛgveda* 10.71.2.

63. See *Taittirīya Brāhmaṇa* 5.8.8.5. Reference to this text and central wording of this sentence come from Jan Gonda, *The Vision of the Vedic Poets* (Berlin: Mouton, 1963; reprint edition, Delhi: Munshiram Manoharlal, 1984), pp. 215–16.

64. *Ṛgveda* 10.71.1.

65. *Ṛgveda* 8.6.32.

66. *Ṛgveda* 2.40.6.

67. *Ṛgveda* 10.64.12.

68. *Atharvaveda* 10.1.8.

69. *Atharvaveda* 3.5.6. "Chariot makers who possess vision" and "imaginative artists" render *dhīvāno rathakārāḥ* and *karmārā manīṣiṇaḥ*, respectively.

70. *Ṛgveda* 1.139.1.

71. *Atharvaveda* 7.1.1.

72. The process of the manifestation of the divine here is similar to what later philosophers and contemplatives were to regard as the graded descent of the unified Word into increasingly material forms of language: the transcendent sublime (Parā) descends first into the sublime level of being (Paśyantī, "that which is seen" but not yet heard), which descends into an intermediate range of creation between unmanifest and manifest (Madhyamā, the "middle"), which becomes the physical level of language (Vaikharī), namely, oral speech.

73. For discussions of this hymn, see Frits Staal, "Ṛgveda 10.71 on the Origin of Language," in Harold Coward and Krishna Sivaraman, eds., *Revelation in Indian Thought: A Festshrift in Honour of Professor T. R. V. Murti* (Emeryville, Calif.: Dharma Publishing, 1977), pp. 4–6; Wendy O'Flaherty, *The Rig Veda: An Anthology* (Harmondsworth: Penguin Books, 1981), pp. 61–62; F. B. J. Kuiper, "The Ancient Aryan Verbal Contest," *Indo-Iranian Journal* 4, number 4 (1960); Manilel Patel, " A Study of Ṛgveda X.71," *Viśvabharati Quarterly* 4, number 4 (August–October 1938).

74. The Śakvarī meter consists of eight syllables repeated seven times.

75. On this topic, see also H. D. Velankar, "Mind and Heart in the Rgveda (Manas and Hrd)," *Proceedings and Transactions of the All-India Oriental Conference*, 22nd Session (Gauhati), edited by by Maheswar Neog (Gauhati: All-India Oriental Conference, 1966), volume 2, pp. 1–5.

76. *Atharvaveda* 6.41.1.

77. *Ṛgveda* 1.163.5–6.

78. See *Ṛgveda* 10.85.9, which refers to Sūryā's mindfulness in the sense of "willing appreciation" for her lord, Soma. See also 5.83.3, in which the poet states that "my mind trembles in fear."

79. *Ṛgveda* 1.109.1a–b.

80. *Ṛgveda* 1.109.1c–d.

81. *Ṛgveda* 10.81.4.

82. *Ṛgveda* 10.58.12.

83. *Ṛgveda* 10.57.3.

84. *Ṛgveda* 10.57.5.

85. *Ṛgveda* 10.57.4.

86. It is consistent, therefore, that the verbal root *man-,* which gives rise to the words *manas*, *manasin*, and *manīśin*, leads also to the Sanskrit *manana*, "meditation" in the sense of "contemplation on a reverent thought," as well as to *mantra*, "instrument of thought, speech, sacred language," and to *manman*, "possessing the power of effective thought."

87. See *Ṛgveda* 2.40.3, 4.48.4, 6.49.5, 7.69.2.

88. *Ṛgveda* 7.100.1. See also 8.2.37.

89. *Ṛgveda* 7.64.4.

90. In classical Hindu thought, the primordial ancestor of all human beings—the Vedic Adam, if you will—is known as Manu.

91. *Ṛgveda* 10.123.6.

92. *Ṛgveda* 5.4.10.

93. *Ṛgveda* 7.33.9.

94. For similar observations, see R. N. Dandekar, *Der Vedische Mensch: Studien zu Selbstauffassung des Inders in Ṛg- und Atharvaveda* (Heidelberg: C. Winter, 1938) pp. 48, 62f.; Velankar, *Ṛgveda Maṇḍala VII*, p. 4; Gonda, *Vision of the Vedic Poets*, pp. 278–79.

95. *Ṛgveda* 10.5.1.

96. *Ṛgveda* 10.123.6.

97. *Ṛgveda* 10.47.7. For the idea that poetry touches the gods' hearts, see also *Ṛgveda* 1.16.7.

98. *Ṛgveda* 10.91.13.

99. *Ṛgveda* 6.16.47.

100. *Ṛgveda* 10.91.14.

101. *Ṛgveda* 1.60.3.

102. *Ṛgveda* 2.35.2.

103. *Ṛgveda* 3.39.1.

104. *Ṛgveda* 10.64.2.

105. *Ṛgveda* 10.71.8.

106. According to H. D. Velankar, "the deliberative wisdom and thoughts of the mind seek confirmation from the natural wisdom of the heart." See Velankar, *Ṛgveda Maṇḍala VII*, p. 5.

107. *Ṛgveda* 10.71.2 and 10.71.3.

108. Soma is described in the *Ṛgveda* by such words as *andhas* ("herb": see, for example, 9.18.2 and 9.55.2), *aṁsu* ("vegetal filament": see 1.91.17 and 10.17.12.), *giriṣṭhā* ("residing in the mountains:" 9.18.1), and *parvatāvṛddha* ("growing in the rugged heights": 9.46.1). Scholarship is uncertain regarding the identity of this plant, if it existed at all. Internal textual references have suggested to Raimundo Panikkar, for example, that the *soma* plant may have been *Ephedra intermedia* (a theory presented earlier by Sir Aurel Stein) while R. Gordon Wasson's studies suggest to him that it was *Amanita muscaria* (the "Fly agaric" mushroom). See Panikkar, *The Vedic Experience: Mantramañjarī* (Berkeley and Los Angeles: University of California Press, 1977), p. 364; Wasson, *Soma: Divine Plant of Immortality*, Ethno-mycological Studies, number 1 (New York: Harcourt Brace Jovanovich, 1968). For related discussion, see John Brough, "Soma and Amanita Muscaria," *Bulletin of the School of Oriental and African Studies* 34 (1971), pp. 331–62.

109. *Ṛgveda* 9.33.5.

110. See *Ṛgveda* 4.26.

111. For imagery of filtering, see, for example, *Ṛgveda* 9.51.1 and 9.67.19. Of many references to the clarity and purity of the *soma* such filtering brings, see, for example, 9.78.1.

112. Such terms include *candra* ("glittering, shining"), *darśata* ("beautiful to look at"), *dyumat* ("bright, splendid"), *śuci* ("shining, radiant"), and *śubhra* ("brilliant, resplendent").

113. *Ṛgveda* 9.107.4.

114. *Ṛgveda* 9.69.6.

115. *Ṛgveda* 9.77.1.

116. For a number of images of *soma*'s expansive nature, see the many hymns in book Nine of the *Ṛgveda*.

117. *Ṛgveda* 9.59.4.

118. The Sanskrit *amṛta,* (*a-mṛta,* "not-dead") derives from the root *mṛ-*, to "decease," from the Indo-European **mer-,* to "die." The Indo-European root appears also in the Latin stem *mort-* and thus the English *mortal* and *im-mortal* as well as in the Greek *a-mbrotos* and therefore the English *ambrosia.*

119. *Śatapatha Brāhmaṇa* 9.5.1.8.

120. *Ṛgveda* 8.79.1–2.

121. *Ṛgveda* 9.1.1 and 9.1.3.

122. *Ṛgveda* 9.86.22.

123. *Ṛgveda* 9.1.10.

124. For interpretive discussion of the Soma hymns as a group, see Shrikrishna Sakharam Bhawe, *The Soma Hymns of the Ṛgveda,* Baroda Research series (Baroda: University of Baroda, 1957–62).

125. *Ṛgveda* 9.3.1.

126. Relevant Sanskrit terms here would include *vicakṣaṇa* ("clear-sighted" and so on), *viśvavedas* ("all-knowing"), and *vipascit* ("one with energetic consciousness").

127. *Ṛgveda* 19.91.2.

128. *Ṛgveda* 9.107.3.

129. *Ṛgveda* 9.86.29.

130. *Ṛgveda* 9.12.4.

131. *Ṛgveda* 8.79.1.

132. *Ṛgveda* 9.107.7.

133. *Ṛgveda* 8.48.6.

134. *Ṛgveda* 9.104.5.

135. *Ṛgveda* 8.48.12.

136. *Ṛgveda* 8.48.5.

137. *Ṛgveda* 8.48.6 and 8.48.2.

138. *Ṛgveda* 8.48.3.

139. Vedic commentarial tradition views the speaker here to be Indra. Certainly, the imagery is reminiscent of Indra's heroic character. But it may be that the god speaking here is Agni, the god of fire, who carries gifts from the human world to that of the gods. Such would be suggested by verse 13: "A well-stocked house, I leave now, carrying the gift to the gods. Have I not drunk the *soma*?"

140. The Sanskrit here would be *vṛṣan* (powerful), *śuṣmin* (vigorous), *sahāvat* (possessing transformative strength), *sāsahi* (successful, victorious), and *āśu* (speedy, direct).

141. Such words include *cāru* (shimmeringly beautiful) and *priya* (pleasing, delightful).

142. *Ṛgveda* 1.139.2.

143. The Sanskrit is *somasya sevebhir akṣabhiḥ.*

144. *Ṛgveda* 6.47.2–3.

145. *Ṛgveda* 3.38.6

146. *Ṛgveda* 9.75.2.

147. See *Ṛgveda* 9.44.6, 9.63.24, 9.86.48.

148. See *Ṛgveda* 9.64.24, 9.66.3, 9.84.5, 9.100.5.

149. *Ṛgveda* 9.9.1.

150. *Ṛgveda* 9.96.18.

151. *Ṛgveda* 5.29.1.

152. See, for example, *Ṛgveda* 1.12.6.

153. *Ṛgveda* 6.7.7.

154. *Ṛgveda* 6.49.7.

155. As they did Soma, Vedic poets also described Agni as *kratuvid*, "granting mental skill." See *Ṛgveda* 2.39.2, 9.108.1, 10.2.5.

156. See *Ṛgveda* 1.31.16.

157. *Ṛgveda* 4.11.2–3b.

158. *Ṛgveda* 4.5.3.

159. *Ṛgveda* 8.48.3.

160. *Ṛgveda* 1.23.24.

161. *Ṛgveda* 5.52.13–14.

162. Later philosophers of aesthetics in India, in fact, were to characterize beautiful art as that which allows the artist and the connoisseur to be of the "same heart," *sahṛdaya*, and thereby to share the essence of a sublime emotion.

163. *Ṛgveda* 9.76.4.

164. *Ṛgveda* 6.9.2–3.

165. *Ṛgveda* 6.9.5.

166. *Ṛgveda* 3.53.9.

167. *Ṛgveda* 8.72.8 (*Vālakhilya* 8.83.8).

168. See *Ṛgveda* 3.54.16, 8.18.19, 8.27.10. The phrase *of the same lineage* translates *sājātya*.

169. *Ṛgveda* 1.105.9.

170. *Ṛgveda* 1.139.9.

171. See *Ṛgveda* 6.8.1.

172. See *Ṛgveda* 1.87.5.

173. *Ṛgveda* 9.95.5.

174. *Ṛgveda* 6.47.3. See also 9.96.7.

175. *Ṛgveda* 1.126.1.

176. *Ṛgveda* 7.4.1.

177. *Ṛgveda* 7.13.1. It may be that the Sanskrit verbs in these passages, all of which derive from the root *bṛh-*, to "bear," are used in the context of ritual: to "bear" here would be to bring an offering to a god.

178. *Ṛgveda* 6.16.37.

179. On related discussion, see P. S. Sastri, "The Rigvedic Theory of Beauty," *Proceedings and Transactions of the All-India Oriental Conference, Twelfth Session, Benares Hindu University, 1943–44*, edited by A. S. Altekar (Benares: Benares Hindu University, 1946), pp. 232–39.

180. *Ṛgveda* 10.50.7.

181. The phrase translates *brahmakṛta* in *Ṛgveda* 10.54.6.

182. *Ṛgveda* 7.29.2.

183. *Ṛgveda* 7.22.9.

184. *Ṛgveda* 7.15.4

185. *Ṛgveda* 6.32.1.

186. *Ṛgveda* 10.23.6.

187. *Ṛgveda* 1.38.1.

188. *Ṛgveda* 2.28.5

189. *Atharvaveda* 10.8.38.

190. *Ṛgveda* 7.94.1.

191. *Atharvaveda* 3.17.1–2. See also *Ṛgveda* 10.101.4, *Vājasaneyi Saṁhitā* 12.67. For discussion of the poetry of the Atharvans, see N. J. Shende, *Kavi and Kāvya in the Atharvaveda*, Publications of the Centre of Advanced Study in Sanskrit, class B, number 1 (Pune: University of Poona, 1967).

192. *Ṛgveda* 1.130.6.

193. *Ṛgveda* 5.73.10.

194. *Ṛgveda* 1.111.1.

195. *Ṛgveda* 5.2.11.

196. *Ṛgveda* 5.29.15.

197. *Ṛgveda* 10.39.14.

198. *Ṛgveda* 1.61.4–5b.

199. *Ṛgveda* 2.31.7.

200. *Ṛgveda* 1.38.1.

201. *Ṛgveda* 1.62.13.

202. *Ṛgveda* 1.114.9.

203. "Skillfully with skillfulness" translates *sukṛtaḥ sukṛtyayā.*

204. *Ṛgveda* 1.161.9.

205. Literally, "striding over the back of Ṛta."

206. *Ṛgveda* 10.123.3c, d–4.

207. *Ṛgveda* 9.75.2.

208. This interpretation of this verse comes from Gonda, *Vision of the Vedic Poets*, p. 74.

209. *Ṛgveda* 5.29.15.

210. *Ṛgveda* 5.7.3.

211. *Ṛgveda* 3.2.8.

212. See *Ṛgveda* 1.123.13, 6.55.1, and 7.66.12, respectively.

213. *Ṛgveda* 9.94.2.

214. On Ṛta as the truth underlying the songs sung in the ritual ("die Wahrheit des Kultliedes"), see Lüders, *Varuṇa*, part 2, pp. 420–85.

215. For passages on verses that are *anṛta*, see *Ṛgveda* 1.105.5, 1.139.2, 1.151.1, 1.151.3, 2.24.7, 7.65.3, 10.10.4, 10.87.11.

216. For passages noting verses that are "crooked" (*vṛjina*), see *Ṛgveda* 4.1.17d, 4.23.8, 5.12.5, 6.51.2c, 7.60.2d. For "wayward" (*yātu*) and thus "evil" singers who stray from the truth, see *Ṛgveda* 5.12.2; 7.34.8; 7.104.7,12, 13, 14, 20; 10.87.11. For mention of songs that are "injurious" or demonic (*druh*), see *Ṛgveda* 1.23.22, 1.122.9, 2.23.17, 5.68.4, 10.61.14.

CHAPTER FOUR

1. *Ṛgveda* 1.164.11 uses just this metaphor of the turning wheel to describe Ṛta.

2. *Śatapatha Brāhmaṇa* 2.2.4.1.

3. *Śatapatha Brāhmaṇa* 11.1.6.1.

4. *Atharvaveda* 12.1.1. The close association between Ṛta and *satya* is reflected in such passages as *Ṛgveda* 5.57.8, which describes the aerial Maruts as divine "poets [who are] knowers of Ṛta [and] hearers of *satya*," while *Ṛgveda* 3.54.3 asks of heaven and earth, "May your sacred order [Ṛta] be faithful to the truth [*satya*]." The *Śatapatha Brāhmaṇa* is quite succinct when at 6.4.4.10 it instructs a priest to intone repeatedly, *ṛtaṁ satyam ṛtaṁ satyam*: "[This is] order, [this is] truth; order, truth."

5. T. G. Mainkar has concluded that "the Ṛgvedic poet was a wise man well conversant in the life around him. . . . [H]is similes cover a wide field and reveal a considerable variety of theme, coming as they do from religion, sacrifice, nature, home and war. The Ṛgvedic poet . . . was not a mere cobbler of words, but knew much and had first hand experience of the life around him. . . . [L]ife with all its complexities was known to him and this fact is reflected in his poetical compositions." See Mainkar, *The Ṛgvedic Foundations of Classical Poetics* (Delhi: S. Balwant for Ajanta Publications, 1977), p. 51.

6. See, for example, *Ṛgveda* 1.119, 5.41.17, 6.74.2.

7. The derivation of the word *vrata* is somewhat uncertain because in Sanskrit there are two identical verbal roots, *vṛ-*, which have quite different meanings: one means to "choose"; the other, to "cover" or "envelop." If it derives from the former, then *vrata* can be understood to be associated in some way with the effective power of the will; thus it comes to mean in classical Sanskrit "solemn vow," "holy practice," or "sacralizing conduct." If it derives from the latter, then *vrata* has the sense of an encompassing, overarching authority or protective guidance, and thus "sanctifying rule." For discussion of *vrata* as solemn vow (and thus as "commitment" or "offering": *Gelübde*), see Hanns-Peter Schmidt, *Vedisch vratá und awestisch urvăta* (Hamburg: Cram, de Gruyter & Co., 1958), pp. 21–72; as "commandment" or "obligation," see

Joel P. Brereton, *The Ṛgvedic Ādityas*, American Oriental series, volume 63 (New Haven, Conn.: American Oriental Society, 1981), pp. 70–81; as "ordinance, charter, command" (*Satzung, Gebot*), see Bernfried Schlerath, review of Schmidt, *Zeitschrift der Deutschen Morgenländischen Gesellschaft* 110 (1960), p. 193, and Stanley Insler, *The Gāthās of Zarathustra* (Teheran-Liege: Bibliotheque Pahlavi, 1975), pp. 175f.

8. *Ṛgveda* 5.69.4.

9. *Ṛgveda* 1.62.10.

10. *Ṛgveda* 3.4.7.

11. *Ṛgveda* 10.124.3.

12. *Ṛgveda* 6.70.1

13. There are variants to this noun: *manuṣa, manus, manuṣya*. All derive from *man-*, to "think."

14. See, for example, *Ṛgveda* 1.36.19, 1.139.9, 1.76.5.

15. The word *sacrifice*, "to make holy," derives from the Latin *sacrificium*: from *sacere*, "sacred," plus *facere*, "to do, to make."

16. *Ṛgveda* 5.26.6

17. *Ṛgveda* 8.43.24.

18. It may be of interest to note that the Sanskrit word *ṛta* is distantly related, not only to the English words *art* and *harmony* as well as to *order*, *coordinate*, and *ordain*, but also to *rite* and thus to *ritual*.

19. *Ṛgveda* 6.21.11. See also 5.41.6, 6.50.2, 7.56.12, 10.154.4, 10.66.8.

20. *Ṛgveda* 2.11.12.

21. *Taittirīya Saṁhitā* 1.6.10.2.

22. *Atharvaveda* 7.5.1–2.

23. *Atharvaveda* 7.5.3.

24. Public *yajña*s were known therefore as *śrauta* rites, that is, as "based on *śruti*."

25. *Ṛgveda* 2.28.5.

26. *Ṛgveda* 5.29.15.

27. Namely, *sthā-*.

28. This point is argued at some length by J. C. Heesterman, *The Broken World of Sacrifice: An Essay in Ancient Indian Ritual* (Chicago: University of Chicago Press, 1993), especially pp. 1–85.

29. *Śatapatha Brāhmaṇa* 2.4.3.3.

30. *Ṛgveda* 1.164.41.

31. The phrase *aty atiṣṭhad daśāṅgulam* (verse 1, rendered here as "[he] reached beyond it the distance of ten fingers") could also be translated as "he presided over the place of ten fingers breadth," namely, the heart. This would suggest the idea that Puruṣa lives within one's inner being. For this interpretation, see W. Norman Brown, "The Sources and Nature of *Puruṣa* in the Puruṣasūkta," in *India and Indology*, edited by Rosane Rocher (Delhi: Motilal Banarsidass, 1978), p. 8, appearing first in *Journal of the American Oriental Society* 51 (1931), pp. 108–18.

32. See, for example, *Śatapatha Brāhmaṇa* 10.6.5.9, which describes the *brahman* as *svayambhu*, "self-existing."

33. *Atharvaveda* 10.2.25.

34. See, for example, *Śatapatha Brāhmaṇa* 11.2.3.1–3.

35. *Ṛgveda* 1.164.45–46.

36. See, for example, *Ṛgveda* 1.31.18 (compare *Atharvaveda* 13.1.33 and 17.1.14), 1.52.7, 1.80.1, 1.93.6, 1.117.11, 1.185.6, 5.80.1, 6.23.5–6, 7.22.7, 8.1.3, 10.4.7, 10.49.1.

37. See *Ṛgveda* 7.36.1, for example: "May the *brahman* issue from the seat of Ṛta."

38. See *Atharvaveda* 1.19.4, 5.8.6; *Ṛgveda* 6.75.19.

39. *Ṛgveda* 10.2.25.

40. See *Ṛgveda* 7.33.11.

41. See *Ṛgveda* 2.12.14, 1.31.18.

42. See *Taittirīya Brāhmaṇa* 2.8.9.6–7.

43. Note that Brahman is identified in this verse as feminine. See also verse 31.

44. *Chāndogya Upaniṣad* 3.8.10.

45. Jan Gonda quotes the *Laws of Manu* 1.98: "The very birth of a *brahman* is an eternal incarnation of the dharma." See Gonda, *Notes on Brahman* (Utrecht: J. L. Beyers, 1950), p. 51.

46. *Śatapatha Brāhmaṇa* 5.1.1.11: *brahma hi brāhmaṇah.*

47. See, for example, *Ṛgveda* 10.107.6 and *Taittirīya Saṁhitā* 6.6.1.4.

48. See *Ṛgveda* 10.125.5.

49. See, for example, *Kauśītaki Brāhmaṇa* 6.11, which notes that the "brahmin becomes a brahmin through that sap of brilliance that he developed from his threefold knowledge," that is, from his knowledge of the *Ṛgveda, Sāmaveda,* and *Yajurveda.*

50. "Lustrous in sacred knowledge" here translates *brahmavarcasa.* See, for example, *Śatapatha Brāhmaṇa* 13.1.9.1.

51. "Knowledge of all sacred things" renders *sarvavidyā.* See, for example, *Taittirīya Brāhmaṇa* 3.10.11.4.

52. *Śatapatha Brāhmaṇa* 1.5.1.12.

53. *Śatapatha Brāhmaṇa* 1.8.1.28.

54. See *Aitareya Brāhmaṇa* 5.32.4. The phrase *brahmin's essence* translates *brahmatva.*

55. *Śatapatha Brāhmaṇa* 14.6.1.7.

56. Jan Gonda, *Notes on Brahman*, p. 57.

57. *Kauṣīkaki Brāhmaṇa* 6.11, translated here by Heesterman in *The Broken World of Sacrifice*, p. 150. In a note Heesterman refers also to *Ṣaḍviṁśa Brāhmaṇa* 1.6.5, *Hiraṇyakakeśin Śrauta Sūtra* 10.8,106, *Bharadvāja Śrauta Sūtra* 3.15.6, *Āpastamba Śrauta Sūtra* 14.8.3, and *Śatapatha Brāhmaṇa* 5.5.5.16.

58. Relevant Sanskrit terms here include *payus* ("joint") and *antardhi* ("interim"). For discussion, see Heesterman, ibid., pp. 150–51.

59. "Expiatory rite" translates *prāyascitta*; "healer" translates *bhiṣaj.*

60. For discussion of the "connective" function of the *brahman*-priest, see Heesterman, *The Broken World of Sacrifice*, pp. 152–57.

61. As Heesterman says, "Vedic ritual is essentially the cult of fire. Given the fire's obvious importance to the life of the household it stands to reason that it should have pride of place in the domestic or *gṛhya* ritual—and so it has. Installed at the time of marriage, it defines the household as a unit and accompanies it until the demise of the *paterfamilias* when it renders its last service at his cremation and a new phase starts with the next generation, equally marked by kindling and maintaining the fire. But the pivotal role of the fire is even more conspicuous in the sacrificial *śrauta* ritual. Still apart from the burnt offerings the care of the fire—readying the hearths, making fire or taking it from elsewhere, distributing it over the hearths, elaborately refueling it, and verbally worshipping it—forms the thread that holds the sacrificial proceedings together. The *śrauta* ritual turns on the fire." See Heesterman, *The Broken World of Sacrifice*, p. 86.

62. *Bṛhadāraṇyaka Upaniṣad* 1.4.15.

63. *Ṛgveda* 5.25.1–2.

64. See *Ṛgveda* 1.143.2, 7.5.7.

65. *Ṛgveda* 3.3.14.

66. See *Ṛgveda* 1.14.3, 6.2.6, 6.4.2, 6.12.1, 7.3.6, 7.8.4, 8.7.36.

67. See *Ṛgveda* 8.43.32.

68. *Ṛgveda* 6.8.2.

69. *Ṛgveda* 6.6.2.

70. *Ṛgveda* 8.91.5 (*Vālakhilya* 8.102.5).

71. *Ṛgveda* 3.5.3.

72. *Ṛgveda* 8.60.11.

73. *Ṛgveda* 8.49.10. See also 4.1.5, 7.15.1.

74. *Ṛgveda* 1.127.1. See also 7.16.3, 8.19.23, 8.43.10.

75. *Ṛgveda* 7.43.2. See also 4.6.2.

76. *Ṛgveda* 7.11.5.

77. See also *Ṛgveda* 7.7.2, which mentions Agni's descent from the heavens, and 10.98.11, which notes his ascent into the divine heights.

78. See also *Ṛgveda* 3.3.2, 3.6.5, 3.8.9, 4.7.8, 7.2.3.

79. In the *Ṛgveda* the Ādityas are usually numbered at seven—Varuṇa, Mitra, Aryaman, Bhaga, Dakṣa (or Dhātṛ), Aṁśa, and Sūrya/Savitṛ—each associated with one of the seven bodies of heaven (see, for example, *Ṛgveda* 9.114.3: "seven regions have their seven suns; seven are the Āditya gods"), although sometimes they are listed as eight or more. In the Brāhmaṇas they are numbered at twelve, each identified with the sun in the different months of the year.

80. On the Ādityas as protectors of the *vratas*, see Brereton, *The Ṛgvedic Ādityas*, pp. 70–80.

81. See *Ṛgveda* 7.104.3.

82. *Ṛgveda* 1.53.8.

83. For studies of the Agnihotra, see H. W. Bodewitz, *The Daily Evening and Morning Offering (Agnihotra) according to the Brāhmaṇas* (Leiden: E. J. Brill, 1976); P.-E. Dumont, "The Agnihotra (or Fire-God Oblation) in the Taittirīya-Brāhmaṇa: The First Prapāthaka of the Second Kāṇḍa of the Taittirīya-Brāhmaṇa with Translation," *Proceedings of the American Philosophical Society* 108 (1964), pp. 337–53.

84. On the Darśapūrṇamāsa-iṣṭi, see P.-E. Dumont, "The Full-moon and New-moon Sacrifices in the Taittirīya-Brāhmaṇa," *Proceedings of the American Philosoph-*

ical Society 101 (1957), pp. 216–43; 103 (1959), pp. 584–608; 104 (1960), pp. 1–10; H. G. Ranade, "Some Darśapūrṇamāsa-Rites in the Śatapatha Brāhmaṇa and in the KātŚS," *Bulletin of the Deccan College Research Institute* 35 (March 1976), pp. 121–26; Alfred Hillebrandt, *Das altindische Neu- und Vollmondopfer in seiner einfachsten Form* (Jena: Gustav Fischer, 1879).

85. Regarding the Cāturmāsya. See V. V. Bhide, *The Cāturmāsya Sacrifices* (Pune: University of Poona, 1979).

86. For a study of the Agnyādheya and Punarādheya rites, see Hertha Krick, *Das Ritual der Feuergründung*, Österreichische Akademie der Wissenschaften, Philosophisch-historische Klasse, Sitzungsberichte, Band 399 (Vienna: Österreichische Akademie der Wissenschaften, 1982).

87. On the Agniṣṭoma, see Wilhelm Caland and V. Henry. *L'Agniṣṭhoma: Description complete de la forme normale du sacrifice de Soma dans le culte védique*, 2 volumes (Paris: Ernest Leroux, 1906).

88. Regarding the Agnicāyana, see Frits Staal, *Agni: The Vedic Ritual of the Fire Altar*, 2 volumes (Berkeley: Asian Humanities Press, 1983); P.-E. Dumont, "The Special Kinds of Agnicayana (or Special Methods of Building the Fire-Altar) according to the Kaṭhas in the Taittirīya-Brāhmaṇa: The Tenth, Eleventh, and Twelfth Prapāṭhakas of the Third Kāṇḍa of the Taittirīya-Brāhmaṇa with Translation," *Proceedings of the American Philosophical Society* 95 (1951), pp. 628–75.

89. On the Vājapeya, see Krick, *Das Ritual der Feuergründung*, pp. 132–33.

90. For discussion and bibliography on this same theme, see Smith, *Reflections on Resemblance, Ritual and Religion*, pp. 54–69.

91. On the idea of the self-sacrifice, see J. C. Heesterman, "Self-Sacrifice in Vedic Ritual," *Gilgul: Essays on Transformation, Revolution, and Permanence in the History of Religions, Dedicated to R. J. Zwi Werblowsky*, edited by Shaul Shaked et al. (Leiden: E. J. Brill, 1987), pp. 91–106; Ananda K. Coomaraswamy, "Ātmayajña: Self-Sacrifice," *Harvard Journal of Asiatic Studies* 6 (1942), pp. 358–88; reprinted in *Coomaraswamy*, volume 2: *Selected Papers, Metaphysics*, edited by Roger Lipsey (Princeton: Princeton University Press, 1977), pp. 107–47.

92. See *Ṛgveda* 10.81.6.

93. On Prajāpati, see Brian K. Smith, "Sacrifice and Being: Prajāpati's Cosmic Emission and Its Consequences," *Numen* 33 (1986), pp. 65–99; Smith, *Reflections on Resemblance, Ritual and Religion*, pp. 54–70; Santi Banerjee, "Prajāpati in the Brāhmaṇas," *Vishveshvaranand Indological Journal* 19 (June–December 1981), pp. 14–19; S. Bhattacharji, "Rise of Prajāpati in the Brāhmaṇas," *Annals of the Bhandarkar Oriental Research Institute* 64 (1983), pp. 205–13; Jan Gonda, "The Popular Prajāpati," *History of Religions* 22 (November 1982), pp. 129–49; Gonda, *Prajāpati and the Year* (Amsterdam: North Holland Publishing Co., 1984); Gonda, *Prajāpati's Rise to Higher Rank* (Leiden: E. J. Brill, 1986); J. R. Joshi, "Prajāpati in Vedic Mythol-

ogy and Ritual," *Annals of the Bhandarkar Oriental Research Institute* 53 (1972), pp. 101–25; A. W. Macdonald, "A propos de Prajāpati," *Journal Asiatique* 240 (1952), pp. 323–38; R. T. Vyas, "The Concept of Prajāpati in Vedic Literature," *Bhāratīya Vidyā* 38 (1978), pp. 95–101.

94. *Śatapatha Brāhmaṇa* 10.4.2.2.

95. As an analogy, one might think of a human body in which the many and various cells have become disconnected from each other: the cells would each have their own particular existence, and yet there would be no body, no whole, no unified structure of being.

96. *Śatapatha Brāhmaṇa* 7.1.2.1.

97. As Brian Smith says, "creation is not cosmos." See Smith, *Reflections on Resemblance, Ritual and Religion*, p. 54.

98. *Śatapatha Brāhmaṇa* 6.1.2.12–13.

99. *Śatapatha Brāhmaṇa* 7.1.2.2.

100. A similar passage from another text, *Taittirīya Brāhmaṇa* 1.2.6.1, substitutes for *vīrya* and *prāṇa* the terms *tejas* and *rasa*: "luminous energy" and "essence of life." Reference in Smith, *Reflections on Resemblance, Ritual and Religion*, p. 65.

101. *Śatapatha Brāhmaṇa* 7.1.2.6.

102. *Śatapatha Brāhmaṇa* 7.1.2.7–8.

103. *Śatapatha Brāhmaṇa* 7.1.2.13–14.

104. *Śatapatha Brāhmaṇa* 7.1.2.12.

105. *Śatapatha Brāhmaṇa* 6.1.2.17.

106. *Śatapatha Brāhmaṇa* 7.1.2.9–11.

107. *Śatapatha Brāhmaṇa* 7.1.2.11.

108. The *anuṣṭubh* consists of four lines of eight syllables each. It is common Vedic meter used in praises of the deities.

109. *Śatapatha Brāhmaṇa* 7.1.2.21.

110. *Śatapatha Brāhmaṇa* 1.3.2.1.

111. *Śatapatha Brāhmaṇa* 1.2.5.14.

112. This is the Pravargya or "moving forth" ceremony. On this rite, see J. A. B. van Buitenen, *The Pravargya: An Ancient Indian Iconic Ritual*. Deccan College Building Centenary and Silver Jubilee series, number 58 (Pune: Deccan College, 1968).

113. See *Śatapatha Brāhmaṇa* 7.4.1.1–18.

114. *Āpastamba Śrauta Sūtra* 15.1.16.10.

115. *Śatapatha Brāhmaṇa* 10.1.2.1.

116. *Śatapatha Brāhmaṇa* 9.1.2.33–40.

117. *Śatapatha Brāhmaṇa* 10.1.2.3.

118. *Śatapatha Brāhmaṇa* 7.4.1.1.

119. The typical verb here is *upadadhāti*, "he lays out."

120. The phrase *structural connection* here translated *bandhu*, otherwise "bond." For a study, see Jan Gonda, "*Bandhu-* in the Brāhmaṇas," *Adyar Library Bulletin* 29 (1965), pp. 1–29

121. The world the sacrifice fashioned was sometimes described as *apūrva*, that is, as "unprecedented." The patron (*yajamāna*) was usually a person of wealth, for the complicated rituals typically employed many priests and went on at times for over a year; sometimes the patron was the king, who supported the performance in service of the entire community. Typically, the *yajamāna* was identified in some way with Prajāpati.

122. See Jan Gonda, *Loka: World and Heaven in the Veda* (Amsterdam: N. V. Noord-Hollandsche Uitgevers Maatschappij, 1966), p. 7.

123. The word derives from the Sanskrit verbal root *lok-*, which means to "see" or to "behold." It is related through the Indo-European **leuk-* ("light, brightness") to the English *light*, *illuminate*, and *lucent*. See Morris, ed., *The American Heritage Dictionary*, pp. 1526–27; Julius Pokorny, *Indogermanisches etymologisches Wörterbuch* (Bern: A. Francke, 1959), vol. 2, p. 687.

124. *Pañcaviṁśa Brāhmaṇa* 18.3.1.

125. *Taittirīya Brāhmaṇa* 1.1.4.7.

126. *Taittirīya Saṁhitā* 6.2.1.1.

127. *Aitareya Brāhmaṇa* 7.10.

128. On this point it is worth quoting Heesterman at some length. "So what is the relationship between sacrifice and ritual? . . . In the simplest of terms, sacrifice deals with the riddle of life and death, which are intimately linked and at the same time each other's absolute denial. The riddle cannot be resolved, it can only be reenacted by the participants in the 'play' of sacrifice, whose stakes are the 'goods of life' as against death. . . . [S]acrifice is the catastrophic center, the turning point of life and death, deciding each time anew, through endless rounds of winning, losing, and revanche, the state of human affairs here and in the hereafter. The world of sacrifice is a broken world. Broken at its very center, it is forever hovering on the brink of collapse. . . . If sacrifice is catastrophic, ritual is the opposite. It is called upon to control the passion and fury of the sacrificial contest and to keep such forces within bounds." See Heesterman, *The Broken World of Sacrifice*, pp. 2–3.

129. *Jaminīya Brāhmaṇa* 2.69. See J. C. Heesterman, *The Inner Conflict of Tradition* (Chicago: University of Chicago Press, 1993), pp. 53–54.

130. *Jaiminīya Brāhmaṇa* 2.69–70. Reference, translation, and discussion in Heesterman, *The Inner Conflict of Tradition*, pp. 32–33. For a related discussion, see Heesterman, *The Broken World of Sacrifice*, pp. 53–54.

131. See, for example, *Śatapatha Brāhmaṇa* 5.1.3.11.

132. On Prajāpati as "all" or "this all," see *Śatapatha Brāhmaṇa* 1.3.5.10, 13.6.1.6; *Kauṣītaki Brāhmaṇa* 6.15, 25.12; *Jaiminīya Upaniṣad Brāhmaṇa* 1.46.2.

133. See, for example, *Śatapatha Brāhmaṇa* 3.2.2.4, 5.2.1.2, 6.4.1.6, 14.2.2.18; *Taittirīya Brāhmaṇa* 3.2.3.1, 3.7.2.1.

134. Of many instances, see *Śatapatha Brāhmaṇa* 1.3.2.1.

135. *Chāndogya Upaniṣad* 3.16.1–5.

136. *Prāṇāgnihotra Upaniṣad* 33–34, 38, 40.

137. *Chāndogya Upaniṣad* 8.5.1–3.

138. *Kauṣītaki-Brāhmaṇa Upaniṣad* 2.5.

139. *Śatapatha Brāhmaṇa* 11.5.6.1. On the Five Great Sacrifices (*pañca mahāyajñas*), see P. V. Kane, *History of Dharmaśāstra*, volume 2, pp. 696–756.

140. See *Taittirīya Āraṇyaka* 2.10.

141. *Āśvalāyana Gṛhya Sūtra* 3.1.1–4.

142. *Śatapatha Brāhmaṇa* 11.5.2.2–3.

143. See *Āpastamba Dharma Sūtra* 2.4.9.5–6.

144. See *Laws of Manu* 3.92–93.

145. *Taittirīya Upaniṣad* 1.11.2.

146. *Taittirīya Upaniṣad* 3.10.1. Guests were not to make a nuisance of themselves. The *Laws of Manu* 3.102 interprets the word for "guest," *atithi*, as one who will not stay a whole day (*a-tithi*: "not-day"), and says that "a guest is a brahmin who stays for only one night."

147. On the *pitṛyajña*, see *Viṣṇu Dharma Sūtra* 67.23.25; *Āśvalāyana Gṛhya Sūtra* 1.2.11; *Laws of Manu* 3.91.

148. See *Laws of Manu* 3.82–83.

149. *Taittirīya Āraṇyaka* 2.10. See also *Āpastamba Dharma Sūtra* 1.4.13.1; *Baudāyana Dharma Sūtra* 2.6.4; *Gautama Dharma Sūtra* 5.8–9.

150. See *Laws of Manu* 3.70.

151. *Āśvalāyana Gṛhya Sūtra* 1.2.2. For a similar but slightly different list, see *Mānava Gṛhya Sūtra* 2.12.2.

152. *Śatapatha Brāhmaṇa* 11.5.6.3.

153. See *Śatapatha Brāhmaṇa* 11.6.6.4–7.

154. *Śatapatha Brāhmaṇa* 11.6.6.3.

155. *Śatapatha Brāhmaṇa* 11.5.6.8.

156. See *Taittirīya Āraṇyaka* 2.11.

157. *Taittirīya Āraṇyaka* 2.12.

158. P. V. Kane, *History of Dharmaśāstra*, Volume 2, p. 703, in reference to *Āśvalāyana Gṛhya Sūtra* 3.4.

159. *Śatapatha Brāhmaṇa* 11.5.6.3.

160. *Taittirīya Brāhmaṇa* 3.10.11.

161. The *Śatapatha Brāhmaṇa* notes at 5.7.4–8 that, in addition to passages from those collections, the person undertaking *svādhyāya* is to study the various sacred stories (*itihāsas* and *purāṇas*) and songs in praise of heroes.

162. *Śatapatha Brāhmaṇa* 11.5.7.10.

163. Such oblations are to be performed *upāṁśu*, "in a low voice, as a whisper," or *tūṣṇīm*, "quietly." On the "unuttered" or "silent" (*anirukta*) in this context, see Louis Renou and Lillian Silburn, "Nirukta and Anirukta in Vedic," in J. N. Agrawal and B. D. Shastri, eds., *Sarūpa-Bhāratī, or Homage of Indology: The Dr. Lakshman Sarup Memorial Volume* (Hoshiapur: Vishveshvaranand Institute Publications, 1954), pp. 68–79. Appreciation is here expressed to Brian K. Smith, who gave me these references in a personal conversation.

164. *Śatapatha Brāhmaṇa* 6.2.3.9.

165. *Kauśītaki Brāhmaṇa* 6.11. For further discussion, see above.

166. *Vāc* and *manas*, respectively. See *Chāndogya Upaniṣad* 4.16.1.

167. *Chāndogya Upaniṣad* 4.16.3–6.

168. *Bṛhadāraṇyaka Upaniṣad* 3.1.9.

169. *Jaiminīya Upaniṣad Brāhmaṇa* 1.14.2.

170. *Brahma Upaniṣad* 4. "[All of this] exists in the heart, in the sparkling of consciousness" translates *hṛdi caitanye tiṣṭhati.*

CHAPTER FIVE

1. *Ṛgveda* 3.38.3.

2. *Atharvaveda* 11.8.18.

3. *Aitareya Upaniṣad* 2.3.

4. *Brahma Upaniṣad* 4.

5. For a classical set of instructions to the *vānaprastha*, see *The Laws of Manu* 6.1–32.

6. For a typical set of instructions, see *Āpastambha Dharmasūtra* 2.9.22.9.

7. For an example of such instructions, see *Taittirīya Āraṇyaka* 2.11. Reference in Kane, *History of Dharmaśāstra*, volume 2, pp. 701–2.

8. *Śvetāśvatara Upaniṣad* 2.8–10.

9. For an analysis of the twelve components of the *Praṇava* (to which it refers as *nāda*, the universal "tone" or "sound"), see *Nādabindu Upaniṣad* 6–18.

10. *Kṣurikā Upaniṣad* 3–4b.

11. *Yogaśikhā Upaniṣad* 2–3. This is a reworked rendering of Paul Deussen's, *Sixty Upaniṣads of the Veda*, translated by V. M. Bedekar and G. B. Palsule (Delhi: Motilal Banarsidass, 1987), vol. 2, p. 710.

12. For discussion of the *sadhamāda*, see Chapter Three, above.

13. We see an example of the intricate complexity such *brahmodyas* in *Śatapatha Brāhmaṇa* 13.5.2.12–20, in which the various priests ask each other such questions as "Whose light is equal to the sun?" "Into what things has Puruṣa entered?" "What was the first to be born?" "Who is the tawny one?" "How many kinds of sacrifice are there, how many syllables?" and so on. Other priests respond by saying, "Brahman is the light equal to the sun," "Puruṣa has entered into five things, and they are established in Puruṣa," "The sky was the firstborn," "The night is the tawny one," "There are six kinds of this sacrifice [and] a hundred syllables." The theological disputation continues with the *udgātṛ* asking the *brahman*-priest, "Who knows the navel of the world? Who knows the birthplace of the great sun? Who knows the moon, where it was born?" The *brahman*-priest replies, "I know the navel of this world." The ritual's patron then asks the *adhvaryu*, "I ask you about the farthest end of the earth. I ask you about the navel of the world. I ask you about the seed of the virile horse. I ask you about the highest realm of speech" to which the *adhvaryu* replies, "This altar-ground is the farthest end of the earth. This sacrifice is the navel of the world. This *soma* extract is the seed of the virile horse. This *brahman*-priest is the highest realm of speech." The disputation ends with the assertion that "This, truly, is the complete attainment of speech, the *brahmodya*." Another example of a *brahmodya* appears in *Śatapatha Brāhmaṇa* 11.5.3.1–13, in which Śauceya Prācīnayogya and Uddālaka

Āruṇeya trade questions of each other in the context of the performance of the sacrifice. Śauceya asks Uddālaka, "What is like the cow [in the] Agnihotra? What is like the calf? What is like the cow joined by the calf? What is like their meeting? What is like [the milk] when being milked? What is like that which is brought [from the cowpen]? What is like the light that is thrown upon it?" and so on. Uddālaka responds: "My Agnihotra cow is Iḍa, the daughter of Manu. My calf is the nature of the god of the wind [Vāyu]. The [cow] joined to the calf is in the conjunction [of Iḍa and Vāyu]. Their meeting is the Virāj. When it is being milked [the milk] belongs to the Aśvins, and when it has been milked to the Viśvedevas. When brought [from the cowpen] it belongs to the god of the wind. When it is placed on the fire it belongs to Agni." See also 13.2.6.10–17.

14. The word itself suggests the act of sitting at the feet of a teacher. It is formed from the verbal root *sad-* ("sit"), joined by the prefixes *upa* and *ni*, both of which in this case suggest a certain respectful proximity and may be translated here as "nearby."

15. That such teachings were to be heard only by disciplined and responsible students is demonstrated by the texts themselves. For example, after presenting a series of teachings, *Muṇḍaka Upaniṣad* 3.2.10–11 says,

> Those who perform the rites, who are learned in the scriptures, who are well established in [their cultivation of knowledge of] the Absolute, who with faith offer themselves to the sole seer: to them alone may one declare this knowledge of the Absolute. . . . This [*upaniṣad*] is the truth. . . . Let none who has not maintained the [sacred] vow think on this. Homage to the highest seers; homage to the highest seers.

Such lessons were therefore not for everybody, but rather for those who earnestly yearned to understand. In fact, synonyms and appositions of the word *upaniṣad* include not only such phrases as "the truth of the truth" (*Bṛhadāraṇyaka Upaniṣad* 2.1.10), but also "that which is hidden" (*Nṛhsiṁhottaratāpanī Upaniṣad* 8) and "that which is a supreme secret" (*Kaṭha Upaniṣad* 3.17).

16. Although nearly 250 texts call themselves Upaniṣads, Indian commentators generally have recognized anywhere from ten to more than a hundred works that can justly be called Upaniṣads (for a stock list of 108 such texts, see the enumeration given by *Muktikā Upaniṣad* 1.30–39). The dates of these texts fall into two general periods. The so-called major Upaniṣads date roughly from the eighth to the first centuries BCE ("[major" because they have been interpreted by most classical Indian philosophers and because virtually all Indian commentators regard them as legitimately connected with the Vedic tradition). Other Upaniṣads—we might call them the "minor" Upaniṣads—date from roughly 100 BCE to 1100 CE. The latter would include the Sāmānya-Vedānta Upaniṣads, the Yoga Upaniṣads, the Saṁnyāsa Upaniṣads, the Mantra Upaniṣads, the Śaiva Upaniṣads, the Vaiṣṇava Upaniṣads, and the Śākta Upaniṣads. In this chapter we will make reference to both the major and minor Upaniṣads.

For an introduction to Upaniṣadic literature and teachings, see William K. Mahony, "Upaniṣads," in *The Encyclopedia of Religion*, edited by Mircea Eliade et al.,

16 volumes (New York: Macmillan, 1987), volume 15, pp. 147–52, from which some of the wording in this and the previous note is taken.

17. *Chāndogya Upaniṣad* 3.5.4.

18. See *Bṛhadāraṇyaka Upaniṣad* 1.3.28.

19. *Maitrī Upaniṣad* 4.4. The terms for "knowledge," "contemplative fervor," and "meditation" are *vidyā, tapas,* and *cintā,* respectively.

20. *Tejobindu Upaniṣad* 4.

21. *Kaivalya Upaniṣad* 16.

22. See the opening of Chapter Four, above. The general idea offered in this paragraph is similar to one presented by Panikkar in *Mantramañjarī*, pp. 631–33.

23. *Ṛgveda* 9.113.7–11.

24. This paragraph continues to share a line of thought with Panikkar, *Mantra-mañjarī*, p. 633.

25. *Ṛgveda* 9.11.7.

26. See *Bṛhadāraṇyaka Upaniṣad* 3.1.1.

27. See *Bṛhadāraṇyaka Upaniṣad* 3.1.2–5.

28. *Bṛhadāraṇyaka Upaniṣad* 3.1.6.

29. *Kaṭha Upaniṣad* 4.1–2.

30. *Kaṭha Upaniṣad* 1.12. For other examples of negative imagery in Upaniṣadic depictions of heaven, see *Bṛhadāraṇyaka Upaniṣad* 5.10, *Chāndogya Upaniṣad* 8.4.1–2, *Śvetāśvatara Upaniṣad* 2.12.

31. *Chāndogya Upaniṣad* 3.13.7.

32. *Kaṭha Upaniṣad* 1.13.

33. *Kaṭha Upaniṣad* 1.14. "Abiding in the cave of the heart" translates *nihitam guhāyām*, more literally perhaps "placed in the secret place." But the word *guhā* also refers more figuratively both to the heart and to a cave, thus the current translation, "in the cave of the heart."

34. See *Ṛgveda* 10.164.46.

35. *Mahānārāyaṇa Upaniṣad* 10.1, 10.3, and 10.7. The translation is a reworked rendering of Paul Deussen, *Sixty Upaniṣads of the Veda*, translated by V. M. Bedekar and B. B. Palsule (Delhi: Motilal Banarsidass, 1980), pp. 254–55.

36. *Kaṭha Upaniṣad* 3.15.

37. *Kaṭha Upaniṣad* 3.15.

38. *Taittirīya Upaniṣad* 3.1.

39. See, for example, *Śatapatha Brāhmaṇa* 10.6.5.9, which describes Brahman as *svayambhū*, "self-existing."

40. *Atharvaveda* 10.2.25.

41. *Bṛhadāraṇyaka Upaniṣad* 3.9.1–11.

42. See, for example, *Śatapatha Brāhmaṇa* 5.1.3.11.

43. *Bṛhadāraṇyaka Upaniṣad* 5.3.1.

44. *Chāndogya Upaniṣad* 8.3.3.

45. *Śvetāśvatara Upaniṣad* 1.15.

46. *Brahma Upaniṣad* 16.

47. *Brahmabindu Upaniṣad* 12–14.

48. *Chāndogya Upaniṣad* 3.12.7–9.

49. *Bṛhadāraṇyaka Upaniṣad* 4.4.5. The phrase *sa vā 'ayam ātmā brahma* ("Truly, this Ātman is Brahman") has come to be known as a *mahāvākya*, that is, as a "great teaching" that encapsulates in one short phrase the essence of Upaniṣadic thought as a whole.

50. *Chāndogya Upaniṣad* 3.14.3.

51. *Bṛhadāraṇyaka Upaniṣad* 5.6.1.

52. *Adhyātma Upaniṣad* 46.

53. *Muṇḍaka Upaniṣad* 2.2.9.

54. *Muṇḍaka Upaniṣad* 3.1.7. On the phrase *cave of the heart*, see note 33, above.

55. *Kaṭha Upaniṣad* 5.12. "Wise" here translates *dhīra*.

56. *Kaṭha Upaniṣad* 5.15.

57. See *Bṛhadāraṇyaka Upaniṣad* 1.5.20: "The breath of life [*prāṇa*] enters him from out of the moon and water. Truly, that is the breath of life which, neither moving nor still, is neither disturbed nor injured. He who knows this becomes the Self [*ātman*] of all beings."

58. See *Bṛhadāraṇyaka Upaniṣad* 3.7.3.–3.7.23.

59. *Kauṣītaki Upaniṣad* 4.20.

60. See *Chāndogya Upaniṣad* 6.9.1–6.16.3.

61. *Praśna Upaniṣad* 3.6.

62. *Īśā Upaniṣad* 1, 5–7.

63. *Śvetāśvatara Upaniṣad* 4.1–2.

64. *Subāla Upaniṣad* 7–9.

65. *Śvetāśvatara Upaniṣad* 6.11–12.

66. *Śvetāsvatara Upaniṣad* 4.10.

67. *Śvetāśvatara Upaniṣad* 4.11 and 4.14–16.

68. *Śvetāśvatara Upaniṣad* 3.9 and 3.13.

69. Śaiva Upaniṣads include the *Akṣamālaka, Atharvaśikhā, Atharvaśira, Kālāgnirudra, Kaivalya, Gaṇapati, Dakṣiṇāmūrti, Pañcabrahma, Bṛhajjābāla, Bhasmajābāla, Rudrahṛdaya, Rudrākṣabābāla,* and *Śarobha* Upaniṣads.

70. Vaiṣṇava Upaniṣads include the *Anyakta, Kalisaṁtaraṇa, Kṛṣṇa, Garuḍa, Gopālapūrvatāpanī, Gopālottaratāpanī, Tripādvibhūtimahānārāyaṇa, Dattātreya, Nṛsiṁhapūrvatāpanī, Nṛsiṁhottaratāpanī, Rāmapūrvatāpanī, Rāmottaratāpanī, Vāsudeva,* and *Hayagrīva* Upaniṣads.

71. Śākta Upaniṣads include the *Tripurā, Tripurātāpanī, Tripurārahasya, Sarasvatīrahasya, Saubhāgyalakṣmī, Bhāvanā, Bahvṛcā, Devī,* and *Sītā* Upaniṣads.

72. *Tripurā Upaniṣad* verses 1, 6, and 10. Translated here by Douglas Renfrew Brooks, *The Secret of the Three Cities: An Introduction to Hindu Śākta Tantrism* (Chicago: University of Chicago Press, 1990), pp. 151, 164, 174.

73. *Bahvṛcā Upaniṣad* 5–8. This is a later Upaniṣad influenced by Śākta Tantric thought. The reference to the "Three Cities" reflects the Tantric idea that the Absolute assumes triadic form and function as it devolves from primordial unity: as will (*icchā*), action (*kriyā*), and knowledge (*jñāna*), for example; or as creator, creation, and the process of creativity; or as the knower, the object of knowledge, and the process of knowing. There are other triadic formulations as well. For discussion of this theme, see Brooks, *Secret of the Three Cities*, p. 97, and references in that Index, *s.v.* "Tripurā."

74. *Śvetāśvatara Upaniṣad* 2.11.

75. *Maṇḍalabrāhmaṇa Upaniṣad* 2.1.10.

76. Both *citra* and *cit* derive from the verbal root *cit-*, to "perceive, fix the mind on, understand."

77. Savitṛ's name derives from the verbal root *su-*, to "set in motion, vivify, stimulate."

78. The terms *dhī-* (with a hyphen) and *dhī* (without a hyphen) can be confusing. The former represents a Sanskrit verbal root, that is, a phoneme that does not appear in actual use but on which meaningful words are built. The latter is the undeclined form of a noun built on that verbal root. In order to avoid this confusion, some writers prefer to use the nominal form of the noun, *dhīḥ*, to distinguish it from its root, *dhī-*. See, for example, Gonda, *Vision of the Vedic Poets*, pp. 68–169 and *passim.*

79. *Muṇḍaka Upaniṣad* 1.1.6.

80. *Ṛgveda* 1.62.12.

81. *Ṛgveda* 6.49.7.

82. See, for example, *Śvetāśvatara Upaniṣad* 1.3: "Those who practiced the discipline of meditation [*dhyāna-yoga*] saw the power of the divine Self."

83. *Mahā Upaniṣad* 2.58.

84. *Brahmavidyā Upaniṣad* 13.

85. The reference here is probably to underground streams flowing hidden under dry riverbeds.

86. *Śvetāśvatara Upaniṣad* 1.15–16.

87. *Śvetāśvatara Upaniṣad* 1.12–14.

88. *Tejobindu Upaniṣad* 2.

89. *Śvetāśvatara Upaniṣad* 1.3.

90. *Muṇḍaka Upaniṣad* 3.2.4–5 and 3.2.9.

91. *Muṇḍaka Upaniṣad* 3.1.7.

92. The phrase "nine doorways" refers to the nine openings in the human body (eyes, ears, nostrils, mouth, and places of evacuation). The "three strands" may suggest the three qualities of physical existence—purity, energy, and darkness (*sattva, rajas,* and *tamas,* respectively)—on which the Sāṁkhya school of Indian philosophy was later to base much of its metaphysical thought. Alternatively, they may refer to the skin, nails, and hair. For these interpretations, see William Dwight Whitney, trans., *Atharva Veda Saṁhitā*, 2 volumes, reprint edition (Delhi: Motilal Banarsidass, 1971), volume 2, pp. 601 and 1045.

93. *Atharvaveda* 10.8.43–44.

94. *Chāndogya Upaniṣad* 3.14.1–2.

95. *Kaṭha Upaniṣad* 2.12.

96. *Maitrī Upaniṣad* 6.24.

97. *Kauṣītaki Upaniṣad* 3.2.

98. *Śvetāśvatara Upaniṣad* 3.14–17.

99. *Maṇḍalabrāhmaṇa Upaniṣad* 1.1.9.

100. *Aitareya Upaniṣad* 3.2–3.

101. The phrase *satyaṁ jñānam anantam brahma* ("Brahman is truth, knowledge, and infinity") from this, an early Upaniṣad, stands as a precursor for what was to become a well-known Vedāntic description of Brahman as *sat-cit-ānanda*: "Being, Consciousness, and Bliss." Some later Upaniṣads were to make use of the latter formula. See, for example, *Nṛsiṁhottaratāpanī Upaniṣad* 4.3: "This Ātman, the highest Brahman . . . shines forth . . . filled with Being, Consciousness, and Bliss"; and 7.2: "This whole world consists of Brahman, which consists of Being, Consciousness, and Bliss." See also *Rāmapūrvatāpanī Upaniṣad* 92.

102. *Taittirīya Upaniṣad* 2.1.

103. *Varāha Upaniṣad* 2.45–47.

104. *Muṇḍaka Upaniṣad* 1.1.7–9. See also 2.1.1: "This is the truth. Just as sparks of similar shape arise forth by the thousands from a blazing fire, even so many different kinds of beings arise forth from the Immutable, and to it they return as well."

105. See also *Muṇḍaka Upaniṣad* 2.1.9, which adds "By him is the inner soul supported, along with the elements."

106. *Mahānārāyaṇa Upaniṣad* 10.3 and 10.7.

107. See *Maitrī Upaniṣad* 7.1.

108. *Taittirīya Upaniṣad* 2.1.1.

109. *Taittirīya Upaniṣad* 2.1.1.

110. *Taittirīya Upaniṣad* 2.3.1. "Consists of the breath of life" translates *prāṇamaya.*

111. *Taittirīya Upaniṣad* 2.1.4–5. The phrases *consists of thought* and *consists of understanding* translate *manomaya* and *vijñānamaya*, respectively.

112. *Taittirīya Upaniṣad* 2.1.5. "Consisting of bliss" renders *ānandamaya.*

113. See *Kaṭha Upaniṣad* 5.7.

114. *Bṛhadāraṇyaka Upaniṣad* 4.3.7.

115. Some of the wording in this sentence is similar to Paul Deussen's phrasing in *The Philosophy of the Upanishads*, reprint edition (New York: Dover Publications, 1966), p. 296.

116. *Bṛhadāraṇyaka Upaniṣad* 4.3.9–10. "For one is indeed a creator" translates *sa hi kartā.*

117. *Bṛhadāraṇyaka Upaniṣad* 4.3.13.

118. *Bṛhadāraṇyaka Upaniṣad* 4.3.14.

119. *Bṛhadāraṇyaka Upaniṣad* 4.3.20. The phrase *this is imagined through ignorance* translates *tad atrāvidyayā manyate.*

120. *Bṛhadāraṇyaka Upaniṣad* 4.3.21.

121. *Bṛhadāraṇyaka Upaniṣd* 4.3.30.

122. *Bṛhadāraṇyaka Upaniṣad* 4.3.32.

123. *Bṛhadāraṇyaka Upaniṣad* 4.3.15–17.

124. *Māṇḍūkya Upaniṣad* 3–7. Regarding this interpretation of the state of Prājña, "Wisdom," compare *Bṛhadāraṇyaka Upaniṣad* 4.3.21, which we noted previously refers to one "who is in the embrace of the wise Self."

125. *Māṇḍūkya Upaniṣad* 12.

126. *Māṇḍūkya Upaniṣad* 7.

127. *Kaṭha Upaniṣad* 3.10b–11. Compare *Kaṭha Upaniṣad* 6.6–8:

> Knowing the separate nature of the senses,
> their appearing and disappearing,
> and their separate emergence,
> the wise person understands, and sorrows not.
> Higher than the senses is the mind;
> Higher than the mind is the pure being.
> Higher than the true being is the great self;
> Higher than the great is the unmanifest.
> Higher than the unmanifest, however, is the [supreme] Person,
> pervading all things and without any distinguishing characteristics:
> He who knows him is liberated [from the cycles of change]
> and attains immortality.

128. The metaphysical stance taken here is similar to that subsequently taken by Sāṁkhya schools of Indian philosophy. The *Maitrāyaṇa Upaniṣad* draws explicitly on such ontologies when, at 3.2, it explains the notion of rebirth:

> The five subtle elements are known by the term *bhūta* [an elemental component of being]. But then, the five Mahābhūtas [the gross elements] are also known by the term *bhūta.* The combination of all these [elements] is what is known as the body. He who dwells within the so-called body is referred to as the elemental self [*bhūtātman*]. The immortal Ātman remains untouched, like a drop of water on a lotus petal. However, the threads of material nature overwhelm this Ātman. Overwhelmed in this way, [a person] becomes confused and, because of this confusion, forgets the sublime Creator dwelling within his own self. Pushed by

the flood of material being, dirtied and deluded, he becomes uncertain and unsteady, weakened, full of greed, uncomposed and dissolving into the illusion [that he possesses a separate self]. He thinks, "I am this, this is mine," and he traps himself with his self, like a bird in a net. Encumbered by the effect of his actions, he enters into a good or a bad womb and transmigrates upward or downward, overwhelmed by oppositions and contrasts.

129. The word *buddhi* derives from the root *budh-*, "awake."

130. See Chapter One for discussion of the gods' power of imaginative creativity, *māyā*, according to the Vedic Saṁhitā literatures.

131. *Tripurātāpanī Upaniṣad* 5.6.

132. *Muṇḍaka Upaniṣad* 3.1.9–10.

133. *Yogakuṇḍalī Upaniṣad* 3.4.

134. *Chāndogya Upaniṣad* 3.14.1. Referring to Śaṅkara's commentary on this passage, Radhakrishnan (*The Principal Upaniṣads*, p. 391) glosses *kratv-anurūpam phalam*: "As we will, so will our reward be."

135. *Kaṭha Upaniṣad* 3.3–6.

136. *Kaṭha Upaniṣad* 3.7–9.

137. The Prologue to the *Adhyātma Upaniṣad* and verses 1, 19–20.

138. *Adhyātma Upaniṣad* 65.

139. *Kaṭha Upaniṣad* 5.13.

140. *Muṇḍaka Upaniṣad* 3.1.9.

141. *Chāndogya Upaniṣad* 8.1.1–6, 8.3.3–4.

142. *Tejobindu Upaniṣad* 1.1.

143. *Trīpurātāpanī Upaniṣad* 1.39.

144. *Praśna Upaniṣad* 3.6. For other passages in the major Upaniṣads on the heart and its channels, see *Bṛhadāraṇyaka Upaniṣad* 2.2.19, 4.2.2–3, 4.3.20, and 4.4.8–9; *Chāndogya Upaniṣad* 8.6.1–3 and 8.6.6 (also *Kaṭha Upaniṣad* 6.16); *Taittirīya Upaniṣad* 1.6.1; *Kauśītaki Upaniṣad* 4.19; *Maitrī Upaniṣad* 6.21, 6.30, and 7.11.

145. *Muṇḍaka Upaniṣad* 2.2.1 and 2.2.6.

146. These five forms of breath are known as *prāṇa*, *apāna*, *vyāna*, *samāna*, and *udāna*, respectively.

147. *Subāla Upaniṣad* 4.1.

148. *Yogakuṇḍalī Upaniṣad* 1.82.

149. Terms for such wheels or centers of consciousness vary somewhat. The most common names are: the *Mūlādhāra* ("root-support"), located at the base of the spine; the *Svādhiṣṭhāna* ("based in its own abode"), at the level of the sexual organ; the *Maṇipūra* ("bejeweled") at the navel; at the level of the heart turns the *Anāhata* (where the silent, "unstruck" universal sound is heard); the *Viśuddha* ("untainted") is at the throat; the *Ājñā* ("command") lies between the eyebrows; and finally the *Sahasrāra,* the resplendent "thousand-petalled" lotus, unfolds its blossom above the head.

150. *Saubhāgyalakṣmī Upaniṣad* 3.1–9 lists the *cakra*s in this way. The *Ādhāra-cakra* sits at the base and is to be envisioned as a flame. The *Svādiṣṭhāna-cakra* is at the level of the genital organ; one is to meditate on it as resembling a growth of coral. The *Nābhi-cakra* or *Maṇipūraka-cakra* lies at the navel. One is to contemplate it as a whirlpool in the shape of a serpent that shines with the light of millions of suns. The *Hṛdaya-cakra* at the heart is to be envisioned as a lovely and enchanting swan. At the *Kaṇṭha-cakra*, located at the throat, the *iḍā-*, *piṅgalā-*, and *suṣumnā-nāḍī*s weave through each other. Within the wheel of the *Tālu-cakra* at the level of the palate is a small bell; meditating on the hollow within the space of that bell one dissolves the gross movements of the mind. In the *Bhrū-cakra* at the eyebrow one contemplates a tongue of flame, gaining thereby power over words. The *Brahmarandhra-cakra* at the top of the head is to be envisioned as a wisp of smoke, thinner than a needle. The ninth, the *Ākāśa-cakra* or "wheel of space," consists of a lotus with sixteen petals, facing upward; in it one should envision the rising power of *śakti* into the supreme and vast emptiness of the universe.

151. The relevant Sanskrit terms here are *antarlakṣya* ("to be seen inwardly"), *bahirlakṣya* ("to be seen outwardly"), and *madhyalakṣya* ("to be seen in between").

152. *Maṇḍalabrāhmaṇa Upaniṣad* 1.2.3–6.

153. *Maṇḍalabrāhmaṇa Upaniṣad* 2.2.7–12.

154. *Maṇḍalabrāhmaṇa Upaniṣad* 2.1.7–9. That the divinity within is called Khecarī here (literally, "she who moves through the atmosphere") suggests that she lives in this quiet place of the heart where the breath has been stilled. The epithet also suggests the *khecārī-mudrā*, a yogic practice in which one's breathing is so thoroughly controlled that it slows effectively to a stop. The breath as vital force then remains calm in the heart and mind.

155. *Yogaśikhā Upaniṣad* 4–7. This translation is a reworked rendering of that found in Paul Deussen, *Sixty Upaniṣads of the Veda*, translated by V. M. Bedekar and G. B. Palsule, 2 volumes (Delhi: Motilal Banarsidass, 1980), vol. 2, p. 710.

156. *Varāha Upaniṣad* 5.31–35. "What is thought of by the mind is accomplished by the mind itself" translates *manasā cintataṁ kāryaṁ manasā yena sidhyati.*

157. *Chāndogya Upaniṣad* 3.13.7.

158. *Kaṭha Upaniṣad* 3.10b.

159. *Kaṭha Upaniṣad* 3.13.

160. *Śvetāśvatara Upaniṣad* 1.10. "Cessation of the imaginary world formed by the fluctuations of the mind" translates *viśvamāyānivṛttiḥ*.

161. *Śāṇḍilya Upaniṣad* 1.7.14–21.

162. *Amṛtabindu Upaniṣad* 14. This is a rendering of Paul Deussen's translation in *Sixty Upaniṣads of the Veda*, vol. 2, p. 694. For a representative list in a late Upaniṣad of the eight central practices of classical Yoga, see *Śāṇḍilya Upaniṣad* 1.2, which lists *yama (*restraint and forbearance) *niyama* (spiritual discipline and the performance of religious obligations), *āsana* (body posture), *prāṇāyama* (control of the breath), *pratyāhāra* (withdrawal of the senses inward), *dhyāna* (contemplative focusing of the mind), and *samādhi* (inward absorption).

163. *Śāṇḍilya Upaniṣad* 1.10. "With qualities" translates *saguṇa*, "without qualities" renders *nirguṇa*.

164. *Maṇḍalabrāhmaṇa Upaniṣad* 1.3.1. "Without the use of the mind" translates *amanaska*.

165. *Maṇḍalabrāhmaṇa Upaniṣad* 5.1.1–3.

166. *Tripurātāpanī Upaniṣad* 5.7–8.

167. *Maitrī Upaniṣad* 6.24.

168. *Maitrī Upaniṣad* 6.34.(1–9).

169. *Brahma Upaniṣad*, concluding verses.

CHAPTER SIX

1. For a discussion of the difference in the Vedic world between "creation" and "cosmogony," see Brian K. Smith, *Reflections on Resemblance, Ritual and Religion* (New York: Oxford University Press, 1989), pp. 54–69.

2. Thus, for example, *saṁyuj-*, conjoin, link; *saṁkṛ-*, put together, compose; *saṁkḷp-*, arrange; *saṁtan-*, join together, connect; *saṁdhā-*, fasten together, unite; *sampad-*, bring together. I take this point from Smith, *Reflections on Resemblance, Ritual and Religion*, p. 63, who also refers to Lilian Silburn, *Instant et cause: Le Discontinue dans la pensée philosophique de l'Inde* (Paris: Libraire philosophique J. Vrin, 1955), p. 56.

3. *Ṛgveda* 6.47.3b–4.

4. *Ṛgveda* 4.56.3.

5. *Ṛgveda* 8.41.3.

6. *Ṛgveda* 5.63.6.

7. *Ṛgveda* 3.38.3.

8. *Śvetāśvatara Upaniṣad* 4.9b–10.

9. *Taittirīya Brāhmaṇa* 2.8.8.4.

10. *Pañcaviṁśa Brāhmaṇa* 10.14.2.

11. *Śatapatha Brāhmaṇa* 10.5.3.1–5.

12. *Ṛgveda* 10.125.7–8.

13. *Ṛgveda* 10.125.3d–5.

14. *Ṛgveda* 10.190.1–3.

15. *Ṛgveda* 9.9.1.

16. *Ṛgveda* 9.86.29.

17. *Ṛgveda* 6.7.7.

18. *Ṛgveda* 5.85.2

19. *Ṛgveda* 9.96.18.

20. *Ṛgveda* 1.62.12.

21. *Ṛgveda* 1.68.5/.

22. *Ṛgveda* 3.53.9.

23. *Ṛgveda* 7.33.11.

24. See, for example, *Ṛgveda* 5.29.15, which uses the adjectives *navya* (new), *bhadra* (sparkling), and *sukṛta* (well-formed) to describe the prayerful songs Gaurivīti Śāktya sang to Indra.

25. *Ṛgveda* 7.94.1.

26. See *Ṛgveda* 3.26.8.

27. See *Ṛgveda* 10.67.10.

28. See, for example, *Ṛgveda* 10.98.2–3.

29. *Ṛgveda* 7.15.4.

30. *Ṛgveda* 10.23.6

31. *Ṛgveda* 6.32.1.

32. *Śatapatha Brāhmaṇa* 1.2.5.14.

33. *Śatapatha Brāhmaṇa* 7.4.1.15.

34. *Śatapatha Brāhmaṇa* 7.4.1.18.

35. As the Brāhmaṇas assert, the performance of the ritual is "for gaining a firm foundation [*pratiṣṭhāna*]." Of many examples, see *Aitareya Brāhmaṇa* 4.21, *Pañcaviṁśa Brāhmaṇa* 5.5.4–5, 18.10.10.

36. *Śatapatha Brāhmaṇa* 7.4.1.1.

37. *Brahma Upaniṣad* 4.

38. *Aitareya Upaniṣad* 3.1.2–3.

39. *Taittirīya Upaniṣad* 2.3.1.

40. *Taittirīya Upaniṣad* 2.4.1–2.5.1.

41. *Varāha Upaniṣad* 2.45–47.

42. *Ṛgveda* 6.47.18.

43. *Ṛgveda* 10.71.4 and 10.71.7.

44. *Ṛgveda* 1.39.1.

45. For examples, see *Ṛgveda* 1.164.11–14 (turning wheel), *Ṛgveda* 10.125 (universal Word); *Ṛgveda* 10.90 (cosmic Person), *Atharvaveda* 10.8 (cosmic pillar), and *Atharvaveda* 4.1 (Brahman).

46. See *Ṛgveda* 7.76.2.

47. *Ṛgveda* 6.9.6.

48. *Ṛgveda* 7.33.9.

49. *Ṛgveda* 10.125.2.

50. *Ṛgveda* 7.64.4.

51. *Ṛgveda* 4.11.2–3b.

52. I take the following interpretation of *Ṛgveda* 1.164 from W. Norman Brown, "The Creative Role of the Goddess Vāc in the Ṛg Veda," in *Pratidānam: Indian, Iranian and Indo-European Studies Presented to F. B. J. Kuiper* (The Hague: Mouton, 1968), pp. 393–97, reprinted in *India and Indology,* edited by Rosane Rocher (Delhi: Motilal Banarsidass for the American Institute of Indian Studies, 1978), pp. 75–78.

53. *Ṛgveda* 1.164.41–45.

54. See *Śatapatha Brāhmaṇa* 9.2.1.21 and 14.3.2.24.

55. *Ṛgveda* 1.164.4–5.

56. See also *Ṛgveda* 10.5.7.

57. See *Ṛgveda* 1.164.5–10.

58. See *Ṛgveda* 1.164.13–14 and 1.164.26–30.

59. *Mahānārāyaṇa Upaniṣad* 1.11.

60. *Chāndogya Upaniṣad* 3.13.7.

61. *Muṇḍaka Upaniṣad* 2.2.9.

62. *Kaṭha Upaniṣad* 4.12.

63. *Kaṭha Upaniṣad* 4.1b–2.

64. *Muṇḍaka Upaniṣad* 2.29.

65. *Kaṭha Upaniṣad* 2.20–23.

66. *Śatapatha Brāhmaṇa* 7.1.2.1.

67. *Ṛgveda* 3.39.1.

68. *Ṛgveda* 5.29.15.

69. *Ṛgveda* 10.39.14.

70. *Atharvaveda* 3.17.1–2.

71. *Ṛgveda* 7.94.1.

72. *Ṛgveda* 10.64.2.

73. *Ṛgveda* 1.139.2.

74. *Śatapatha Brāhmaṇa* 7.1.2.12.

75. *Śatapatha Brāhmaṇa* 7.1.2.9–11.

76. Smith, *Reflections on Resemblance, Ritual and Religion*, p. 65 in reference to *Taittirīya Brāhmaṇa* 1.2.6.1.

77. *Brahmabindu Upaniṣad* 11.

78. *Kaṭha Upaniṣad* 2.1 and 2.5.

79. *Śvetāśvatara Upaniṣad* 2.8–10.

80. *Subāla Upaniṣad* 4.1.

81. *Varāha Upaniṣad* 5.31–34.

82. *Maṇḍalabrāhmaṇa Upaniṣad* 2.1.10.

83. *Maṇḍalabrāhmaṇa Upaniṣad* 2.1.6.

84. *Śāṇḍilya Upaniṣad* 1.7.14–21.

85. *Ṛgveda* 9.113.7–9.

86. *Śatapatha Brāhmaṇa* 10.6.5.8.

87. *Muṇḍaka Upaniṣad* 3.2.9.

88. See *Pañcaviṁśa Brāhmaṇa* 24.11.2. See also *Jaiminīya Brāhmaṇa* 1.117: "Prajāpati emitted the creatures, who were emitted hungry. Being hungry, they ate each other." References in Smith, *Reflections on Resemblance, Ritual and Religion*, p. 59n.

89. *Kaṭha Upaniṣad* 4.2.

90. *Ṛgveda* 1.164.10 and 1.164.37.

91. *Aitareya Upaniṣad* 1.3.1.

92. See *Ṛgveda* 1.164.47.

93. See *Ṛgveda* 9.113.2.

94. *Ṛgveda* 1.114.9.

95. *Ṛgveda* 10.123.3c, d–4.

96. *Ṛgveda* 1.23.24.

97. *Ṛgveda* 8.48.3.

98. *Śatapatha Brāhmaṇa* 11.2.3.1–3.

99. *Śatapatha Brāhmaṇa* 11.2.3.4–6.

100. *Ṛgveda* 5.15.2.

101. *Taittirīya Āraṇyaka* 1.23.8.

102. *Maitrī Upaniṣad* 6.17.

103. *Muṇḍaka Upaniṣad* 3.2.4–5.

104. *Aitareya Upaniṣad* 1.3.11.

105. *Bṛhadāraṇyaka Upaniṣad* 1.4.10. So, too, the Upaniṣadic sage could affirm any of the other *mahāvākyas* ("great teachings") of the Upaniṣads: *sa vā ayam ātmā brahma,* "Truly, the Brahman is this Ātman" (*Bṛhadāraṇyaka Upaniṣad* 4.4.5); *tat tvam asi*, "That, thou art" (*Chāndogya Upaniṣad* 6.8.7, etc.); *sarvaṁ khalvidaṁ brahma*, "Verily, this whole world is Brahman" (*Chāndogya Upaniṣad* 3.14).

106. See *Bṛhadāraṇyaka Upaniṣad* 3.9.26, 4.2.4, 4.4.22, 4.5.15.

107. *Chāndogya Upaniṣad* 3.14.4.

108. *Kaṭha Upaniṣad* 3.15.

109. *Kaṭha Upaniṣad* 5.8.

110. *Śvetāśvatara Upaniṣad* 4.19–20.

111. *Bahvṛcā Upaniṣad* 5–8.

112. *Muṇḍaka Upaniṣad* 3.2.5.

113. *Kaṭha Upaniṣad* 5.12–14.

Bibliography

SANSKRIT TEXTS

Unless otherwise noted, all translations in the preceding pages are mine. For readers who wish to consult other renderings or to read larger portions of these works than those included in this study, I have included here reference to selected translations where they are available.

Adhyātma Upaniṣad. In *The Sāmānya Vedānta Upanishads*. Edited by Pandit A. Mahadeva Sastri. Madras: The Adyar Library, 1921. Translated by K. Nārāyaṇasvāmī Aiyar. In *Thirty Minor Upanishads*. Madras: K. Nārāyaṇasvāmī Aiyar, 1914. Reprint edition, El Reno, Okla.: Santarasa Publications, 1980.

Aitareya Āraṇyaka. Edited and translated by Arthur Berriedale Keith. Oxford: Clarendon Press, 1909. Reprint edition, Oxford: Oxford University Press, 1969.

Aitareya Brāhmaṇa. 2 volumes. Ānandāśrama Sanskrit Series, number 32. Poona: Ānandāśrama, 1931. Translated by Arthur Berriedale Keith. In *Ṛgveda Brāhmanas*. Harvard Oriental Series, Volume 25. Cambridge, Mass.: Harvard University Press, 1920. Reprint edition, Delhi: Motilal Banarsidass, 1971.

Aitareya Upaniṣad. In *Daśopaniṣad-s*. Revised edition. Edited by the Pandits of The Adyar Library under the supervision of C. Kunhan Raja, revised by A. A. Ramanathan. 2 volumes. Madras: The Adyar Library and Research Centre, 1984. Volume 1. Translated by Patrick Olivelle. In *Upaniṣads*. Oxford and New York: Oxford University Press, 1996.

Amṛtabindu Upaniṣad. Translated by Paul Deussen (as the *Brahmabindu Upaniṣad*). In *Sechzig Upaniṣad's des Veda*. Leipzig: F. A. Brockhaus, 1897, 1921. Sanskrit text in a much longer recension appears in *The Yoga Upaniṣads*. Edited by Pandit A. Mahadeva Sastri. Reprint edition, Madras: The Adyar Library and Research Centre, 1968.

Āpastamba Dharma Sūtra. Edited by U. C. Pandey. Kashi Sanskrit Series, number 59. Varanasi: Chowkhamba Sanskrit Series Office, 1971. Translated by Georg Bühler. In *The Sacred Books of the Āryas.* Sacred Books of the East, volume 30. Oxford: Oxford University Press, 1886. Reprint edition, Delhi: Motilal Banarsidass, 1964.

Āpastamba Śrauta Sūtra. Edited by Richard Garbe. 3 volumes. Calcutta: Royal Asiatic Society of Bengal, 1882–1902. Translated into German by Wilhelm Caland. 3 volumes. Calcutta: Vandenhoeck and Ruprecht, 1921. Reprint edition, Wiesbaden: Dr. Martin Sandig, 1969.

Āśvalāyana Gṛhya Sūtra. Edited and translated by N. N. Sharma. Delhi: Eastern Book Linkers, 1976. Translated by Hermann Oldenburg. In *The Gṛhya Sūtras.* Sacred Books of the East, volume 29. Oxford: Oxford University Press, 1866. Reprint edition, Delhi: Motilal Banarsidass, 1964.

Atharvaveda Saṁhitā (Paippalāda recension). Edited by Raghu Vira. New Delhi: Meharchand Lachmandas, 1976.

Atharvaveda Saṁhitā (Śaunaka recension). Edited by V. Bandhu. 4 volumes. Hoshiarpur: Vishveshvaranand Vedic Research Institute, 1960–62. Translated by William Dwight Whitney. 2 volumes. Harvard Oriental series, volumes 7 and 8. Cambridge, Mass.: Harvard University Press, 1905. Reprint edition, Delhi: Motilal Banarsidass, 1971.

Bahvṛcā Upaniṣad. In *The Śākta Upaniṣads.* Second edition. Edited by Pandit A. Mahadeva Sastri. Reprint edition, Madras: The Adyar Library and Research Centre, 1986. Translated by A. G. Krishna Warrier. In *The Śākta Upaniṣad-s.* Adyar: The Adyar Library and Research Centre, 1967.

Baudhāyana Dharma Sūtra. Edited by U. C. Pandeya. Kashi Sanskrit Series, number 104. Varanasi: Chowkhamba Sanskrit Series Office, 1972. Translated by Georg Bühler. In *The Sacred Books of the Āryas.* Sacred Books of the East, volume 14. Oxford: Clarendon Press, 1879. Reprint edition, Delhi: Motilal Banarsidass, 1965.

Brahma Upaniṣad. In *The Sāmānya Vedānta Upanishads.* Edited by Pandit A. Mahadeva Sastri. Madras: The Adyar Library, 1921. Translated by Paul Deussen. In *Sechzig Upaniṣad's des Veda.* Leipzig: F. A. Brockhaus, 1897, 1921.

Brahmabindhu Upaniṣad. In *Upaniṣat-Saṁgraha.* Edited by J. L. Shastri. Delhi: Motilal Banarsidass, 1970. Reprint edition, 1984.

Brahmavidyā Upaniṣad. In *The Yoga Upaniṣads.* Edited by Pandit A. Mahadeva Sastri. Reprint edition, Madras: The Adyar Library and Research Centre, 1968.

Translated by Paul Deussen. In *Sechzig Upaniṣad's des Veda.* Leipzig: F. A. Brockhaus, 1897, 1921.

Bṛhadāraṇyaka Upaniṣad. In *Daśopaniṣad-s.* Revised edition. Edited by the Pandits of The Adyar Library under the supervision of C. Kunhan Raja, revised by A. A. Ramanathan. 2 volumes. Madras: The Adyar Library and Research Centre, 1984. Volume 2. Translated by Patrick Olivelle. In *Upaniṣads.* Oxford and New York: Oxford University Press, 1996.

Chāndogya Upaniṣad. In *Daśopaniṣad-s.* Revised edition. Edited by the Pandits of The Adyar Library under the supervision of C. Kunhan Raja, revised by A. A. Ramanathan. 2 volumes. Madras: The Adyar Library and Research Centre, 1984. Volume 2. Translated by Patrick Olivelle. In *Upaniṣads.* Oxford and New York: Oxford University Press, 1996.

Devī Upaniṣad. In *The Śākta Upaniṣads.* Second edition. Edited by Pandit A. Mahadeva Sastri. Reprint edition, Madras: The Adyar Library and Research Centre, 1986. Translated by A. G. Krishna Warrier. In *The Śākta Upaniṣads.* Reprint edition, Adyar: The Adyar Library and Research Centre, 1975.

Dhyānabindu Upaniṣad. In *The Yoga Upaniṣads.* Edited by Pandit A. Mahadeva Sastri. Reprint edition, Madras: The Adyar Library and Research Centre, 1968. Translated by Paul Deussen. In *Sechzig Upaniṣad's des Veda.* Leipzig: F. A. Brockhaus, 1897, 1921.

Gautama Dharma Sūtra. Edited by Manmatha Nath Dutt. In *The Dharma Śāstra Texts.* Calcutta: M. N. Dutt, 1908. Translated by Georg Bühler. In *The Sacred Books of the Āryas.* Sacred Books of the East, volume 14. Oxford: Clarendon Press, 1879. Reprint edition, Delhi: Motilal Banarsidass, 1965.

Gopatha Brāhmaṇa. Edited by R. Mitra and H. Vidyabhusana. Calcutta: Bibliotheca Indica, 1872. Reprint edition, Delhi: Indological Book House, 1972.

Īśā Upaniṣad. In *Daśopaniṣad-s.* Revised edition. Edited by the Pandits of The Adyar Library under the supervision of C. Kunhan Raja, revised by A. A. Ramanathan. 2 volumes. Madras: The Adyar Library and Research Centre, 1984. Volume 1. Translated by Patrick Olivelle. In *Upaniṣads.* Oxford and New York: Oxford University Press, 1996.

Jābāladarśana Upaniṣad. Edited by J. L. Shastri. In *Upaniṣat-saṁgrahaḥ.* Delhi: Motilal Banarsidass, 1980.

Jaiminīya Brāhmaṇa. Edited by R. Vira and L. Chandra. Nagpur: Sarasvati Vihara series, 1954. Incomplete translation by H. Bodewitz. In *Jaiminīya Brāhmaṇa I:1–65.* Leiden: E. J. Brill, 1973. Incomplete translation by H. Bodewitz. In *The Jyotiṣṭoma Ritual: Jaiminīya Brāhmaṇa I:66–364.* Leiden: E. J. Brill, 1990.

Jaiminīya Upaniṣad Brāhmaṇa. Edited and translated by Hanns Oertel. *Journal of the American Oriental Society* 16 (1896), pp. 79–260.

Kaṭha [*Kaṭhavallī*] *Upaniṣad*. In *Daśopaniṣad-s*. Revised edition. Edited by the Pandits of The Adyar Library under the supervision of C. Kunhan Raja, revised by A. A. Ramanathan. 2 volumes. Madras: The Adyar Library and Research Centre, 1984. Volume 1. Translated by Patrick Olivelle. In *Upaniṣads*. Oxford and New York: Oxford University Press, 1996.

Kāṭhaka Saṁhitā. Edited by V. Santavalekar. Bombay: Bhāratamudraṇālayam, 1943.

Kauṣītaki Brāhmaṇa. Edited by H. Bhattacharya. Calcutta Sanskrit College Research Series, number 73. Calcutta: Sanskrit College, 1970. Translated by Arthur Berriedale Keith. In *Ṛgveda Brāhmaṇas*. Harvard Oriental Series, Vol. 25. Cambridge, Mass.: Harvard University Press, 1920. Reprint edition, Delhi: Motilal Banarsidass, 1971.

Kauṣītaki [*Kauṣītakibrāhmaṇa*] *Upaniṣad*. In *The Sāmānya Vedānta Upanishads*. Edited by Pandit A. Mahadeva Sastri. Madras: The Adyar Library, 1921. Translated by Patrick Olivelle. In *Thirteen Principle Upaniṣads*. Oxford and New York: Oxford University Press, 1996.

Kena Upaniṣad. In *Daśopaniṣad-s*. Revised edition. Edited by the Pandits of The Adyar Library under the supervision of C. Kunhan Raja, revised by A. A. Ramanathan. 2 volumes. Madras: The Adyar Library and Research Centre, 1984. Volume 1. Translated by Patrick Olivelle. In *Upaniṣads*. Oxford and New York: Oxford University Press, 1996.

Kṣurikā Upaniṣad. In *The Yoga Upaniṣads*. Edited by Pandit A. Mahadeva Sastri. Reprint edition, Madras: The Adyar Library and Research Centre, 1968. Translated by Paul Deussen. In *Sechzig Upaniṣad's des Veda*. Leipzig: F. A. Brockhaus, 1897, 1921.

Laws of Manu. See *Manu Smṛti*.

Mahānārāyaṇa Upaniṣad (Atharva recension). In *Upaniṣat-Saṁgraha*. Edited by J. L. Shastri. Delhi: Motilal Banarsidass, 1970. Reprint edition, 1984.

Mahānārāyaṇa Upaniṣad (Draviḍa recension). Translated by Paul Deussen. In *Sechzig Upaniṣad's des Veda*. Leipzig: F. A. Brockhaus, 1897, 1921.

Maitrāyaṇī Saṁhitā. 4 volumes. Edited by L. von Schroeder. Leipzig: F. A. Brockhaus, 1883–86. Reprint edition, Wiesbaden: Franz Steiner Verlag, 1970–72.

Maitrāyaṇī (*Maitrāyaṇa*) *Upaniṣad*. In *The Sāmānya Vedānta Upanishads*. Edited by Pandit A. Mahadeva Sastri. Madras: The Adyar Library, 1921. Translated by Paul Deussen. In *Sechzig Upaniṣad's des Veda*. Leipzig: F. A. Brockhaus, 1897, 1921.

Maitreyī Upaniṣad. In *Upaniṣat-Saṁgraha*. Edited by J. L. Shastri. Delhi: Motilal Banarsidass, 1970. Reprint edition, 1984.

Maitrī [*Maitrāyaṇīya*] *Upaniṣad*. In *The Principal Upaniṣads*. Edited and translated by S. Radhakrishnan. Reprint edition, London: George Allen & Unwin; New York: Humanities Press, 1978.

Maṇḍalabrāhmaṇa Upaniṣad. In *The Yoga Upaniṣads*. Edited by Pandit A. Mahadeva Sastri. Reprint edition, Madras: The Adyar Library and Research Centre, 1968. Translated by K. Nārāyaṇasvāmī Aiyar. In *Thirty Minor Upaniṣads*. Madras: K. Nārāyaṇasvāmī Aiyar, 1914. Reprint edition, El Reno, Okla.: Santarasa Publications, 1980.

Māṇḍukya Upaniṣad. In *Daśopaniṣad-s*. Revised edition. Edited by the Pandits of The Adyar Library under the supervision of C. Kunhan Raja, revised by A. A. Ramanathan. 2 volumes. Madras: The Adyar Library and Research Centre, 1984. Volume 1. Translated by Patrick Olivelle. In *Upaniṣads*. Oxford and New York: Oxford University Press, 1996.

Manu Smṛti. Edited by J. H. Dave. Bhāratīya Vidyā series. Bombay: Bhāratīya Vidyā Bhavan, 1972–82. Translated as *The Laws of Manu* by Georg Bühler. Sacred Books of the East, volume 25. Oxford: Clarendon Press, 1886. Reprint edition, New York: Dover Publications, 1969.

Muktikā Upaniṣad. In *The Sāmānya Vedānta Upanishads*. Edited by Pandit A. Mahadeva Sastri. Madras: The Adyar Library, 1921. Translated by K. Nārāyaṇasvāmī Aiyar. In *Thirty Minor Upaniṣads*. Madras: K. Nārāyaṇasvāmī Aiyar, 1914. Reprint edition, El Reno, Okla.: Santarasa Publications, 1980.

Muṇḍaka Upaniṣad. In *Daśopaniṣad-s*. Revised edition. Edited by the Pandits of The Adyar Library under the supervision of C. Kunhan Raja, revised by A. A. Ramanathan. 2 volumes. Madras: The Adyar Library and Research Centre, 1984. Volume 1. Translated by Patrick Olivelle. In *Upaniṣads*. Oxford and New York: Oxford University Press, 1996.

Nādabindu Upaniṣad. In *The Yoga Upaniṣads*. Edited by Pandit A. Mahadeva Sastri. Reprint edition, Madras: The Adyar Library and Research Centre, 1968. Translated by Paul Deussen. In *Sechzig Upaniṣad's des Veda*. Leipzig: F. A. Brockhaus, 1897, 1921.

Nṛsiṁhapūrvatāpinīya Upaniṣad. In *The Vaiṣṇava Upaniṣads*. Edited by Pandit A. Mahadeva Sastri. Second edition. Adyar: The Adyar Library and Research Centre, 1979. Translated by Paul Deussen. In *Sechzig Upaniṣad's des Veda*. Leipzig: F. A. Brockhaus, 1897, 1921.

Pañcaviṁśa Brāhmaṇa. 2 volumes. Edited by P. A. Cinnaswami Sastri and P. Pattabhirama Sastri. Kashi Sanskrit Series, number 105. Benares: Sanskrit Series Office, 1935. Translated by W. Caland. Bibliotheca Indica, number 255. Calcutta: Asiatic Society of Bengal, 1931.

Prāṇāgnihotra Upaniṣad. In *The Sāmānya Vedānta Upanishads*. Edited by Pandit A. Mahadeva Sastri. Madras: The Adyar Library, 1921.

Praśna Upaniṣad. In *Daśopaniṣad-s*. Revised edition. Edited by the Pandits of The Adyar Library under the supervision of C. Kunhan Raja, revised by A. A. Ramanathan. 2 volumes. Madras: The Adyar Library and Research Centre,

1984. Volume 1. Translated by Patrick Olivelle. In *Upaniṣads*. Oxford and New York: Oxford University Press, 1996.

Rāmapūrvatāpanīya Upaniṣad. In *The Vaiṣṇava Upaniṣads*. Edited by Pandit A. Mahadeva Sastri. Second edition. Adyar: The Adyar Library and Research Centre, 1979. Translated by Paul Deussen. In *Sechzig Upaniṣad's des Veda*. Leipzig: F. A. Brockhaus, 1897, 1921.

Rāmottaratāpanīya Upaniṣad. In *The Vaiṣṇava Upaniṣads*. Edited by Pandit A. Mahadeva Sastri. Second edition. Adyar: The Adyar Library and Research Centre, 1979. Translated by Paul Deussen. In *Sechzig Upaniṣad's des Veda*. Leipzig: F. A. Brockhaus, 1897, 1921.

Ṛgveda Saṁhitā. Edited by Theodor Aufrecht. Published as *Die Hymnen des Rigveda*. 2 volumes. Reprint edition, Vienna: Otto Harrassowitz, 1988. Edited by F. Max Müller. 4 volumes. Chowkhamba Sanskrit Series, volume 99. Reprint edition, Varanasi: Chowkhamba Sanskrit Series Office, 1966. Translated by Karl Friedrich Geldner. *Der Rig-Veda aus dem Sanskrit in Deutsche übersetzt*. 4 volumes. Harvard Oriental Series, volumes 33–36. Cambridge, Mass.: Harvard University Press, 1951–57. Translated into English by Ralph T. H. Griffith. *The Hymns of the Ṛgveda*. New revised edition, edited by J. L. Shastri. Delhi: Motilal Banarsidass, 1973. Partial translation by Wendy Doniger O'Flaherty. *The Rigveda: An Anthology*. Harmondsworth: Penguin Books, 1981.

Ṣaḍviṁśa Brāhmaṇa. Edited by B. R. Sharma. Kendriya Sanskrit Vidyapeetha Series, 9. Tirupati: Kendriya Sanskrit Vidyapeetha, 1967.

Śāṇḍilya Upaniṣad. In *The Yoga Upaniṣads*. Edited by Pandit A. Mahadeva Sastri. Reprint edition, Madras: The Adyar Library and Research Centre, 1968. Translated by K. Nārāyaṇasvāmī Aiyar. In *Thirty Minor Upaniṣads*. Madras: K. Nārāyaṇasvāmī Aiyar, 1914. Reprint edition, El Reno, Okla.: Santarasa Publications, 1980.

Sarasvatīrahasya Upaniṣad. In *The Śākta Upaniṣads*. Second edition. Edited by Pandit A. Mahadeva Sastri. Reprint edition, Madras: The Adyar Library and Research Centre, 1986. Translated by A. G. Krishna Warrier. In *The Śākta Upaniṣad*-s. Adyar: The Adyar Library and Research Centre, 1967. Reprint edition, 1975.

Śatapatha Brāhmaṇa (Mādhyandina recension). 5 volumes. Bombay: Laxmi Venkateshwar Steam Press, 1940. Translated by Julius Eggeling. 5 volumes. Sacred Books of the East, volumes 12, 26, 41, 43, 44. Oxford: Clarendon Press, 1882–90. Reprint edition, Delhi: Motilal Banarsidass, 1963.

Saubhāgyalakṣmī Upaniṣad. In *The Śākta Upaniṣads*. Second edition. Edited by Pandit A. Mahadeva Sastri. Reprint edition, Madras: The Adyar Library and Research Centre, 1986. Translated by A. G. Warrier. In *The Śākta Upaniṣads*. Adyar: The Adyar Library and Research Centre, 1967. Reprint edition, 1975.

Subāla Upaniṣad. In *The Sāmānya Vedānta Upanishads.* Edited by Pandit A. Mahadeva Sastri. Madras: The Adyar Library, 1921. Edited and translated by S. Radhakrishnan. In *The Principal Upaniṣads.* London: George Allen & Unwin; New York: Humanities Press, 1953. Reprint edition, 1978.

Śvetāśvatara Upaniṣad. In *The Śaiva Upaniṣads.* Edited by Pandit A. Mahadeva Sastri. Madras: The Adyar Library and Research Centre, 1950. Translated by Patrick Olivelle. In *Upaniṣads.* Oxford and New York: Oxford University Press, 1966.

Taittirīya Āraṇyaka. 2 volumes. Ānandāśrama Sanskrit Series, number 38. Poona: Ānandāsrama, 1978.

Taittirīya-Brāhmaṇa. 3 volumes. Ānandāśrama Sanskrit Series, number 37. Poona: Ānandāśrama, 1979. Partial translation by P.-E. Dumont. In *Proceedings of the American Philosophical Society* 92, 95, 98, 101, 107–9, 113.

Taittirīya Saṁhitā. 8 volumes. Ānandaśrama Sanskrit Series, number 42. Poona: Ānandāśrama, 1978. Translated by Arthur Berriedale Keith. *The Veda of the Black Yajus School.* Harvard Oriental series, volumes 18 and 19. Cambridge, Mass.: Harvard University Press, 1914. Reprint edition, Delhi: Motilal Banarsidass, 1967.

Taittirīya Upaniṣad. In *Daśopaniṣad-s.* Revised edition. Edited by the Pandits of The Adyar Library under the supervision of C. Kunhan Raja, revised by A. A. Ramanathan. 2 volumes. Madras: The Adyar Library and Research Centre, 1984. Volume 1. Translated by Patrick Olivelle. In *Upaniṣads.* New York and London: Oxford University Press, 1996.

Tejobindu Upaniṣad. In *The Yoga Upaniṣads.* Edited by Pandit A. Mahadeva Sastri. Reprint edition, Madras: The Adyar Library and Research Centre, 1968. Translated by Paul Deussen. In *Sechzig Upaniṣad's des Veda.* Leipzig: F. A. Brockhaus, 1897, 1921.

Tripurā Upaniṣad. In *The Śākta Upaniṣads.* Second edition. Edited by Pandit A. Mahadeva Sastri. Reprint edition, Madras: The Adyar Library and Research Centre, 1950, reprint edition, 1986. Translated by A. G. Warrier. In *The Śākta Upaniṣad*-s. Adyar: The Adyar Library and Research Centre, 1967. Reprint edition, 1975. See also Douglas Renfrew Brooks, *The Secret of the Three Cities: An Introduction to Hindu Śākta Tantrism.* Chicago: University of Chicago Press, 1990. Pp. 149–190.

Tripurātāpinī Upaniṣad. In *The Śākta Upaniṣads.* Second edition. Edited by Pandit A. Mahadeva Sastri. Madras: The Adyar Libary and Research Centre, 1950, reprint edition, 1986. Translated by A. G. Warrier. In *The Śākta Upaniṣad*-s. Adyar: The Adyar Library and Research Centre, 1967. Reprint edition, 1975.

Upaniṣat-Saṁgraha. Edited by J. L. Shastri. Delhi: Motilal Banarsidass, 1970. Reprint edition, 1984.

Vājasaneyi Saṁhitā. Third Edition. Edited and translated by Devi Chand. New Delhi: Munshiram Manoharlal, 1980.

Varāha Upaniṣad. In *The Yoga Upaniṣads*. Edited by Pandit A. Mahadeva Sastri. Reprint edition, Madras: The Adyar Library and Research Centre, 1968. Translated by K. Nārāyaṇasvāmī Aiyar. In *Thirty Minor Upaniṣads*. Madras: K. Nārāyaṇasvāmī Aiyar, 1914. Reprint edition, El Reno, Okla.: Santarasa Publications, 1980.

Yogakuṇḍalī Upaniṣad. In *The Yoga Upaniṣads*. Edited by Pandit A. Mahadeva Sastri. Reprint edition, Madras: The Adyar Library and Research Centre, 1968. Translated by K. Nārāyaṇasvāmī Aiyar. In *Thirty Minor Upaniṣads*. Madras: K. Nārāyaṇasvāmī Aiyar, 1914. Reprint edition, El Reno, Okla.: Santarasa Publications, 1980.

Yogaśīkhā Upaniṣad. Translated by Paul Deussen. In *Sechzig Upaniṣad's des Veda*. Leipzig: F. A. Brockhaus, 1897, 1921.

Yogatattva Upaniṣad. In *Upaniṣat-Saṁgraha*. Edited by J. L. Shastri. Dehli: Motilal Banarsidass, 1970. Reprint edition, 1984. Translated by K. Nārāyaṇsvāmī Aiyar. In *Thirty Minor Upaniṣads*. Madras, K. Nārāyaṇsvāmī Aiyar, 1914. Reprint edition, El Reno, Okla.: Santarasa Publications, 1980.

SECONDARY STUDIES

Agrawala, V. S. *The Thousand-Syllabled Speech*. Part 1: *Vision in Long Darkness*. Varanasi: Vedāraṇyaka Ashram (distributed by Prithivi Prakashan, Varanasi), 1963.

Airi, Ragunath. *Concept of Sarasvatī*. Delhi: Munshiram Manoharlal, 1977.

Alper, Harvey P., ed. *Understanding Mantra*. Albany: State University of New York Press, 1989.

Aguilar, H. *The Sacrifice in the Ṛgveda*. Delhi: Bharatiya Vidya Prakashan, 1976.

Banerjee, A. C. *Studies in the Brāhmaṇas*. New Delhi: Motilal Banarsidass, 1963.

Banerjee, Santi. "Prajāpati in the Brāhmaṇas." *Vishveshvaranand Indological Journal* 19, numbers 1–2 (June–December 1981), pp. 14–19.

Barua, B. M. "Art as Defined in the Brāhmaṇas." *Indian Culture* 1 (July 1934–April 1935), pp. 118–20.

Basu, J. *India in the Age of the Brāhmaṇas*. Calcutta: Sanskrit Pustak Bhandar, 1969.

Bedekar, D. K. "The Revelatory Character of Indian Epistemology." *Annals of the Bhandarkar Oriental Research Institute* 29 (1948), pp. 64–84.

Bergaigne, Abel H. J. *La réligion védique d'après les hymnes du Rig-Veda*. 3 volumes. Paris: F. Vieweg, 1878–83. Translated by V. G. Paranjpe as *Abel Bergaigne's Vedic Religion*. 4 volumes bound together. Delhi: Motilal Banarsidass, 1979.

Bhandarkar, Ramakrishna Gopal. "The Veda in India." *Indian Antiquary* 3 (May 1874), pp. 132–35.

Bhargava, P. L. *India in the Vedic Age: A History of Aryan Expansion in India.* Second revised and enlarged edition. Aminabad: Upper India Publishing House, 1971.

Bhattacharji, Sukumari. "Rise of Prajāpati in the Brāhmaṇas." *Annals of the Bhandarkar Oriental Research Institute* 64 (1983), pp. 205–13.

Bhattacharya, D. "Cosmogony and Rituo-Philosophical Integrity in the Atharvaveda." *Vishveshvaranand Indological Journal* 15 (March 1977), pp. 1–12.

Bhattarcharya, Kamaleswar. "Le 'Védisme' de certains textes hindouistes." *Journal Asiatique* 225 (1967), pp. 199–222.

Bhattarcharya, V. C. "On the Justification of *rūpasamṛddha ṛk-* Verses in the Aitareya Brāhmaṇa." *Our Heritage* 4 (1956), pp. 99–106, 227–37; 5 (1957), pp. 119–46.

Bhawe, Shrikrishna Sakharam. "The Conception of a Muse of Poetry in the Ṛgveda." *Journal of the University of Bombay* 19, number 2 (1950), pp. 19–27.

———. *The Soma Hymns of the Ṛgveda.* Baroda Research Series. Baroda: University of Baroda, 1957–62.

Bhide, V. V. *The Cāturmāsya Sacrifices.* Pune: University of Poona, 1979.

Biardeau, Madeleine. *Théorie de la connaissance et philosophie de la parole dans le brahmanisme classique.* Paris: Mouton, 1964.

———, and Charles Malamoud. *Le Sacrifice dans l'Inde ancienne.* Bibliothèque de l'Ecole des Hautes Etudes, Sciences religieuses, volume 79. Paris: Presses Universitaires de France, 1976.

Blair, Chauncy. *Heat in the Rig Veda and Atharva Veda.* New Haven, Conn.: American Oriental Society, 1961

Bloomfield, Maurice. *The Atharva-Veda and the Gopatha Brāhmaṇa.* Strassburg: Karl J. Trübner, 1899. Reprint edition, New Delhi: Asian Publication Services, 1978.

———. "The Mind as Wish-Car in the Veda." *Journal of the American Oriental Society* 39 (1919), pp. 280–82.

———. *The Religion of the Veda.* New York: G. P. Putnam's Sons, 1908.

Bodewitz, H. W. *The Daily Evening and Morning Offering (Agnihotra) according to the Brāhmaṇas.* Leiden: E. J. Brill, 1976.

Böhtlingk, Otto, and Rudolf Roth. *Sanskrit-Wörterbuch.* 7 volumes. Petrograd: Kaiserliche Akademie der Wissenschaften, 1868.

Breckenridge, Carol A., and Peter van der Veer, eds. *Orientalism and the Postcolonial Predicament.* Philadelphia: Pennsylvania University Press, 1993.

Brereton, Joel P. *The Ṛgvedic Ādityas*. American Oriental Series, volume 63. New Haven, Conn.: American Oriental Society, 1981.

Brooks, Douglas Renfrew. *Auspicious Wisdom: The Texts and Traditions of Śrīvidyā Śākta Tantrism in South India*. Albany: State University of New York Press, 1992.

———. *The Secret of the Three Cities: An Introduction to Hindu Śākta Tantrism*. Chicago: University of Chicago Press, 1990.

Brough, John. "Soma and Amanita Muscaria." *Bulletin of the School of Oriental and African Studies* 34 (1971), pp. 331–62.

Brown, W. Norman. "Agni, Sun, Sacrifice and Vāc: A Sacerdotal Ode by Dīrghatamas (Rig Veda 1.164)." *Journal of the American Oriental Society* 88 (1988), pp. 199–218. Reprinted as "Dīrghatamas's Vision of Creation," in Rosane Rocher, ed., *India and Indology* (see below), pp. 53–83.

———. "The Creative Role of the Goddess Vāc in the ṚgVeda." In *Pratidānam: Indian, Iranian and Indo-European Studies Presented to F. B. J. Kuiper*. The Hague: Mouton, 1968. Pp. 393–97. Reprinted in Rosane Rocher, ed., *India and Indology* (see below), pp. 74–75.

———. "The Sources and Nature of *Puruṣa* in the Puruṣasūkta." *Journal of the American Oriental Society* 51 (1931), pp. 108–18. Reprinted in Rosane Rocher, ed., *India and Indology*. Delhi: Motilal Banarsidass for the American Oriental Society, 1978. Pp. 5–10.

Buitenen, J. A. B. van. *The Pravargya: An Ancient Indian Iconic Ritual*. Deccan College Building Centenary and Silver Jubilee Series, number 58. Pune: Deccan College, 1968.

Burckhardt, Titus. *Art of Islam: Language and Meaning*. Westerhan, England: World of Islam Festival Trust, 1976.

Burrow, Thomas. *The Sanskrit Language*. Second edition. London: Faber and Faber, 1965.

Caland, Wilhelm, and Victor Henry. *L'Agniṣṭoma: Description complète de la forme normale du sacrifice de Soma dans le culte védique*. 2 volumes. Paris: Ernest Leroux, 1906.

Chaudhary, Radhakrishna. *Vrātyas in Ancient India*. Chowkhamba Sanskrit Studies, volume 38. Benares: Chowkhamba Sanskrit Series Office, 1964.

Coomaraswamy, Ananda K. "Ātmayajña: Self-Sacrifice." *Harvard Journal of Asiatic Studies* 6 (1942), pp. 358–88. Reprinted in Roger Lipsey, ed., *Coomaraswamy*, volume 2: *Selected Papers: Metaphysics*. Princeton, N.J.: Princeton University Press, 1977. Pp. 107–47.

Coward, Harold G., ed. *"Language" in Indian Philosophy and Religion.* SR Supplements, 5. [Toronto?]: Corporation Canadienne des Sciences Religieuses/Canadian Corporation for Studies in Religion, 1978.

———, and Krishna Sivaraman, eds. *Revelation in Indian Thought: A Festshrift in Honour of Professor T. R. V. Murti.* Emeryville, Calif.: Dharma Publishing Co., 1977.

Dandekar, R. N. *Der Vedische Mensch: Studien zu Selbstauffassung des Inders in Ṛg- und Atharvaveda.* Heidelberg: C. Winter, 1938.

Das, Veena. "Language of Sacrifice." *Man* (New Series) 18 (September 1983), pp. 445–62.

de Nicolás, Antonio T. *Avatāra: The Humanization of Philosophy through the Bhagavad Gītā.* New York: Nicolas Hays, Ltd., 1976.

———. *Four-Dimensional Man: Meditations through the Ṛgveda.* Stony Brook, N.Y.: Nicolas Hays, Ltd., 1976.

Deussen, Paul. "Das Einheitslied des Dīrghatamas, Ṛigv. 1.164," in *Allgemeine Geschichte der Philosophie* 1.1. Leipzig: Brockhaus, 1920. Pp. 105–19.

———. *The Philosophy of the Upanishads.* Translated by A. S. Geden. Reprint edition, New York: Dover Publications, 1966.

———. *Sechzig Upaniṣad's des Veda.* Leipzig: F. A. Brockhaus, 1897, 1921. Translated by V. M. Bedekar and G. B. Palsule as *Sixty Upaniṣads of the Veda.* 2 volumes. Delhi: Motilal Banarsidass, 1987.

Devasthali, G. V. *Religion and Mythology of the Brāhmaṇas.* Pune: University of Poona, 1965.

Dorson, Richard M. "The Eclipse of Solar Mythology." In Thomas A. Sebeok, ed., *Myth: A Symposium.* Bloomington: Indiana University Press, 1958.

Drury, Naama. *The Sacrificial Ritual in the Śatapatha Brāhmaṇa.* Delhi: Motilal Banarsidass, 1981.

Dumont, Louis. "World Renunciation in Indian Religions." *Contributions to Indian Sociology* 4 (1960), pp. 33–62. Reprinted in *Religion/Politics and History in India: Collected Papers in Indian Sociology.* The Hague: Mouton, 1970. Pp. 33–60.

Dumont, P.-E. "The Agnihotra (or Fire-God Oblation) in the Taittirīya-Brāhmaṇa: The First Prapāṭhaka of the Second Kāṇḍa of the Taittirīya-Brāhmaṇa with Translation." *Proceedings of the American Philosophical Society* 108 (1964), pp. 337–53.

———. "The Full-moon and New-moon Sacrifices in the Taittirīya-Brāhmaṇa." *Proceedings of the American Philosophical Society* 101 (1957), pp. 216–43; 103 (1959), pp. 584–608; 104 (1960), pp. 1–10.

———. "The Iṣṭis to the Nakṣatras (or Oblations to the Lunar Mansions) in the Taittirīya-Brāhmaṇa with Translation." *Proceedings of the American Philosophical Society* 98 (1954), pp. 204–23.

———. "The Special Kinds of Agnicayana (or Special Methods of Building the Fire-Altar) according to the Kaṭhas in the Taittirīya-Brāhmaṇa: The Tenth, Eleventh, and Twelfth Prapāṭhakas of the Third Kāṇḍa of the Taittirīya-Brāhmaṇa with Translation." *Proceedings of the American Philosophical Society* 95 (1951), pp. 628–75.

Eliade, Mircea. *The Myth of the Eternal Return or, Cosmos and History*. Translated by Willard R. Trask. Princeton, N.J.: Princeton University Press, 1954.

———. *The Sacred and the Profane*. Translated by Willard R. Trask. New York: Harcourt, Brace and World, 1959.

———. *Yoga: Immortality and Freedom*. Second edition. Translated by Willard R. Trask. New York: Harcourt, Brace and World, 1959.

Falk, Maryla. *Nāma-rūpa and Dharma-rūpa: Origin and Aspects of an Ancient Indian Conception*. Calcutta: University of Calcutta, 1943.

Filliozat, Jean. "La Force organique et la force cosmique dans le philosophie médicale de l'Inde et dans le Véda." *Revue Philosophique* 116 (1933), pp. 410–29.

Findly, Ellison Banks. "*Mántra kaviśastá*: Speech as Performative in the Ṛgveda." In Harvey P. Alper, ed., *Understanding Mantra*. Albany: State University of New York, 1989. Pp. 15–47.

Frykenberg, Robert E. "The Emergence of Modern 'Hinduism' as a Concept and as an Institution: A Reappraisal with Special Reference to South India." In Günther D. Sontheimer and Hermann Kulke, eds., *Hinduism Reconsidered*. Delhi: Manohar, 1989. Pp. 29–49.

Geldner, Karl Friedrich. "Willens- oder Verständiskraft." *Der Rigveda in Auswahl*. Volume 1. Stuttgart, W. Kohlheimer: 1907.

Gonda, Jan. "All, Universe and Totality in the Śatapatha Brāhmaṇa." *Journal of the Oriental Institute (Baroda)* 32 (September–December 1982), pp. 1–7.

———. *Ancient-Indian ojas, Latin *augos and the Indo-European nouns in -es-/-os*. Utrecht: N. V. A. Oosthoek's Uitgevers Mij., 1952.

———. "*Bandhu-* in the Brāhmaṇas." *Adyar Library Bulletin* 29 (1965), pp. 1–29.

———. *Change and Continuity in Indian Religion*. Disputationes Rheno-Trajectinae 9. Berlin: Mouton, 1965. Reprint edition, New Delhi: Munshiram Manoharlal, 1985.

———. "The Creator and His Spirit." *Wiener Zeitschrift für die Kunde Südasiens* 27 (1983), pp. 5–42.

———. *Four Studies in the Language of the Veda.* Disputationes Rheno-Trajectinae 4. 's-Gravenhage: Mouton, 1959.

———. "In the Beginning." *Annals of the Bhandarkar Oriental Research Institute* 63 (1982), pp. 43–62.

———. "The Indian Mantra." *Oriens* 16 (1953), pp. 244–97. Reprinted in Jan Gonda, *Selected Studies, Presented to the Author by the Staff of the Oriental Institute, Utrecht University, on the Occasion of His Seventieth Birthday.* 4 volumes. Leiden: E. J. Brill, 1975.

———. *Loka: World and Heaven in the Veda.* Amsterdam: N. V. Noord-Hollandsche Uitgevers Maatschappij, 1966.

———. *Notes on Brahman.* Utrecht: J. L. Beyers, 1950.

———. *Pūṣan and Sarasvatī.* Amsterdam: North Holland Publishing Co., 1985.

———. "Reflections on *Sarva-* in Vedic Texts." *Indian Linguistics* 16 (November 1955), pp. 53–71.

———. "The 'Original' Sense and the Etymology of Skt. *Māyā.*" In *Four Studies in the Language of the Veda.* 's-Gravenhage: Mouton, 1959. Pp. 119–94.

———. "The Popular Prajāpati." *History of Religions* 22 (November 1982), pp. 129–49.

———. *Prajāpati and the Year.* Amsterdam: North Holland Publishing Co., 1984.

———. *Prajāpati's Rise to Higher Rank.* Leiden: E. J. Brill, 1986.

———. *Some Observations on the Relations between "Gods" and "Powers" in the Veda a propos of the Phrase 'Sūnuḥ Sahasaḥ.* 's-Gravenhage: Mouton, 1957.

———. "Vedic Gods and the Sacrifice." *Numen* 30 (July 1983), pp. 1–34.

———. *Vedic Literature (Saṁhitās and Brāhmaṇas).* Volume 1, fascicle 1 of Jan Gonda, ed., *A History of Indian Literature.* Wiesbaden: Otto Harrassowitz, 1975.

———. *The Vision of the Vedic Poets.* Berlin: Mouton, 1963. Reprint edition, Delhi: Munshiram Manoharlal, 1984.

Gopal, Ram. *The History and Principles of Vedic Interpretation.* New Delhi: Concept Publishing, 1983.

Grassmann, Hermann. *Wörterbuch zum Rig-Veda.* Wiesbaden: Otto Harrassowitz, 1976.

Halbfass, Wilhelm. *Tradition and Reflection: Explorations in Indian Thought.* Albany: State University of New York Press, 1991.

Hastings, James et al., eds. *Encyclopedia of Religion and Ethics.* 13 volumes. Edinburgh: T. & T. Clark; New York: C. Scribner's Sons, 1908–26.

Hauer, J. W. *Der Vrātya: Untersuchungen über die nichtbrahmanische Religion altindiens.* 2 volumes. Stuttgart: W. Kohlhammer, 1927.

Haug, Martin. "Vedische Räthselfragen und Räthselsprüche (Übersetzung und Erklärung von Rigv. 1.164)," *Sitzungsberichte der philosophisch-philologischen Classe d. bayerischen Akademie der Wissenschafen zu München,* 1875, pp. 457–515.

Heesterman, J. C. *The Ancient Indian Royal Consecration: The Rājāsūya Described according to the Yajus Texts and Annoted* [sic]. Disputations Rheno-Trajectinae, volume 2. 's-Gravenhage: Mouton, 1957.

———. "Brahman." In *Encyclopedia of Religion.* 16 volumes. New York: Macmillan, 1987. Volume 2, pp. 294–96.

———. *The Broken World of Sacrifice: An Essay in Ancient Indian Ritual.* Chicago: University of Chicago Press, 1993.

———. *The Inner Conflict of Tradition.* Chicago: University of Chicago Press, 1985.

———. "On the Origin of the Nāstika." *Wiener Zeitschrift für die Kunde Süd- und Ostasiens* 12–13 (1968–69), pp. 171–85.

———. "Priesthood and the Brahmin." *Contributions to Indian Sociology* (New Series) 5 (1971), pp. 43–47.

———. "Self-Sacrifice in Vedic Ritual." In Shaul Shaked et al., eds., *Gilgul: Essays on Transformation, Revolution and Permanence in the History of Religions. Dedicated to R. J. Zwi Werblowsky.* Leiden: E. J. Brill, 1987. Pp. 91–106.

Heimann, Betty. "The Supra-Personal Process of Sacrifice." *Rivista degli studi orientali* (Rome) 32 (1938), pp. 731–39.

Henninger, Joseph. "Sacrifice." In Mircea Eliade et al., eds., *Encylopedia of Religion.* New York: Macmillan and The Free Press, 1987. Volume 12, pp. 544–57.

Henry, Victor. *Les Livres VIII et IX de l'Atharva-Veda,* traduits et commentés. Paris: J. Maisonneuve, 1894.

Hillebrandt, Alfred. *Das altindische Neu- und Vollmondopfer in seiner einfachsten Form.* Jena: Gustav Fischer, 1879.

———. "Brahman." In James Hastings, ed., *Encyclopedia of Religion and Ethics.* New York: Charles Scribner's Sons, 1910. Vol. 2, pp. 796–99.

Inden, Ronald. "Orientalist Constructions of India." *Modern Asian Studies* 29 (1986), pp. 401–46.

Insler, Stanley. *The Gāthās of Zarathustra.* Teheran-Liege: Bilbliotheque Pahlavi, 1975.

Johnson, Willard. "On the Ṛg Vedic Riddle of the Two Birds in the Fig Tree (RV 10.164.20–22) and the Discovery of the Vedic Speculative Symposium." *Journal of the American Oriental Society* 96, number 2 (April–June 1976), pp. 248–58.

———. *Poetry and Speculation of the Ṛg Veda*. Berkeley and Los Angeles: University of California Press, 1980.

Joshi, J. R. "Prajāpati in Vedic Mythology and Ritual." *Annals of the Bhandarkar Oriental Research Institute* 53 (1972), pp. 101–25.

Kaelber, Walter O. "The 'Dramatic' Element in Brāhmaṇic Initiation: Symbols of Death, Danger, and Difficult Passage." *History of Religions* 18 (August 1978), pp. 54–76.

———. *Tapta Mārga: Asceticism and Initiation in Vedic India*. Albany: State University of New York Press, 1989.

Keith, Arthur Berriedale. *Religion and Philosophy of the Veda and Upanishads*. Harvard Oriental Series, 31. Cambridge, Mass.: Harvard University Press, 1925. Reprint edition, Delhi: Motilal Banarsidass, 1976.

Klostermaier, Klaus. "The Creative Function of the Word." In Harold G. Coward, ed., *"Language" in Indian Philosophy and Religion*. SR Supplements, 5. Toronto: Corporation Canadienne des Sciences Religieuses/Canadian Corporation for Studies in Religion, 1978. Pp. 5–18.

Knipe, David. *In the Image of Fire: Vedic Experiences of Heat*. New Delhi: Motilal Banarsidass, 1975.

Krick, Hertha. *Das Ritual der Feuergründung (Agnyādheya)*. Österreichische Akademie der Wissenschaften. Philosophisch-historische Klasse. Sitzungsberichte, Band 399. Veröffentlichungen der Kommission für Sprachen und Kulturen Südasiens, Heft 16. Vienna: Österreichische Akademie der Wissenschaften, 1982.

Kunhan Raja, C. *Asya Vāmasya Hymn (The Riddle of the Universe) Ṛgveda 1.164, with the Commentaries of Sāyana and Ātmānanda*. Madras: Ganesh and Co., 1956.

———. *Poet-Philosophers of the Ṛgveda, Vedic and Pre-Vedic*. Madras: Ganesh and Co. 1963.

Kuiper, F. B. J. "The Ancient Aryan Verbal Contest." *Indo-Iranian Journal* 4, number 4 (1960).

———. *Ancient Indian Cosmogony*. New Delhi: Vikas Publishing House, 1983.

Lévi, Sylvain. *La Doctrine du sacrifice dans les Brāhmaṇas*. Second edition. Bibliothèque de l'Ecole des Hautes Etudes, Sciences religieuses, volume 73. Paris: Presses Universitaires de France, 1966.

Lincoln, Bruce. "Death and Resurrection in Indo-European Thought." *Journal of Indo-European Studies* 5 (Summer 1977), pp. 247–64.

———. *Death, War and Sacrifice.* Chicago: University of Chicago Press, 1991.

Lommel, H. "Baumsymbolik bei altindischen Opfer." *Paideuma* 6 (1957), pp 490–99.

Lüders, Heinrich. *Varuṇa.* 2 volumes. Volume 1: *Varuṇa und das Wasser*; volume 2: *Varuṇa und das Ṛta.* Göttingen: Vandenhoeck & Ruprecht, 1959.

Macdonald, A. W. "A propos de Prajāpati." *Journal Asiatique* 240 (1952), pp. 323–38.

Macdonald, K. S. *The Brāhmaṇas of the Vedas.* Reprint edition, Delhi: Bharatiya Book Corporation, 1979.

Macdonell, Arthur A. *The Vedic Mythology.* Grundriss der Indo-Arische Philologie und Altertumskunde, volume 3, part 1A, edited by Georg Bühler. Strassburg: K. J. Trübner, 1893. Reprint edition, Varanasi: Indological Book House, 1963.

Mahony, William K. "Dharma: Hindu Dharma." In Mircea Eliade et al., eds., *Encyclopedia of Religion.* 16 volumes. New York: Macmillan and The Free Press, 1987. Volume 4, pp. 329–32.

———. "Soul: Indian Concepts," In Mircea Eliade et al., eds., *Encyclopedia of Religion.* 16 volumes. New York: Macmillan and The Free Press, 1987. Volume 13, pp. 438–43.

———. "Upaniṣads." In Mircea Eliade et al., eds., *Encyclopedia of Religion.* 16 volumes. New York: Macmillan and The Free Press, 1987. Volume 15, pp. 147–52.

Mainkar, T. G. *The Ṛgvedic Foundations of Classical Poetics.* Delhi: S. Balwant for Ajanta Publications, 1977.

Mayrhofer, Manfred. *Kurzgefasstes etymologisches Wörterbuch des Altindischen.* 4 volumes. Heidelberg: Carl Winter Universitäts Verlag, 1956–80.

Monier-Williams, Monier. *A Sanskrit-English Dictionary.* Oxford: Clarendon Press, 1899. Reprint edition, 1974.

Morris, William, ed. *The American Heritage Dictionary of the English Language.* Boston (and other cities): Houghton Mifflin, 1981.

Müller, Max. *Chips from a German Workshop.* 4 volumes. New York: Charles Scribner and Co., 1869.

———. *Contributions to the Science of Mythology.* 2 volumes. London: Longmans, Green and Co., 1897.

———. *India: What Can It Teach Us? A Course of Lectures Delivered before the University of Cambridge.* London: Longmans, Green and Co., 1883.

———. *Introduction to the Science of Religion.* London: Longmans, Green and Co., 1897.

———. *Lectures on the Origin and Growth of Religion*. London: Longmans, Green and Co., 1880.

———. *Natural Religion*. London: Longmans, Green and Co., 1892.

———. *Three Lectures on the Vedanta Philosophy*. London: Longmans, Green and Co., 1898.

Mus, Paul. "Où finit Puruṣa?" *Mélanges d'Indianisme à la mémoire de Louis Renou*. Paris: E. de Boccard, 1968. Pp. 539–63.

Narahari, H. G. *Ātman in Pre-Upaniṣadic Vedic Literature*. Adyar: The Adyar Library, 1944.

Nārāyaṇasvāmī Aiyar, K. trans. *Thirty Minor Upanishads*. Madras: K. Nārāyaṇasvāmī Aiyar, 1914; reprint edition, El Reno, Okla.: Santarasa Publications, 1980.

O'Flaherty, Wendy Doniger. *Dream, Illusion and Other Realities*. Chicago: University of Chicago Press, 1983.

———. *The Rig Veda: An Anthology*. Harmondsworth: Penguin Books, 1981.

———. *Tales of Sex and Violence: Folklore, Sacrifice, and Danger in the Jaiminīya Brāhmaṇa*. Chicago: University of Chicago Press, 1985.

Oguibenine, B. L. *Structure d'un mythe védique: le mythe cosmogonique dans le Ṛg Veda*. The Hague: Mouton, 1973.

Oldenberg, Hermann. *Vorwissenschaftliche Wissenschaft: Die Weltanschauung der Brāhmaṇa-Texte*. Göttingen: Vandenhoeck and Ruprecht, 1919.

Pandeya, Rajendra P. "The Vision of the Vedic Seer." In *Hindu Spirituality: Vedas through Vedanta*, edited by Krishna Sivaraman. Volume 6 of *World Spirituality: An Encyclopedic History of the Religous Quest*. New York: Crossroad, 1989. Pp. 5–28.

Panikkar, Raimundo. *The Vedic Experience: Mantramañjarī*. Berkeley and Los Angeles: University of California Press, 1977.

Paranjpe, V. G. *Abel Bergaigne's Vedic Religion*. 4 volumes bound together. Delhi: Motilal Banarsidass, 1979.

Parpola, Asko. "On the Symbol Concept of the Vedic Ritualists." In H. Biezais, ed., *Religious Symbols and Their Functions*. Stockholm: Almquist and Wiksell, 1979. Pp. 139–53.

Patel, Manilel. "A Study of Ṛgveda X.71." *Viśvabharati Quarterly* 4, number 4 (August–October 1938).

Patton, Laurie L., ed. *Authority, Anxiety, and Canon: Essays in Vedic Interpretation*. Albany: State University of New York Press, 1994.

Pokorny, Julius. *Indogermanisches etymologisches Wörterbuch*. 2 volumes. Bern: A. Francke, 1959.

Pollack, Sheldon. "Deep Orientalism?: Notes on Sanskrit and Power beyond the Raj." In Carol A. Breckenridge and Peter van der Veer, eds., *Orientalism and the Postcolonial Predicament.*. Philadelphia: Pennsylvania University Press, 1993. Pp. 76–133.

Radhakrishnan, Sarvepalli. *The Principal Upaniṣads*. London: George Allen & Unwin; New York: Humanities Press, 1978.

Raghavan, V. *Ṛtu in Sanskrit Literature*. Delhi: Shri Lal Bahadur Shastri Kendriya Sanskrit Vidyapeeth, 1972.

Ramanathan, A. A., trans. *The Saṁnyāsa Upaniṣads*. Madras: The Adyar Library and Research Centre, 1978.

Ranade, H. G. "Some Darśapūrṇamāsa-Rites in the Śatapatha Brāhmaṇa and in the KātŚS." *Bulletin of the Deccan College Research Institute* 35 (March 1976), pp. 121–26.

Ravi Varma, L. A. "Rituals of Worship." In H. Bhattacharya, ed., *The Cultural Heritage of India*. Second edition. 5 volumes. Calcutta: Ramakrishna Mission Institute of Culture, 1953. Volume 4, pp. 445–63.

Ray, Pramod Chandra. *Theory of Oriental Beauty (with Special Reference to Ṛg Veda)*. Sambalpur: First Orissa Sanskrit Conference, 1974.

Regnaud, P. "La *māyā* et le pouvoir créateur des divinités védiques." *Revue de l'Histoire des Religions*. 1885, pp. 237ff.

Renou, Louis. "'Connexion' en védique, 'cause' en bouddhique." *Dr. C. Kunhan Raja Presentation Volume*. Madras: The Adyar Library, 1946. Pp. 55–60.

———. *The Destiny of the Veda in India*. Edited and translated by Dev Raj Chanana. Delhi: Motilal Banarsidass, 1965.

———. *Etudes védiques et pāninéennes*. 17 volumes. Paris: Publication de l'ICI, 1955–69.

———. *Hymnes spéculatifs du Veda*. Paris: Gallimard, 1956.

———. *Histoire de la langue sanskrite*. Lyon: Editions IAC, 1956.

———. "On the Word *ātman*." *Vāk* 2 (1952), pp. 151–57.

———. *Vedic India*. Translated by Philip Spratt. Delhi: Indological Book House, 1971.

———, and Lilian Silburn. "Nirukta and Anirukta in Vedic." In J. N. Agrawal and B. D. Shastri, eds., *Sarūpa-Bhāratī, or Homage of Indology: The Dr. Lakshman Sarup Memorial Volume*. Hoshiapur: Vishveshvaranand Institute Publications, 1954. Pp. 68–79.

——— , with Lilian Silburn, "Sur la notion de brahman," *Journal Asiatique* 237 (1949), pp. 7–46.

Rocher, Rosane, ed. *India and Indology: Selected Articles by W. Norman Brown.* Delhi: Motilal Banarsidass, 1978.

Rönnow, K. "Ved. *kratu-*." *Le Monde Oriental* 26 (1932), pp. 1–90.

Said, Edward W. *Orientalism.* New York: Vintage, 1979.

Sastri, P. S. "The Rigvedic Theory of Beauty." *Proceedings and Transactions of the All-India Oriental Conference, Twelfth Session, Benares Hindu University, 1943–44*, edited by A. S. Altekar. Benares: Benares Hindu University, 1946. Pp. 232–39.

———. "The Vision of Dīrghatamas." *Prabuddha Bhārata* 62 (February 1957), pp. 63–66.

Sharvananda, Svami. "The Vedas and Their Religious Teaching." In *The Cultural Heritage of India*, vol. 1: *The Early Phases*. Second edition revised and enlarged. Calcutta: The Ramakrishna Mission Institute of Culture, 1958; reprint edition, 1982, pp. 182–98.

Schayer, Stanislov. "Die Struktur der magischen Weltanschauung nach dem Atharva-Veda und den Brāhmaṇa-Texten." *Zeitschrift für Buddhismus* 6 (1925), pp. 259–99.

Schlerath, Bernfried. Review of Hanns-Peter Schmidt, *Vedisch vratá und awestisch urvă̄ta* (see below), *Zeitschrift der Deutschen Morgenländischen Gesellschaft* 110 (1960), pp. 192–94.

Schmidt, Hanns-Peter. *Bṛhaspati und Indra: Untersuchungen zur vedischen Mythologie und Kulturgeschichte.* Vienna: Otto Harrassowitz, 1968.

———. *Vedisch vratá und awestisch urvă̄ta.* Hamburg: de Gruyter, 1958.

Schmidt, Wilhelm. *Der Ursprung der Gottesidee.* 12 volumes. Münster: Aschendorff, 1926.

Sebeok, Thomas A., ed. *Myth: A Symposium.* Bloomington: Indiana University Press, 1958.

Sen, Chitrabhanu. *Dictionary of the Vedic Rituals based on the Śrauta and Gṛhya Sūtras.* Delhi: Concept Publishing, 1978.

Sharma, B. R. "Symbolism of Fire Altar in Vedas." *Annals of the Bhandarkar Oriental Research Institute* 33 (1952), pp. 189–96.

Sharma, Hriday R. "The Spirituality of the Vedic Sacrifice." In Krishna Sivaraman, ed., *Hindu Spirituality: Vedas through Vedanta.* New York: Crossroad, 1989. Pp. 29–39.

Sharpe, Eric J. *Comparative Religion: A History*. New York: Charles Scribner's Sons, 1975.

Shende, N. J. *Kavi and Kāvya in the Atharveda*. Publications of the Centre of Advanced Study in Sanskrit, class B, number 1. Pune: University of Poona, 1967.

———. *Religion and Philosophy of the Atharva Veda*. Pune: Bhandarkar Oriental Research Institute, 1952.

Silburn, Lilian. *Instant et cause: Le Discontiue dans la pensée philosophique de l'Inde*. Paris: J. Vrin, 1955.

Smith, Brian K. *Classifying the Universe: The Ancient Indian Varṇa System and the Origins of Caste*. New York: Oxford University Press, 1994.

———. *Reflections on Resemblance, Ritual and Religion*. New York: Oxford University Press, 1989.

———. "Sacrifice and Being: Prajāpati's Cosmic Emission and Its Consequences." *Numen* 33 (1986), pp. 65–99.

Smith, Frederick M. *The Vedic Sacrifice in Transition: A Translation and Study of the Trikāṇḍamaṇḍana of Bhāskara Miśra*. Poona: Bhandarkar Oriental Research Institute, 1987.

Sontheimer, Günther D., and Hermann Kulke, eds. *Hinduism Reconsidered*. South Asia Institute, New Delhi Branch, Heidelberg University, South Asian Studies, number 24. New Delhi: Monohar Press, 1989.

Staal, Frits. *Agni: The Vedic Ritual of the Fire Altar*. 2 volumes. Berkeley: Asian Humanities Press, 1983.

———. "Vedic Mantras." In Harvey P. Alper, ed., *Understanding Mantra*. Albany: State University of New York Press, 1989. Pp. 48–95.

———. "Ṛgveda 10.71 on the Origin of Language." In Harold Coward and Krishna Sivaraman, eds., *Revelation in Indian Thought: A Festshrift in Honour of Professor T. R. V. Murti*. Emeryville, Calif.: Dharma Publishing, 1977.

Thieme, Paul. "Brahman." *Zeitschrift der Deutschen Morgenländischen Gesellschaft* (Leipzig) 102 (1952), pp. 91–129.

Upadhyaya, Suresh A. "The Word Manīṣā in the Ṛgveda." *Proceedings and Transactions of the All-India Oriental Conference* 21 (1961), pp. 21–30.

Velankar, H. D. "Mind and Heart in the Rgveda (Manas and Hrd)." *Proceedings and Transactions of the All-India Oriental Conference,* 22nd Session (Gauhati), edited by Maheswar Neog. Gauhati: All-India Oriental Conference, 1966. Volume 2, pp. 1–5.

———. *Ṛg Veda Maṇḍala VII*. Bombay: Bharatiya Vidya Bhavan, 1963.

Verpoorten, Jean-Marie. "Unité et distinction dans les spéculations rituelles védiques." *Archiv für Begriffsgeschichte* 21 (1977), pp. 59–85.

Vesci, Uma. *Heat and Sacrifice in the Vedas*. New Delhi: Motilal Banarsidass, 1985.

Voiqt, Johannes H. *Max Müller, The Man and His Ideas*. Calcutta: Firma K. L. Mukhopadhyay, 1967.

Vries, Jan de. *Perspectives in the History of Religions*. Translated by Kees W. Bolle. Berkeley: University of California Press, 1977.

Vyas, R. T. "The Concept of Prajāpati in Vedic Literature." *Bhāratīya Vidyā* 38 (1978), pp. 95–101.

Wasson, R. Gordon. *Soma: Divine Plant of Immortality*. Ethno-mycological Studies, number 1 New York: Harcourt Brace Jovanovich, 1968.

Wheelock, Wade T. "The Mantra in Vedic and Tantric Ritual." In Harvey P. Alper, ed., *Understanding Mantra*. Albany: State University of New York Press, 1989. Pp. 96–122.

Whitney, William Dwight, trans. *Atharva Veda Saṁhitā*. 2 volumes. Harvard Oriental Series, numbers 7 and 8. Cambridge, Mass.: Harvard University Press, 1905; reprint edition, Delhi: Motilal Banarsidass, 1962.

Index and Glossary

A

Abhijñā (superior wisdom), 6
Absolute, the: unity of, 162–170; encompassing the identity of Brahman and Ātman, 162–167; identified with the supreme deity, 167–170; as dwelling within the heart, 164–167; as associated with the mind, 165–166; eternal nature of the, 172; as universal Consciousness, 175–177; as "not this, not this," 227; as encompassing all things, 228. *See also* Ātman; Brahman
Adhvaryu priest. *See* Brahmin, types of
Aditi (mother of the gods), 38, 125, 129
Ādityas (the divine sons of Aditi), 28, 59, 212, 238, 247, 264; as omniscient, 71; as protectors of Ṛta, 47; as deities of expansive life, 125–128, 130. *See also* Mitra; Varuṇa
Agni (the god of fire), 18, 21, 26, 28, 55, 59, 66, 72, 75, 76, 79, 81, 82, 84, 128, 132–133, 147, 194, 209, 211, 213, 244; as domestic hearth fire, 21, 122; as bird, 94; and light, 63, 71; and the earth, 53; and the Gāyatrī, 110; and the gods' *māyā,* 35–36; and Ṛta, 101–102, 122, 123; as bearer of offerings to the gods, 84, 122–123; as cosmic priest, 36, 121; as physical fire, 20–21, 27; as name of the "One Reality," 55; as a poet, 90, 123, 205, 251; as source of poetic inspiration, 91, 94; as Vaiśvānara, 73; as (the god of) lightning, 35; as the god of the sun, 25–27, 35–36; central role in the ritual, 121–124; and the *brahman,* 121–122; and the heavens, 122; as protector of vows, 122; as bringer of the dawn, 137; and inner light, 170; as the divine falcon of the sky, 207; as first-born of Ṛta, 213; as wealth-giver, 248; as an *ṛtudevata,* 248. *See also* Fire
"Agni, Laud of" (*Ṛgveda* 1.1), 122–124
Agni, the Oblation to (the *Agnihotra*), 130, 141, 145, 154, 264. *See also* Inner Oblation to Agni, the
Agnicayana. See Building the Fire Altar Ceremony, the
Agnihotra. See Agni, the Oblation to
"Agnim īḷe Sūkta." See "Agni, Laud of"
Agniṣṭoma. See Praise of Fire Ceremony, the

B

Brahmin *(continued)*
who concentrates the ritual within himself, 121; as the mind of the sacrifice, 149–150; *hotṛ* (one who invokes the gods), 120, 142, 149; *purohita* (domestic priest), 123; *ṛtvij* (one who performs seasonal rites), 123; *udgātṛ* (one who sings chants), 120, 142, 149, 270; and Vāc, 120; as protector of *yajña*, 120; as "the mind of the sacrifice," 120; and the *bráhman*. *See also* Priest(s)
Brahmodya (enigmatic disputation regarding Brahman), 155, 270
Breath, living, 118, 134, 135, 150, 166, 178, 179, 190, 273, 376; fashioned by Word, 204. *See also* Prāṇa
Bhṛgus (a class of semi-divine poets), 96, 217
Bṛhadukta (name of a visionary poet), 94
Bṛhaspati (Lord of the Expansive Power, Lord of Prayer), 38, 62–63, 76, 111, 126–127, 132, 205
Broken world, 11–12, 15–16, 56, 111, 132–134, 162, 199, 216, 224, 230. *See also* Chaos, Struggle
Buddhi (intelligence), 10–11, 184; derivation of the word, 278
Buddhism, Zen, 13
Building the Fire Altar Ceremony, the (*Agnicayana*), 83, 130, 137, 149, 265
Bull: as image of the "One," 53; as image of the sun, 33–34

C

Cakras (centers of consciousness in *yogī*'s body), 191–192; names and locations of, 279
Candra (shimmeringly beautiful), 244, 255
Caru (bright, beautiful), 257
Cāturmāsya. *See* Four-month Rite, the
Cave of the Heart, 166, 174, 177, 179, 187, 190, 215, 223, 272, 273. *See also* Heart
Chalice: as image of poetic and ritual imagination, 98–99
Chandas (pleasing chant), 236
Chaos, 12, 47, 88, 136, 140, 200–201, 212. *See also* Anṛta; Broken world
Chariot, 86, 216; as image of Ṛta, 101; as image of a sacred song, 70, 76, 80, 96–97; as link between human and divine worlds, 101; as vehicle for the gods, 60; as vehicle for the sun, 50–51; poet likened to chariot maker, 96–97, 100, 253; as image of controlled mind, 154, 186, 220
Cit (consciousness, supreme Consciousness), 171. *See also* Consciousness
Citra (sparkling, shimmering, beautiful), 72, 170–171; etymological relationship to *cit*, 274
Competition. *See* Sadhamāda; Struggle
Consciousness: sparkling of, 150–151; light of, 153; as residing in the heart, 153, 176, 177; within all things, 176; as Brahman, 176; the Absolute as, 176–177; universal pulse of, 182; and *kuṇḍalinī*, 191–192; as the foundation of all that is, 208–209; and truth and bliss, 221, 276. *See also* Sat-cit-ānanda
Contemplation, 148–151, 170–172, 180, 152–199; imagination and contemplative vision, 188–194
Contemplative sage, vii, viii, 2, 150. *See also* Meditator
Contest, poetic. *See* Sadhamāda; Struggle
Cosmology. *See* Metaphysics
Cow, 34, 75, 99, 104; mother of the gods as, 38; Sarasvatī as, 39; Vāc as, 37–38, 55; as image of the forces of life, 126; as image of sacred sound, 127; as image of creative divine Voice, 212

E

F

G

H

R

S

T

U

V

W

Y